The Lost Education of Horace Tate

ALSO BY VANESSA SIDDLE WALKER

Their Highest Potential: An African American School Community in the Segregated South

Hello Professor: A Black Principal and Professional Leadership in the Segregated South

Race-ing Moral Formation: African American Perspectives on Care and Justice (co-editor with John R. Snarey)

The Lost Education of Horace Tate

UNCOVERING THE HIDDEN HEROES WHO FOUGHT FOR JUSTICE IN SCHOOLS

Vanessa Siddle Walker

THE NEW PRESS
NEW YORK
LONDON

Published in the United States by The New Press, New York, 2018
Distributed by Two Rivers Distribution

ISBN 978-1-62097-105-5 (hc)
ISBN 978-1-62097-106-2 (ebook)

CIP data is available

The New Press publishes books that promote and enrich public discussion and understanding of the issues vital to our democracy and to a more equitable world. These books are made possible by the enthusiasm of our readers; the support of a committed group of donors, large and small; the collaboration of our many partners in the independent media and the not-for-profit sector; booksellers, who often hand-sell New Press books; librarians; and above all by our authors.

www.thenewpress.com

Composition by Westchester Publishing Services
This book was set in Minion Pro Regular

Printed in the United States of America

10 9 8 7 6 5 4 3 2 1

To “Mother” Virginia Tate, without whom
Dr. Tate could not have advocated and
I could not have written

CONTENTS

PART III. THE EDUCATION OF A PEOPLE

The Lost Education of Horace Tate

INTRODUCTION

FINDING THE HIDDEN PROVOCATEURS

"You have to talk to Dr. Horace Tate." By January 2000, I had heard this from colleagues several times but had not yet complied. I was an Emory professor who had already spent twelve years probing the story of the segregated schooling of African American children. During that time, I had argued that history already captured the problems imposed on these schools but failed to uncover the resilience of black school communities. In *Their Highest Potential*, I chronicled the story of professional educators, high expectations, caring school climates, and parental support, a story that resonated with the memories of many in black communities throughout the South.

Perhaps an article in the *Atlanta Journal-Constitution* about my work that appeared shortly before I, impulsively, first called Dr. Tate helped me gain access. I knew he had been the head of the black educational organization in Georgia in the years before he formally entered politics, and I had become convinced that my continued inquiry into segregated schools required his perspective. Although I would later learn he was an avid daily reader of newspapers, I was not thinking about the article when I finally mustered the courage to dial the number I had been given. I expected to leave a short message with an answering service or a secretary. When, to my surprise, he said "Hello," I was ill prepared to explain why I wanted to see him. It was the first of many entry errors, most of them ones I admonished graduate students to avoid.

Dr. Tate agreed to meet with me someplace he called "the building." I remember being impressed on the first visit as I ascended the stairs and entered the suite leading to the executive offices of the former black teachers association. We settled at a long table in a formal boardroom beneath the smiling portraits of deceased people I did not know. In front of us on the table as we began to talk was a small stack of papers. I explained my work on black education. He listened, nodded, and sometimes gave me a hint of a smile. "You've got part of the story," he finally said.

Then he launched into his own memories. He spoke of dark roads and secrets, Horace Mann Bond and U.S. presidents, board meetings and Martin Luther King Jr. Occasionally he nodded toward the portraits on the wall, suggesting that something was important about the leadership of those individuals. I listened respectfully. I knew he was talking about something. I just could not figure out what that something was, despite my years of research on segregated schooling.

As I prepared to leave, he said I could take the stack of materials on the table that he had never once referenced. I promised to copy and return them, thanked him, and left. I knew materials on black schools were scarce, so I understood these documents were important, even after I looked at them and they seemed to have nothing to do with his stories.

When I returned a few weeks later to continue our conversation, a new stack of materials sat on the table, a bit higher than the first set. In succeeding months, the stacks grew taller. Eventually he allowed me to enter his former office and peruse the materials on the bookshelves, and he opened the door to the old artifact closet. I still remember the time he placed a complete set of *Heralds*—the magazine of the Georgia Teachers and Education Association (GT&EA)—in my hand as we stood at the top of the stairs before I left one day. I accepted them with emotional and fumbling gratitude.

My conversations with Dr. Tate lasted two years. In the beginning, we met at "the building." When his health began to decline, he would call me at home and launch into accounts as I grabbed my computer and began to type. "Am I boring you?" he would sometimes ask. Even if he was in the middle of a story I had heard before, I assured him that he was not.

"When I am dead," he announced during one session, "I want you to go to my wife and tell her to let you see the things in the basement of our home." At that time I had not yet met his wife, Mrs. Virginia Tate, and could not imagine how I would execute his wish. I breathed a huge sigh of relief when I finally passed her "test" for inquisitive researchers and was allowed to follow Dr. Tate for the first time into the sacred hollows of their home basement. I was in research heaven.

His stories continued from this new location. While I still could not connect his life with the material accounts I was given, I continued to listen. Somewhere during every visit, he would join me and the doctoral students I had brought along to help me as I began to comb through documents in his home two or three days a week. He would emerge slowly, wearing a freshly starched and pressed white shirt with a pen in the chest pocket.

He'd take a seat and wait for me to ask questions about materials I had read. Before I finished going through the materials in the basement, however, he died.

Even after his death I continued to pursue the trail he had left. The insights from his stories led me throughout America and around the world. Black educators were everywhere I had not looked before. They were in the Library of Congress, at the White House, with attorneys and civil rights activists, in Europe and Africa. But they had been out of the frame of a lens focused primarily on segregated schoolhouses. It took me sixteen additional years beyond his death to push through the secret door he had opened for me and find them.

When I did, I discovered a hidden world of courageous black educational leaders. Through their organizations, these men and a few women created networks of advocacy that mirrored the networks created by the white educational associations in which they were denied membership. Like white organizations, they hosted national meetings, state meetings, regional meetings, and local meetings in all the states across the South. As one educator said, "We saw each other all the time." But the black organizations operated with different actors and intent. These educators had problems to tackle without the kind of support white educators took for granted.

This black organizational network helped birth the advocacy undergirding both the *Brown v. Board of Education* decision and the civil rights movement. Necessarily invisible to prying eyes, black educators provided the plaintiffs, money, and data for the National Association for the Advancement of Colored People (NAACP) to generate the education cases. Although the national office always wanted its local NAACP chapters to be the agents of change, local and state networks of black educators, working covertly, provided the operating structure within southern states that allowed the legal cases to unfold. The bottom-to-top functioning of these networks allowed local parents to access nationally known attorneys to litigate their school-related grievances. Local NAACP chapters often provided the shield by lending their names, since they were already highly visible advocates who had enough distance from schools to lessen the concerns about retaliation by those who were determined to maintain the status quo.

Through this organizational network, black educators also stimulated a vision to demand equal rights in an unequal America. This time working from top to bottom in their networks, they crafted forms of purposeful education that infused black schools with a civic and literary curriculum, and with a power of purpose to fight for their full freedom absent in white schools. “You have to know somebody did something to you,” one of the principals explained. Once you know, you can ask, “Who did it and what did they do?”[1]

Generations of students who were quietly taught how to recognize they were being denied their rights and armed with the resilience to believe they did not have to be diminished by America’s perverse form of “justice for all” laid the groundwork for subsequent generations to demand equality. Reflecting on the curriculum in the local black high school, the *Atlanta Daily World* wrote in 1932 of the activities of its educators: “If the young people of today are trained in the use of the ballot . . . these same young people . . . will not sit passively . . . and let themselves be barred from complete citizenship.”

Of course, the black educators could not always publicly discuss what they were actually working toward. Doing so would cripple change before it could begin to take hold. Instead, the black educators used their organizations to mask their activities. And the individuals they elected to lead those organizations were shameless and almost intuitive about their adaptation of old West African aesthetics and norms to achieve their desired results. While white children read Brer Rabbit tales as bedtime stories, black educators deftly appropriated the West African trickster figure who’d survived the Middle Passage and used him strategically.

Robert Moton, Booker T. Washington’s successor at Tuskegee Institute, captured their unspoken use of the strategy well. The Negro was “voluntarily admitted” into every phase of the white man’s life, he explained in his book *What the Negro Thinks*. Much of Negro behavior was “nothing more” than the Negro’s “artful and adroit accommodation of his manners and methods to what he knows to be the weaknesses and foibles of his white neighbor.” For his revelation of the strategy all the black educators knew was essential when engaging powerful opponents in critical moments, the NAACP awarded Mr. Moton its prestigious Spingarn Medal. Too often history scripted these educators as Uncle Toms. They called themselves provocateurs.[2]

Had I not had access to Dr. Tate, I would not have thought to look for these educators who employed a visible network to operate secret strategies utilized by every generation from Reconstruction to desegregation. Yet when I did, they were evident in a story just beneath the surface of memory. In Richmond, I talked twice with esteemed NAACP attorney Oliver

Hill. Attorney Hill was emphatic in his attribution of agency as he described his litigation in education. "It was the teachers," he twice explained as he described the activity veiled in public memory. "The educators were organized."[3]

I met with Attorney Hill's Georgia counterpart, Donald Hollowell. Together they worked to litigate school desegregation cases in the 1960s to force the South to implement *Brown v. Board of Education.* Attorney Hollowell offered a confirmatory assessment. "The educators got the plaintiffs," he explained as I sat with him in his home in Atlanta. "We groomed them for the witness stand."[4] Both blind at the time of their reflective reports, the two attorneys could easily see a truth America missed. "Should we tell them what we are doing?" a black leader in the educational network once asked Thurgood Marshall at a private meeting with the heads of the black educational associations from across the South. The minutes reflect no response, but Attorney Marshall soon issued a press release lauding educators for their work with the NAACP.

Not until decades after the black educators paid the cost for their activism with lost jobs, diminished advocacy, and dismantled networks did a former black principal (reconvening with his colleagues at the headquarters of Georgia's black educators' association) speak frankly of the invisible source of agency for black children. "They knew we were the key to everything," the principal explained. That was why they were fired.[5] His words eerily presaged those of civil rights icon Dr. C.T. Vivian. Of the power of the hidden provocateurs in black communities, the Presidential Medal of Freedom recipient posited unwaveringly: "Black educators were key."[6]

The story of these whispered truths is one America has largely missed. Instead, the country has been almost unilaterally steeped in a story repeatedly told and almost universally accepted: the NAACP protested injustice and crafted the successful *Brown v. Board of Education* Supreme Court case that was supposed to deliver black children from poor schools to new opportunities. Grassroots movements of citizens tired of injustice erupted after *Brown* and demanded that America deliver on its promises of equality. The memory—of brilliant attorneys, courageous ministers, and a handful of private citizens who protested injustice as plaintiffs or through civil disobedience—remains seared in America's collective consciousness.

This memory threads through high school and college curricula and continues barely challenged into graduate school and beyond. It dominates history as well as artistic and media portrayals, and it undergirds policy.

One sees it in museums and hears it asserted as indisputable fact. Although a few books, articles, or people suggest a more complicated narrative, this little-challenged memory remains the basis of commonly accepted truth and provides a dangerously incomplete background upon which current efforts to achieve justice for black children—and all children—are founded.

America's memory of courageous actors, legal justice, and civil rights is not incorrect. However, it is insufficient. It diminishes on record the role of black educators, their organizations, and their leaders advocating for black children in America's changing justice terrain. It forgets to interrogate the power of perception and the creation of illusion as ways to effect change. It has left buried a story that Dr. Tate knew needed to be told.

PROLOGUE

BEFORE THE END

Tall, brown-skinned, stately, and beginning to show the weariness of the fight in his eyes, the executive director of the twelve-thousand-member black Georgia Teachers and Education Association, Dr. Horace Edward Tate, leaned in toward the podium to make an unneeded introduction. It was 1967, when America was engaged in a bloody war in Vietnam, and the world's most recognized and decorated voice for nonviolence waited silently in the Municipal Auditorium in downtown Atlanta for his turn to speak.

"And when the time comes," Dr. Tate ended with great flourish as he prepared to welcome the next speaker, "we are going to try to put you in office as president!" The five thousand black educators in the audience applauded, and the well-timed chords of an unseen organ rang loudly.

It was a singular, stellar moment of collective enthusiasm as Rev. Martin Luther King Jr. stepped forward, thanking his "good friend, Dr. Tate." Rev. King was shorter than Dr. Tate, the difference immediately obvious as he assumed his place behind the fresh-cut flowers framing the front of the podium and the array of gleaming microphones. The relationship between the two men was balanced nonetheless.

"He is a giant of integrity, a giant of competence, and a giant of leadership ability," Rev. King said emphatically, returning the commendations of Dr. Tate. "Already Horace Tate has carved for himself an imperishable niche in the annals of the educational history of our state and this nation." Enthusiastically the audience agreed.

He was vintage Rev. King on that evening as he began his talk, his voice gradually ascending to the elevated, punctuated, and staccato phrasing recognized the world over. But the message Rev. King delivered about black education and black educators was a message America missed.

He and other blacks were done with segregation "henceforth and forever more," Rev. King proclaimed to the audience of black educators. No one among them wanted a return to second-class citizenship. However,

Rev. King continued, repeating the words these educators had heard Dr. Tate say numerous times at state and regional meetings, integration must be two-way: a "genuine integration."

"Integration doesn't mean the liquidation of everything started and developed by Negroes," he went on. The audience applauded.

"Now there are too many Americans," Rev. King enunciated emphatically, "whites and Negroes, who think of integration merely in aesthetic and romantic terms, where you just add a little color to a still predominantly white-controlled power structure. We must see integration in political terms where there is shared power. And I am not one that will integrate myself out of power."

The audience burst into more applause as Rev. King spoke directly to the educators' long-standing concerns, the ones overshadowed in the public press by a civil rights movement that imagined black educators as passive observers: "We have got to see that integration is genuine integration, where there is shared power." Rev. King knew the educators confronted just such a crisis in school integration, that they were calling for equality in myriad domains of school integration "with all [their] might." He understood that black educators were at that very moment being forced to pay the penalty for their decades of seeking equality of opportunity for black children.

"I think you are on sound ground in saying that this integration process must not mean Negro annihilation," he affirmed. "And it is just as important to have Negro principals at formerly all-white schools as it is to have white principals at formerly all-Negro schools. I want to stress this point because this is very important! Integration must lead us to a point where we share in the power that all of our society will produce."

With increasing vigor, Rev. King spoke of how the South retained white schools in its implementation of the *Brown v. Board of Education* decision while black schools were discarded. He could not understand why Negro children should be sent to formerly all-white schools while no white children were required to come to improved Negro schools. Dismantling all the organizational structures and pedagogical precepts of black educators seemed to be the price for the Supreme Court decision intended to eradicate inequality, and it was wrong.

"No," he thundered. "We want it alllllllll the way!"

Real integration was what the audience also wanted—not "outer-gration," as Dr. Tate deprecatingly called it. The assembly exploded into more applause.

The evening was one to remember. As Rev. King returned to his seat, the audience stood and clapped in jubilant affirmation. Rev. King's ideas were precisely the points Dr. Tate and other black educational leaders across the fourteen southern states had been emphasizing since the South turned its back on justice and refused to implement *Brown* fairly.

At previous state and regional meetings of the Negro educators in Georgia, when Dr. Tate was particularly energized by some new inequality, he had crisply recalled for the GT&EA membership the role that black educational organizations across the South had always played in protecting the interests of black children. Since Reconstruction, Dr. Tate reminded them, black educators had been teaching black children to believe they could become full participants in American democracy—and those same educators were also leading the fight for equitable facilities, school bus transportation, teacher training, salaries, textbooks, and curricula. Yes, educators had sometimes appealed directly to southern state boards of education and political leaders, but they also quietly supplied plaintiffs and money to the NAACP and maneuvered secretly in myriad ways to gain resources and access. Through their organizations, black educators had been masterly tricksters who fought injustice with the dual weaponry of the appearance of reasoned public petition and stealthy daggers that challenged failed democratic practices. Meanwhile, as revered community leaders, they skillfully used curriculum to teach children to believe they could be full U.S. citizens. Black educators were quietly behind every movement for equality over a period of almost a hundred years.

"No one . . . but GT&EA worked to set in motion [what the children needed] for first-class citizenship," Dr. Tate often crescendoed in educational meetings as he wrapped up his list of the activities of generations of black educators. "No one else has done it for us," he would conclude as older members in the audience nodded appreciatively.

But in 1967 few Americans knew black schools were the sites where protests against school inequality had been birthed, or that black educators were the unseen midwives. Even fewer knew these black educators' latest and last fight was an organized protest against the inequitable implementation of the thirteen-year-old *Brown v. Board of Education* Supreme Court decision. The public knew only what the press reported, and the press did not report the ways southern states deliberately recast a Supreme Court decision designed to protect black children into one that protected the interests of white children. Nor did the press alert the public to the ways the federal government and white educational organizations quietly condoned these new forms of inequality sweeping the South.

"I want you to wake up and listen," Dr. Tate had told the waiting audience of black educators just before he welcomed Rev. King to the stage on that day in 1967. "Negroes cannot and will not be free or integrated if all that they have is relinquished or emasculated or given up or abandoned." With a punctuated enunciation every bit as eloquent as King's, he pointed out the ways blacks were being promoted into subservience in the very era when America was embracing a national rhetoric marked by a commitment to equality. Black children were gaining access to the buildings, books, and equipment long sought, but they were losing prematurely the advocacy base that helped them gain that access in the first place. The result would never produce long-term educational successes for the masses of black children, Dr. Tate prophesied. Real school integration was just and right; its current implementation was evil and wrong.

Like voices ringing in an otherwise silent canyon, Dr. Tate's words and Rev. King's words echoed one another that evening, overlapped, and joined in a single plea.

For one shining moment, it seemed their orchestrated collective call to awaken America to its latest injustice against black children might work. With the most noted voice in the world in agreement with their concerns and present at the podium, the message black educators repeatedly tried to publicize might make national news. For where Rev. King went, cameras and the press went. Maybe Rev. King could alert America to the invidious covert undermining of the original intent of *Brown v. Board of Education*.

But justice can be cruel sometimes, especially if you are black in America, and the moral arc leading to it can seem frustratingly long. As the audience enthusiastically applauded at the end of Rev. King's speech, Mr. Tate crossed his legs thoughtfully. This night, when justice just might triumph, had been a long time coming.

Part I

THE EDUCATION OF A YOUNG PRINCIPAL

I will make justice the measuring line.
—Isaiah 28:17

1

IN THE SHADOW OF HIS SMILE

Dark roads cover secrets and darkness hides people, especially black people.[1] The local Negro principal in Greensboro, Georgia, H.E. Tate, needed both on the third, or maybe fourth, in a series of trips he made in 1949.

The sun slanted downward in the winter sky as Mr. Tate gathered his belongings from his office and headed out the front door of the colored community's spanking new school. The school was a cement block structure boasting eight classrooms and an auditorium that seated four hundred people. With corridors, thermostat-controlled heat, stage and curtains, modern lights, bathrooms, inside drinking water, and even a janitor to keep it clean, people all over the town talked about the new Negro school.[2]

By 1949 standards, it was a substantial building for Negro children, and white people in the little Georgia town of Greensboro especially loved boasting about the Negro school. In fact, they were so proud of the $75,000 bond issue they had passed for its construction that they regularly invited other white people from all around the neighboring area to come investigate for themselves. More than 130 times in the first six months after its opening, Mr. Tate stopped his work with the Negro children and teachers to escort groups of white visitors through the building. Some came from more than 150 miles to tour the school. White people in Greensboro wanted to be sure other white folk could see for themselves what "we had constructed for our Negroes."[3]

Mr. Tate sometimes smiled inwardly at the naiveté of his visitors. But today the tricks he had orchestrated along with the Negro community stayed in the recesses of his consciousness. As he walked briskly to his car, placing his personal items inside, he had other plans, ones more far-reaching than those he had devised in order to get the new building.

Mr. Tate routinely drove his car onto the school's campus even though the house he rented with his new wife was close enough to the school to walk. Having the car right there made it easier to make the necessary trips to the white part of town to pick up the mail and run all the other errands required of a Negro principal who was expected to manage a school with no secretary.[4] Today having the car served him well, for he had a tight schedule if he was to make all the connections. He settled in the 1936 black Buick bought used from his brother and prepared to leave town. His thirteen-year-old "new" car could be temperamental at times—hopefully tonight would not be one of them.[5]

He passed the sprawling oak tree as he navigated down the steep hill leading from the school to the public street, then paused briefly as he prepared to turn away from the direction of his home and onto dusty Canaan Street. The people in this small community loved him. He knew how to nod deliberately, smile broadly, and throw up his hand to anyone he saw as he passed through, and they responded in kind. To them, he was "Fessor Tate." "Fessor" was the Negroes' shortened version of "Professor" and a term of respect and esteem.[6] People who really liked the principal just said "Fess Tate." At twenty-seven, he was their acknowledged community leader. The elderly Negro physician in the town, Dr. Calvin Baber, though making no obvious display of transferring leadership, had ceded the development of the community to Fessor Tate shortly after the young college graduate's arrival four years earlier.

The Fessor made a left at the first intersection and eased his car onto the paved street signaling the beginning of the white side of town. Soon he passed pleasantly through the town's center, driving past Hunter's Drug Store on his right, with the large sign on the side urging everyone to enjoy the refreshing taste of Coke. The Negro-owned shoe repair shop, another notable feature in the town and a hangout spot for both races, was around the corner. Whites called the proprietor "Peg Leg Joe" in acknowledgment of a missing leg; he was so good at repairing shoes that a white store owner provided a storefront for him to practice his trade. By day Negroes and whites lined up to get their shoes fixed by the congenial Peg Leg Joe. At nightfall, Peg Leg Joe assumed the title by which he was known in the Negro community—that of Mr. Fambro. And, as Mr. Fambro, he had proven an able accomplice to Fessor Tate in school matters over the years.[7]

Fessor Tate continued to throw his hand up to wave at the folk as he drove through the town. Even Negroes from Canaan Street convened in these public spaces, enjoying a break from work and visiting with neighbors in this little town, where race relations worked well until someone

In Greensboro, Georgia, black community members sit next to the drugstore in the town center. Mr. Tate passed this building on his travels to Atlanta and back to transport Mr. Harper. *Library of Congress*

challenged the status quo. After clearing the area, the Fessor nosed his car innocently toward Route 278 and Atlanta. In 1949, before the four-lane interstate could whisk drivers along at a substantially more rapid rate, Route 278 was the only road to Atlanta. This curving two-lane road would lead him away from town and out of sight. Behind him, nothing lingering in the dust his car had kicked up on the dirt roads of the black community or in the series of turns in the white community betrayed his mission.[8]

Of course, there were white folk in the town who were starting to become suspicious. Some said the tall young principal with the earnest eyes and tilted eyebrows was behind the ruckus their Negroes had been creating in regard to education in the erstwhile peaceful town of Greensboro, Georgia. "Before ole Tate came to Greensboro, the Negroes were satisfied with their school and their status," some whispered.

In other words, some whites were content with the three frame buildings previously used to educate Negro children since just after Reconstruction. Local whites had not had to build the schools, since the Negro community had donated them to the school board, and they certainly had not expended any energy keeping them repaired. One of them, a dilapidated two-story building with four classrooms, had been condemned forty years earlier but torn down only the previous year. Even the white local newspaper had pronounced the building "unfit" to be a school and said it was a "fire trap."[9]

However, while some whites visiting the new building expressed their approval of a new Negro school to replace the old, falling-down structures, others worried about the result of having let the Negro community prevail in the series of petitions and posturings that had resulted in the construction of the school, especially when the new school came with nice extras such as an auditorium. Some whites wondered if they had let the Negroes go too far: "[Next] they will want a gym!"[10]

Other whispers in the white community about the young principal went to the heart of the matter. They wondered if somebody was trying to disrupt the racial distance that separated Negroes and whites, in effect trying to get Negroes educated to be "as good as we are." Among whites across the South, the very idea generated venom: "The next thing you know, those niggers will want to be going to school with our boys and girls!"[11]

Anything that hinted of equality could be a problem in a town still steeped in old southern traditions.[12] Soothed by continued Negro compliance in their day-to-day affairs, some whites in Greensboro failed to recognize the changing race relations ushered in by the Second World War. One young white pilot from Greensboro wrote his mother of the "strange world" he and other white southern soldiers faced, one in which they had "dark-complected allies." He said he checked skin tones to determine whether he should shoot, even if it meant bringing down a dark-skinned ally by mistake.[13]

While white Greensboro shifted uncomfortably at a democracy that included darker people, Negroes in Greensboro were listening to President Franklin Roosevelt talk about freedom of speech, freedom to worship, freedom from fear, and freedom from want, and they took his words seriously—for themselves and for their children. These Negroes rejected the submission depicted in the *Amos n' Andy* shows, by minstrels, or in *Gone with the Wind.* They wanted to know why their children could not be protected from the people who wished to strip their freedoms as Americans.[14] And with smart Negro attorneys in far-off New York City through an organization called the "N Double A CP" now gaining admission for Negroes to schools previously all-white, Negroes in Greensboro less willingly accepted the blatant inequality that defined "freedom" in Greensboro for themselves and for the last two generations.

The different views of Negroes and whites about race in Greensboro collided in an episode down at the new Greenland Theatre. At the "grand affair" of the plush theater's opening, whites filled the downstairs and Negroes filled the balcony. During the feature presentation, everybody leaned back in comfortable new seats and enjoyed the feature-length film. But when the lights came on and one of the white city officials walked onstage to congratulate the community and the theater's owners on the beautiful new building, his remarks about the spacious balcony and the "traditional good conduct of the colored people" covered some of the same points a subsequent white town leader wanted to make. Perturbed, the second white speaker complained that what he wanted to say had already been said, and that his predicament reminded him of "an old nigger who . . ."

To the surprise of whites below, a loud voice hailed from the Negro balcony: "Callin' us niggers again!" Then, to the befuddlement of whites, the Negroes got up from the plush seats after the remark and left, reportedly creating so much commotion that whites downstairs could not hear well the rest of what was being said.

Whites were baffled, then angered, by the episode. They had been calling Negroes "niggers" all this time. What was the problem now? Meanwhile, as weeks passed and the Negroes refused to return to any movie, the white owners of the theater wanted answers. They needed Negro money to pay for their investment. Soon talk of "race trouble" in Greensboro brewed.

In these years before and during the Second World War, Negroes believed they should be treated differently, even in Greensboro, Georgia. As one old Negro resident dared report to inquiring whites, if he was at work and called "nigger," he was willing to put up with that, as he figured part of his pay included the name-calling. However, he did not believe he should be made "uncomfortable" in the theater when he had gone "for an evening of relaxation." When he paid his own money, he thought, he should be treated with more respect. The idea that Negroes expected better treatment baffled many whites. Some unnamed leader must be behind Negroes' refusal to go to the theater. Soon a delegation of whites went to talk with some of the older Negroes in town. These whites asked repeatedly about Negro leadership but got no answers. They were vexed by their failure to locate a leader. To whites, the whole situation seemed an "exodus without a Moses."[15]

The same concerns generated questions about leadership in other arenas. Negroes had agitated for this new school after the war, and somebody had to be behind it. Some of them were beginning to think that Principal Tate could be the veiled leader. But as one of them said, "We can't prove it," at least not yet.[16] And the Fessor gave no fodder for their speculation as he began his new venture on this particular day.

By now Mr. Tate was several miles outside the city limits, the road descending slightly downward past the small country store on his right. Soon he approached the narrow two-lane bridge that sat too close to the top of the water. The sun was beginning to disappear and the shadows of darkness starting to fall in the crisp air. By the time he came back, it would be pitch dark. Darkness was good. If the plan proceeded punctually, his and Mr. Fambro's accomplice, Mr. Cecil Jackson, the mortician, would be waiting for them near the bridge when he returned.

Once on the other side of the bridge, Mr. Tate settled into the first leg of the journey, the twenty-six miles between Greensboro and the small, quaint, stately town of Madison. Madison boasted more than fifty antebellum homes, including a Greek Revival mansion built in 1811, and it carefully preserved the Romanesque Revival schoolhouse where Oliver Hardy, the comedian of Laurel and Hardy fame, had attended first grade in 1898.[17] From Madison, he drove along the curvaceous stretch of country road that led to Atlanta. The newly paved roads helped his progress. White folk in Greensboro had voiced protests to make sure they got their share of the miles of new paving in the state.[18]

Of course, even if traveling on paved roads, drivers had to assume the pace of any farm equipment commanding more than its share of the highway—or of any other vehicles going nowhere in a hurry. Some folk said country people liked to drive their cars slowly enough to watch the corn grow.[19] Maybe they did, and the odds were Mr. Tate contended with his fair share of corn watchers and cows crossing the road. But Mr. Tate never complained about any of it. He was on a mission, and as long as no one stopped him, he could wait patiently to get around obstacles. He had a lot to think about anyway. The drive to Atlanta gave him plenty of time to rehearse in his mind the events that had led to this journey.

"Fess, I want my children to ride school buses just like the white kids!" The farmer in the door of his office that morning drove his children to school each day from the country. Of the 595 Negro children in the Negro Greensboro school in 1945–46, most lived in Greensboro, but not all children lived so close by. Some children from surrounding Negro neighborhoods walked as much as six miles daily to get to school; in one family, the three children each walked fourteen miles daily to attend school.

The new building exacerbated the problem. Enrollment climbed further as students from the small towns and rural areas of Union Point, Jones Central Community, and Siloam traveled to town to attend the Greensboro High School. The Greensboro city school district and the county school district worked together to allow Negro children from the county to come into the city schools after they reached the highest grade available elsewhere in the county. It was the county's justification for not providing an adequate number of Negro high schools. The Negro man standing at the door of the principal's office had children in the city school, but he lived in Greshamville, a forty-five-minute drive away.[20]

The farmer had not even said good morning when he presented himself at Mr. Tate's office just after the school day started. The farmer had a problem—a school problem. In those times, a school problem was also a race problem, which meant the farmer needed to seek out the Negro community leader. While whites focused on trying to determine exactly who the leader was, Negroes knew exactly where to go.

Notably, the farmer had not sought out a local NAACP branch in order to seek justice for his children. For one thing, no branch of the NAACP existed in Greshamville, nor in Greensboro. In fact, only a few NAACP chapters functioned anywhere across Georgia's 159 counties. When branches did seek to correct some injustice, education typically did not dominate the list of concerns. In fact, even the more vocal Atlanta branch had little sustained educational activity.[21]

Plus, white folk in the South hated the NAACP, and local people knew their northern champions could not prevent southern retaliation. A Negro man had been shot in Georgia just because he said he wanted to work by the day instead of by the month. Another Negro man was in his own house when two white men came through his yard to rob him; the man shot from

Because buses were not available, black children routinely walked back and forth to school. These children are going home from their school in Greensboro, Greene County, Georgia, in 1941. *Library of Congress*

his window to protect himself but ended up jailed for his efforts at self-protection. The national NAACP knew about these Georgia crimes and wanted the local people to write letters of protest to their congressmen or gather data and litigate the crimes so that the perpetrators could be brought to justice. In Georgia, such activities were dangerous, involving possibly the loss of a job and worse.[22]

To be sure, local Georgia Negroes *loved* the justice for which the NAACP stood and were proud of the Negro attorneys in New York litigating the rights of Negro people. And the local NAACP in some of the larger cities did occasionally investigate and challenge injustices in matters related to policemen, peonage, or unfair trials. But to get things done for education in Dixie, well, the Negro people had their own way of attacking problems.[23]

So the farmer came where most other Negro people who had a school-related problem had gone for the last fifty years—to their own school, talking to their own principal. It was the way things had worked for more than two generations.[24]

Mr. Tate, sitting behind his desk, was startled to hear the farmer's words, and while he welcomed them, he had to be cautious, for the farmer could be laying a trap. Mr. Tate looked at the man and weighed him. He might have been sent by the superintendent to see if they could finally "prove" who was behind the forward movement of the Negro community these last years.

Mr. Tate listened quietly as the farmer launched into his frustration.[25]

"Every morning when I am working hard on my farm, I have to stop what I am doing and spend approximately 1½ hours bringing my children to school and getting back home. Then in the afternoon, I have to spend another 1½ hours coming for them. I am tired of this," he said, "especially when a school bus coming to Greensboro passes right by my house in the morning and afternoon."

As the farmer spoke, his voice became more agitated.

"I am a taxpayer just like everybody else in Greene County who owns land, and if taxpayers' money can buy buses for transporting white children to school, that same money can purchase buses for transporting Negro children to school."[26]

Mr. Tate's pleasure grew, coming from somewhere deep inside his soul. He had wanted to agitate for school bus transportation for more than three years, but despite discussing the topic with many people and trying hard to locate someone with children who might be willing to bring a complaint, he had always come up empty-handed.

Nonetheless, Mr. Tate betrayed none of this emotion to the farmer. Instead, his eyes narrowed and his brows slanted, and he asked the farmer to repeat the whole story. He looked as though he needed to untangle all the facts. In truth, Mr. Tate hoped to determine if the man was serious, if he was sincere.

Undaunted, the farmer responded. "Fessor Tate, ain't nothing to relate. I am a working farmer. I work hard for my living. I work in order to try to educate my children, and almost every day I lose three or four hours bringing my children to school and coming back to get them. I could be making a lot of food and cotton during the hours that I spend coming from Greshamville to Greensboro and back.

"Tain't nothing to relate jess except that I want my children to ride to school on school buses like the white children do."

God knows I agree with him, Mr. Tate thought. But his tone and expression remained noncommittal. Talk like this was risky, so he used one more test to confirm the man's sincerity and to see whether the visit was a trap.

"I have several reports to work out for today," he told the farmer, "but I will be happy to discuss this situation fully with you on Wednesday morning. Could you come back at the same time, 9:15, tomorrow?"

The farmer said he could and left after Mr. Tate graciously bid him goodbye. Mr. Tate let him walk out the door of his office, out the door of the school, and get into his truck. Then the principal headed directly to his own car as the farmer drove down the hill past the old oak tree and turned on the dusty roads. The farmer was still in sight as Mr. Tate cranked his own car engine. He pulled off and eased into a comfortable pace behind him—far enough behind not to be noticeable but close enough to monitor the farmer's route. As old black people versed in trickery often say, "Every goodbye ain't gone."[27]

Mr. Tate trailed the man through town, past the big Coke sign in the town center, then over the too-close-to-the-water bridge just outside the city limits, and approximately five of the eighteen miles back out to the farming village. A few miles after he crossed the bridge, the farmer turned left in the direction of Greshamville. Not until then did Tate smile inwardly. The farmer passed the test. He had not gone to the superintendent's office. He was heading straight home.

With a potential plaintiff in mind, the principal could put in motion the steps he had learned from his first few years as a member of the statewide Negro educators' association. Called the Georgia Teachers and Education Association, or "GT and EA," as he had heard people say it, this organization had taught him the steps he needed to take to help the farmer. At its recent regional and state meetings, he had learned that this group of educators desired community members willing to use their names for lawsuits regarding transportation or any other matter of inequality.[28] Fessor Tate had been inspired, but he hadn't been successful in spurring indignation about school bus transportation. It seemed providential that someone had come to him.

As promised, on Wednesday morning, the farmer—Mr. Ward was his name—returned. He was still determined, maybe more so, that his children ride buses to school. This time, instead of showing restraint, Mr. Tate now congratulated Mr. Ward on his decision. And then they talked earnestly but quietly. Even inside a Negro school, their conversation must not be overheard.

Mr. Tate told Mr. Ward he was proud of him and that the cause he was championing was important. He explained to Mr. Ward the effort would require some personal sacrifice on his part to resolve the matter. Despite whites having voted to build the new school in Greensboro for Negroes, school inequality still reigned supreme. He then shared the procedures they would use to seek school bus transportation. First, just as he had done when a small group conspired to get the new school, several meetings needed to be held. This was the "organization" mandate the head of the educators' organization had explained at a recent meeting.[29] Afterward, Mr. Ward and others would make a formal request to the school board. Mr. Tate explained all these details to Mr. Ward, outlining the procedures with such precision one might have assumed he had seen Thurgood Marshall's memo on procedures for legal cases that the national NAACP office had recently mailed to the local branches.[30] But Mr. Tate had not seen the memo.

Finally, Mr. Tate told the farmer he needed to confer with his "GT and EA" contacts in Atlanta, noting that a suit might need to be filed and that they would need to raise some funds for the court costs. He ended with the most grueling challenge: that Mr. Ward would likely be harassed and criticized by the white citizens of Greensboro and that he should probably prepare for the worst.

To Mr. Tate's pleasure, Mr. Ward did not flinch. Like other farmers in the Greshamville community, he raised hogs and chickens and grew rye, wheat, and cotton.[31] He knew he could take care of himself and his family should trouble arise. He was one of the men who followed the advice given by Negro educators at the turn of the century to acquire their own farms. The only way to become an independent class of citizens and withstand the increasing competition from immigrants who would eventually come south was for Negroes to acquire land. Intellectuals including W.E.B. Du Bois and H.A. Hunt confirmed the extent to which such ideas were heeded. In Georgia alone in 1901, Negroes had purchased 66,000 acres of land and added $380,000 to the value of farmland.[32] As was true for other Negro farmers, having land fueled Mr. Ward's courage and commitment to education for all Negro children. He said he did not care about the cost or the number of sacrifices. He had made up his mind. He was ready. He was willing.[33]

When Mr. Ward left his office on that day, Mr. Tate did not trail him.[34]

A tenant farmer in Greene County, Georgia, in the 1940s is shown taking home bags of fertilizer. Unlike independent farm owners, a tenant farmer would have more difficulty bringing a suit against school inequality. *Library of Congress*

But Mr. Tate did pick up the phone to contact his mentor, and that phone call was what led him down the lonely dark road to Atlanta again. Mr. Tate was on his way to get Charles Harper.

By the time two hours of driving and thinking had passed, Mr. Tate was navigating slowly into Atlanta and onto its busy and well-known Auburn Avenue, or "Sweet Auburn"—a place where Langston Hughes's character Jesse B. Simple might have said black people could "live at peace."[35] Mr. Tate relished the sight of the collective power of the 121 or more black-owned businesses and, on another day, might have stopped to linger at some of the restaurants, drugstores, entertainment centers, clothing shops, automotive service stations, or other places where people who looked like him could buy what they needed without harassment. Today, however, time mattered, and he had to focus. He was looking for one among the several dozen black professionals on the street, the man he had called about school bus transportation: Mr. Harper. He knew Mr. Harper lived in one of the two-story houses on Auburn Avenue, in the same block as M. L. King Sr. Today, however, Mr. Tate was headed to the GT&EA office, number 250 in the block-long Odd Fellows Building.[36]

Mr. Tate had heard the stories about how Mr. Harper had been a "fessor" himself. He knew that Mr. Harper had stood up for teacher salary equalization at the school where he was principal: Booker T. Washington, the first public high school for Negroes in Georgia. Before he became full-time leader of the Negro educators across the state, Mr. Harper had championed salary equalization at a faculty meeting, and no teacher stood with him when the superintendent came to discuss the matter. A few years later, the school board forced Mr. Harper to accept "mandatory retirement," despite 5,000 citizens and his 4,200 students twice petitioning that he be retained.[37]

Harper's ouster, however, reignited a new phase in a struggle that had already been ongoing since Negro educators in Georgia first asked for equal school funds in 1878 and for equal salaries in 1920. His friend Benjamin Mays, the esteemed Morehouse College president, said Mr. Harper simply could not sit content by his fireside, reflecting on past achievements and settling down as a worn-out citizen. He was "possessed" to go on missions. Mr. Harper used his forced retirement to launch a statewide campaign against inequality using his leadership in the educational organization as a platform.[38] As the first full-time executive director whose salary was fully paid by Negro teachers, Mr. Harper could operationalize their collective will and align it with national movements. Most important, he was no longer vulnerable to being fired by disgruntled whites.

Mr. Harper's presence loomed large in the educators' annual and regional GT&EA meetings—places where the young Mr. Tate met him. It was in these settings that he taught courageous young principals like Mr. Tate how to agitate. But those who knew Mr. Harper best declared he seemed to have been "in his greatest glory with small groups of citizens, discussing their common and personal problems, in the most remote sections of the state." Thus, when Mr. Tate called needing his assistance for a problem in Greensboro, Mr. Harper quickly made plans to respond.[39]

Mr. Tate elected to drive from Greensboro to Atlanta to pick him up. Mr. Harper did not drive, so either anyone in the 159 counties in Georgia who needed his assistance picked him up or the shorter-than-average-height graying man with the gentle smile, quiet faith, and monumental fortitude cheerfully took the bus, hitchhiked, or hopped a ride with some other educator.[40] Mr. Tate could have let Mr. Harper take the bus to Greensboro and save himself the cost of travel. He did not, however, and he had no regrets about that choice. He had been picking up Mr. Harper for years anyway, ever since he first started agitating for changes in Greensboro.

When Mr. Harper, seventy-two, climbed into the car, he greeted the young professor—one-third his age—with the bright and kind smile that was his trademark. He had by this time been diagnosed with Charcot-Marie-Tooth disease, an illness that progressively atrophied the muscles of his lower legs and caused him to walk with a high step, but he maneuvered his five-foot-four-inch frame into the car. Soon he was resting comfortably on the passenger side after his own full day of work on GT&EA business.[41]

A colleague had once asked him if he was tired of all the fighting. The American demon of inequality bested many—sending them to an early grave, ruining longtime relationships, or prompting them to reach for the bottle. "No," Mr. Harper replied. "A tired man is no good to himself nor to anyone else."[42]

The drive back to Greensboro gave the elder and the younger man time to talk. Mr. Tate admired Mr. Harper for his leadership of GT&EA. He viewed him as a role model, and from Mr. Harper he was learning the strategies to fight oppressive forces by using a set of secret conspirators acting under the innocent cover of a teachers' organization.

Their conversation in the car continued their earlier phone call. Mr. Tate explained that he had had two conversations with the farmer, Mr. Ward, and thought he was sincere in his desire to do whatever was necessary to make it possible for his children and other Negro children to ride school buses. Mr. Harper listened and agreed that the man sounded sincere. Greensboro, the seat of Greene County, could certainly be a place to push the GT&EA agenda for getting school buses.

In what must have seemed short order, the low bridge that led to Greensboro appeared in the distance. Immediately after crossing the Oconee River, but before reaching the Greene County line, Mr. Tate carefully maneuvered his car to the side of the road, onto the grass and dirt of a church parking lot. In the shadows, a second vehicle driven by the Negro mortician Cecil Jackson waited quietly. Funeral directors could be out at all hours of the night unquestioned.

More than four hours had now passed since Fessor Tate had first left his office. Lapsed time had let the sun slip quietly over the waters, and shadows now covered both cars. With his slight limp, Harper emerged stealthily from Mr. Tate's car, with only soft talk piercing the darkness as he eased into the other car. Both drivers confirmed the time for the return rendezvous. Then both cars pulled onto the highway to go their separate ways.

All the men involved knew that too much lingering risked exposure. Although the transfer had been arranged several miles outside the Greensboro city limits, an unexpected car with suspicious riders might pass at any moment. The principal's car, after all, was well known around town, and his presence on the dark highway could be just the evidence inquiring white minds were seeking. If a black community wanted to keep its leader, that leader had to be protected. While Fessor Tate turned his car toward Greensboro and back into town, the mortician headed in the opposite direction, toward Greshamville.

Mr. Tate had three hours to kill. He knew his Atlanta passenger was by now safely ensconced in a remote location talking to parents from the Greensboro Colored School. Mr. Tate could not be present without risking exposure. Even for a cause as important as their children, some Negroes could not be counted on to stay tight-lipped.

A tediously long time passed as Mr. Tate piddled around with tasks that held little immediate interest. He drove back to his home, where his wife busied herself with evening tasks. Finally he checked his gold Elgin watch and saw that it was time.[43] Mr. Tate drove his car quietly past the now-silent Hunter's Drug Store and, with an even pace, rounded the curves leading out of town. Soon he passed the country store and approached the river and lonely stretch of road where he had left Mr. Harper.

On cue, Mr. Jackson pulled his car into the meeting spot and Mr. Harper quietly changed automobiles before both drivers headed their separate ways. Now, at about 10:30 p.m., Fessor Tate was beginning the long journey back to Atlanta.

The weariness of two men who had both worked long days could have set in as they traveled the dark, winding country roads. Probably it did not. Mr. Tate had youthful energy, indignation, curiosity, and hope fueling him. Mr. Harper, the son of an ex-slave who was raised on farmland in nearby Sparta, enjoyed farmers, was fully at home in their midst, and never showed any exhaustion on drives such as this. Years later, another conspirator recalled Mr. Harper's face during a similar excursion into a remote area in southern Georgia. Mr. Harper was full of energy, jovial, sharing the happenings of the day, "laughing heartily and freely like a boy of twelve."[44]

Tonight, as Mr. Harper shared his account of the meeting with the young fessor, the secret collaboration energized them both.

It was after 2:00 a.m. by the time Mr. Tate finally pulled his black Buick up to the front of his house in Greensboro. Across the way was the school where the journey had begun long hours ago. Just across the yard, barely visible in night, Mr. Jackson's car sat undisturbed in the garage of his funeral home. Except for himself, Mr. Jackson, and probably Mr. Fambro, no one knew the automobiles had been part of a quiet meeting earlier that evening.

Fessor Tate wearily opened the door of his small house, passed the heater in the center of the house with some unburned coals remaining, and pushed the door open to the bedroom. His wife, a member of his faculty at the Greensboro Colored School, slept lightly, waking just enough to know he was home. Like other Negro men involved in these activities, he would provide her few details about his night vigils—for her own protection. Questioned by either inquiring whites or reporting Negroes, she would have no answers to give.[45]

Fortunately, the one-eyed jack coal heater in the bedroom offered a bit more heat on the cold evening as he prepared for sleep. Somewhere before 4:00 a.m., Fessor Tate finally climbed into bed and succumbed to fatigue. He had spent about a tank of gas and eight hours on the road since leaving the segregated school on the hill.

In a few hours, he would grab the wash pan for a bath, shave, dress neatly, and drive the short distance over to his job.[46] There he would reenter the cement block building that was the pride of all the citizens of Greensboro, walk briskly down the corridor to his office, and begin taking care of the multiple demands of running a Negro school. Nothing in his face would betray his lack of sleep from his previous night's mission as he cheerfully greeted students and faculty. It was business as usual for a Negro principal.[47]

Meanwhile, back in Atlanta, Mr. Harper compiled the information from Greensboro with that of other black communities across the state. In an earlier communication, he had written a longtime acquaintance: "My dear Attorney Marshall . . . The Georgia Teachers and Education Association is planning on moving in on several boards of education in the matter of discrimination against Negroes."[48]

2

NOW YOU SEE ME, NOW YOU DON'T

Rummaging through the documents on the paper-laden desk from which he orchestrated the activities of educators across the state, the brown-skinned man with gentle eyes, graying hair and eyebrows, and a fully gray mustache sometimes confused the letterhead of the educators' organization, the Georgia Teachers and Education Association, with that of the local NAACP branch in Atlanta where he was president. Scribbling hurriedly, his mind distracted by all the factors involved in creating an organization that could respond to every opportunity to make a difference in Negro education, Mr. Harper wrote on whatever stationery lay close to his fingertips.[1]

White Georgia newspapers blared about the problem they did not know had started in Mr. Harper's office. Over in Irwin County, Negro parents had filed suit against the Irwin County school board and school superintendent demanding equal educational opportunities, inclusive of buildings, equipment, teachers, courses of study, and transportation. It was the second southern case filed—the first suit had been filed in Virginia—and would cost millions if the federal courts sided with the Negro plaintiffs.

State officials confirmed to Irwin County board members and the superintendent that they would have the "advice and assistance" of the state legal department "in fighting [the] suit demanding equal education for Negroes." In fact, the Georgia attorney general, Eugene Cook, declared the state would "fight in every way possible" the suit filed by the Negroes.[2]

The governor fought back as well, with specious reasoning and rhetoric aimed at agitators. In his Saturday morning radio talk on October 22, 1949, Governor Eugene Talmadge invoked an argument that had been statistically refuted by Dr. Du Bois and others during Reconstruction: that whites paid more taxes and thus deserved better schools. In Irwin County, colored citizens were receiving "far more educational benefits than they will ever contribute in taxes," the governor incorrectly pointed out to his listeners. Everyone knew "wide inequalities" existed among white schools also, he claimed, with better facilities offered in urban areas. "The value of a school is determined by the training pupils get—not by its physical facilities," he posited.

The governor needed to address these matters. Headlines like the one in the *New York Times* in January 1949 that proclaimed "Negro, White Schools in the South Held $545,000,000 Apart in Value" made southerners nervous. The South would need money from somewhere if the southern states were actually going to make good on the "equal" part of the "separate but equal" decree in the 1896 *Plessy v. Ferguson* Supreme Court decision. Now, an even worse potential Supreme Court decision was possible—one that might require integration. The South was just beginning to be aware of the demands for equality attacking their cherished traditions, and southerners in Georgia were eager to identify the source of their problems.

This "first assault directly made upon the segregation laws of Georgia," as he characterized it on the Saturday morning program, was crafted by the "iniquitous organization know[n] as The National Association for the Advancement of Colored People, with headquarters in New York City."[3] They had their local accomplices also, he explained: the Negro attorney Austin T. Walden was "southern counsel" for the NAACP. He gave Attorney Walden's address, 200 Walden Building, and explained that this attorney was responsible for filing the case. Signing the complaint with him was Thurgood Marshall, 40 West 40th Street, New York, also a Negro, and "national counsel" for the NAACP. The governor said he wanted "to make it plain to the white people and the negroes of Georgia just what people and what organizations are back of this suit." They were associated with organizations that "in devious ways" were furthering Soviet and Communistic policy. They were attempting to drive a wedge as the beginning of an effort to "break down" segregation in the southern states. They were "disgruntled agitators from Northern States" and they were seeking to "destroy all that the far-seeing white and Negro people have accomplished in progress in the last few generations."[4]

As Governor Talmadge bristled over "plots" to disrupt southern educational practices in his expansive office under the glittering gold dome of the Georgia state capitol, he had no idea that in fact the "outside agitators" he accused of disrupting peaceful southern relationships were headquartered only a few blocks away.

The truth was that the local NAACP chapter in Irwin County was not the source of the governor's problem, despite the broad publicity about the NAACP's demands and the publicity Irwin County was receiving nationally. To be sure, the national NAACP *wanted* its local branches to be effective advocates against race problems and hoped very much these branches would be local leaders. But the local NAACP chapters at this stage in the fight for equality mostly left education matters to the educators. It had been that way since the formation of the NAACP in Georgia.

James Weldon Johnson, former Florida principal and the NAACP field director, had traveled south in 1917, during the national fever of the Great War, and planted NAACP local chapters across Georgia. His speech skills greatly improved since his Atlanta University days, when he had been terror-stricken at the thought of public speaking, Mr. Johnson spoke to communities with a calm, dispassionate reasoning that beguiled audiences and solicited new branches and membership. With even Georgians exuberant about President Woodrow Wilson's proclamations of freedom, the Georgia branches he planted in homes like that of educator Lucy Laney in Augusta became part of a greatly increased NAACP membership. By 1919, the national association boasted 47,000 members with 328 branches in 43 states.[5]

But as the world war ended, talk of equality died as President Wilson segregated Washington, America ceased to put into practice its language of equality and democracy, and thousands of Negro Georgians became part of the migration north. The new Georgia branches organized during and after the war, the ones that often included Negro educators as leaders and members, began to shrivel and cease functioning right as Georgia moved to the top of the list in lynchings. Within only a few months or years after they began, and having undertaken just a smidgen of activity, Georgia local NAACP branches joined the one hundred to two hundred mostly dead or "practically dead" NAACP branches across the South that the national office lamented in 1923. If not dead, the branches were certainly "soundly asleep."[6]

It cannot be said that Negro southerners did not care about the activity of the NAACP. They did, as evidenced by Atlanta's demands to bring the NAACP national meeting to Atlanta in 1920. The Atlanta educators Henry Hunt and Lucy Laney had been among the speakers at the national meeting in Cleveland in 1919, and the city pulled together to cheat a northern contender out of the coveted 1920 meeting. Those at the meeting "spoke as they always did," the NAACP leaders proclaimed, the southern site notwithstanding. But that public talk with educators on the stage was before the South gelled its intent to repress Negro gains, the result of the frenzy of World War I rhetoric and the loss of a black workforce heading north to help with the war industry.[7]

As the 1920s unfolded, Negroes in the remaining southern NAACP branches who still were without the right to vote could not participate in their communities as democratic citizens in the ways northern branch members could. Outside of Atlanta, which did have the vote, southern branches could not simply write petitions to the president of the United States, as requested by the national office, or object when white Georgia senators refused to support the much-needed anti-lynching bill that was consistently pursued by the national office.

"Can't you all prove that [a man who was lynched] did not have an ax and attempt to bring the murderer to justice?" the national office, colloquially known as "the National," queried of one local branch. The answer was no: the local branch's members could not do that without risking livelihood or even life, possibly becoming another on the list of Georgia lynching cases.

One member told the National to send materials in his wife's name. He knew postal workers noted correspondence arriving from the NAACP, though he did not specify his reasons for putting his wife at risk. Surely he believed her less subject to retaliation. Some asked whether they could do NAACP work under another name entirely. The National understood these problems. Once they even sought to insure their office representatives traveling in southern states against "bodily injury resulting from personal assault," but they could not obtain a policy.[8]

Even into the 1940s, the Georgia NAACP had yet to achieve the full statewide organization James Weldon Johnson had aspired to decades prior and which the new legal counsel for the NAACP, Charles Houston, emphatically reminded the National's new head, Walter White, that the organization needed. A World War I veteran, Houston explained to White that the organization should be like an army, "divided and subdivided into smaller units," with White at the top and succeeding layers of state and local organization that would network Negro communities.[9]

Like Mr. Johnson, Mr. White tried to create such a tightly networked organization. With the National desperately in need of money as contributions from philanthropists such as Julius Rosenwald, George Peabody, and others dried up in the 1930s, Mr. White reached out to defunct Georgia chapters to generate support. "You need the NAACP, and the NAACP needs you!" Walter White pleaded with Negro leaders in Georgia, where chapters had been so long deceased that new organizers did not even know an earlier chapter had ever existed in their community.[10]

Some cities responded. But these new chapters continued the path chartered by those chapters long forgotten. They held fund-raisers and supported the Christmas Seals drive. They hosted large meetings when national staff traveled south, and dutifully sent money to the National to support the litigation campaign and budget deficits.

Yet rarely did local chapters delve deeply into education—not even in Irwin County, which was receiving all the publicity that was making the governor nervous and mad. The local Georgia NAACP simply did not have the network to carry out an education campaign. Even in Atlanta, where members of the local chapter could vote and Mr. Harper served as the chapter's leader, the branch focused primarily on inequalities related to policemen, recreation, and juvenile delinquency.[11]

Something else was driving the fight against school inequality, some organized structure that *could* reach across the state and organize protest. That structure was as invisible to the governor's prying eyes as Mr. Tate's clandestine trips to Atlanta.

In 1917, a few months after James Weldon Johnson planted NAACP chapters across the state of Georgia, Henry Alexander Hunt, his former baseball teammate from Atlanta University, began the task of reinventing the defunct Negro educational organization originally active after Reconstruction.

During Reconstruction, Negroes had been able to vote. Angered by the inequality ushered in after the 1877 Hayes Compromise facilitated the withdrawal of northern supervision over southern problems, Negro educators across the state organized in 1878 under the leadership of Richard Wright to protest the inequality in distribution of school funds between Negro and white children. By 1879, two hundred Negro educators were protesting. For more than a decade, the educators continued to speak publicly about their demands for education. But disenfranchisement at the turn of the century disrupted the educators' public advocacy. With no political voice, the Georgia educational association barely survived.[12]

As the climate surrounding World War I invited more open dialogue about equality, however, a new generation of Negro educators took advantage of the possibilities. In Fort Valley, Georgia, philanthropists determined to solve the southern problem by imposing industrial education on Negro youth hired Henry Alexander Hunt to train students to be docile, industrial workers. Mr. Hunt appeared to do so, at least in the early years. But he also gradually introduced the liberal arts into Fort Valley High and Industrial School, emphasized civic education, started a student NAACP chapter, and, in the late 1930s, oversaw the transformation of the school into a junior college; it would eventually become a four-year college.[13]

Henry Hunt had been an older classmate of James Weldon Johnson at Atlanta University during the days when young men housed in the institution's South Hall resided in rooms with wooden slop buckets, oilcloth mats, and beds with thick mattresses filled with sweet-smelling straw and imagined how they would change the world for Negroes.[14] Lifelong colleagues who ultimately would die within months of each other, both Mr. Johnson and Mr. Hunt were part of the Amenia Conference in 1916 at Troutbeck, the beautiful home of Joel E. Spingarn in Amenia, New York. Booker T. Washington had died in 1915, and Negroes needed a collective strategy. With no reporters, no uninvited guests welcome, and even the promise of not publishing the name of anyone present without his or her consent, the group met near a three-acre pond, gathering under a white tent that transformed itself from auditorium to dining room each day at noon. Dr. Du Bois sent the invitations, having scribbled on James Weldon Johnson's, "Please come." Meanwhile, Mr. Hunt rode with one of the philanthropists who gave money to the NAACP and consciously ignored introduction of a liberal arts curriculum into his school. Together, Mr. Hunt and George Foster Peabody took the eighty-five-mile, two-and-a-half-hour train ride from Grand Central Station in New York, then climbed aboard a carriage for the final two-and-a-half-mile journey to join the others for a "free and frank discussion" in late August 1916.[15]

In the open air, amidst majestic views of good green earth, pale blue sky, and alluring waters, the attendees talked intimately, joked together, and even made repartee in the midst of serious argument as they "laughed any poseur off the rostrum." Their stated goal was to create "the most advanced position that all can agree upon and hold as vantage ground from which to work for new conquests by colored Americans." By agreement, no proceedings were ever published. But one of the outcomes, as Dr. Du Bois,

Mr. Hunt, and Mr. Johnson knew, was that the Negro leaders enjoying themselves under the clear blue skies had agreed to organize.[16]

The very next year, in 1917, James Weldon Johnson showed up in Georgia to organize local NAACP chapters. He was adjusting to his new role as the NAACP's field organizer. That same year, Mr. Hunt began to reorganize the black educators in Georgia using the idea of "key people." Perhaps not coincidentally, the term was one also utilized by Mr. Johnson in private communications. Mr. Hunt pretended that the idea of having key people out front to speak for education had developed spontaneously from one of the farmers' conferences he hosted at his school in middle Georgia, Fort Valley High and Industrial School, but a contemporary knew better.

"It was Mr. Hunt's idea," the colleague said, "that since the Negro teachers were voteless and also employees of the city, county or state, they were helpless to make any contribution toward significant changes in the educational pattern. He, therefore, organized an educational group that included non-teaching citizens such as physicians, heads of fraternal organizations, representatives of insurance companies and other self-employed persons."[17] The idea was to attack educational injustice using as visible protesters Negroes whose financial status made them less vulnerable to white retaliation, all while orchestrating the protest under the auspices of educators.

Mr. Hunt imported the old Br'er Rabbit script from West Africa in which the little rabbit had to outsmart his more powerful opponent. Without the vote, Negro people likewise had to think their way out of problems, Mr. Hunt once said when lecturing an Atlanta University audience. "Does the Negro think it is his lot by divine decree . . . ?" he asked. No, but the Negro was the victim of "crooked thinking," and needed to use mental acumen when dealing with an opponent who had on his side the country's laws, wealth, and educational opportunities. Organizing key people was one such strategy.

A new educational organization that could use key people to represent the masses' needs for education was "just the thing" needed, according to the *Savannah Tribune*, a Negro paper, in an article announcing the need for an "Educational Awakening." The educators' agenda was to use the organization to "bear upon the public authorities of the state all the influences we possibly can to the end that more liberal appropriations be made and better facilities provided for the education of Negro youth." The newspaper concurrently reported confidently on the "good work" the educational group was doing. Their strategy was sure to "reach every home, however humble, in the matter of education."[18]

After a series of large public meetings over two years, Mr. Hunt's plan became operationalized by 1919 as the availability of federal aid combined with the worry of Georgia's whites about losing the "best labor they ever had"—more than sixty thousand Negroes from the state had migrated north to fill the factory demands of World War I.[19] Fully aware of the "opportune moment" created by the climate, Mr. Hunt and a group of "distinguished" Negro citizens from other professions personally petitioned the state school board with a written memorial.[20] Mr. Hunt, who had the respect of Georgia's governor and whose school received support from the Episcopal Church, not state coffers, led the delegation.

The men expressed to the Georgia State Board of Education the "deep concerns" they had about the deplorable conditions of black education. They wanted higher salaries for teachers, longer school terms, better school buildings to replace the "tumble-down old shacks and unsanitary old churches," and a state normal school to train Negro teachers. In a "manly" way, the *Savannah Tribune* reported, the leaders spoke directly to the white state school board. "There is a feeling among Negroes generally though perhaps expressed only to themselves," the leaders emphasized to the men capable of making changes in education, "that Georgia does not mean to do the square thing by her Negro citizens." Then they elaborated on their three pages of requests.

Concurrently, Mr. Hunt continued to garner the support of Negro citizens across Georgia. In 1921, as the new educational organization met in Atlanta at his church, Big Bethel AME, Mr. Harper presided over the meeting. Mr. Hunt's presidential address reflected the organization's slogan: "The Negro Youth of Georgia Shall Be Educated." Present were educators who had been part of the original black educational organization, one that featured curricular topics, not political issues, among the matters addressed at its meetings. Present also were key people, inclusive of business leaders, social workers, and professional men and women. All attended the multiple sessions that would become foundational in the new organization, and all embraced the need for "co-operation" between educational and religious forces. A young local attorney, A. T. Walden, a graduate of Fort Valley, outlined the minimum that education associations should ask for Negro education from the public authorities. Other presenters discussed the steps the people needed to take to "share more largely in bond issues" that distributed public funding for education.[21]

This strategy of key people operated in Atlanta as well, even during the hopeful days of World War I. A youthful and exuberant Walter White, recently graduated from Atlanta University, reported to James Weldon Johnson shortly after the formation of the Atlanta NAACP that word had come to them that the seventh grade was being taken away in the Atlanta schools, so the new branch had decided to begin its fight with education. The Atlanta school board would eliminate seventh grade for Negro children, White said, "over the bodies of the Atlanta Branch of the N.A.A.C.P."—"figuratively speaking," of course. With absolute confidence he proclaimed that the NAACP branches in Boston, Washington, and New York would have to "take our dust."[22]

Later the same day, White—then a young insurance agent at Atlanta Life—wrote Mr. Johnson again. An emergency committee of the NAACP chapter had been appointed to take charge of the seventh grade situation, he reported. He said the committee had appeared before the city board of education earlier in the day and protested strongly to the white leaders of Atlanta. In response, Atlanta's white businessmen and educational leaders affirmed that what their "dear colored brethren" said was true, and they "definitely agreed" to maintain the seventh grade.

"We certainly feel jubilant," Mr. White wrote, "and if the N.A.A.C.P. does no more, it has earned its right for existence. And we have just begun to fight."[23] Next they would make the streetcar owners "open their eyes," he announced. And if that did not work, "other more stringent measures will be adopted." The new NAACP chapter was committed to getting "some real results."[24]

But with the exception of a few photographs documenting inequalities, Mr. White's anticipated fight did not materialize. Neither was there evidence of support for his plan to have the three hundred members of the Atlanta NAACP write individual letters of protest to the school board about the double sessions, which required some students to attend school in the morning and others in the afternoon, in Negro schools. In fact, except for Mr. White's own protest letter, which "aroused interest" among white and colored people when it appeared in the *Atlanta Independent*, the Atlanta branch did little the rest of the year.

Atlanta began to look a lot like the other Georgia NAACP chapters that were drying up. Before the end of 1917, the National alluded to Atlanta's inactivity with gentle encouragement: "I am glad to hear that the Branch is taking up active work again." But a year after the supposed new activity, the Atlanta branch needed to be gotten back on a "firm basis" again. As late as 1925, despite membership drives and some registration activity, the National expressed that it was "troubled" about the Atlanta branch.[25]

But there were other issues involved, as an article in the *Savannah Tribune* indicated. The paper reported the 1917 school meeting as a "well-thought out and well-directed attack," one that was "thoroughly grounded and fortified in facts." The newspaper said the petitioners, representing a local committee of ministers and the NAACP, with one spokesman from each body, achieved the "excellent response" by careful preparation and interracial cooperation. The local report, relying on a first-person account from one of the participants, diverged in subtle but important ways from Mr. White's description of NAACP men "protest[ing] sharply" or telling the board they knew their rights and "what they demanded."[26] The truth was that the emergency committee assigned to explore the school question was not appointed until the Thursday *after* the organization meeting, and the members of the emergency committee only learned that same morning of the need to meet before the 3:00 p.m. school board meeting. Furthermore, the Atlanta branch did not even have its charter when it "won" its fight.[27] Nor did NAACP-affiliated ministers have at their disposal the extensive data on educational inequality that could be delivered to the emergency committee. In truth, the NAACP supplied the public agency, but behind the scenes were players from education. Indeed, the tone of the meeting was a southern strategy of manly direct appeal based on reason—like Mr. Hunt's request to the school board—and not confrontational challenge.

Key people or organizations dominated the public stage, but they did not act alone. Mr. Hunt alluded to the strategy in his letter to James Weldon Johnson, whom he addressed as "My Dear Jim," shortly after the "wonderful" meeting held by the educators in Atlanta. His organization was dedicated to "objective improvement" of Negro public schools, with all that implied—better salaries, longer school terms, better school buildings and equipment, and supervisors. His method was simple, he explained. The education organization was arousing the people to the "supreme importance of taking greater interest in the education of Negro youth" and bringing "influence to bear in every way possible upon public officials for a more equitable distribution of public school funds."[28]

The plan was classic Mr. Hunt. "Now, I want to ask you to take hold of the matter for me and see what you can find out," he once wrote another old college classmate when he faced obstacles to get the resources he needed.

"You need not confine your activities in this matter to any particular individual or set of individuals but [first?] set in motion *any and all forces* which you think may bring about the desired result."[29] In other words, his friend was to get the result without showing Mr. Hunt's hand in the plan. Mr. Hunt used the same approach with President John Hope of Morehouse. In a letter to the president and several others, Mr. Hunt emphasized the need for Negroes to be part of a particular public meeting in Atlanta. Mr. Hunt explained that, if they were in agreement, they should be in contact with Attorney Walden, whom Mr. Hunt had already requested to "take charge of the correspondence and call a meeting." To the southern public, it would appear that Attorney Walden was the source of the idea.[30] In reality, it was Mr. Hunt.

The victorious 1917 NAACP strategy that saved the seventh grade looked a lot like a quiet cooperation between Mr. Hunt's new education organization and the NAACP. But full public disclosure of how these key people operated was not part of the strategy. Too much was on the line.

From the national office—exuberantly broadcasting the work of the Atlanta branch—had come the request that the local president provide a "direct narrative of just how the Branch went about its fight on the school question and just what results it obtained."[31] The branch did not comply. However, when the branch reactivated, the national office took credit for building the first black high school in Atlanta, the Booker T. Washington High School—the school to which Mr. Harper had been appointed principal (and from which he was subsequently fired). Indeed, not until years later would the *Atlanta Daily World* make public a truth insiders such as Mr. Hunt, Mr. Johnson, and Mr. Harper already knew: a young principal who appeared publicly at none of the meetings was actually one of the "moving spirits" behind the establishment of the high school. That young principal had been Mr. Harper.[32]

Just as Mr. Tate would one day observe him, Mr. Harper had watched Mr. Hunt maneuver. He had worked with Mr. Hunt in GT&EA as he ascended to its leadership. Mr. Harper knew well what a frustrated governor did not: that the source of the major schooling changes afoot in Georgia was, in part, the work of an unseen network of black educators.[33]

3

MY DEAR MR. MARSHALL

From his small office in the Odd Fellows Building on Auburn Avenue, Mr. Harper knew exactly how to help Mr. Tate and the citizens of Greensboro. He worked only a few blocks away from where the youthful Walter White had written his exuberant letters to the NAACP office in 1917, highlighting NAACP activity but never saying a word to James Weldon Johnson about the role the educators had played.

"Dear Mr. Marshall," Mr. Harper wrote to the NAACP's special counsel after the meeting of the Executive Board of the GT&EA in July 1947. He went on to inform Attorney Marshall that "the committee in charge" planned to challenge discrimination by "having patrons affected to file a petition with the local boards of education seeking a correction of the disadvantages which their children suffer." In other words, his committee of educators still planned to use key people.

Mr. Hunt's key people plan had worked through the years to address some modicum of the injustices. In the 1920s, when the rhetoric about equality died not long after the Negro soldiers who had given their lives in the Great War and Negro Georgians could no longer publicly demand the delivery of the NAACP magazine, the *Crisis*, the educators turned to the philanthropic monies available through the foundation established by the Sears and Roebuck merchant and German Jewish immigrant Julius Rosenwald. Mr. Rosenwald contributed to the NAACP during the Great War, but then turned his attention to the Rosenwald Fund's school building program, initially conceived with Booker T. Washington in 1912 and designed to use monetary contributions to encourage Negro communities to donate land, labor, buildings, and money to obtain school buildings they were denied by the state. In 1920 the program's offices moved from Tuskegee to Nashville and expanded under new leadership.

GT&EA had gone to work, calling on its key people in communities across the state. Their journal for educators, the *Herald*, sent the message to teachers across the state. Teachers needed to be the ones to tell parents "it is their duty to go before the Local Board when it meets on the first Tuesday in the Courthouse and ask for things that are fair and just and in keeping with the needs of your school."[1]

Negro parents responded. By the time the Rosenwald Fund's school building program ended officially in 1937, with the Eleanor Roosevelt School in Warm Springs, Georgia, as the last to be erected, Negroes had built 259 schools in 103 of the 159 counties in Georgia. Collectively, they obtained $5,165,281 in funds for the Negro school building program from the Rosenwald program.[2]

As the Rosenwald program came to an end, the GT&EA adopted a similar strategy with President Roosevelt's New Deal money. The president enjoyed his "Little White House" in Warm Springs for years; he would drive gleefully along country roads and stop to talk to both whites and Negroes about southern problems. Mr. Hunt was among the people with whom he chatted. As the Georgia-informed perspectives evolved into the New Deal programs to aid Americans suffering from the effects of the Depression, GT&EA quickly crafted a Georgia slogan aligned with the president: "A New Deal for the Negro Child."

Officially the organization wrote superintendents reminding them of the first allotment of $10 million provided to Georgia through a federal work relief program run by the Works Progress Administration. Among the projects approved by the Georgia National Emergency Council to receive some of this money were Negro school buildings. But GT&EA also turned to its key people, sending them letters saying that the GT&EA is "writing to you" as one of the "key people of our group in the state in the interest of better school buildings for our children." They enclosed a copy of the letter they had already written to superintendents reminding them of money available for Negro schools, then urged Negro people all over the state to take advantage of this opportunity to obtain funding. "Act now," the letter to the key people concluded. "Inform and organize our people. Formulate Projects . . . Hurry. Tomorrow is too late."[3]

GT&EA president Agnes Scott Jones outlined some of the remaining inequalities. She provided details on the number of consolidated schools for Negroes compared to whites, per pupil expenditure for Negroes as compared to whites, teacher certificates for Negroes as compared to whites, teacher salaries for Negroes as compared to whites, and more. The "weight of this disparity," she wrote, made it difficult for the Negro child to start abreast with white children. "Therefore, *the task of the Georgia Teachers and Education Association is to narrow the gap between these two extremes in equipment, facilities, in professional qualifications and in salary schedules.*"[4]

And that was precisely what Mr. Harper sought to accomplish via a litigation campaign. What he needed, though, was a larger, more representative, more cohesive body of educators to support the effort. Mr. Hunt's district organization had worked for its era, disseminating ideas in annual and district meetings and through its quarterly publication. Philanthropic money and federal money had indeed been channeled to Negro schools.[5] But because school districts allowed small pockets of vocal residents to determine the way forward, he needed a way to strengthen representation that would allow the organization to include the voice of all educators in every town and community in the state. Mr. Harper turned to Horace Mann Bond, the new president of Fort Valley State College, who had replaced Mr. Hunt after his death in 1938.

Dr. Bond partnered with Mr. Harper on the plan to strengthen the organization beyond the district structure designed by Mr. Hunt. Dr. Bond's assignment was to propose and write an amendment to the organization's constitution that would shift GT&EA to a new model that allowed for regional representation. Before presenting the amendment Dr. Bond consulted with the Georgia Education Association, the statewide organization of white educators. Negro educators consistently wanted the appearance of aligning structurally with their white counterparts. It provided credibility and masked the ways they used similar structures for different ends. However, despite the public show of consultation, the truth was that Dr. Bond had already written his own plan.[6]

As required by the GT&EA constitution, Dr. Bond presented his proposal for a Representative Assembly at the 1941 annual meeting in Augusta, with 1,900 people in attendance. He argued the organization needed to get away from the "small clique" that dominated annual sessions and resulted in "ballot box stuffing" at biennial election meetings and in "high pressure farces with votes." Moving to a regional structure would be the way to create a "powerful state organization that will be in [a] position to increase educational facilities for Negro people in every section of Georgia." It was through the local units that the educators would be able to "weld together all elements of our people in any area and through their joint action accomplish results on a large scale." He argued that the proposed new structure would also allow the organization to align itself with the efforts of other educators across the South to revive their state organizations.[7] In the *Herald*, Dr. Bond countered the accusations that his constitutional revisions would prioritize urban control by pointing out that the interests of Negro children were "too desperate to allow Negro teachers to have the great issues they face be clouded by an artificial appeal to urban or rural suspicions."[8]

"If [the amendment] is voted down," Bond proclaimed in the *Herald*, "well and good." But, despite expectations of a "spirited clash" over what came to be called the "Bond Amendment," Negro educators at the 1942 meeting at Booker T. Washington High School passed the amendment. His efforts would wind up increasing GT&EA membership from 32 percent to 60.1 percent of black teachers in Georgia, an increase that boosted the organization's strength from 2,000 members to 8,500, during the years Mr. Harper served as executive secretary (1942–55).[9] After the 1942 vote, a grateful Mr. Harper wished to express thanks for Dr. Bond's efforts and wrote to Mrs. Bond asking her to purchase "some gift for him" with the $20 he enclosed in the letter.[10]

By the time Mr. Harper became executive secretary, the new Executive Board represented the eleven GT&EA regions across the state. Its elected members communicated regularly with unit presidents of the local groups and visited schools. The board met quarterly, with the members reporting to Mr. Harper on matters of concern in their region.

What's more, the structure of the board gave its eleven members full authority to represent the will of the educators in their respective regions, which allowed local educators to deny involvement in any actions the organization would undertake. Mr. Harper was the group's connection to the NAACP and other national movements. The organization was a mask that concealed their strategy of advocacy and protection.[11]

In the 1940s, the state conference of the NAACP was not yet sufficiently organized to advocate for Negro children's education, so the educators themselves would have to do it. The networked organization of educators was the way the new plan to achieve justice for Negro children could be implemented. The new NAACP branch chapters that had begun to take shape during the 1940s would be the public face of these efforts, providing a focal point for white anger and keeping attention away from the activities of the educational organization. On the ground, the chapters would

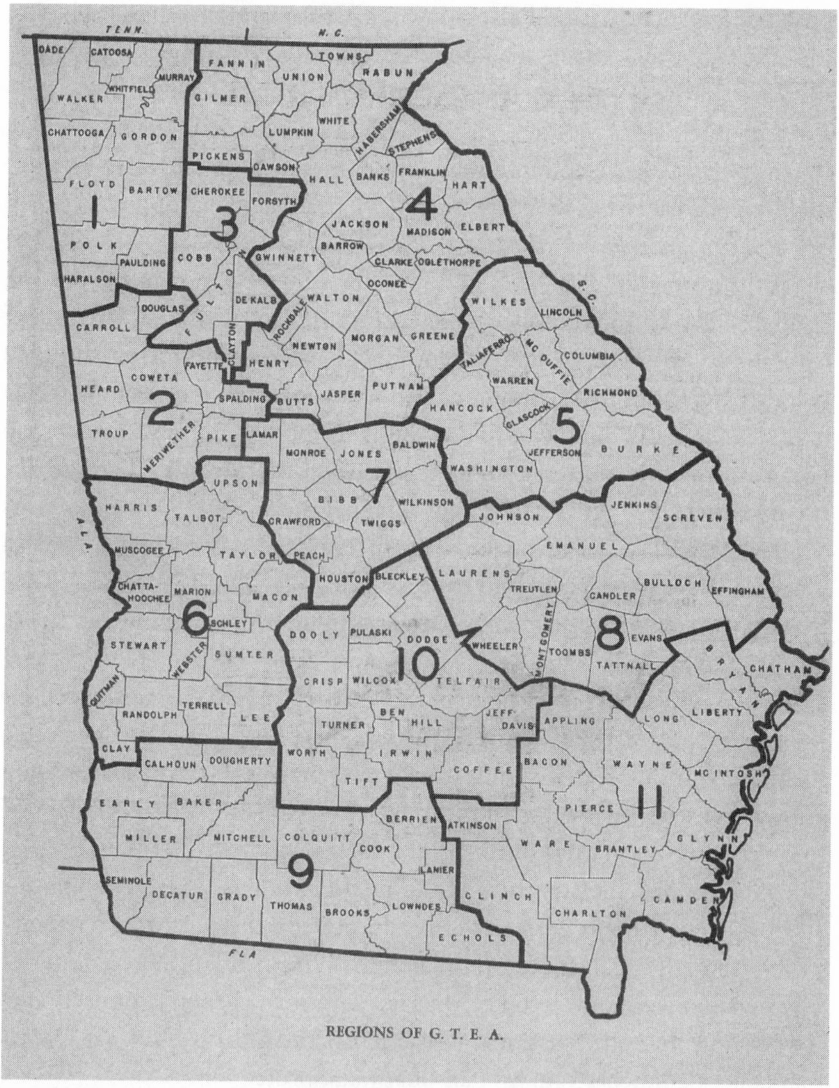

REGIONS OF G. T. E. A.

Dr. Bond and Mr. Harper convinced GT&EA to dispense with the former district organization and to adopt a regional representative organization for the association. They believed regional representation would create a more democratic process of representation. Shown here is the original map created and distributed to GT&EA members across the state. It allowed members to easily locate their county association within a regional area. *Herald*, October 1946. *GT&EA Collection* continue to do what they had always done: hold fundraisers, report their dues to the National, and host high-profile speakers to help spur membership campaigns.[12]

"If the Association does not get satisfactory results through these petitions," Mr. Harper and his board wrote in the 1947 letter to Thurgood Marshall, "the board of directors, in cooperation with local NAACP branches and patrons, plan to take these superintendents and Boards of Education into the Federal Courts. In that instance, they would turn to your office for legal assistance." Mr. Harper wanted Mr. Marshall to make sure the petition was "encouched in such terms and language as to make it legally sound."[13]

The national office of the NAACP did not respond to the GT&EA Board of Directors in time for its August 2 meeting, held in Albany, as the educators had requested. The Executive Board then sent a more detailed follow-up request to the NAACP on August 3. They reiterated the intent of the educational association to equalize educational opportunities in the state, emphasizing they represented a professional organization of seven thousand members and that they had already created a special committee to complete a survey of inequalities in the 159 county boards and the 50 independent boards of education. They knew with certainty the "most vulnerable places" in Georgia discriminating in Negro education. And they again specified what they wanted from the lawyers.

"This letter should attempt to do several things," the communication read, "including the following." They wanted him in part one of the letter to set forth the legal basis for their petition. "This part of the letter should be so general that it could be sent to all boards of education." In another part of the letter, they needed a skeleton, or suggested format, where they could fill in the details. "For example, in one county we would like to call attention specifically to the lack of transportation for Negro pupils. In another county it might be the length of term. Still in another county it might be discrimination as reflected in teachers' salaries." The point was that they already had "the detailed information that we might fill in" for this section.

Finally, the GT&EA Executive Board addressed tone. "We would want the letter of course to end with this section by setting forth a frank warning that if we do not get results with this procedure the G.T.E.A. is prepared to take the next steps which might involve legal procedures."

One day after the second letter arrived at the national office in New York, Assistant Special Counsel Franklin H. Williams responded to Mr. Harper. He apologized for the long delay, noting staff on vacation and the pressure of a number of cases. However, he had prepared the petition that morning. "It will be necessary in each instance where this petition is used to fill in the blanks with the appropriate matter. Each inequality complained of, e.g., school term, salaries, etc., ought to be set out in a separate paragraph." He hoped the document would "serve their purposes."

Meanwhile, the NAACP's Robert Carter—an attorney whom GT&EA board members knew and said they would work with if Attorney Marshall was busy—responded the day after to the chair of the GT&EA committee. He noted that he hoped the materials sent would serve their purpose and that Mr. Harper should already have a copy of it. "Of course," he ended, "it goes without saying, you have our wholehearted support and cooperation. If the petition and suggestions are not satisfactory or if we can assist you further in any way, kindly let us know."[14]

The GT&EA board put into place exactly the strategies Attorney Marshall had carefully outlined in his New York memo to the southern NAACP branches in 1943. To equalize educational opportunities, every branch should have a local legal committee that would make a study of school laws in the state (including provisions for equality, the ways school funds were raised and distributed, and the procedure for protesting local school budgets). Once this information had been collected and made public, the local NAACP chapter should give the national office the information so they could publicize the inequalities and build up public support. They should contact the Negro press. They should hold mass meetings to acquaint the public with the inequalities and garner their support. Only after these steps were completed could they begin the campaign of formal petitions to the local school boards. The public petitions would bring wide publicity. Copies would be given to the press and to all individuals present at each of the school board meetings.[15]

Attorney Marshall had written the important and comprehensive memo, but he failed to capture the strategy in which the educators were the invisible agents behind the whole operation. No one was offended, as they were aware that public and behind-the-scenes behaviors did not always align. As executive secretary, for example, Mr. Harper traveled across the state, always making sure that the courageous school principals working quietly behind the more public parental advocacy had the information they needed to coordinate activities and adapt orders to their local circumstances.

Mr. Harper had the reputation of appearing on local scenes "by bus, horse and wagon or in a 'tin lizzie.'" He often made jokes, not just to pass the time but also to help him avoid becoming overwhelmed by the immensity of the challenges they faced.

Mr. Harper already had what he needed from other local school districts across the state. Across his desk were strewn copies of the carefully typed and signed petitions from trusted key people in their local school districts. They read just like the memo he and the board had requested from Attorney Marshall.

From Albany, Georgia, a memo to the superintendent and members of the Board of Education of Dougherty County:

> This petition of your petitioners respectfully shows:
>
> 1. That we are tax payers, Negro patrons and other Citizens of Dougherty County interested in the Education of the youth of our county and state.
> 2. That there are 1775 white children of Dougherty County, who attend the City schools of Albany . . . That the school buildings in Albany are of brick construction. That the county operates only one school for white children with a frame building and that all of these schools have flush toilets. That three of these schools have auditoriums and one, a gymnasium. That all of these schools except one have libraries . . . On the other hand . . . Negroes children attend classes in 23 buildings [all] of which are frame construction except one. That 13 of these schools are one teacher schools . . . That all save one have pit toilets and are without libraries, gymnasium and auditorium.

The thin eleven-by-fourteen-inch sheets enumerated seven complaints before getting to the point they wished to make: "Because these discriminations in the education of white and Negro Children of Dougherty County by the County Board of Education are contrary to the laws of the state of Georgia, and of the United States, we your petitioners pray the Board of Education to cease these long standing discriminations by providing the following facilities among others for Negro children of our country." The petition went on to list the requests, and concluded with community signatures.

File Copy

Petitions

Lincolnton, Ga. Jan. 1949

To: The Superintendent of Schools and the President and Members of the Board of Education of Lincoln County:

Your petitioners respectfully show:

1. That we are citizens of Lincoln County and many of us are patrons of the public schools of Lincoln County and all are interested in the education of all the people.

2. Your petitioners also show that there is but one consolidated school for white children in Lincoln County which has 2 brick buildings and 2 frame buildings. That there are 21 schools for Negro children in Lincoln County most of which are of the inferior one and two-teacher type, and none having any brick structures, all being of the cheaper frame buildings.

3. We show further that the school building in which white children are taught has an auditorium, running water and flush toilets, but that none of these conveniences is to be found in any of the 21 Negro schools.

4. It is shown that there are 4035 volumes in the white school with a value of $5200. In the 21 Negro schools there a re but 505 volumes in libraries, valued at $350.

5. Your petitioners wish also to call your attention to these discriminations based on race; that the laboratory equipment provided by the Board for the white school is valued at $1800; the equipment for home making, vocational, agricultural classes and trade classes in the white school has the considerable value of $5000; the lunch room equipment is worth $1500 and the food processing equipment $2000. This makes a total of $8500 invested in these 4 items alone for white children, but the records fail to reveal a single dollar spent by the Board to provide similar equipment for Negro children.

6. We show that the value of the schoolplant for white children is $107,500; that of all the plants for Negro children, $12,191.50. This is an investment per white child of $166.00 in contrast to plant investment of $14 per Negro child. For every dollar invested in school plants per Negro child, there is invested more than 11 dollars per white child.

Petitions for potential cases arising in local communities are among the records of the GT&EA. The petitions vary in the type of request parents make to the school boards based on the needs in individual areas. However, all of them have in common the general template delivered by the NAACP legal defense team at the request of the GT&EA Executive Committee and Mr. Harper. *GT&EA Collection*

7. It is further shown that the Board of Education of Lincoln County operates the white school for a term of 176 days; but all Negro schools are operated for only 138 days, a difference of 38 days. This is done despite the fact that the State Board of Education would pay salaries for the two extra months and that the Board of Lincoln County has additional funds which could be used to extend the term in Negro schools to 9 months.

8. We respectfully show that 12 private buses and 1 car were used by the Board of Education to transport 554 children a total of 75,539 miles to white schools at a cost of $17,315.13. On the other hand the Board did not provide a dollar for transportation of any of the Negro children.

9. Your petitioners would also show that the 11th. grade in the white school is 41 per cent of the number in the 1st. grade, there being 37 enrolled in the 11th. grade and 89 in the first grade. Although there are 299 enrolled in the first grade in Negro schools, there are only 9 in the 11th. grade or a bare 3 per cent of the number enrolled in the first grade. For every white child who dropped out of school approximately 13 Negro children dropped out. This is a fact that must shock the Board as well as the parents of these children who have failed to continue their education.

10. This fearful loss of children from school is due to the discriminations cited above; poor housing, inefficient one and two-teacher schools; lack of teaching aids, lack of ample library facilities and lack of equipment for various purposes; lack of transportation, the seven month term and other inequalities.

11. We show that these inequalities in education are based on race and are in violation of the laws of the State of Georgia and of the United States.

12. In order to provide equal facilities in education for Negro children in Lincoln County, your petitioners, most respectfully petition the Board of Education to take the following steps forthwith:

(a) Set up modern consolidated schools instead of the outmoded small schools and equip these schools with modern equipment.

(b) Erect a modern high school with auditorium, cafeteria and other requirements of a standard high school so that it may meet the requirements of the Southern Association.

(c) Provide bus transportation for Negro children as is provided white children, using the same type and model of buses as are used for other childreh and employing Negro bus drivers of good repute at the same salaries paid operators of other buses.

(d) Extend the 7 months school term now existing for Negro children to 9 months as provided for other children.

(e) Improve the teaching personnel so that better teaching may take place in the Negro schools.

(f) Enforce the Compulsory school law in Negro schools as it is being enforced in other schools.

(g) Do away with all other existing inequalities in the two school systems based on race.

. We do not seek to enter our children in schools provided by the Board for white children, but we do most earnestly seek the educational advantages that Justice and the Law claim we are entitled to. The little black boys and girls of Lincoln Cou nty are as dear to our hearts as the little white children are to yours. We have been forbearing and of long patience. Now we a ppeal to you as Christian gentlemen who believe in fair play and who take your sacred obligation seriously to correct the inequalities that our children suffer in education and give them a chance to grow to full economic, intellectual, cultural and moral maturity here in Lincoln County and the Sunny South.

Our country is beset by growing and powerful aggressor nations. She will have need of everything that our children will be able to offer. The conflict is between Communism and Democracy. Ignorance makes for Communism; intelligence and loyalty for Democracy. The Negro today and tomorrow, like the Negro from Bunker Hill to this day must stand for Old Glory and be prepared to defend it in peace or war.

Most respectfully,

The petition to the board of education in Hancock County was much the same: "This petition shows that your petitioners are citizens and tax payers of Hancock County, Georgia and that many of us are patrons of the public schools of Hancock County and that we are interested in the education of all children of whatever race or color." It went on to detail the contrast in the education provided for white and black children, listing concretely at the end the steps the petitioners wished the board to take to improve Negro education. It concluded: "Your petitioners pray the board to remove all other discrimination in the school system of Hancock County."

Another petition was sent to the superintendent in Troup County, outlining the concerns about the resources provided for Negro children compared to the resources provided for white children. The document enumerated the items requested and concluded: "As our neighbors and as Christian Gentlemen, we call upon you to work together with the Negro people."

Other documents sent to authorities in Lincolnton, Cordele, and elsewhere followed the same pattern. The writers established themselves as petitioners, provided contrasting statistics for Negro and white education, made requests specific to the location—in Greensboro, for example, the document requested school bus transportation—and concluded with the threat of a lawsuit, as well as an appeal to Christian principles and/or an appeal to fair and democratic behavior.[16]

As soon as Mr. Tate could find the time and money to transport him back to Greshamville, Mr. Harper would have to get the Greensboro petition back out to the small farming community. Other local residents needed to sign the form before the request could be presented to the school board.[17]

As they talked during their late-night rides, Mr. Harper explained to Mr. Tate some of the matters that were not spoken about publicly in the meetings. He probably talked about some of the risks too.

Mr. Harper knew the problems that could occur for those assuming leadership in matters of race. In 1921, during a period when the NAACP was struggling to remain viable in Atlanta, the branch secretary, Mrs. Canady, who was in the office on a Saturday afternoon to prepare cards for the membership drive, died in an inexplicable fire. Writing his friend James Weldon Johnson, Mr. Hunt said she had "stepped on a match which ignited her skirt," but he said nothing about how the flame had suddenly appeared in the office. He only noted that he thought it "dangerous" to give publicity to the event, as it might disrupt "still further" the struggling NAACP membership campaign in Atlanta.[18] Mr. Harper had been a founding member of the chapter. He knew what had happened.

Mr. Harper's pastor apparently did not heed Mr. Hunt's advice. Rev. Richard Henry Singleton wrote a glowing tribute to Mrs. Canady's life, then moved the Atlanta NAACP offices to the safe haven of the massive Big Bethel AME Church where Mr. Harper was a member and where Mr. Hunt's large education association meeting had been held. But in February 1923 fire mysteriously erupted in Big Bethel as well, destroying the local office yet again, along with the church sanctuary. The collapsed six-story tower left the inner sanctum helplessly opened to the sky. Rev. Singleton died later that year. From the national offices in New York, James Weldon Johnson sent condolences to Big Bethel and to Rev. Singleton's widow, but expressed privately his shock at hearing of Rev. Singleton's passing for he had "thought him possessed of vigorous health." He had been, at least before the second burning of the local NAACP headquarters, which had destroyed much of his church and left the pastor emotionally bereft. Such were the reprisals that accompanied effort.[19]

Even years later, the risks of such work had not diminished. Mr. Hunt died at age seventy-two in 1938 of a pre-dawn heart attack at the home in Washington, DC, he used when he was working on federal government matters; some speculated that his heart had broken under the strain of race work. His quiet collaborator, James Weldon Johnson, who sometimes needed the tranquility of a sea voyage to or from Europe to ease jittery nerves, had died just a few months earlier. Georgians understood the gaping hole left by both deaths; the Atlanta University president proclaimed in the university bulletin that the race had lost two great leaders in one year.[20]

Mr. Harper had also seen how venom could be aroused by educational matters. In 1940, while he was still principal at Booker T. Washington High School, a fire destroyed a new $25,000 ten-room brick elementary school for Negro students in Atlanta and left 450 students without a school. By the time policemen arrived, thirty minutes after the Negro community's desperate call, the entire roof had caved in. The origin of the fire at the elementary school was publicly proclaimed to be "shrouded in mystery," but its impact on Mr. Harper was anything but. Mr. Harper had to accept eighty of

Mr. Henry Alexander Hunt, principal of Fort Valley Normal and Industrial School, was the leading figure in re-creating the teachers' organization in Georgia in 1917. His national and cross-national relationships allowed Georgia's advocacy efforts to align with those in other states. *Henry A. Hunt Library, Fort Valley College, Fort Valley, Georgia*

the older displaced students in his own school, which was already overcrowded.[21]

Mr. Harper understood that driving back and forth between Greensboro and Atlanta was risky business for the young Principal Tate. Although newspapers reported that the national NAACP's court victories had no dire effect on race relations in the South, Mr. Harper understood southern truths. NAACP attorneys were courteously treated in courtrooms. But local actors—even those trying to fly under the radar—who attempted to challenge inequality could pay with their livelihoods, their health, and sometimes their lives.[22]

Thus Mr. Harper and Mr. Tate's complex race work had to be covert. The work required a group who knew the people in their communities, including who in particular would be willing to be plaintiffs in litigation and who would not. This group had to be highly organized. With a connected leader, the group could get the key people into the right legal hands. However, that group had to operate outside the suspicion of local authorities invested in the status quo.

Mr. Harper had great confidence in the young Mr. Tate. He knew Mr. Tate would not delay in making the necessary connections with the local people, despite the enormous risks.

After all, Mr. Ward and his accomplices were waiting.

4

THE BALM IN GILEAD

Before Mr. Harper introduced him to the inner workings of an educational organization, Mr. Tate didn't have strategies for achieving justice for Negro children, for himself, or for anyone else. He just had anger.

For almost as long as he could remember, Mr. Tate had been mad about inequality. He hated the textbooks with Ralph Emerson but no Paul Lawrence Dunbar. He despised seeing Shirley Temple's name but not Lena Horne's. Everywhere, white people seemed determined to make him believe he was a second-class citizen, despite his having learned in the Elberton Colored School down the dusty streets from his neighborhood that it was "self-evident" he should live in freedom.[1]

He liked his stately two-story brick school for the Negro children in Elberton. He never connected it with the World War I climate of advocacy created by Mr. Hunt and GT&EA, never even imagined his own parents might have been some of the key people who lobbied for the school and obtained the land for it from local wealthy white sisters. But he did know that, despite being a nice school for Negro children in comparison to the structures Negro children were consigned to in other parts of the state, it still paled in comparison to the sprawling brick white school nearby. The city had attended to every detail of the construction of the massive school for white children, including being sure its windows were oriented in a way that allowed just the right amount of sunlight into the classrooms to facilitate learning. Despite the lessons his principal and teachers lovingly taught, the stark difference between the schools made clear that not everyone believed in freedom and justice for all.

He had been no more than nine or maybe ten the Christmas season when he accompanied his father to the musty old Galant/Belk store nestled between the one- and two-story brick buildings comprising the quaint town center of Elberton. Outside, and looming large, was the rebuilt

Confederate monument on the grassy square. The new monument was a replacement for the earlier one destroyed by citizens who said the face looked too much like a Yankee.

Inside the store near the corner of the square, the scene looked just as it should only a few days before Christmas in a small southern town. On one side of the store, men searched for the tools and the seed they needed to maintain small family farms. On the other side, women purchased household and clothing items. In those pre-Depression years, the strand of exquisite blue granite in the ground below that made the little town the "Granite Capital of the World" ensured adequate income for many among the town's citizens, allowing them to enjoy shopping during the holiday season.[2]

A red-suited Santa had claimed little Horace's attention. While his father shopped, Horace had naively joined the line where children of a lighter hue waited excitedly for their turn to sit on Santa's knee. Once settled, they nodded with certainty when asked if they had been very good, and with bright smiles they listed the items they wanted for Christmas. No other Negro children stood in the line, though it never occurred to Horace he should not.

Eventually the single colored child reached the front of the line.

"Ho ho ho," Santa said as Horace approached. Then he rose abruptly and announced, "Old Santa wants a glass of water."

Horace stood innocently as Santa walked away, his belly bulging over the black belt and the curls of his white beard dangling. Horace assumed Santa really was thirsty and waited. Ten or more minutes passed before he noticed the white boys and girls behind him in line were moving away, and he was left alone.

Eventually sounds from the other side of the store seeped to where he stood. Quietly ushered away by the adult gatekeepers of segregation, the white children had reconvened with Santa on the other side of the store. Children who had been behind him in line had already climbed onto his lap and shared their wishes for Christmas as Santa listened carefully. A surprised Horace stood motionless.[3] Without being told, he knew not to go stand in the other line. But as his father grasped his hand and ushered him silently out the door, the episode seeped into his heart. He did not know how to fight the anger he felt developing inside of him.

* * *

"You know you better get off that sidewalk," his sister whispered emphatically one day when he failed to follow accepted southern protocol. He was eight or nine, and by this age he should have known to step aside to allow white ladies to pass as they walked the broad sidewalks of the gently curving road up to the town center where the Confederate soldier still dominated the grassy square. The street boasted majestic colonial homes with shaded porticos and sprawling yards enjoyed by prosperous white citizens of the town. However, his older sister knew that whether they walked on this street, where whites lived, or on Elbert Street, a parallel street where Negroes lived and conducted business, not getting out of the way for white people violated southern expectations for Negro behavior.[4]

Usually Horace complied with southern norms. Like the other Negro boys, he scattered from his game in the dirt street in front of his home when the police showed up, knowing no matter what was asked or how he answered, he could be hollered at and told, "Boy, don't talk back to me!" or "You don't have any business in the road!"

All the Negro boys knew the police would tell a lie about them if they said anything other than they were sorry. The police might say they threw something at the car, even though they were only playing between their houses and breaking no law. Every time he and his friends saw a policeman, they scattered. And they were especially leery of the four-hundred-pound (or so they thought) illiterate policeman who could not even write a subpoena without going downtown for help. All the boys knew that if they didn't avoid him, they could wind up in jail and their parents would have to come get them out.[5] Horace conducted himself like everyone else and just avoided the police.

As a child, he had been mistreated at the post office too. "You're not supposed to be ahead of white people," an older white man waiting in line behind him instructed him as he stood in line to buy stamps. He was flabbergasted. But he dutifully got out of line so no whites had to wait. On this day on the sidewalk, however, years of indignation welled up. He ignored his sister.[6]

As the two met the white ladies coming toward them on the street, Horace kept his eyes pointed ahead and refused to step off the sidewalk. He knew right from wrong. He had been taught fairness at home. If he did not have to get out of the street for Negro adults who passed, why should he have to get out of the street for white adults who passed?[7]

The ladies passed without challenging him, and his chest puffed in smug satisfaction. When his older sister stopped getting off the sidewalk too on later trips to town, he bristled with victory.

Walking resolutely past white ladies was a small act, really, only a minor form of resistance in the grand scheme of things. But it was all a little boy knew to do. Not until college did he learn that his southern Negro elders, including his principal at the Elberton Colored School, had developed their own ways to channel their anger at the injustices Negro children faced, more intricate than challenging the politics of sidewalks or Santas.[8]

Some things were providential, or so Horace always believed. Perhaps that was how he found himself at Fort Valley State College. It was the college Mr. Hunt had led—and where the new educational organization of 1917 had been born.

He certainly had no substantive answer to the question in the Fort Valley admission package about what he really wanted to do with his life. In fact, he had picked Fort Valley, twenty-nine miles south of Macon, over Paine College in Augusta, which his beloved high school principal had recommended and where many of his high school friends had gone.[9]

It was October 1, 1940, and Horace, almost nineteen years old and a sophomore, walked appreciatively over the carefully laid pathways of Fort Valley's grassy campus, passing under the canopy of the majestic oaks planted as seedlings by Mr. Hunt and paying little attention to the intricate architectural designs of the brick buildings the industrial students had built in the years before him. Fort Valley boasted a beautiful campus, once referred to as a refreshing oasis by a white visitor weary of traveling the flat and fertile but dreary farmlands that surrounded it.[10]

He climbed the few steps of the relatively new $100,000 Academic Building, swung open the heavy door, and began making his way past the state-of-the-art classrooms and science lab on the main floor. Ten o'clock classes had been canceled for the day, making the classrooms empty or nearly empty as he and other students converged in the assembly hall, with its shiny hardwood floor.

Students sometimes convened in this assembly hall for fun—to watch movies, to play basketball, or to have parties. Once a year, the hall hosted the annual "Ham and Egg Show," aimed at helping farmers with meat and egg production. In earlier years, this show had been embodied in the farmers' conferences, which had grown so popular that *Life* magazine carried a feature article about them for the world to see. During these conferences, when the Negro community from the surrounding areas came to campus for these events, large cured hams hung upside down all around the room, their smell so alluring that rumbling stomachs ached for a taste.[11]

However, as Horace moved toward his assigned seat among the sets of four wooden chairs bound together for easy moving, he was aware that this assembly was neither for fun nor about food. Today he and the other 324 students gathered for their second annual Founders' Day Program.[12]

Horace loved these required assemblies, along with vespers on Tuesdays and Sundays. They featured pioneering educators and activists such as Mary McLeod Bethune and Charlotte Hawkins Brown, political figures such as Atlanta attorney A.T. Walden, or presidents and professors from a variety of Negro colleges, who spoke on ideas and events that inspired his interest and taught him how to think about the world and his place in it. He even enjoyed the presentation by white professor Josiah Crudup, who used cords and current to demonstrate electricity. Horace was convinced he was obtaining an excellent education at the school—that it was "top notch." As he settled into his seat with the other students, his usual anticipation bubbled. Today's speaker was W.E.B. Du Bois.

The robed fifty-member Fort Valley choir stood at the front of the auditorium, facing him and the other students and guests seated either on the main floor or in the slightly sloping balcony overhead. The choir's exquisite professional concert series could be heard on the local radio station, WMAZ. Horace knew nothing about the history of the choir, whose songs were skillfully chosen to appeal to the tastes of whites and thereby elicit their financial support for the school, but he thoroughly enjoyed the melodious voices. With their repertoire of spirituals and classical music, the choir summoned the student body to reflection at the start and close of assemblies.[13]

Negro colleges, like African colleges, exuded pomp and formality, and today's assembly was no exception. The faculty entered through the back doors in formal procession and made their way to the front rows. Following their entrance, the president and guest speakers emerged from a hidden door at stage left. The new Fort Valley president, Horace Mann Bond, who held a Ph.D. from the University of Chicago, had inherited the results of Mr. Hunt's behind-the-scenes successes: in 1939, just before Mr. Tate entered as a freshman, Fort Valley had become a four-year state-supported college.

Like the other students, Horace admired the youthful President Bond, who brought with him new ideas about curriculum and solid scholarship. He had published *The Education of the Negro in the American Social Order* in 1934, and his second book, *Negro Education in Alabama: A Study in Cotton and Steel*, came out the year he arrived at Fort Valley. For the latter work, he even received a citation for outstanding contributions to education research from the white American Educational Research Association. He had written numerous other articles, and he was encouraging faculty scholarship and development as well.[14]

Though he was not formally trained as an administrator, the school was growing under his leadership. During Dr. Bond's first year, Horace's freshman year, fifty-two more students than the college had planned on showed up; in his second year, sixty-six above the number planned for arrived. Even Dr. Bond was stunned by the rapid growth. By the end of the first day of registration in the fall of 1939, he had resorted to radio announcements to warn away other students who might have wished to enroll. After a week, he had simply closed the registration process, an act unprecedented in Georgia schools—Negro or white. "We felt we had to do so," the new president confessed. Dormitories were flooded with newcomers, with the women's dorm in particular "stocked far beyond capacity." The school simply had no more room.[15]

But the students sitting quietly in the hall were paying attention not just because President Bond was a scholar or a good administrator, or even because the U.S. government had ranked their institution among the twenty-five leading Negro colleges.[16] They liked President Bond as a human being. He was energetic and progressive. He was friendly and approachable. He was an "indefatigable worker," and he was modest. Like Mr. Hunt, who was said to have sometimes rounded up young migrant workers during their off season and allowed them to enjoy the campus sports facilities, Dr. Bond believed he had a mission tied to the young people he served in the Fort Valley community. He played games and sports with them. Sometimes he went over to the boys' dorm where Horace lived, Ohio Hall, which housed 150 students, and shared his jazz collection.[17]

The aging Dr. Du Bois sat quietly as President Bond introduced him as a "lifelong scholar and happy warrior."[18] In the fall of 1940 Dr. Du Bois was out of favor with the NAACP organization he had helped found, because of an explosive article he had published while serving on the advisory board of GT&EA: "Does the Negro Need Separate Schools?" In that article he analyzed how Negro schools' purposeful supplementation of state curricula and caring school climates that made Negro children aspire to compete, despite the restrictions of segregation, might be beneficial. The national NAACP felt that the article did not advance the legal campaign to demand equality.[19]

The Fort Valley president was Dr. Du Bois's former mentee from the days when he needed a research assistant. In his introduction Dr. Bond championed Dr. Du Bois as one of the "two great scholars of the race" for their respective generations (the other was Dr. Charles S. Johnson, a colleague who worked on interracial committees to help advance Negro education and who would be speaking to the students during another assembly three days later).[20]

At the conclusion of President Bond's introduction, Dr. Du Bois stepped forward, the tassel on his cap gently swaying with each step. Dr. Du Bois was no stranger to Fort Valley or to Georgia. As his eyes scanned the receptive students, he launched into an address about a man he simply called his friend. He titled the lecture "On the Significance of Henry A. Hunt."

He needed to tell an emerging generation about Henry Hunt, for although Hunt was buried on the campus in a small grove of trees and bushes, neither Horace nor most of the other students knew much about him. Two years earlier, while Horace had been enjoying his senior year at Elberton Colored School, the Negro people of Fort Valley were mourning a fallen leader, whose body was transferred from the Washington train and slowly driven amidst the crowds to the college's quaint white president's home, where it would rest overnight.

Neither Horace nor the students knew of the relationship between Mr. Hunt and the NAACP: the way the organization had solicited him to participate in national meetings, consulted him for advice on southern matters, and placed him atop the list of southern people whom they knew they could count on. In one of the many telegrams that deluged the small campus in the wake of Mr. Hunt's death, Walter White had declared himself to be "heartbroken." Negroes and whites alike had waited in line on the steps of the library building, Carnegie Hall, to say goodbye to the statesman, considered a friend to the rural farmer and to Eleanor Roosevelt alike, a man who served as a delegate to the Republican National Convention and who had reinvented the GT&EA, who had organized the community to make the Negro "articulate on his demands for education."[21]

In his talk, Dr. Du Bois emphasized that the new generation needed commitment if they were going to solve the education problems that remained, despite decades of fighting by their predecessors. As he listened, Horace's head tilted slightly and his right eyebrow arched, as both always did when he was intent.

At the time, Horace was not aware that when Mr. Hunt came to Fort Valley in 1904 he had publicly stated that he intended to make it an industrial school like Booker T. Washington's Tuskegee Normal and Industrial Institute in Alabama. The former principal, John W. Davidson (a former classmate of Mr. Hunt's at Atlanta University who had left college a few months before graduation), had not been very successful in his efforts to camouflage his liberal arts bent, and so he had resigned as philanthropists began to court Mr. Hunt to take the job of creating a first-class industrial school in middle Georgia. Had he known about the first years of Mr. Hunt's tenure at Fort Valley, he might have wondered about the friendship between him and Dr. Du Bois, who had publicly challenged the industrial model of Tuskegee that Mr. Hunt supposedly came to champion.[22]

"I knew Henry Hunt personally and with fair intimacy for more than twenty-five years," Dr. Du Bois began. They had lived in "contemporaneous" days, he explained to the students, by which he meant not merely that both had graduated from college in 1890 and that both had presented the commencement addresses for their respective institutions, Harvard and Atlanta University.[23] Rather, Dr. Du Bois sought to explain to the young students the era during which both had been young men and how this era influenced their actions.

Both graduated from college during an era when Negro accomplishment and potential success characterized their worlds. In the North, "sharp, powerful, uninhibited and resourceful individuals" could grow up to become millionaires, or so people proclaimed. Even a progressive South referred to slavery as an "illogical institution," and southern states proclaimed the destiny of the white and Negro bound together. Their era—the one in which the first Negro teachers' organization was organized in Georgia in 1878 by Richard Wright and teachers publicly protested inequality in school funding—had been one where it seemed rapid advance of the race was possible.

But both men also shared the vexation of a time when the Reconstruction period of accomplishment for Negroes was hit with "sudden catastrophe." Supreme Court decisions, state segregation laws, disenfranchisement, and white opinion galvanized against the southern Negro at the turn of the century, and advancement halted. Negroes banded together across the South, creating national networks of Negro educators to share ideas across states in the hope of making some progress collectively. Dr. Du Bois had come to Atlanta University during that period and created the esteemed Atlanta University publications that yearly updated Negroes and whites on the progress and needs of the race. In 1911, Mr. Hunt had been the opening speaker for the Atlanta University conference on education, and he and Mr. Hunt had together written the resolutions articulating Negroes' needs and demands, including federal aid. Dr. Du Bois explained to the students how this increasingly more restrictive era had been a "sort of culmination of forces loosened in the first generation, riding high on the winds of success, and smashing again to even greater disaster."

Either man might have chosen to give up on achieving justice for Negro children during this dismal time, but neither did. When Mr. Hunt had come to Fort Valley on a chilly, rainy night in February 1904 he had been greeted by flat black, muddy water flooding the campus and mounds and mounds of pebbles; there were no trees, shrubbery, or grass. The institution's few original buildings stood like boxcars on a railroad track: ugly, bare, and unprotected. Meanwhile, the community whispered of indiscretions on the part of Mr. Davidson, while simultaneously viewing the arriving Mr. Hunt with suspicion, especially his questionable Episcopalian religion. Yet, in trickster maneuvers that Horace and the other students were not aware of, Mr. Hunt had coaxed from philanthropists the donations needed to build the beautiful and debt-free campus the current students enjoyed, containing eighteen buildings on ninety-one acres of land. Like the better-known Dr. Du Bois, Mr. Hunt had committed his life to creating real opportunities for his generation, even though he might have made a different choice.[24]

"If he had chosen to join the white race in his earlier years," Dr. Du Bois observed to the students, "he could have done so without question." He explained that Mr. Hunt was the descendant of a mulatto mother and was named for his white father, who reportedly maintained a conjugal relationship with his mother back on Hunt Hill in Georgia.[25] Mr. Hunt looked fully white, and he could have easily chosen to live the privileges of a white life.

Had he abandoned the race, Dr. Du Bois emphasized, he would have not been alone. "Thousands of men and women like him have done so." These mulattoes were the ones he and Walter White had described as simply "disappearing" every year from the census. They did not migrate north, nor did they die. Rather, as James Weldon Johnson had provocatively revealed in his 1912 *Autobiography of an Ex-Colored Man,* these Negroes had simply become white by choice.

The young people in the audience knew the truth he spoke. As Charles Johnson had written in the introduction to Mr. Johnson's *Autobiography,* pretty much every southern Negro could count among his acquaintances someone who had elected to pass. Sometimes they passed temporarily to get a hotel room or a meal or a job but retained all social connections with the Negro community. Sometimes they married into the white race, severed all ties, and became one of the missing.[26]

Dr. Du Bois impressed upon his young listeners that Mr. Hunt did not have to live as a Negro in an era when Negroes were being so severely mistreated, since the path of disappearance was open to him. In fact, one of Mr. Hunt's four siblings married a white woman. Mr. Hunt could have escaped the oppression. It was a "deliberate choice," Dr. Du Bois proclaimed, to refuse to deny his fully black grandmother and to cast his lot with the Negroes.[27] The cost Mr. Hunt paid was one Dr. Du Bois wanted to be sure the brown faces looking at him fully understood.

Since Mr. Hunt looked like a typical Georgia white man, Dr. Du Bois explained, he found himself consistently facing situations where he was treated by other whites as a peer, only to later face ostracism and insult when they discovered he openly identified himself with the Negro race. The situation was an ongoing challenge to Mr. Hunt—whether to stand on his right to be judged as a man and not tell who he was or to be judged as engaging in "unforgivable deception" if he did not. Yet, despite the denigration he received for naming himself, Mr. Hunt refused to be anything other than a Negro man.[28]

Most of the students in the audience would not face similar choices, Dr. Du Bois explained. However, the question of *where* they should serve was a choice they all would have to make.

"If, for instance, I asked this audience: how many of you would prefer to live in New York rather than Fort Valley, the vote in favor of New York, if it were open and honest, would be overwhelming," Dr. Du Bois noted. Indeed, Horace had older brothers who had gone to New York before Horace was born and who, for reasons he did not know, had never come back to the little town of Elberton. Most others in the mostly poor, rural audience also knew people who had gone north and had heard of the thrilling city of "magnificent civilization" that was New York. Dr. Du Bois's words painted what their eyes had not seen, allowing them for a moment to imagine what it might be like to live and work in a place of such beauty, power, efficiency, comfort, and convenience. He explained that Mr. Hunt might have also been personally lured by its invitation to liberation, and that Mr. Hunt—even as a Negro—could certainly have succeeded in that great city. His brother-in-law had done so.[29]

But Mr. Hunt had deliberately chosen the rural life, Dr. Du Bois explained. He had eschewed the fads and luxuries of city life and made a conscious decision to live in rural Georgia, a place where the resistance was most bitter and the battle most fierce—and, consequently, where the victory could be most glorious."[30] In choosing to address the education problem of Negroes in rural areas, Mr. Hunt had made a decision that cost him convenience, friendship, and money.[31]

It was certainly true that life in the country offered quiet, fresh air, sunlight, and wholesome good food, Dr. Du Bois observed. But Fort Valley was substantially more rural than the Biddle College campus in Charlotte, North Carolina, and the surrounding middle-class Negro community from which Mr. Hunt had come. At Biddle, Mr. Hunt had the respect of the administration and philanthropists, lived on a well-maintained and beautiful campus, and was admired by the young men living in the dorm he supervised, who appreciated the commitment he and his wife had made to their development. He supervised Biddle's baseball teams, enjoyed a regular salary, was promoted to more responsibility, and participated in a variety of formal events in the stately chapel of a recognized and successful Negro college. When he arrived via buggy at the dreary Fort Valley campus, Mr. Hunt surely could have decided to go back to Biddle, where his wife and three children could have had more substantial comfort and better opportunities for their education.[32]

Yet, Dr. Du Bois explained, Mr. Hunt had stayed in Fort Valley in pursuit of a higher purpose. The education problem for Negroes was primarily a rural one. Somebody, Dr. Du Bois explained to students relatively unaware of the challenges before their time, needed to "take hold of rural life and re-make it and re-build it." Otherwise, in the long run city life would be "entirely without support and reason for being." Mr. Hunt had decided his greatest usefulness could be to attack "this country's problem," even though it required giving up money and comfort. He had even given up a position in Africa awaiting him upon college graduation because he thought he could do more good in the South.[33]

"There is something peculiar about sacrifice in human living," Dr. Du Bois continued,

> about the deliberate surrender of certain obvious advantages and pleasures so that greater opportunity will come to someone else. It is not logical and there is no use pretending that it is. . . .
>
> The man who faces the possibility of sacrifice for great ends would better make up his mind and grip his courage and say I am giving up something. It is mere pretense; it is "pie in the sky by and by" to deny the real sacrifice. It is worth while because I am willing to do something of this sort if it makes life broader and easier for other folk, such as I am, who are going to follow me.

Before leaving the idea of sacrifice, Dr. Du Bois wanted to make one other point, and that was the matter of money. Turning to his long-standing concerns about economics, he noted that there was a "small minority of people who make the matter of income, their chief thought: income for themselves and for their children." Income, he conceded, was important because poverty led to disease, death, ignorance, crime, quarreling, and even despair. As a result, "a considerable group of people give a large part of their time and effort to being sure that they and their children get an income large enough so that they can live decently and in a civilized manner and educate their children and clothe and house them and give them that guidance and advice which will make them healthy and normal folk."

However, he explained, Mr. Hunt had had to sacrifice income in the choices he made. During the Depression years, faculty had witnessed Mr. Hunt and other top-level administrators emerging tight-lipped from back-room meetings at which a serious shortfall of funding had been discussed. Like his predecessor at Fort Valley and like countless other Negro educators sacrificing to help children, Mr. Hunt had used personal funds and disposed of family property to supplement teacher salaries and help keep the school afloat during difficult seasons. In fact, Dr. Du Bois had even contributed some of his own personal funds to Fort Valley.

Dr. Du Bois proclaimed it "unfortunate" that the very people working to change the world would be "exceptional" if they managed to live even in ordinary comfort. However, he did emphasize that the success Mr. Hunt had experienced in his life had been possible only because "men of vision" were "willing to sacrifice something of present comfort for the advantage of future generations."

As a young Horace sitting in the audience listened intently, Dr. Du Bois outlined the challenge that would define the life of the young face he would never come to distinguish from the others in the crowd. "The problem that he, therefore," Dr. Du Bois said, "leaves to you is a problem as to how you are going to see to it that not only such work is done for the people who need it and in the places where the need is greatest but also that that work is going to be so paid for that the persons who do it can do it well and not sacrifice health and strength and happiness in this duty."

For those like Horace who brought anger to the problem of inequality, Dr. Du Bois acknowledged the life of the Negro as one fraught with "unusual difficulty." It was easy, as President Bond once wrote, to have hot and indignant responses, to vent the pent-up feelings.[34] It certainly took more energy, ambition, and determination for the Negro to accomplish a task than a white man. Dr. Du Bois conceded the point.

However, there were also "clear advantages" he believed to be attached to the obvious disadvantages of being a Negro. For a moment, Dr. Bu Bois allowed his mind to return to his days as an undergraduate student at Harvard, and taking these southern students with him on his mental journey, he recalled bumping over the cobblestones between Boston and Cambridge as he and a classmate headed back to campus. Dr. Du Bois explained he assumed the classmate to have all the advantages of a fortunate mortal: "good-looking, healthy, cultured, rich, and white." And yet, as they jostled over the streets together, the classmate confessed to an aghast Du Bois that he really didn't know what he wanted to do when he finished college because there was nothing in which he was "particularly interested."

As he recalled the incident, Dr. Du Bois explained to the listening students the advantage of the Negro over his directionless white classmate. The former classmate's lack of ambition was an example of "one of the disadvantages of those people in the world who do not see or realize the world's injustice, who think of themselves as the privileged and who lose their opportunities because of the very abundance."

In contrast, as Negroes, they had a distinct opportunity the white man lacked.

Because the country violated its proclaimed commitment to citizenship rights for all, it created a people "always conscious of injustice." That awareness had fueled Mr. Hunt in his time, and he had determined to act against it. Dr. Du Bois hoped the listening students might act also. Social reform would not be "providential" or "a matter of chance," he noted. It would be "a matter of planning."

Since most of the students facing him were preparing to be teachers, he ended his lecture with a concrete example for their lives. What must the teacher do when he encountered a country school where the community needed a new schoolhouse, better attendance, better clothes, and more books? Suppose a teacher wanted a better salary but was disappointed by the "deliberate discrimination" he witnessed and knew he could not count on economically impoverished Negro patrons of the school to help?

Dr. Du Bois explained this was the dilemma Mr. Hunt had confronted often in his life. It was "always in his mind," something that had frequently emerged "in their talks together." Since the educational inequalities still existed, this generation of young Negroes would need to address them. Like Mr. Hunt, they would need a plan for advancement. Unless they had commitment to such a constructive plan, it could "mean frustration in much of the work which you young people undertake."

"If, reasoning logically," he concluded,

> a man proposes to work for himself alone and other men follow his example, we shall have a world in which there will be much comfort and happiness because one of the difficulties today is that so many of us do not even attend to our own best interests. But on the other hand, if we have in the world an increasing number of people who are willing really and definitely to sacrifice, not all but a considerable part of their comfort and happiness in order that the number of people to whom happiness and comfort is possible may be largely increased; then not only is the sum total of happiness increased but the world is a much better place to live. . . . The quest as to who is to make that sacrifice is, as the life of Henry Hunt teaches, a matter not of compulsion, not of threat, but of inner individual choice.[35]

With respect for the wisdom of his speech, the students clapped heartily for Dr. Du Bois at the conclusion of his talk, the sound multiplying as it bounced off the hardwood floors and walls. Then the faculty and students solemnly processed out of the Academic Building and assembled around the brick tomb that contained the remains of Dr. Du Bois's colleague and friend. Amidst the towering oak trees, the Fort Valley choir lifted its voices in reverent song. The hymn had been Mr. Hunt's favorite: "Sometimes I feel discouraged and think my work's in vain, but then the Holy Spirit revives my soul again."[36]

Trained in piano before first grade, Horace loved music and enjoyed singing. He stood among the crowd of students and added his voice to the others swelled in harmony. "There is a balm in Gilead," they sang collectively, "to make the wounded whole."[37] Mr. Hunt's memory provided a symbol of silent struggle for young Negroes who knew they were mistreated but who did not yet know how to fight effectively.

Standing with Dr. Bond close to the tomb, Dr. Du Bois knew there were certain aspects of the life of Henry Hunt he had failed to speak of. He knew Mr. Hunt had been part of the synergy that helped stop national oppression during the World War I era. A delegate of the Georgia educators, Mr. Hunt had been one of the speakers in 1921 at the Pan African Congress Dr. Du Bois convened in London when Negro men from around the world discussed the need to organize.[38]

Dr. Du Bois had recommended Mr. Hunt for the position of assistant to the governor of the Farm Credit Administration (FCA) during the Depression era. Mr. Hunt had studied cooperatives in Denmark, and Dr. Du Bois was convinced no one knew better how to lift Negro farmers out of Depression woes. The position also put Mr. Hunt among the members of President Roosevelt's famed "Black Cabinet." During Mr. Hunt's tenure at the FCA, not one Negro who had taken out a loan under the FCA's programs had defaulted.[39]

And, as Dr. Du Bois would explain later when he returned to Fort Valley to talk directly about his disagreements with Booker T. Washington over industrial education, which Mr. Hunt had promoted in his early years at the Fort Valley School, the debate was really a non-debate. As he, Mr. Hunt, and others had agreed at Amenia, it was never a matter of "if" but to what degree industrial education should be utilized.[40]

But the intricacies and nuances of the particular ways to fight were not matters for public disclosure. In public, world-renowned scholar Dr. Du Bois toasted a relatively unknown soldier for equality, his friend H.A. Hunt, with his presence while a new generation watched. It was an echo of the moment in 1921 when he, Mr. Hunt, and other Pan African Congress delegates had laid a wreath together in Paris to reverently salute a fallen unknown soldier from the Great War in the shadows of the Champs-Élysées: "Ici repose un soldat français mort pour la patrie."[41] Mr. Hunt was such a soldier in the United States.

Meanwhile, Horace Tate watched quietly as the tribute came to a close before turning away from the service with the other students and returning to college life. If someone had suggested that Dr. Du Bois had just mapped Horace's own path from anger to effective service, he likely would have been without words.

5

A SIMPLE SCHEME TO DO A "SIMPLE LITTLE"

His senior year, Horace walked briskly to the attractive nine-room white president's house sitting on the edge of the Fort Valley campus near the college's entrance. It had been a year ago that Miss Jones, his boss at the school cafeteria, had dismissed him from his duties and told him to go see President Bond. Like the other students, Horace did whatever Miss Jones said. Miss Jones brooked no nonsense from her employees, demanding precision and perfection—"respect, proper attire and manners"—whether they were serving tables or scrubbing floors in the pristine college cafeteria with its silverware and glasses carefully placed at each setting on the white tablecloths. In her dining hall, employees alternated between fear and reverence.

Miss Jones was also known for her generosity and sincere kindheartedness. She enjoyed a reputation for creating jobs for students in dire need of income and for paying close attention to those who performed in an exemplary manner.[1] Horace had needed a job when he arrived in the middle Georgia flatlands of Fort Valley after the long bus ride from hilly Elberton. He had barely $50 in his pocket from a teachers' scholarship from the Elberton Colored School and the money he made caddying for a professional white golfer who relied heavily on the advice of the young man he paid. The $7 a month he made working in Miss Jones's school cafeteria and the $7 a month his mother somehow "scraped up" helped with the $45 tuition and monthly boarding costs. Horace felt like he had slaved in Miss Jones's kitchen over the years, but that time had also given her ample opportunity to observe him closely.[2] Perhaps her quietly whispered reference explained Horace's sudden new employment.

Horace became a student chauffeur for President Bond. He may have gotten the job because of Miss Jones's recommendation. Alternatively, it could have been because so few young men remained on campus. Two months after the assembly with Dr. Du Bois during his sophomore year, the Japanese bombed Pearl Harbor and President Roosevelt quickly ordered

Americans into the second war in less than twenty-five years. Across the country, as they had in every other war, Negroes supported the war effort, in some cases leading the contributions of America's other citizens.[3]

They were all Americans at war, as President Bond and Mr. Harper had publicly proclaimed in an editorial in the GT&EA magazine, the *Herald*. The world as they had known it was "deader than a duck," President Bond said privately to his friends. He knew he needed to prepare his "boys" for the war's upcoming demands, so he assembled all the young men for some frank talk. President Roosevelt was asking that they risk their lives for a principle of freedom not practiced in the United States. He might as well be truthful, so he spoke directly that night in Jeans Hall, crisply summarizing the contradictions between America's rhetoric and practice.[4]

In the coming months, war did summon many of his Fort Valley boys into the army. President Bond was proud of their progress and said so publicly. "What it takes to make it" his Fort Valley boys "seemed to have," the president said as he toasted the Fort Valley troops. If they could make it in the army, they could make it anywhere. However, as many male classmates left for service, Horace was among the remaining students who regularly saluted the Negro soldiers from the confines of campus. He had been diagnosed with high blood pressure as a teenager and was turned down for service.[5]

While the exact chain of fortuitous events that led to his becoming the chauffeur for the college president remains unknown, Horace loved the job. He walked purposefully to crank the car at the back of the president's house whenever needed and proudly drove him over Georgia's winding roads and rural wooden bridges until they arrived at their destination. On at least one occasion, they went as far as Fisk University, Horace driving him past the beautiful Chattahoochee River as they crossed into Tennessee and winding around the mountainous roads while a pregnant and uncomfortable Mrs. Bond sat in the back urging him to drive a little above the 35 mph "Victory Speed" limit imposed nationwide in order to reduce the consumption of gasoline and rubber. Horace glanced at the quiet father who appeared to be asleep and, taking a chance, drove a little faster.[6]

Occasionally he still reported to his job in the cafeteria, but whenever President Bond needed him, he made his way from the four-story boys' dormitory where he lived, Ohio Hall, walked past Carnegie Hall with its array of magazines and newspapers supplementing the liberal arts curriculum, ventured beyond Mr. Hunt's grave, and over the grassy lawn that would lead him to some up-close, private time with the president. More than once, he had seen Dr. Bond meeting with the head of the various departments in one of the classrooms and had overheard him talking about what needed to be done to educate the students. His school work kept him busy, and his grades tended toward C-pluses and B-minuses. From the president's talks, he knew the faculty was working hard to create a superior educational program at the school.

But in the car, Horace received an education exceeding any he could obtain in a class, club, or job. Often during their rides Dr. Bond took the time to induct the young driver into the world of Negro leadership.

"Mr. Tate, what would you do if you had a problem?" Dr. Bond asked unexpectedly one day.

Horace had known how to be angry about the race problem since he was a kid. Dr. Du Bois and other assembly speakers had talked about commitment. But he did not know how to answer President Bond's question.

He thought for a minute. He could go to his advisor, he finally suggested.

"Where else could you go to?" the president probed.

"I could go see the academic counselor," Horace offered tentatively.

President Bond remained silent. The miles rolled by.

Eventually the president spoke again. "Mr. Tate, I asked you a while back where you would go if you had a problem."

Understanding that his earlier answers had been insufficient, Horace reflected quietly. Finally he muttered, "I guess I could go see you."

Pleased, Dr. Bond said no more. The way to solve a problem was to go to the top.

While Horace might not have fully absorbed the point in the car that day, the idea was behind a seemingly inexplicable situation that had occurred at a campus assembly two years earlier, when Horace was a sophomore. For reasons baffling to students, to Mr. Hunt's widow, to one of Dr. Bond's colleagues over at Atlanta University, and to countless others, Dr. Bond decided to invite the race-baiting governor of Georgia, Eugene Talmadge, to come deliver the Hubbard Day address at Fort Valley. Hubbard Day honored William Merida Hubbard, the venerable old Negro educator whose school, the State Teachers and Agricultural College for Negroes, had been merged with Fort Valley when it became a state-supported institution in 1939. The governor had known Mr. Hubbard since boyhood, and Mr. Hubbard had spoken of the governor with feelings of kindness and affection, Dr. Bond noted in his letter of invitation to the governor.[7]

When the governor surprised many by accepting the invitation and the negative responses to the invitation began to surface, President Bond responded nervously. The governor had just vetoed a bill that would have used state money to support the Training School for Negro Delinquent Girls at Macon, a move sponsored by Mrs. Hunt and the Colored Women's Clubs. Negro women had already turned over the school's land and building to the state and begun to celebrate when the governor decided to veto the project as part of his "economy" platform.

Negroes believed the governor was a racist. Horace remembered a radio address from his childhood in which the governor blatantly pronounced there was "no nigger anywhere that was worth more than ten cents a day." The speech did not gain the governor friends among Negroes, Horace included.[8]

A colleague at Atlanta University spoofed Dr. Bond's incredible decision to bring the governor to Fort Valley at a time when Negroes were so angry. In a note, he created fictitious news stories about the looming event.

> May 9th: As preparations were being made at the Fort Valley State College for the reception of Governor Talmadge, the President, H.M. Bond, could not be reached. His office reported that he had cancelled all engagements on account of a slight nervous indisposition.
>
> . . .
>
> May 10th: President H.M. Bond left here for an unannounced destination this morning. It was said that he had gone off to recover from a recent high nervous strain.

Privately, President Bond was feeling exactly as his colleague's lampoon suggested: he was worried that his bright idea to invite the top leader in the state was about to blow up in his face. The unkind little joke did little to assuage his worries.

Neither did a confidential note from Mrs. Hunt delivered a half hour before the official event. Mrs. Hunt said her grandson Charlie, a current student, had reported that the students were planning to get up and walk out if the governor "used the word 'nigger' in his remarks." Of course, Governor Talmadge was well rehearsed in the use of "nigger," so President Bond's stress heightened further.

President Bond had been counting on the presence of Mr. Hubbard, with his long relationship with the governor, to help keep the governor's language appropriate. But Mr. Hubbard had unexpectedly—and inconveniently—died shortly after the governor accepted the invitation.[9] President Bond would have no assistance from that quarter.

As the governor entered Assembly Hall, eight hundred black faces stared at the visitor in obvious hostility. President Bond had suggested to the students that they come wearing neat and clean outfits but not so dressed up that it would look as though they were putting on a show. He had neglected to warn them to control their facial expressions.

The event did not begin smoothly for anyone. As the governor walked in, he appeared shocked to hear a Negro organist's beautiful rendition of Handel's "Largo." Meanwhile, the president continued to worry that the governor might say "nigger" and all of the students would get up and walk out. At the beginning of the assembly, he told the audience to remain seated as they sang "America the Beautiful."

The responsive reading was little better. President Bond had intentionally chosen a dark-skinned little boy to lead the scriptural selection. The little boy read very carefully, very loudly, and very well: "At the same time came the disciples unto Jesus, saying, 'Who is the greatest in the kingdom of heaven?'" In response, Horace and the other students in the audience answered loudly and defiantly: "And Jesus called a little child unto him, and set him in the midst of them."

After the boy read the next verse, the audience replied, "The greatest among you shall become as a child," glaring at the governor.

The boy read the next verse, and the audience nearly roared the response: "But whoever shall offend one of these little ones which believe in me, it were better for him that a millstone were hanged about his neck, and that he were drowned in the depth of the sea."

Having made their point with their volume and expressions, the students sat back down in their assigned wooden seats.

Dr. Bond introduced the speaker by carefully saying "Negro" several times in order to "familiarize Brother Talmadge with the sound, just in case he had never heard it before pronounced like that." Sitting close by, his wife worried that President Bond would make a Freudian slip and himself say "nigger." Thankfully, the nervous president did not.

Altogether, it was a trying introduction. And it was followed by an equally awkward speech by the governor. Those who had heard Governor

Talmadge speak before said he seemed to be a different man before the eyes of eight hundred black audience members "looking at him as though he were some sort of monster." He tried first one tack, and then another.

"The Negro is the best labor, with intelligent supervision, in the world," he started, carefully pronouncing the word "Negro." The audience stiffened in a manner not unnoticed by the governor.

The governor tried again. "Under intelligent supervision, the patience, endurance, and capacity for work of the Negro is what makes him the best labor in the world. That's the highest compliment I feel I can pay to anyone."

The audience did not relax at all, so he changed his tack once more. "Hubbard was a religious man. You know, the Christian church is the most important institution in the world."

And here, as President Bond later reported, "at last on safe grounds, he extolled the glories of the church for ten minutes, and sat down—the briefest speech, I have heard, that the Governor ever had made in his life." He was so relieved that the governor made it through the belabored pronunciations of "Negro" that he clapped madly. His wife told him later that his relief was too apparent.

The Fort Valley choir sang several spirituals. The chancellor of the state university system spoke, and one of the regents proclaimed Fort Valley to be worth many times over the money the state was paying. The guests then adjourned so that the governor could dedicate the cooperative building recently built with money from the Rosenwald Fund and pose for some pictures. Mr. Talmadge's words at the dedication were "very enthusiastic, if somewhat dumbfounded."[10] But the most important consequence of that day was that the governor was photographed with young adult Negro students at a Negro college. And those pictures of the state's top man were all President Bond needed to solve his immediate problem.

Across Georgia, Governor Talmadge had been vehemently accusing the Rosenwald Fund of corrupting the morals of the South by preaching "racial amalgamation through the University of Georgia and several of the white teachers' colleges." In an inflamed political environment, President Bond expected Fort Valley to be ruined. The deal Mr. Hunt had privately facilitated to transfer Fort Valley to state control utilized the assistance of a large Rosenwald Fund grant along with "assurance" of continued additional and larger support by both the state and the Rosenwald Fund.[11] In the few years since Dr. Bond had taken over the presidency, Fort Valley had received more money from the Rosenwald Fund than had any other institution in the state—indeed, more than all of the rest of Georgia combined.

President Bond said the idea of inviting the top man who could help the school survive amidst political fights about philanthropic money came from a Fort Valley white man, a friend of the late Mr. Hunt who appeared to be a Talmadge supporter but was not.[12] This man owned an automobile dealership and supplied a nice car for the governor to ride to campus in; he attended the event himself, as did other white leaders and one typical tobacco-spitting Talmadgite. But the real goal of the event was to photograph Governor Talmadge with Dr. Bond and as many other Negroes in as many poses as possible.

"The plot we carried out to perfection," Dr. Bond gleefully said years later. "To my great pleasure, we photographed Mr. Talmadge dedicating a building which had just been erected with funds provided by the Rosenwald Fund." For all the world to see, "Old Gene" stood beaming on the steps of the Hubbard Cooperative Building with the Negro president.

The scheme worked. "During the rest of the bitter campaign," President Bond recalled, "Mr. Talmadge raised hell about the Rosenwald Fund, and its nefarious activities . . . Not once did he refer to the Fort Valley State College."[13]

President Bond had worked the "demands of strategy." "If it is permissible for a commanding general to reduce the pressure upon the most formidable defenses of the enemy, and to center his attack upon the weaker and more exposed portions, it was certainly legitimate . . . to do likewise . . . for the betterment of the Negro . . . Shall we thrust with . . . a keen rapier, hilt to hilt, to the bloody death, or shall we study cannily the disposition of the opposing forces understanding the psychology of the opponent, take advantage of his prejudices, seize upon them for our own devices."[14]

As Horace Tate witnessed this event and others, he was seeing the trickster strategy in operation in the older generation. He was absorbing lessons he could not articulate at the time. He knew President Bond wasn't a "kowtowing person who would tell white folk one thing and do another," and he liked that. But the president also thought through matters as problems that needed to be solved, and manipulated the levers needed to get the problems solved. "Think it out before you speak it out," Mr. Hunt would have said.

President Bond adroitly coined slogans such as "Help One Million Georgians Help Georgia." Georgia with its 1.5 million Negroes had the largest African American population east of the Mississippi. More than

200,000 Negroes lived within fifty miles of Fort Valley. In the beginning, Horace did not fully understand the phrase: "Help One Million Georgians Help Georgia."

In a private conversation, Horace queried the president: "What about these other people who need help?" he asked.

The president explained that he needed a slogan that would help him explain why he needed the programs he requested at Fort Valley. It was easier to say to the Board of Regents he wanted to educate the kids in the college to help Georgia's Negro students. That was how he could get more teachers, more facilities, better libraries.[15]

It was lessons like these, lessons not written anywhere in his textbooks, that Horace learned his senior year as he drove President Bond. Basically, Dr. Bond was using two of America's dominant values, Christianity and democracy, to the school's advantage. In one report on the school's progress, every section heading quoted the scriptural verses against hurting little children that Dr. Bond had selected for the event with Governor Talmadge. The report ended with a request for money and a heading that was set in all capital letters: "TAKE HEED THAT YOU DESPISE NOT ONE OF THESE LITTLE ONES."[16]

President Bond was retooling an old strategy. Mr. Hunt had used exactly the same words when he appealed to top businessmen and philanthropists for money in the hundreds of slick flyers and letters he had sent north. "Inasmuch as ye have done it unto one of the least of these my brethren, ye have done it unto me," Mr. Hunt had begun one appeal.

> Are you interested in this work of ministering to the needs of "the least of these my brethren"?
>
> Do you feel inclined to help?
>
> Please yield to the promptings of the generous impulse.
>
> Please use the pledge card and self-addressed envelope.
>
> Please do it now.

Giving money to the Negro children at Fort Valley could "serve the Master through serving those who need."[17]

Both Fort Valley presidents were playing upon an American vulnerability, characterizing the country's dismissal of Negro children as contrary to the biblical imperative to care for all the children of God.

President Bond employed a similar strategy using the American value of democracy. He enjoyed taking photographs and had been out on a Saturday afternoon when he ran across a most charming little Negro boy. Of the fifteen or more little boys he could have photographed that afternoon, he selected this particular child, who seemed to convey a joy for life, natural grace, and shy charm. The boy's picture became the cover for an issue of the GT&EA journal, the *Herald*, and the journal's editor, President Bond, used the photograph to talk about being a Negro child in a democratic country.

President Roosevelt had just spoken to America about the four freedoms that were the rights of all people: freedom of speech, freedom of worship, freedom from want, and freedom from fear. This pronouncement had come from a president who had supported the building of a school for white children in Warm Springs, the town not far from Fort Valley where his Little White House was located, long before he asked the Rosenwald Fund to reopen its coffers to build a school for Negro children in Warm Springs. Despite being revered by many Negro citizens for his New Deal programs, he was also the president who repeatedly ignored Walter White's requests for presidential support of an anti-lynching bill.

Dr. Bond used President Roosevelt's speech to reflect on the rights white Americans took for granted and how those freedoms the president spoke of applied to the little Negro boy whose picture he snapped.

"I can't think of a thing that this little boy has done to hurt anybody," Dr. Bond editorialized. Of course, he might have thrown a few rocks at the boys or pulled the girls' hair, but aside from these childish activities, "he's never hurt anyone or wished to hurt anyone."

Nonetheless, there were people in the world who sought to hurt this little boy, he pointed out. While President Roosevelt worried about translating the Four Freedoms into world terms, Dr. Bond explained he hankered to translate them into terms of the little boy he had photographed for the cover of the *Herald*.

Would this little Negro child—a "lovely little boy"—have freedom of speech? Would he have freedom from fear? "Does he, or will he, live in a world where the ordered balance of justice and law is such that he will commit no aggression against anyone else, and no one else will commit aggression against him?"

Dr. Bond lamented the world of hatred, oppression, cruelty, and poverty into which this Negro child had been born. He did not want to see him corrupted by this world. "Perhaps he was not born a saint," the president of Fort Valley commented, but "our little boy was not born a criminal" either.[18]

Dr. Bond proclaimed that his job and that of all the educated Negroes in Georgia was to translate the freedoms the president spoke of into realities for this little boy and for all Negro children.[19] It was a fundamental civic right for all Americans, including Negro Americans, despite America's imperfect practice of democracy.

Having highlighted the areas in which America was vulnerable to Negro claims, President Bond emphasized to his students the need for commitment to changing the circumstances of fellow members of their race, as Dr. Du Bois had called for. Fort Valley's president repeatedly explained the reason Horace and the other students were in college. Their job was to improve the life of little Negro children in Georgia. Though principalities and powers worked against the "welfare and happiness and health and intelligence" of the children, Fort Valley students must remain focused on one central theme amidst the "many schemes afoot to save the world."[20]

In his first faculty meeting as the college's president, Dr. Bond expressed his hope that the Fort Valley students would learn a great deal about themselves and the world in which they lived—whether their immediate environs, Peach County, or the legacy of ancient Greece and Rome. They were to learn something of the basic problems of the current social and economic system. But one of the principal functions in teacher training—one not stated in the mission the Board of Regents envisioned for Fort Valley—would be to develop in students the understanding that "the problems of children—and of Negro children—were their principal concern."[21] It was a little, simple scheme really: that of doing "a simple little for little children."[22] Fort Valley students were to see the needs of this community and position themselves to help.[23] They were "to help folk."[24] Reflecting on his efforts to form the students at his university, President Bond once commented to a colleague, the president of Georgia State College, on the sense of purpose a leader gained when he worked diligently at some great task: "May I say in closing, that while not exactly like the Christ Child, I find myself continually growing in wisdom, in bulk if not in statue, and I hope in favor with God and man."[25]

Through both observing Dr. Bond's public actions and conversing with him privately, Horace grasped the message of this president he admired, the man who he was convinced talked the talk and walked the walk. The Fort Valley graduates were to go into the rural and urban areas of the state "to do what can be done to give children a better chance." He and his fellow students understood the contradictions of faith and democracy. They understood the need for strategic, thoughtful leadership. They had absorbed the president's message: "You've got to get into that community and become a leader. You don't get an education just to help yourself."

As Horace drove Dr. Bond from one GT&EA state or regional meeting to another, the same message reverberated. "If you are only going to get an education for yourself, what good have you done?"[26] That attitude became an essential part of the student chauffeur. "He was a smart man . . . brilliant," an observant Horace concluded of Dr. Bond.[27]

Of course, the president lived in a world much larger than the one his mentee or other students had yet seen. President Bond had participated in a meeting with Dr. Du Bois, Mr. Hunt, and other national leaders in Washington, D.C., a few years before Mr. Hunt's death at which they verbally and in writing objected to the long-standing practice of allowing federal money to continue to flow into southern states without any restrictions that demanded equality in the use of the funds. Southern whites had been withholding the full appropriation of Negro money since the beginning of federal support for land grant colleges before the turn of the century. At their Washington meeting, the leaders shared ideas and crafted strategy as they sought to deter the same federal inequalities that had limited opportunities for their predecessors.[28]

In Georgia, after he became president of Fort Valley, President Bond aligned with the new GT&EA president, Mr. Harper, in planning the educational association's strategy. President Bond liked the language Mr. Harper used, and he liked the man's openness. Mr. Harper spoke persuasively of the need "to demand and fight for equal privileges and opportunities" at a meeting in 1942. "We can have these elements," Mr. Harper said, "and we must have them. We are not inferior because of color. Intelligence knows no color."[29] President Bond agreed, of course.

Such a world was still beyond the understanding of the young man who chauffeured the college president. Horace was a senior, after all, and enjoying college life. His class put on a Kiddy Kostume Ball on Halloween night. Ears of corn and pumpkins decorated the Assembly Hall, and eventually showers of corn kernels rained down on unsuspecting goblins and others. In March there was a Barn Dance, complete with "two pigs in a pen, a calf, two hens, and a honest-to-goodness wagon" and plenty of hay about, with the students dressed in farm fashions.

In April, as graduation loomed, the Diet-Elites, a group that was advised by Miss Jordan and of which Horace was a part, hosted a closed affair in the little dining hall. With soft lights, red and white decorations, and melodious tunes from the gramophone, Horace and the other students were definitely "on the beam" at the exclusive affair. Then there was his work as president of the College Players Guild. His senior year they produced four plays, with Horace overseeing the thirty-five student members on everything from acting to stage sets.[30]

As the year neared its close and activities wound down, Horace spent little time reflecting on race matters, even when Dr. Du Bois returned to deliver another lecture. His talks got "better and better," Dr. Bond said of the elder who liked to "dawdle around our little place."[31] But Horace was focused more on graduation.

He had come a long way since the testing, informal group discussions, registration, and orientations that filled his first week as a freshman, and even since the comprehensive examinations in general science, math, English, literary appreciation, southeastern problems and prospects, and study skills that had to be passed to complete the sophomore year. However, graduation depended not on the accumulation of credits, grades, and quality point averages but on the faculty assessment of his progress over the four years in meeting the goals of the institution, as outlined in "The Scope, Objectives, and Suggested Activities of the Fort Valley State College."[32]

Receiving the letter officially congratulating him on completion of the requirements of Fort Valley was a relief. The Fort Valley years provided an excellent training ground. Intellectually, he understood that rising Negro leaders had "no right to sit silently by while the inevitable seeds are sown for a harvest of disaster to our children," as Dr. Du Bois had argued many years before.[33]

But knowing about the challenge to serve and even having absorbed a few isolated ideas about how to serve did not mean that Horace had accepted a commission to serve.

6

TO HELP OUR PEOPLE

"You got a job?" It was the kind of question a Negro mother who sacrificed to help her son go to school could ask when she observed him lounging back at her home, comfortably unemployed.

Elberton was a quaint place that offered reprieve. Nestled in the northeastern quadrant of the state, its location was said to have been selected by turkeys who, following their instincts, flew into trees at nightfall as their owners herded them to market down in Augusta. Only by daylight did the owners discover the striking beauty of the place the turkeys had selected. With a clean conscience, since the land was "ceded by the Cherokees and Creeks," the founders named the place Old Town Springs, later incorporated it as Elbertville, and finally called it Elberton in 1803.[1]

Horace seemed drawn to the place—a bit like the turkeys, perhaps. He had a bachelor of science in education, which had been conferred on May 30, 1943, after a faculty vote. He had taken courses in botany, invertebrate zoology, vertebrate zoology, and general microbiology. But instead of walking into an uncertain future, he nestled into his childhood home. The house had several bedrooms, running water, a bathroom, and a telephone. For Negroes, it was a comfortable house. His mother delighted in the son she had taught "to go on to greater truths than I have ever known." She was a tall, broad-shouldered lady, and usually she was direct but not harsh. Today, however, her question was no gentle inquiry, the sort of thing proud relatives might ask just after the graduation ceremony. It was a demand that necessitated an immediate response.[2]

Horace pondered how to answer. He was supposed to be a teacher who could "help somebody." He was not sure he wanted to be a teacher, though. He had been thinking about whether he should try to save the $4,000 he would need to go to medical school. But he did have one job possibility, though he had given it little thought.[3]

Horace had stayed on at Fort Valley for the summer session after his graduation and had taken a job mopping the floor in Miss Jones's kitchen.

Fort Valley had been his home for four years, and he was in no hurry to leave. Plus, the job provided post-graduation money. To his surprise, a man he did not know approached him one day as he mopped and asked him about going to Union Point to teach.

"Fessor Tate," the white-looking man with the smiling round face and big spectacles addressed him. The man was a Negro principal attending the summer session of Fort Valley in order to obtain his college degree. Horace smiled inwardly; he had just finished school. No one had ever called him "Fessor."

The principal did not ask about Horace's major. He only wanted to know if the young man had a degree. Horace affirmed that he had just graduated.

"I need a Fessor like you to come over and help our boys and girls learn something," the principal told him. Then the principal left without waiting for a response, leaving the young man baffled. Horace did not even know where Union Point was. He returned to mopping.

On the last day of his summer school session, the same principal returned to the cafeteria, found Horace, and restated his summons. "Fessor, I'm expecting you to come over to Union Point when school opens."

Horace remained noncommittal. He still had not looked for Union Point on a map.

However, if his mother considered that a job offer, then Horace figured he had one.

Horace's mother, like many Negro mothers of that era, had sacrificed so their children could go to school, and she was not willing to see him not use his degree. She promptly redirected his thinking. "You out of college now, you got a college degree. You are going to work."

The direct message from his mother was clear. He was too old to be rescued from the harsh reality of needing to make a living. He had to get a job.

Horace found a map and figured out the location of Union Point. He picked up the old black telephone, made certain no one else was talking on the party line, and called Dr. Baber in nearby Greensboro to ask how he might contact the principal at Union Point. He received from Dr. Baber a phone number for the county agent, and eventually left a message with the county agent inquiring about the school's principal. The county agent said he would have to drive over to the school to give the message to the principal because the principal had no phone. Twenty minutes later the principal, Mr. Eli Jackson, returned Horace's call.

"Is this the Fessor calling me?" Mr. Jackson asked affably. "I'm expecting you on Monday." And that was the end of the interview.

By Monday, Mr. Tate had bought his brother's old car and become a new teacher at Union Point.[4]

The frame Negro elementary and high school at Union Point sat in a large grassy area with trees out front. The school facilities paled in comparison to the two-story brick structure where Horace had finished high school back in Elberton, but the Negro teachers behaved similarly. They did not allow the inadequate facilities to limit the children's minds. They believed every Negro child who could communicate could learn, and so they set about the task of making sure the children did so, despite lacking equipment and books. "The teacher is an artist," one of their colleagues wrote in the *Herald*, laying the foundations for tomorrow, working with "the precious clay of unfolding personality." The Negro educators' goal was

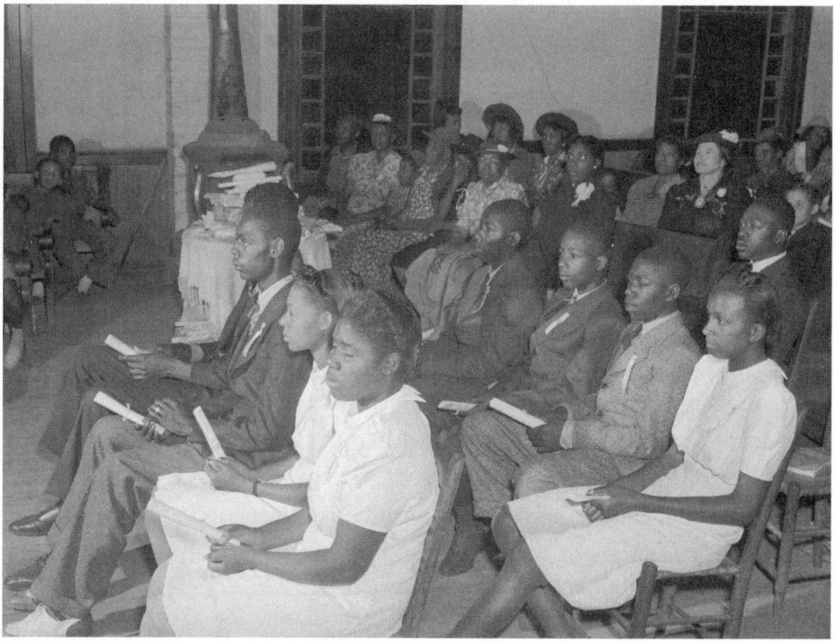

In his first job, Horace Tate was hired at the Union Point Negro High School in Greene County, Georgia. This photograph shows the graduation exercises at a local church for the students in this high school in 1941, one year before his employment. *Library of Congress*

nothing short of "the improvement of society."[5] Horace recognized these ideas from his old professors at Fort Valley and his college-educated teachers at Elberton. The teachers at this school might not have college degrees, and the school might not have had an auditorium or accessible bathroom toilets or what could be called a science room (there was only a Bunsen burner and a microscope), but like Elberton it had core values.[6]

Mr. Tate opened himself to the opportunities before him. He taught classes in math, chemistry, and biology. Like other Negro educators, he believed you could not teach a child you did not know. He involved himself quickly in the local community, attending church and becoming part of the PTA. He coached both boys' and girls' basketball in the afternoons. Some of his zeal reflected the lessons he had learned at Fort Valley. Some mirrored that of his new colleagues. Some linked back to his mother. Now that he had a job, he asked what she wanted him to do for her. Horace expected that she would want to go to New York to see her other sons or that she would want a new dress. He had been flabbergasted when his mother said simply: "Help our people."

Mr. Tate soon found himself experiencing a different kind of introduction to this small, stable Negro community than he had expected. Almost immediately, Mr. Jackson began parading him around to meet Negro leaders and across the railroad tracks to show him off to whites.[7] Mr. Tate was the only person in the whole rural school, including the principal, with a college degree. As the reigning community leader—most Negro principals were leaders in their community—Mr. Jackson wanted to make sure everyone knew it.

He had a "Fessor" at his school, Mr. Jackson said to all of them, a young man who was a college graduate, and he had come to help educate the children at Union Point. In grocery stores, dry goods stores, and banks, the people learned from Mr. Jackson of the new young professor who was going to bring "real education" to the Negro children at Union Point. They didn't care whether his college degree was from Harvard, Yale, or Fort Valley. He had a college degree, and a college degree generated pride in the Negro community. When Mr. Tate began to stand up in the churches to speak about school needs—as was the custom of Negro educators—people respected the young teacher and they listened.[8]

Mr. Jackson introduced Mr. Tate to the GT&EA as well. Not that Mr. Tate had a choice: Mr. Jackson required all his teachers to join the GT&EA. Even before the end of his first month of employment, Mr. Tate was part of the professional association and was attending the local Greene County Teachers Association meetings at three-thirty on Tuesday afternoons to discuss planning.

Though he did not usually run the meeting, Mr. Jackson was a respected leader in this room, which included all the Negro teachers in the county. Quickly Mr. Tate grasped the activities of the local group, operating under the influence of Mr. Jackson. The teachers talked about the programs the state educational association had set out as goals and decided which ones applied to their local situation.

In mid-November, Mr. Jackson introduced Mr. Tate to the annual state principals' conference, held in nearby Augusta. As they drove onto the stately campus of Paine College, Mr. Jackson and Mr. Tate joined well-dressed men in suits, ties, and hats and women in immaculately stylish attire and high heels. These were the people who led Negro elementary and high schools across the state. Although Mr. Jackson was the actual principal representing Union Point, Mr. Jackson brought Mr. Tate everywhere he went, introducing him as his young "whipper-snapper."

Over the day-long principals' meeting, Mr. Tate listened to lectures, ate the cafeteria-style lunch prepared by local Negro women, and met in the afternoon in small groups with other Negro principals from across the state. Attendees in each group spoke freely about the problems in their local communities. Facilitated by an assigned principal in the group, they also discussed how the problems might be solved. In the early 1940s, topics included equalizing salaries, accrediting high schools, and coordinating activity among teachers to have more effective organization. At the end of the long day, each group's appointed secretary reported out at the evening session.[9]

Mr. Tate had entered another world. He learned about the eleven regional meetings operating after President Bond's amendment passed, and GT&EA distributed carefully drawn maps showing which counties belonged to which region. Mr. Tate discovered Union Point was in Region IV, along with eighteen or twenty other counties. In the regional meeting, like in the local meeting, the teachers and principals from across the counties came together to discuss problems in Negro education and how they might be addressed.[10]

Mr. Tate sent the required GT&EA registration form to obtain housing for the spring annual state meeting in Atlanta, and received an assignment of a Negro family with whom he could stay. He was beginning to see that he needed the experiences Mr. Jackson provided. But he failed to grasp just how much he would need the entrée Mr. Jackson provided.

The thirty-four-year-old Principal Jackson was drafted into the army in December 1943, only four months after Mr. Tate began teaching. The superintendent summoned Mr. Tate to his office. Mr. Tate was the only teacher in the Union Point school with a college degree, the superintendent explained—discounting Mr. Tate's lack of experience and his age relative to the other teachers. The superintendent needed Mr. Tate to fill Mr. Jackson's job as principal. The meeting, Mr. Jackson's departure, and his new responsibilities happened so fast. By the time he walked through the doors of the historic Sisters Chapel at Spelman College in Atlanta for his first annual GT&EA meeting, Mr. Tate was the twenty-one-year-old principal of Union Point School.[11]

The oversized four-page program handed to Mr. Tate after registration bespoke the seriousness of these two days in April. Negro educators from across the state joined for this major annual meeting largely because the problems of Negro education remained severe. Although progress had been made in each of the preceding decades, GT&EA continued to focus on the matters that had been central since its inception: demanding better salaries, better teachers, better equipment, more supervisors, longer terms, enforcement of rules mandating compulsory education, larger buildings, better locations for Negro schools, abolishment of one-teacher schools in favor of consolidation, better health services, and appropriations for summer schools. Until the right to vote could be secured, Mr. Hunt had said, the GT&EA would need to continue to pressure southern governments intent on misappropriating school money so that it favored only white children.

On the front page of the program was a picture of the historic Graves Hall of Morehouse College. Inside the program was an array of sessions. Some events were mandatory, such as the musical concert and formal addresses on the first evening. The next morning's session, back at Sisters Chapel at 7:30 a.m., with its music, invocation, and two addresses, was also mandatory.

For a young newcomer, the array of choices at the meeting, themed "Education for Living in a Democratic World," could be dizzying. Mr. Tate could choose to attend a forum on the high school as a democratic organization, covering issues in pupil-teacher planning, faculty meetings, principal-superintendent relationships, pupil organizations and activities, and assembly programs. At the same time, however, was scheduled the Elementary Section meeting, led by Hermese Johnson of Fort Valley. He needed both but could only go to one.

Also on the program were meetings about job opportunities for Negroes; a symposium on juvenile delinquency; a panel discussion on citizenship handicaps for Negroes in Georgia that involved a Rev. M.L. King, the pastor of Ebenezer Baptist Church; and three symposiums that involved health—tuberculosis, venereal disease control, and nutrition. He could choose sessions on how to use films or learn about book services available for schools.[12] He noticed that there would also be sessions with Dr. Bond and sessions with his own former high school principal, Paul J. Blackwell, which must have made it clear to him that teaching black children excellently was also a long-standing tool in the fight for equality for Negro children.

In the opening session, the GT&EA president, I.E. Washington, had been masterful and inspiring. He stated his pleasure at seeing the number of the educators who had come to the meeting despite the wartime travel restrictions and rationing. These were people who had "consecrated" their lives to helping Negro children, despite inadequate salaries.

"You will receive no medal," he said. "Your name will not be emblazoned across the world's great daily papers. Your stories of sacrifice and devotion will not be dramatized over the great radio chains." But these teachers should be about the business of "preparing for the world of tomorrow." The "impressionable minds" entrusted to their care needed inspiration to seek a world of freedom, justice, and equality of opportunity.[13]

Following the president's opening remarks was a speech by A.T. Walden, a Fort Valley graduate and trustee whom Mr. Tate remembered from a presentation at a Fort Valley assembly. Attorney Walden was also the lawyer assisting GT&EA efforts. After Attorney Walden, the executive secretary, Charles Harper, moved to the podium and provided a host of details about the GT&EA's efforts to secure better education for Negro children. With each speaker, Mr. Tate learned more about the organization's purpose and, in this season of advocacy, its fight for salary equalization. Salary inequality had not deterred him from entering education, but the size of his first check, $56.80, bothered him. He listened with intense interest. It was almost like being back at Fort Valley at assemblies.

In the late 1930s, Negro educators had to decide whether to partner with the NAACP and use litigation as a means to seek equality or to continue the direct appeals to state leaders. The NAACP was ready to begin its fight, posited Charles Houston, the Harvard-educated attorney who had trained an elite group of Howard law students to become social engineers. However, the problem with the NAACP's announced plan to begin its fight with education, and to subsequently move on to tackle salary discrimination, was that the National had little money. Without strong organization and money, it was like pounding one's head against a stone wall, said Mr. Houston.[14]

In contrast, educators did have money for their activities. While newspapers offered extensive coverage of the NAACP's litigation campaign, educational organizations across the South quietly paid the price. It was educators who provided the plaintiffs and the money for the efforts, and who suffered the sacrifice when a teacher or principal was fired—although the organizations maintained funds that paid designated plaintiffs one year's salary if they lost the job as a result of the litigation. Attorney Thurgood Marshall captured the extent of the educators' commitment best. Arguing that the National needed a campaign beyond the issue of teacher salaries if it wanted to keep its northern branches viable, Marshall noted that the financial difficulties in the national office were not related to the salary cases. "The teachers were paying for their cases," he said.[15]

In addition to a pool of money, Mr. Tate learned, educators also had information about all kinds of inequality in southern schools. In Mr. Hunt's era, the National sought information about schools from its branches, but received few responses. Yet in President Bond's office, had Mr. Tate been able to see them at the time, were the sort of detailed surveys of educational inequality a litigation team needed.

Date ________ County _______

Q_U_E_S_T_I_O_N_N_A_I_R_E

Name of School _______ No. Teachers ________ Qualifications:

Co. License ____ High School _____ Jr. College _____

Three-year College ____ Four Year College ______ Above ________________

Maximum salary of teachers _________ Minimum salary of teachers _______

No. of checks teachers have received __________ Was State money

supplemented by local funds? ________Assistance given by patrons ________

Kind of building ____________ Equipment ___________________

Total enrollment _______ Approximate daily attendance ________

> What is longest distance pupils have to come to school _______ Is
> Transportation provided for them? ________ How?_________
> Opening Date of school in 1938 _____________Closing date in 1939 ___
> Did white schools close at the same time as Negro schools? ____ When? _____
> Is there any other information that you think would be of value to us in connection with what we are attempting to do?[16]

The forms were carefully filled out, providing data on county after county in Georgia.

After collecting the data in 1939, the GT&EA Executive Board had discussed whether to join educators in other states and pursue salary increases through immediate litigation or to hold off for a time. One issue affecting their decision was a statewide financial crisis in the state that meant some teachers had not received checks for five months; even white teachers and the state superintendent were behind in salary. If GT&EA took "to drastic action" at this time regarding the more general salary issues, these leaders considered, the teachers might not receive the back salaries due them at all. Before taking "definite action," the Executive Board agreed to get "some definite facts."[17]

While GT&EA engaged in internal fighting about the direction the educators should take, Mr. Harper acted. He had been a young principal when he was among the one hundred teachers who went before the Atlanta School Board in 1920 to request salary equalization. Salaries were not equalized. He tried again when the Atlanta superintendent came to his faculty meeting around 1940. That was how he became "retired."

As Mr. Harper moved through the ranks of GT&EA as president and then executive director, the GT&EA had heeded Walter White's demand that it was "imperative" to find a teacher who would bring a suit. They did. That teacher too was dismissed. Another lawsuit—sponsored by a "Citizens Committee" in Savannah and supported by the teachers and principals—was also filed, though not sustained.[18]

At the time of the April 1944 statewide meeting where Mr. Tate was learning details of a world he had not known existed, Mr. Harper quietly coordinated the current Georgia teacher salary case, *Sam Davis v. Atlanta School Board*.[19] National attorneys Oliver Hill, Thurgood Marshall, and Robert Carter had just been in Atlanta with local attorney A.T. Walden and Mr. Harper to discuss strategies. As the young principal listened, he learned that it was the educators and their organization who had been spearheading the salary efforts in Georgia. The National did come in to help, but really "all they had to do was attend a meeting."[20]

At the April 1944 GT&EA meeting, Mr. Harper made the current needs explicit for the audience. To continue the salary litigation, they needed to "raise a fund of $5000 to meet whatever expenses may be incurred in the effort to have the salaries of Negro teachers placed on par with those of other teachers and otherwise to obtain for Negro people of the state educational opportunities guaranteed them by Federal and State laws." He had already sent out a letter to key people across the state for distribution to the teachers that explained the special fund being set up by GT&EA for legal costs.

Each teacher needed to make a minimum contribution of $100 to this special fund. This amount represented approximately two months' salary for many and exceeded the monthly rent of $75 for the GT&EA office. The teachers also needed to "seek financial contributions from interested citizens" and sponsor special projects, programs, or contests to help supplement individual contributions. All money raised should be mailed to the office of the executive secretary at 250 Auburn Avenue, whereupon they would receive a receipt by return mail. Everyone should operate "speedily" to disseminate the information as far as possible before the close of school so that the Board of Directors could "lay their case before the proper authorities without delay."[21]

The teachers appreciated Mr. Harper's advocacy. Never relying on a single strategy, Mr. Harper and members of the Executive Board had already enacted the directive of the Representative Assembly and met with the governor, Eugene Talmadge, in a direct appeal to "seek immediately a one-salary schedule for the teachers of Georgia"; in the following years they would meet repeatedly with the state board on salary matters and also on the issues of trade schools, lengthening of school terms, and textbooks.[22]

As President Washington thanked Mr. Harper and the members of the new Executive Board for their "untiring and unselfish efforts," he reminded the educators of the foundation Mr. Harper had created through the rising membership and democratic regional network, which allowed the resolutions passed by the association at state meetings like this to be implemented.

It was an "ambitious and visionary program" Mr. Tate learned about at his first annual GT&EA meeting, one where all Negro educators could join hands with communities to advance Negro boys and girls.[23] Every principal might not have the courage to challenge inequality. Mr. Tate would be one who did.

In the spring of 1944, as Mr. Tate learned to operate as a professional leader, the Greene County superintendent sent Mr. Tate a letter requesting to meet with the new principal. As he rode to the Greene County courthouse and headed toward the office of Mr. Floyd T. Corry, the new young principal had no idea why he was being summoned, as Mr. Corry had previously expressed confidence in his ability to do the job. When he arrived, he was surprised to find that the principal of the white high school joined the meeting.

"Mr. Tate," the superintendent began, "Mr. Neal, the principal of the Union Point White High School, states that he has received some of your mail. He feels it is because you erroneously used the name of 'Union Point High School' when you ordered stationery and envelopes for your school."

"Well," Mr. Tate said, "I have received several of Mr. Neal's letters at my school. I simply readdress the letters and drop them in the post office so they would reach Mr. Neal. If he receives a letter that has my name on it, all he has to do is redirect the letter to me."

As Mr. Tate soon learned, the problem was not actually about receiving mail.

"Your school is *not* the Union Point High School," the white principal responded—his manner somewhat haughty and hostile, in Mr. Tate's opinion. "It is the Union Point Colored High School. You need to put the word *colored* in your school's name."

Mr. Tate stared, dumbfounded.

The superintendent, who had received accolades from the *Herald* in the 1930s because of his enthusiasm for the Negro school and community program, at that point said, almost meekly, "Mr. Tate, would you have a *problem* placing the word *colored* on your letterhead?"

The twenty-one-year-old principal did have a problem with that, and he said as much. He was the little boy refusing to step off the sidewalk, but now he knew he was backed by an organization and a climate that made staying on the sidewalk possible, so to speak.

He was aware, he explained, that Mr. Neal was the principal of the school the white children attended and he the principal of the school the Negro children attended. But he could not understand why he had to put race in the name of his school while Mr. Neal could simply use the name "Union Point High School."

The white men stared silently for maybe fifteen seconds. Eventually Mr. Tate suggested a resolution. "I will be willing to resolve this problem by placing the word *colored* in my high school's title if Mr. Neal will use 'Union Point *White* High School' as his title."

Mr. Neal did not agree. He did not want to put "white" in his school's name. Unruffled, Mr. Tate said he did not want to put "colored" in his school's name.

After twenty minutes of discussion failed to resolve the issue, the superintendent suggested the matter be postponed until the next meeting. There was no next meeting, however. Mr. Tate had achieved his first professional victory, and he treasured the memory.[24]

One year later, however, his leadership of the Union Point High School was over: World War II had ended, and Mr. Jackson returned to his school.

Having tasted the influence the local Negro principal wielded in helping the Negro community, Mr. Tate could not be satisfied with something else. During the summer break in 1944, he had tried business, working as an assistant manager with the Afro American Life Insurance Company in Athens. The job provided more income than he had ever had but did not give the satisfaction of trying to improve the conditions for Negro children. In June 1945, when he heard from his friend Josephus Johnson about a principal's position opening in the neighboring Greensboro Colored School, he expressed interest.[25]

As he had been taught to do by President Bond, who had stressed to him that "under no circumstances was someone to take someone else's job," Mr. Tate queried the principal, Clara Gay, to confirm that she was indeed leaving. He made the formal call: "Mrs. Gay, I've been asked to apply for a job where you are. Are you leaving?"[26]

Assured she was and "that he should go ahead and apply for it," Mr. Tate met his friend Mr. Johnson at his office in Greensboro in the summer of 1945. Since the superintendent of the city schools, C.C. Wills, was on vacation, Mr. Johnson had offered to drive Mr. Tate the few short miles over to the superintendent's home.[27]

As they drove, Mr. Johnson briefed Mr. Tate on the rules he would need to follow to obtain the principalship. He was to say "yes sir" and "no sir." He should remove his hat and not sit unless he was invited to do so. He should not ask any questions that would antagonize Mr. Wills. Upon arrival, Mr. Tate left the car without comment on the instructions and headed up the walkway to the house.

The horn blew. Mr. Johnson was beckoning at Mr. Tate through the window.

Mr. Tate turned around and returned to the car. "Where are you going?" Mr. Johnson asked.

"I am going to the door," Mr. Tate responded.

Mr. Johnson was incredulous. "You want the job?" He explained that going to the front door would anger the superintendent, and he suggested Mr. Tate go to the back door. "One way not to get the job is to go to the front door," he assured Mr. Tate.

Mr. Tate had listened to Mr. Johnson's earlier suggestions without comment. He had been taught to say "yes sir" and "no sir" to elders of all hues, so according this form of respect to the superintendent would not be a problem. He had no hat to take off. He did not know Mr. Wills, so he had no way of knowing which questions might offend him—which allowed him to ask any questions he wished. But to suggest that a prospective principal who was supposed to be teaching children about first-class citizenship go to the back door to get a job crossed the line.

Somewhat testily, Mr. Tate explained to Mr. Johnson he would not go to the back door, even if he did not get the job. In fact, he said, he would not even want the job as principal of the school if he had to work under a man "with a second-class philosophy, to serve as head of a school where children must be taught first-class citizenship." Mr. Tate was resolute. He had to do a lot of things in a segregated school because custom dictated it, but complying never meant he liked it. If this superintendent did not want a man who was willing to go to the front door, he said, he did not want this principal's job.

"I'm not going to be subservient," Mr. Tate announced.

Mr. Johnson looked puzzled for a moment. "I understand," he finally said. "Go on to the front door and see what happens."

Mr. Tate knocked at the front door. Mr. Wills pushed open the door and joined him on the front porch, where they talked for over an hour. Satisfied, Mr. Wills said he liked him, that he seemed to know what to do with a school, and that he was "impressed with [his] ambitious spirit." If Mr. Tate was willing to accept $100 a month, he had the job, the superintendent said. Then, as the new employee prepared to leave, the superintendent's wife opened the front door and suggested they "sit down and talk a bit" in the living room. Mr. Tate walked inside—through the front door.

"Professor Tate, would you like to have some tea?" she asked. When he said yes, the superintendent's wife served him and the superintendent cookies and tea as the three talked together for another twenty minutes.

Mr. Johnson was sleeping in the warm afternoon Georgia sunshine when Mr. Tate returned to the car around three-thirty from the two o'clock interview. Hesitantly he asked if Mr. Tate had gotten the job. He bolted up in amazement when Mr. Tate said yes.

"Are you kidding me?" Mr. Johnson asked. When Mr. Tate confirmed again that he had been hired, Mr. Johnson shook his head in amazement. This was the first time he had ever seen a Negro man go to the front door and come away with a job.

"And let me tell you something else," Mr. Tate said, and paused. Mr. Johnson waited expectantly. "I went inside the house and was served tea and cookies."

Mr. Johnson was dumbfounded.

"Will wonders never cease?" he finally mumbled.[28]

A week later, Mr. Tate went to pick up the keys to his new school. Mr. Wills had told him his job was to make sure the children could "read, write, count, and . . . have good manners." He gave Mr. Tate permission to recruit eight teachers, understanding they would get the state salary schedule and no supplement—which meant their salaries would not be equal to those of the white teachers. Otherwise, Mr. Wills had said the school was his to run.[29]

Superintendents of Mr. Wills's era had few expectations for the education of Negro children, even if they might like an individual teacher or principal. Turning the door lock on his first visit, Mr. Tate discovered quickly the school wasn't much. Basically, it had three buildings. One of them was a two-story frame structure with four large classrooms and a corridor running through the center with an auditorium upstairs seating about two hundred people. It also had a room large enough for him to convert it to a kitchen. Community members said it had been condemned as "unfit for educating children forty years ago." The other two structures were World War II army surplus. That was it. Anything else he needed—lights, water, materials, supplies, equipment, telephone, athletic equipment, and so forth—he would have to obtain from the parents of his 564 pupils.

Since 1920, when Mr. Hunt had told the educators they needed to work with key people in their communities, teachers and parents had worked together to obtain school supplies and keep the building in repair.

Greensboro, like other small towns in Georgia, was part of the peculiar system Dr. Du Bois and Mr. Hunt had described in 1911 when they coauthored the resolutions at the Atlanta University conference on the Negro school. It was common for whites to believe Negroes were undeserving of schools because they did not pay sufficient taxes, but Negroes actually paid more in taxes than they received in services. Where this occurred, financially strapped Negro parents were actually helping to pay for the education of white children.[30]

More than thirty years after those resolutions had been written, Mr. Tate still did not have the resources he needed in this dilapidated space. But he had Mr. Harper and a southern educational climate increasingly uneasy about the litigation across the South demanding equality. He had the knowledge he had gained from his days at Fort Valley under President Bond, and the introduction to the GT&EA he had received under Mr. Jackson's tutelage.

He was determined to fight.

7

FIGHTING WHITE FOLK

Mr. Tate and eight teachers diligently sought to educate the 594 pupils crowded into the Greensboro school's three buildings in the fall of 1945. Ninety-eight of the students were in the first grade under one teacher. With no library books, or science department, equipment, or textbooks, the teachers created and paid for their own materials.[1]

Mr. Tate drove over to Atlanta to purchase a typewriter from Rich's Department Store for the colored school in Greensboro. Rich's had consistently cashed the worthless checks of white teachers after salary cuts and insufficient money during the Depression, and as a charitable act it accepted bales of cotton as payment for goods, taking a financial loss in doing so. However, Mr. Tate paid from $8 to $10 each month from his own funds for the typewriter. Sometimes his funds were depleted and he made no payment.[2] But with a typewriter, teachers could create lessons to help compensate for the lack of books.

Mr. Tate also drove Route 411 over to Athens and created a credit account at the McGregor store. With this account, he and the teachers pooled funds to purchase a duplicating machine, paper, stencils, styluses, and ink. Whenever supplies ran out, Mr. Tate drove back over to Athens to replenish. He used his own money for gas. The principal hoped the PTA of the school might later be able to reimburse some of the cost for the materials, especially for the teachers, but PTA money was not yet available, and the students were in class now.[3]

The early months passed, and November arrived, bringing with it a challenge neither the collective resources of the principal nor the teachers could overcome. As the autumn weather morphed into chilly mornings and then cold days, the two potbellied stoves in the auditorium of the main building and the single potbellied stove in the center of each of the two classroom spaces stayed cold, as the school had no coal.

Mr. Tate called the superintendent, explained the situation, and asked for coal to heat the building. The Board of Education furnished steam heat for the white school, but the superintendent told Mr. Tate the Board of Education did not furnish fuel for the Negro school. Mr. Tate listened thoughtfully but quietly. He walked through the building again, observing his children bundled up in coats, sweaters, or whatever they had as they tried to learn their lessons.

The next day, he called again for coal. With neither hostility nor arrogance, the superintendent repeated the policy of the Board of Education and said that the PTA or the Negro trustees of Mr. Tate's school should provide fuel. Still new to Greensboro, Mr. Tate did not know his school had trustees. He made some inquiries, finally located the trustees, and discussed fuel. A few gave money, but there was not enough to supply coal for the school.

The next time the temperature dropped, Mr. Tate sent the children home. He had already informed the PTA president and several other parents of his plan to dismiss the children when they had another cold snap, and requested they call the superintendent to complain. On the day the children were sent home early, the parents made the pre-planned phone calls while Mr. Tate waited.

Despite the existing inequalities, white superintendents did not like complaints from Negro parents, especially in the 1940s when the South was paying close attention to the NAACP cases demanding equality. When the Negro parents called to complain about their children being let out of school early by the principal, the superintendent called Mr. Tate.

Mr. Tate confirmed he had sent the children home and told them to remain at home until the weather was warmer or the building was heated. With the earnestness of a more experienced trickster, he explained to the superintendent the children would catch their death in the cold and how he hoped that the kids could come back to school when it was warm enough—or when the county had money for coal.

It was his first time using the shrewd thinking that had characterized an earlier generation. At the local, regional, and state GT&EA principals' meetings he now attended, he joined with other principals who described the problems they were having in their schools, whether with heat or books or other matters. Somebody who had the same problem would talk about how they solved it. At the annual principals' conference or the state meeting, anywhere from sixty-five to seventy principals participated. The principals talked about wanting to have greater jurisdiction over their schools, how they would go to the superintendent to present their schools' material needs and the superintendent would not listen. They talked about getting the cooperation of parents and seeking their support to advocate on behalf of the school and speak openly against the poor facilities. Some of the principals spoke at these meetings, and some did not; some were courageous in how they approached matters, and some were not.

The youngest present, Mr. Tate first sat and listened. He had been only twenty-one when he first became a principal and started attending meetings without Mr. Jackson. Once someone noticed him and asked, "Where did this little fellow come from? How did he get to be a principal?" Mr. Tate simply smiled at them. He had "enough mother wit and intelligence to know not to open [his] big mouth," even when he could formulate in his mind a better solution than the one he heard put forth. Soon the meetings paid dividends. He absorbed a commonly understood truth among Negro community leaders: if a principal got the support of his parents, he or she could get more done for the school than by operating independently.[4]

That November, Mr. Tate's plan worked. Within twenty-four hours, the superintendent delivered five tons of coal to the Negro school.[5]

Coal, however, was only one challenge. The students needed textbooks too. Mr. Tate had requested textbooks his first year, but the superintendent told him no money was available for that. So he bought the typewriter and opened a credit account for duplication materials, and the teachers taught with the materials they could type and reproduce.

For his second year, Mr. Tate decided to plan early. Together, he and his teachers projected enrollment for the 1946–47 school year, and Mr. Tate placed a book order for every pupil slated to attend the Greensboro school. He sent his request for textbooks to Mr. Robert Cousins in Atlanta, a white man who headed the Division of Negro Education for the state. Back in 1919 when Mr. Hunt and his key people had petitioned the state board for the needs of Negro children, they included among their requests a director for Negro education who would be a Negro. The position was filled, but not by a Negro. Instead, a white man was employed who would mediate between the Negro and white communities on matters of inequality. Mr. Cousins operated in the position the same way his boss had before him: he provided the white face that could seek sympathetic support from whites while also providing some aid to Negro schools. In this instance, Mr. Cousins's office promised assistance. He confirmed that the books Mr. Tate requested would be ordered and ready for the pupils when school opened in September.

On the day in August 1946 when the books were to be picked up, four excited boys who had been asked to help appeared in Mr. Tate's office, along with two additional boys who had not even been asked to come. Although Mr. Tate was miffed that the superintendent had made it his responsibility to go pick up the books, his students were excited. They had never had textbooks before. A Negro community member, Alex Smith, owned a half-ton truck and had agreed to accompany Mr. Tate and transport the books.

The procession downtown began with Mr. Smith's truck leading and Mr. Tate trailing in his own car to the superintendent's office. They left the Negro neighborhood and in a few miles pulled up in front of the white high school with its four columns and beautiful dome. The superintendent's office was located in the white school. Together the troop ascended the graceful stairs and walked the spacious corridors to the superintendent's office. Mr. Wills met them. He had been awaiting their arrival.[6]

Mr. Wills escorted the two men and the boys into a large classroom with thousands of books. Standing in the doorway, the superintendent announced: "Tate, you and the boys can take all the books you can find. And take them to your school. I hope you can locate complete sets. I know you didn't have any books last year, and I know how difficult it is to teach *with* books, let alone trying to teach without them."

His brow furrowing, Mr. Tate looked around. He saw books on shelves, books on tables, books in boxes, and books all over the floor. The only problem was that he did not see any new books. His anger began to rise. "Mr. Wills," he said, "is this what you called me to get?" he asked.

Less than ten years before, Mr. Tate would have had little recourse except to keep spending his and the teachers' own money. State school board policy had been that Negro children would only receive textbooks after the white children finished using them. But, thanks to the direct appeals of GT&EA leadership, Mr. Tate knew the state was supposed to provide new textbooks for free. It was "an answer to the prayers of teachers," the *Herald* proudly proclaimed in 1938 when it announced that, "for the first time, teachers [would] have sufficient materials."[7] That promise of state support had been seven years before. Mr. Tate had accepted the response of the superintendent that he had no money to order books in 1945 when he was first hired and school was about to begin, but he would not accept that response now.

"Mr. Wills," he said, "during the spring I ordered a complete set of books for all of the boys and girls who are expected to attend the Greensboro School for Negroes next year, and the books I see in this room are not new."

Mr. Wills responded patiently. He explained the long-standing school board policy relative to Negro schools and white schools and textbooks. He said he thought the still relatively new principal had understood that when new books were ordered, the new books would be issued to the white children, and the colored children would get the old books the white children had previously used.

Etched in Mr. Tate's memory was the evening his father had dared two white policemen to come into the family home. The policemen said they had come to take to jail one of Mr. Tate's older brothers who was accused of a crime. The father explained to the police that his son had not been out of the house at the time of the supposed crime, and he asked for a warrant. Jolted, the policemen said they did not need a warrant to enter the Negro home. Henry Tate had taken a correspondence law course and worked with a white lawyer downtown, and so, without flinching, the father retorted that they would in fact need a warrant.

Mr. Tate had been a little boy peeping from behind the door as the encounter escalated. The policemen said that they were going back to the bedroom where Horace's brother was sleeping—that is, through the living room and into the bedrooms along the left side of the house, off the kitchen—to take him to jail. Undaunted, the father rejoined, "I'll tell you what. You might get him, but I'll guarantee you one thing. You won't get out of here with him. You can come in but you will not come out alive," he said. Henry Tate owned a gun.

Mr. Tate remembered the way the two policemen had stood silently at his father's threat. They knew he had the support of the law and of a white attorney. They also knew white folk called Henry Tate "crazy," which was a term used for any Negro insane enough to expect to be treated with respect. Some people even whispered that the Negro Tates were related to the white Tate family that had helped found the town, and that the white Tates—while not claiming them—provided some kind of protection for the family.

After what seemed like an eternity of hesitation, the policemen turned and left. As far as the young Horace was concerned, his father had refused to act as expected—as though he were merely three-fifths human.[8] Knowledge of the law (mixed with a little courage) could help people stand up sometimes, especially if they were willing to accept the consequences.

Now, years later, as far as these textbooks were concerned Mr. Tate did not see his situation as too far removed from that of his father. He knew he had the law on his side, and on this day courage trumped any tricks. Thanks to the information he had gained at GT&EA meetings and the voracious reading of daily news that he had been taught to do at Fort Valley, Mr. Tate was fully aware of the legitimacy of his demand. "Mr. Wills, these books are old books and these are not the books that I ordered," he said, making no effort to conceal his displeasure. "They've got backs off. I don't know if I'll find enough for a particular class."

Mr. Wills said these books were all he had available.

"I don't want these books," Mr. Tate retorted.

Then he turned his attention away from the startled superintendent. "Boys, you go back on the truck, and Mr. Smith, you may transport the boys back to the school. I ordered new books for our pupils, and I refuse to accept any old books."

The superintendent, speechless, turned red.

Mr. Tate exited shortly after Mr. Smith, leaving the superintendent standing alone in the door of the room with the old textbooks.

Back at the Negro school, Mr. Smith feared Mr. Tate would lose his job. Didn't he know that he could be fired for what he had just done in refusing to accept the books?

Mr. Tate did, but he used the opportunity to teach the six wide-eyed boys a lesson. Speaking to Mr. Smith, though his words were intended for the boys as well, he explained that he had never believed segregated schools were legal or ethical, but because he was in the South he had to put up with it. "But even though I put up with segregated schools, I'll be damned if I am going to accept for my kids . . . books that they have used for two, four, six, eight, ten, or twelve years."

While the boys looked on wordlessly, Mr. Smith responded, "It took a lot of nerve for you to do that. I hope you good luck." And then he left.

Returning to his office inside the school, Mr. Tate telephoned Mr. Cousins in Atlanta and told him about the incident.

"Don't worry about the books," Mr. Cousins said. "I've ordered some books and you will get them."

In a week or two, Mr. Tate had new books from the funds available to Mr. Cousins. They arrived two days after school opened. And for reasons unknown—though perhaps the result of a quiet phone call between the white Mr. Cousins and the white superintendent—Mr. Tate kept his job.[9]

Ultimately, however, shrewd manipulation of people and timing demanded proactivity rather than reactivity. Since GT&EA's earliest days, the organization's leadership had harped on the significance of the Negro vote. Mr. Hunt had said the educators needed to "exercise their right," that they needed to vote. No real progress could be made as long as whites had the power and the money and Negroes could not even challenge the status quo through their elected officials. It was a line straight from Mr. Hunt and Dr. Du Bois.

Mr. Tate hatched his plan to respond in the fall of his first year and seeded it with community leaders as Christmas approached in the small town of about 4,000 people. By January 1946, he was ready to move forward. The Negroes would organize a Citizens Club, sometimes referred to as the Men's Civic Club or the Greene County Civic Club.[10]

Mr. Tate and the pastor of the Ebenezer African Methodist Episcopal Church worked together to prepare for a meeting. Ebenezer was a historic church in the Negro community, having been founded in 1867 by ex-slaves who formerly sat on the back pews and balconies of local white churches. In the years before Mr. Tate arrived, Ebenezer had provided a school for Negro children. Although the church had been blown by a storm to the middle of the dirt road in its early years, it survived, its congregants recovering the structure and placing it back on the same spot. Mr. Tate had joined this church—situated not very far from the room in which he boarded when he first arrived in Greensboro—despite being a member of another Methodist denomination.

Like many Negro principals, Mr. Tate also taught Sunday school. He divided his teaching time between Ebenezer and the Springfield Baptist Church, around the curve and up the hill. Springfield Baptist had also opened in 1867, when whites offered the two hundred colored congregants of their church $200 to go build their own church.[11] Mr. Tate participated in both these historic congregations and visited other congregations as well. Doing so made him well known and respected throughout the community, which made it easier to organize the Negro community.

Mr. Tate and the pastor of Ebenezer spun four to five hundred leaflets on the mimeograph machine and notified people of the upcoming meeting. Greensboro Negroes had many needs: electric lights, water, toilets, and paved roads. But of special concern to all were the schools. The upstairs floor of the main school building vibrated alarmingly whenever Mr. Tate or one of the teachers walked briskly across it. And to hold the auditorium together and make it safe for use, ten steel rods had been installed that ran from one wall to another at the top of the ceiling. Everyone knew the Negro children desperately needed a new school.

Whether the Negro community came to the opening meeting of the Civic Club out of curiosity or out of commitment to the ideas, they did come, with more than a hundred people showing up at the Greensboro school. In the October *Herald*, Mr. Tate had read of key people organizing to get a building, transportation, and health care access. In the December issue of the *Herald*, he read of the Civic Club organized in Treutlen County that helped to advocate for the school.[12] A Civic Club in Greene County was a way to follow the patterns of other communities across the South that were interested in obtaining equality without using the volatile name of the NAACP.

Mr. Tate used this same strategy and remained mostly invisible in the newly formed Civic Club. The local educator's job was to organize the community, as Mr. Harper said. And he did. But Mr. Tate's pastor, Rev. Carter, was elected president of the group. As far as white citizens were concerned, the flyers advertised good "citizenship" in the community, which translated to obeying the laws. Unwritten on the hundreds of flyers was that citizenship for Negroes meant demanding democratic participation and, in this case, demanding decent schools.[13]

"First, get your vision," Mr. Tate scribbled on the notecard he hastily prepared for one of the meetings. "Second, get you a plan by which you may accomplish it." Like Mr. Harper, Mr. Tate was already learning to speak extemporaneously from a few notes. As the initial 122 people dwindled down to 18 men over the next few months, he continued to speak with conviction from his notes to the people who remained committed. "Third . . . go to battle for it and humbly pray that God may give you victory."[14]

Despite Mr. Tate's youth, the men who stayed with the group listened to his counsel and cooperated with the plan of the principal who they knew could not be seen planning. After discussion, among the three top agenda items was voting. Indeed, Mr. Harper's old school, Booker T. Washington in Atlanta, had been built by a community that wielded the power of the vote in city bond elections.

Mr. Tate obtained a copy of the standard list of questions used to qualify potential voters. In addition to information about the organization of federal and state officers and terms of office, the list of thirty questions required applicants to know the names of federal, state, and county elected officials. The details seemed endless, but with a learning guide available, club members and applicants could be prepared as they primed the active Negro network to encourage voter registration throughout the community.[15] By May, the club had already registered six hundred people.[16]

Negroes registered across the county and state after the 1944 *Smith v. Allwright* Supreme Court decision expanded voting rights by eliminating white primaries, but the climbing Negro registration numbers did not please the white man campaigning again for governor. The man who had spoken at the Fort Valley State College assembly several years earlier, Eugene Talmadge, came to Greensboro to seek the support of white voters as part of his quest for a fourth term. "The only way I talk to a Negro is when his hat is in his hand," he told an adoring crowd.[17]

But the man had a sharp political eye that immediately understood the potential impact of Negro registration in Greensboro. Speaking to white Greensboro citizens on Monday, May 31, and hence unrestrained by the audience as he had been at Fort Valley, Mr. Talmadge quickly condemned Negro registration. If they wanted to have "clean county government" in Greene County, he said, they "had better form a citizens committee and challenge every Negro registrant in Greene County who can't meet the requirements of the Georgia law." In two years, he warned them, they would have as many Negroes registered as whites, since the population was about fifty-fifty.

Mr. Talmadge explained Georgia laws to his listeners. A Negro could be legally disqualified under Georgia law if he could not meet the "character and literacy tests," or if he had pled guilty to or been convicted of theft or crime involving "moral turpitude," he said. A Negro could be disqualified for living with a woman without marrying, or for having taken up with one woman without having gotten a divorce from another.

"You can't have good government in your county," he emphasized, "when a law enforcement officer has to contend with a bloc of 1,000 or more Negro voters standing ready as a threat to knife him because he is doing his duty."

Whites needed to eliminate the possibility of any cohesive group of voters standing as a threat to a county or city official and do what was "best for their country." He emphasized that Negroes should get justice in the courts so long as segregation was maintained in schools, in churches, and in a Negro political primary. All the south Georgia counties and the six best lawyers in Georgia agreed that in the "long run" this was the best course for Georgia. "If you white people love your country, you will challenge" the Negroes who registered.[18]

And they did. Somewhere between 1,500 and 2,000 people heard "Old Gene," and within two weeks the Board of Registrars had a meeting to hear a number of cases involving court convictions. At the meeting, the board agreed to print in the paper the registration list before the July 17 primary so that the names of questionable registrants could be challenged under the law in writing to the Board of Registrars.

Mr. Tate carefully clipped the list, but the challenges to Negro voters, mysteriously, were withdrawn before the election; apparently, no reasonable complaint could be sustained. Two weeks later Georgia voters elected Eugene Talmadge as governor of Georgia for the final time. A Greene County newspaper proclaimed him to have run the "greatest race he ever ran in this county," but he lost in the county by 122 votes. "Old Gene" had been defeated in the county by a bloc of 850 Negro voters.[19]

Complaints abounded that colored election managers had assisted in preparing most of the colored votes cast or that marked ballots were brought to the polls by colored voters. Talmadge leaders did not contest the results from the local precinct, but Greensboro whites learned a startling truth: Negro votes could matter. In this context, school board members began to listen to Negro complaints about their school.[20]

Mr. Harper had already told Mr. Tate how to prepare the members of his Men's Civic Club—now registered citizens representing Negro voters—when they met with the school board to request improved facilities. Mr. Harper had the "Outline of Procedure for Legal Cases" that Thurgood Marshall had prepared in September 1943 for local NAACP branches to use. Attorney Marshall had explained that every citizen, "regardless of race," had a right to participate equally in all public educational facilities and that every citizen and taxpayer had a right to full information on the details of the public schools in the community. The local branches were to set up a legal committee that would study the laws, obtain the information needed to compare black and white schools, and then make the inequalities public using the Negro press and by setting up mass meetings.[21] Of course, Mr. Harper knew full well that this fact-finding was done by the educators and that the public mass meeting must be quietly led by the principal.

Consistent with Attorney Marshall's suggestions, the Civic Club would prepare a list of people to represent the community's educational needs before the school board. Mr. Harper would tell Mr. Tate how the men should prepare for the meeting, and Mr. Tate would prepare the men of the Civic Club. Everyone understood the need for secrecy.

"Professor Tate," one said, with all agreeing, "if you work out the plan for securing a new school building, tell us what to do and support us as we proceed; we will do the job." In return for his leadership, they pledged that "no one [would] ever know your role in this project."

Mr. Tate did indeed work out the plan. The first item in his Civic Club meeting notes, underlined, was *"Men to go get Building."* His plan followed the latter part of another memo Attorney Marshall had prepared, "Petition to Local School Boards." As in Marshall's memo, he and the men agreed to concentrate on this one item rather than all the pressing matters. To establish the existence of inequality "with one stroke" would make it easy to continue the campaign for equality.[22]

By September 1947 the eighteen men left in the Civic Club selected a committee of seven Negro men who would be trained in how to approach the school board with the requests for a school building. The men met at Ebenezer on Sunday nights, and Mr. Tate schooled them on the way to respond to certain questions.[23]

Mr. Harper had told Mr. Tate to tell the men that one of the first questions to be asked of the committee spokesman would be, "Boys, who sent you to ask for the school building? You know we have lived together in this community for a long time, and we have always had peace and harmony and good relations. You also know that we have always done right by our Negroes and we always intend to do right. We know you need a school building, but the one you have will last several years longer. Who is behind the effort to force us to build our Negroes a building now?"[24]

The projected scenario played out in Greensboro just as it did in other places in the state. The selected men entered the three-story brick courthouse with its Doric columns and shrubs across the front lawn on the second Monday night in September 1947.[25] Questioning the men, the school board struggled to determine a leader for the movement. The seven men knew their leader was waiting around the corner in his parked automobile. But the strategy required him to play a "backseat role," as they called it, and never let anyone know he was, in fact, leading the effort.

At Ebenezer, the men had practiced their answers to the questions so many times at their strategy session that they could say the words as though they were a song. People recalled later that a man named Garfield Jackson made the following statement.

"Mr. Lewis, we have lived in the city of Greensboro all our lives and when we were children we needed a building. But our parents told us that the city officials told them to wait a little longer to give the city enough time to build a treasury so that there would be enough money to make a good down payment on a school building for us."

The school board knew it was true. While white schools had surged ahead in the intervening years, the same school buildings for Negroes remained.[26]

"All of us are grown men now," the speaker continued, "and some of us have children attending classes in the same building in which we attended classes over 20 years ago." The words lingered in the air.

"Gentlemen, we cannot wait any longer. We must have an understanding that that building will be started within this year. Our children must attend school in a good building like the one that your children have."

Baffled, the school board still was determined to figure out who the leader of this movement was. "You mean to tell us you boys decided all of a sudden that you must have a new building for the Negro children, and that decision is yours and nobody prompted you to make it?"

The Negro men knew how to return blank stares.

Another of the seven men, Ray Tripp, finally spoke up. "*We* decided that we must have a school building for our children not later than next year."

The school board refused to promise a new school, since it said it did not have the money. "But we thank you for coming to our meeting and we'll take your request under advisement."

"When may we have an answer?" asked Joe Fambro.

The school board was not specific about an answer, but did tell the committee's members that they were "welcome back anytime" they wanted to come and "we'll be happy to see you."

One block from the courthouse, Mr. Tate waited in his car, which was parked in front of Dr. Baber's restaurant. Dr. Baber was the man Mr. Tate

While black parents appeared before the school board in the courthouse building, Mr. Tate waited down the street in his car. At the end of the meeting, the group convened with Mr. Tate in a black-owned restaurant to discuss the meeting and plan the strategy for the next meeting. *Library of Congress*

had initially called when he was trying to locate Union Point and who had given him the number for the county agent. He had been the acknowledged leader of the Negro community in the years before Mr. Tate's arrival, but had silently ceded the reins to the capable young principal before his death.

The men arrived to meet him less than fifteen minutes after they left the school board meeting. Convening quietly and unobtrusively in the restaurant, the committee members gave Mr. Tate a full report of the meeting. The men imagined they failed, since they had been told no.

But Mr. Tate congratulated them and pronounced the meeting a success. They had had a breakthrough because they had opened a dialogue *and* received a standing invitation to return. At the next Men's Civic Club meeting, the group decided a committee would return every month and make a request. The men faithfully returned to each meeting of the school board in the fall of 1947.

Finally, the school board made some concessions. The board would construct a building if the community would help pay for it, they informed Mr. Tate, who in his interactions with the superintendent played his role as the nonpolitical principal. The school board's strategy of asking the community to pay for its own school was not new: two decades earlier, the availability of money from the Rosenwald Fund prompted school boards to support the building of new schools as long as Negro communities paid most of the cost. Paying a second time for what they had already paid for with their taxes was one of the items Mr. Hunt and Dr. Du Bois had protested in 1911.

While Mr. Tate knew he could count on the community to give, he also knew they simply did not have enough income to raise the many thousands required. So like Mr. Hunt, who had sent numerous letters around the country seeking funding for Fort Valley, Mr. Tate dutifully set about the task of trying to help the community raise the money via outside support to match the school board's offer.

His letter was meticulously crafted: "The citizens of our city have reached an agreement with the board of education whereby a school building is to be constructed. The agreement is as follows: the board of education promises to give three-fourths of the materials needed in constructing the building if the citizens will supply one-fourth and pay the cost for erecting the building." He explained the Negro citizens had pledged $2,000, but with the cost of the building projected at $10,500, the community needed additional support. "If it is at all possible for you to make a donation at this time, be it large or small," he wrote, "it will be more than appreciated."[27]

Mr. Tate mailed letters to leading business enterprises, politicians, and colleges—anyone and any organization he thought might help. Montgomery Ward, Oldsmobile, General Motors, Ford, Golden State Mutual Guaranty Trust, Kansas Milling Company, and Paul Brown, the U.S. House representative for Greene County, all received letters.

And the responses came back quickly.

The effort had our "complete moral support," wrote Golden State Mutual of Los Angeles, as well as "every hope that you will succeed in raising the total." But it regretted that it could not help. Ford said its responsibilities were to the community in Detroit. The other big companies made similar replies.

From Savannah State, the Negro college begun by Richard Wright, the man who first organized educators in 1878, came a small contribution from the president and a suggestion that Mr. Tate and the committee were already following. Mr. Tate needed to develop a program, the president said, "to stimulate officials in charge of education in the State of Georgia to make adequate provision." That was part of his program at Savannah State, he explained. It was part of Mr. Tate's plans also. He just did not publicly admit it.

In December, Mr. Tate requested donations of $300 from the community to secure the building. Maybe each man could donate $10. Some did, but the total was not enough.

As the principal sought money, the school board read the larger federal and political climate and decided the Negro children did need a building, whether or not the Negro community could raise the sum originally required. A *New York Times* article lamenting the gap in the value of Negro and white schools captured the urgency of the era. It called the matter one "of extreme importance" and said that leaders should be preparing a program of information that "would lay the facts before the Southern people" so that there might be widespread acceptance of the need to put more money into Negro schools.[28]

Greensboro was a quaint town that took pride in the fact that Jefferson Davis, the president of the Confederacy, had once paid a visit to the town. A statue of a Confederate soldier guarded the entrance to the stately old courthouse where the school board met. One could even buy "Dixie Ice Cream," as advertised on a sign near the front of the bank. To preserve these treasured traditions of segregation, Greensboro accepted the challenge to make the Negro schools more equal.

At its January 1948 meeting, the school board suggested the citizens of Greensboro be asked to vote on an $85,000 bond referendum. The local residents were not unaware of the climate nationwide. A report prepared by the Southern Regional Council declared that if Negro schools were to catch up, they would need "more than a proportionate share of school funds." It warned that the white South must either "recognize this fact and act accordingly, or else face the prospect of yielding ungracefully to a series of court rulings."[29] The Greensboro paper supported the bond. If passed, $65,000 of the total amount would be designated for a new school building for the Negro children.[30]

A jubilant committee reported to Mr. Tate, then launched a well-organized campaign involving both black and white citizens to try to get the bond issue passed. As far as anyone could remember, this was the first time in the history of Greensboro that a bond issue had designated most of its income to fund a Negro school. The Greensboro *Herald-Journal* helped. It led an August 6, 1948, article, a little over a week before the big vote, with a summary of the gains the white school would receive and then addressed the Negro school. It reminded readers that more than forty years earlier Negroes had deeded the existing school buildings and grounds to the city, and in that time the "city has never spent anything for this property except to keep it up." The present building, it proclaimed, "is a fire trap and is not adequate nor is it fit to be used as a school."

The position of Greensboro whites on the bond varied. Some proclaimed that Negroes did not need to be educated, that they had enough education already, that if they were educated "they'll be as good as we are." After all, proclaimed one, "if they get too smart, who will do the dirty work?" Others resorted to a protest that had been used a generation earlier: "Negroes don't pay any taxes and hence don't deserve to be educated at tax expense"; this argument had been statistically debunked decades earlier.[31]

Other whites were supportive. They hoped Negroes' manners would improve if they got a school. They believed a good school would help create a better community. "We have some good niggers here," proclaimed one, "and we should try hard to keep them pleased and satisfied."

Whites' opinions were just as varied when it came to the educated principal with the enigmatic smile. Many believed he knew his job as a principal, and most understood the Negro community loved him. They could get rid of him but feared "all hell will break loose in the Negro community" if they did. Or they could pass the bond issue and preserve the segregated peace. Instead of getting rid of him, they decided to pass the bond issue.[32]

The August 20, 1948, issue of the local newspaper headlined the success of the Men's Civic Club and their invisible advisor. "Bond Issue Wins Big Vote," it proclaimed. The new Greensboro High School that would lure children from surrounding rural communities was about to be built.[33]

In January 1949 Mr. Tate invited Mr. Harper to come speak at the third anniversary of the Men's Civic Club. The new school building was progressing nicely, and he hoped Mr. Harper could join them on February 16 for the anniversary gathering.

"Will be pleased to come," Mr. Harper responded, saying nothing about Mr. Tate's request to know the "charges for his services." He did ask about the kind of information Mr. Tate would like him to share. Both Mr. Harper and Mr. Tate understood that Mr. Harper, as the executive director of the educational association, could make certain talking points in this local setting that would be unwise for Mr. Tate to make himself.

In response, Mr. Tate explained the meeting would be one to which members of the school board would be invited. The Men's Civic Club had written in its congratulatory letter to the board complimenting it on building the school that they were interested in "helping, not hindering" the good work being done in Greensboro. If Mr. Harper could let these school board members know about the progress being made in other communities regarding educational opportunities for Negroes it would be helpful, for the school transportation fight was looming.[34]

8

OUT OF THE PUBLIC EYE

In April 1949 Thurgood Marshall spoke at the evening session of the state GT&EA meeting in the Augusta City Auditorium, the meeting at which Mr. Tate joined his fellow educators in their condemnation of Georgia's refusal to pass the Minimum Foundation Program of Education (MFPE). This program would have provided state funding to address the inequalities in teachers, buildings, and transportation that existed in rural white schools and in Negro schools. Without it, inequalities would remain. At the meeting, GT&EA members aligned with other state and educational leaders in arguing that "something must be done to improve living in every community in Georgia."

Attorney Marshall began by declining to use the public address system in the auditorium, despite the capacity audience. "I don't need this," he joked. "I talk too loud and too long."

The educators listened appreciatively as the admired attorney discussed pending cases in Georgia and the new voting laws in the state. He covered details about the Constitution that some potential new voters might need to know in order to meet the qualification requirements, including the wording of the Fourteenth and Fifteenth Amendments and the content of certain articles, and he went over other questions that might be asked, including defining the duty of particular government officials, relating the details of a number of historical events, and even trivia such as how many windows were in the White House. He emphasized that all present must work together to "continue to fight for what is rightfully due us."[1]

In the GT&EA membership, which had increased by that time to 6,500, Attorney Marshall had an audience aligned with his objectives. The teachers were "carefully making" plans at this meeting "to take the necessary steps for achieving the goals desired." Organization leaders encouraged members to "find out the new regulation laws on voting" and set up informational classes in their schools. "Politicians are no fools; they do not want you to vote," Mr. William Boyd of Fort Valley bellowed. Homer T. Edwards,

In addition to state meetings, GT&EA also hosted its clinic for school leaders at the 4-H camp near Fort Valley, Georgia. In an era when overnight hotel accommodations were not widely available, Mr. Hunt was among the leadership that secured the property for black meetings and banquets. In this 1949 gathering, more than 400 educators representing 11 regions and 174 local units convened for the 12th Annual Conference. Dr. John Davis was one of the featured speakers. *GT&EA Collection*

Negro principal of the respected Athens High School, crystallized further the determination of the GT&EA: "If you want to obtain your rights," he said, "then stop no shorter than the courts."[2]

Mr. Tate had already accomplished the voter registration in Greensboro that netted a new school. Greensboro was one of the communities ready to move on to the courts, if needed, to get school bus transportation. When he read the veiled reference in the *Herald* that GT&EA was attending to "important business," Mr. Tate knew exactly what that business was, especially in Greensboro.

While Mr. Harper handled matters in other communities, Mr. Tate continued to follow in Greensboro the steps of the process that Attorney Marshall had outlined for local branches and which Mr. Harper had shared with him. Already Mr. Ward, the farmer from Greshamville, had called a meeting of his fellow citizens and explained the transportation problem, with Mr. Harper present as a consultant. And Mr. Harper had prepared the petition.

On waxy, almost see-through paper, Mr. Harper had typed, "We your petitioners, do earnestly pray that the Board of Education provide the same kind and quality of transportation service for Negro children as for white children," pointing out that differences in services provided were "contrary both to our state and national laws as interpreted repeatedly by the Supreme Court of the United States."

Mr. Harper and Mr. Tate had already consulted with the local attorney representing the NAACP, Austin T. Walden. Thus far, the request for school bus transportation in Greene County was proceeding smoothly.

Of course, some of Attorney Marshall's suggestions needed to be modified for the southern context. They would not give the "widest publicity to the petition and meeting" or send speakers to churches, PTA meetings, or labor unions. Neither would they circulate the petition throughout the community. However, after meeting with Mr. Harper—in Mr. Tate's absence—the group had selected five men who would go to the superintendent's office to make a verbal request for school bus transportation for Greene County's Negro children. And, as planned, when Mr. Ward and the others left the office, he submitted a written request to the superintendent.

Just as the representatives from the Men's Civic Club had done earlier regarding the school building, immediately after the meeting Mr. Ward and the committee reported back to Mr. Tate. Mr. Tate listened, asked questions, and—when necessary—picked up the phone to call Mr. Harper. Together, they planned the next strategic move for the committee of citizens and arranged for the committee to report Greshamville citizens on the progress regarding school transportation. And then the cycle of school board meetings, quiet reports, and new strategic moves would continue until they had completed all the steps Thurgood Marshall had outlined in his memo for local NAACP branches.[3] Never mind they were not technically a chapter of that organization—the work needed to be done.

The next step would be for Greshamville's citizens to file a suit against the school board. The complaint would read like that of the other cases across the state, utilizing the template the legal department of the NAACP had set out.

The GT&EA was prepared to take these school boards to court. As Lucius Bacote said at the August state meeting, they had "the best legal talent as our Legal Advisor." "He will be retained," Mr. Bacote announced, but "you and I must pay for his services." The teachers agreed with Mr. Bacote's proclamation that they were "largely responsible for all that happens more than any other group." The educators were ready to take on the financial cost of retaining Attorney Walden so litigation could be pursued wherever needed.[4]

Mr. Tate confided the matter in a letter to a friend in Arkansas. "I might mention also that our county is planning to file a suit one day next week for equal school facilities. This is strictly on the Q.T., so don't mention this in any of your corresponding with even my closest friends."[5]

By the time Mr. Ward filed his suit, whites had realized that the power of Negroes in Greene County had grown. In two and a half years, the Negro vote had increased from 10 to 1,300. Across the state, school boards and politicians scrambled to find ways to funnel money to local school boards so that they might equalize facilities and preserve segregation. One way to address the problem was for the state to pass the MFPE it had turned down in an earlier election. State funding could assist local school boards attempting to equalize facilities. But state funding had not yet been provided, and Greene County had a suit looming.[6]

In the midst of the crisis, the superintendent came to see Mr. Tate.

"Tate, you may or may not know that we got a fellow up there in Greshamville that wants his children to ride school buses," Mr. Corry announced. Mr. Tate looked blank and let Mr. Corry tell him about the suit.

"We don't have any money, but I can't deny that they ought to be riding to school on buses," Mr. Corry confided. He needed Mr. Tate's help. He needed Mr. Tate to "go up there" and see if he couldn't "talk Ward into holding off, not fighting so fast." Mr. Corry clearly did not know that the Negro principal from whom he was seeking help in dealing with the Negro community had in fact engineered the difficulties he was now confronting.

Mr. Tate responded cautiously. First he wanted to know what kind of promises the school board would make.

The superintendent responded, "We're going to have some bus transportation . . . within eighteen months to two years."

"What else?" Mr. Tate asked.

"We will buy a station wagon so Mr. Ward can transport his children," the superintendent said.

"He'll buy a station wagon for me?" Mr. Ward asked. The day after the superintendent's visit, Mr. Tate drove along Route 41 through town, over the bridge where he and Mr. Harper rendezvoused with the funeral home director late at night, and made the left out to Greshamville so he could consult with Mr. Ward.

"What do you think about that?" Mr. Tate asked. The final decision, after all, was not Mr. Tate's to make.

The farmer stood firm. "I can't take that," he said. "I want all the children to ride on buses."

That answer confirmed Mr. Tate's respect for the farmer. He was worth all that the late-night drives had cost Mr. Tate in both money and lost sleep. "Mr. Ward, if you had said anything else, I would have been disappointed. I think you are right."[7]

While matters were heating up in Greensboro, Mr. Tate followed closely the GT&EA case in Irwin County, which had made the national press. He cut out articles from the Atlanta papers, taping together the ones that covered several pages. One headline from the *Atlanta Constitution* blared, "School Suit May Cost 100 Millions."

The lawsuit filed against the Irwin County school board in the federal district court at Valdosta by the NAACP represented eighteen Negro children. According to the paper, the suit demanded equal educational opportunities—meaning equality in buildings, equipment, teachers, courses of study, and transportation. While Georgia's leaders voted to defend the county school board and local superintendent, whites debated the merits of the case, some bringing up once again the long-standing complaints about Negroes not paying enough in taxes to justify receiving equality, others wondering whether there should be a similar suit on behalf of white rural children who also were not receiving adequate schooling. It was clear that the entire South was watching: should Negroes win this Irwin County case—as they won a similar case in King George County, Virginia, the previous year—it would affect all of Georgia and all of the South.[8]

One possible outcome, a newspaper pointed out, might be that counties would be ordered by the courts to implement equal systems but would not be able to meet the state requirements to issue bonds to cover the cost. The result would be that Negroes could obtain the use of white schools. White school standards could be lowered. White school officials could be jailed for failure to comply. Worst of all, integration could be ordered.[9]

A white editorialist in Atlanta, Ralph McGill, pointed out what might happen because the white South failed to follow its own laws about separate equality. "The chicken of failure to do that now is coming home to roost," he proclaimed. He hoped the ruling in the Irwin County case would be delayed for a while, but the state needed to think carefully and plan responsibly for what it would do if the court ruled against the county school board, although "I know it is not pleasant to discuss unpleasant facts." Other editorials across the state of Georgia agreed with him. Not supporting equal education had been a mistake, and something needed to be done soon.[10]

A result of similar worries, the bond issued in Greensboro for the construction of the Negro school reportedly had been the first of its kind in Georgia. But the bond did not pay for transportation. So after Mr. Ward refused the board's offer of a car for the transport of his children, he, Mr. Tate, and the other Negro men involved awaited the school board's response.

When the response came, it was clear that they would still need the help of Mr. Harper. As one of the key Negro men involved in the issue, Mr. Jackson, wrote to Mr. Harper: "Mr. Ward brought me this letter that he received from the board. I am sending this to you so that you might see it and send information as to what steps to take now." The letter, from the superintendent of the Greene County schools to the state school superintendent, noted that after conferring with a committee representing "some of the colored schools," the school district had made "some arrangements" that would be "satisfactory to both parties." The proposed arrangement involved per diem payments from the school to Negro parents to cover the cost of transporting the Negro students.

However, in the letter Mr. Jackson reiterated to Mr. Harper that, as they had discussed earlier that day via phone, the Negro was not, in fact, satisfied with the proposed agreement, even though the letter from the superintendent seemed to imply they were. "Whatever action" they had to take next, he said, needed to be initiated "at the present time, while interest is still high." And while they were leaving to Mr. Harper the decision as to what they should do, he needed to reply quickly, because "Mr. Ward will be back to me Saturday to receive his instructions."[11]

After consultation with Mr. Harper and their invisible agent, Mr. Tate, the committee of Negro men seeking school bus transportation wrote to the president of the Greene County Board of Education, H.H. Tappan. "This is to inform you . . . that we do not agree to the proposed arrangements whereby the Board of Education would grant a per diem payment for transporting Negro children. We agree to the same kind and quality of transportation as is provided white children, only. No other would be fair or legal, and hence would not be acceptable."[12] And they asked the board to provide the transportation immediately.

The school board rejoined that it could not, that it did not have the money to buy buses immediately for the Negro children. This argument, that there was no money available, had been used frequently by school boards across the South to explain their lack of investment in Negro schools.

The solution the board proposed mirrored the action that had been taken by the school board in Treutlen County in 1946. To avoid litigation, the Treutlen County school board paid 25 cents for any child attending school who lived more than a mile and a half outside the city limits until they could provide buses. That arrangement had netted the Negro Civic Club $175 a month for a bus the club operated to transport county students.[13]

In Greensboro, the settlement meant Mr. Tate had a new job for the remainder of the 1949–50 school year. Each month, he created a handwritten summary of students attending school, organized by grade. Painstakingly, he used the Greene County transportation formula to calculate the money owed each student and wrote the student a check from the school's account at the Bank of Greensboro. The state was paying 10 percent of the original cost of a bus, one cent per day for each child transported, a one-way mileage allowance of two cents on paved roads and four cents on unpaved roads. If a passenger car was used, they paid one cent per day per child and a one-way mileage allowance of three cents.[14] The formula meant that Mr. Tate wrote the students checks that ranged from 75 cents to $4.50. In his reports, "High School Children from County in Attendance at the Greensboro High School," he indicated the amount of money paid each month. On November 23, 1949, he paid $166.75 in individual checks to students. Between October 1949 and February 1950, the school board averaged $149.81 per month paid for transportation costs at the Greensboro school. The whole situation was ironic, as the money the school board was paying for transportation was more than the combined salaries of all his teachers.[15]

As the Negro community's demands became more visible and more expensive, Mr. Cousins, the head of the state's Division of Negro Education, may have had an inkling about Mr. Tate's role and become concerned that his position as principal might now be precarious. He wrote Mr. Tate as early as July 1949: "Superintendent Rupert Langford, [of] Augusta, told me yesterday that he was looking for a good man to serve as principal of one of the large elementary schools in Richmond County." They may have discussed the job, but Mr. Tate loved Greensboro and did not pursue the Richmond County job.[16]

There was, indeed, increasing speculation about how and why the Negro community had suddenly became so insistent on receiving the rights due them as citizens of Greene County. "Before old Tate came to Greensboro, the Negroes were satisfied with their school and their status," commented one person. Said another, "We should get rid of Tate and we won't have to build a school building for those niggers."[17]

Mr. Tate knew he had the support of the Negro community and that of many of the "well thinking white people" in the town. He did his best to remain in the shadows, directing others in their direct requests for better conditions and in litigation when those requests were not satisfied. But he was having trouble remaining silent.

"I had a heated discussion yesterday with a member of the board of education concerning my salary," he wrote his confidant in Arkansas in September 1949. At the GT&EA meetings, Mr. Tate had learned that the new state salary scale Georgia had just implemented narrowed the gap between the salaries of Negro and white teachers. The new scale especially favored Negro teachers holding a master's degree. Mr. Tate had been attending Atlanta University every summer to obtain a master's degree, which meant that he would soon be eligible for a salary increase. Evidently the board member had found whatever Mr. Tate said to him about his salary distasteful, and so Mr. Tate wrote to his friend, "It might be necessary for me to seek another position within another few days."[18]

But the days passed, and Mr. Tate remained in his post. Later that fall he requested the use of the white football field, since his school did not have a football field, and Mr. Corry granted the request. But even though the Negro schoolchildren practicing outside with Mr. Tate as coach had won three district basketball championships for girls and two for boys and were co-champions in two other years, the superintendent appeared to be reaching his limit. "Please don't ask to use the gymnasium at the white school," Mr. Corry said.

Mr. Tate didn't. For the remainder of 1949, he continued with his usual responsibilities. He helped with the Boy Scouts, taught chemistry, algebra, and biology, supervised the lunchroom, coordinated school activities, and helped with dramatics. His students won district and state dramatic programs and oratorical contests, and he helped seniors go to college. Every student in the Negro school could read before they reached the fourth grade. The superintendent never complained about his performance as an administrator, and, as some more forgiving whites noted, "There is one thing to be said about Professor Tate and that is that he knows his job and he is for his people."[19]

But not everyone agreed.

As the school year came to an end, Mr. Tate received a message in his office. "You tell Tate," came the message via an informant, that "I know he is behind all this, and the Negro children will ride on school buses over my dead body." The message supposedly came from the chairman of the school board.

Mr. Tate did not flinch.

"You go back and tell Mr. Tappan," he said, "that Professor Tate said he must not be planning to live long."[20]

9

SEASONS OF OPPORTUNITY

Having made his retort, Mr. Tate gave the matter little further thought. Surely in the spring of 1951, a Negro man could be a man. As he drove from Greensboro past the newly sprouting green countryside on his way southwest to Macon, Georgia, he believed his was the era of the Negro comeback. He relished the achievements of people such as Joe Louis, George Washington Carver, and Marian Anderson. These iconic race representatives evoked pride and proved that European domination in America had not diminished the potential of those whose origins lay in the raped African continent. He enthusiastically read histories of Egyptian people who looked like him, such as King Tut. In the years since his graduation from Fort Valley, as he grew to manhood in the principalship, some people in America seemed to be finally recognizing the evils of segregation. Surely his generation's fight against oppression presaged victory.

As far as Mr. Tate was concerned, any man or woman, whether Negro or white, could plainly see that ushering a fellow human being to the stinking, rat-infested, hard-seat balconies of theaters while others enjoyed soft, comfortable seats downstairs was morally wrong. And any person who allowed the yellow-painted school buses to roam the rural areas of the state picking up white boys and girls and delivering them to their schools while refusing to transport black boys and girls could see that it was wrong. He certainly knew it was wrong.

Mr. Tate had driven some of these roads during the days when he chauffeured Dr. Bond from the Fort Valley campus to GT&EA meetings. Back then, as a student, he had not been aware of the ways the organization, led by Mr. Harper and Dr. Bond, had been fighting for opportunity, justice, fairness, influence, and representation. As an insider, he now understood. Or so he thought.

"What are you fighting for?" someone had once asked him. Now that he was a principal, he could reply, and tie his answer to a movement that had begun before he was born. For years GT&EA had been leading the fight for transportation, salaries, facilities, equipment, vocational schools, and so much more. He did not know all the leaders who had come before him, but he did know he agreed with the struggle. His commitment to the purposes of the educators' organization made this trip—a drive of several hours to Macon and staying with an unknown Negro family for several days while he attended the GT&EA's annual meeting—not a repugnant idea. These meetings were a pillar in the formula for resistance.[1]

Mr. Tate could see the results of GT&EA's work locally and the NAACP's work nationally as he pulled into the wide driveway of Ballard-Hudson Senior High School, the new and immaculately maintained brick structure that would be hosting the 1951 annual meeting. Only a year old, the school occupied a twenty-six-acre campus in a quiet and accessible part of town. The land sloped to the south and east, and the classrooms in the group of four buildings were constructed so that as many of the windows as possible looked over the rolling fields. He remembered the shabby buildings he had encountered when he first arrived in Greensboro. But now it was a new day, and someone cared about windows in a school building for Negro children.

The school boasted two classroom buildings. One was approximately four hundred feet long and held twenty-two classrooms and toilets. The other housed science classrooms, with laboratories for biology, chemistry, and physics. Additional buildings, with covered concrete paths so the children would not get rained on as they walked from class to class, dotted the campus. One administrative building boasted a general office and a private one for the principal, as well as lounges for male and female teachers. Another contained a cafeteria and kitchen plus shop classrooms. In another space was the gymnasium/auditorium that would host the GT&EA annual meeting.[2]

As he navigated the circular driveway, designed to decrease vehicular congestion, Mr. Tate surely understood that this new building for Negro children had not appeared simply because white people in Macon had had a revelation about practicing democracy or Christianity. Nor was the new school simply the result of GT&EA's well-worded position statements, presented by the Resolution Committee each year during their representative assemblies. Yes, Mr. Harper used these statements to represent the will of Negro educators to the powers that be: the state board of education, state school superintendent, the state board of regents, city and county boards of education, state legislators, and the governor, all of whom listened carefully and judged Mr. Harper's presentations to be "intelligent." But their attention and comments would not have built the school Mr. Tate was preparing to enter had Mr. Harper not craftily aligned an agenda of local and national legal protest with these crucial educational meetings.

At the annual state meeting the previous year, the GT&EA Representative Assembly adopted resolutions giving Mr. Harper the crisp mandate to utilize the legal language of the NAACP in his petitions. Mr. Harper was to report to public officials that he represented petitioners who were citizens of the United States, taxpayers, Negroes, and teachers of the children attending the public schools and colleges of Georgia and who wanted relief in the continuing discrimination on the basis of race and color that persisted in Georgia in construction, equipment, facilities, libraries, transportation services, curriculum, length of school day, and accreditation status. Mr. Harper should explain that, under the Fourteenth Amendment of the United States Constitution as interpreted by the Supreme Court of the United States, boards of education were under "a positive duty not to discriminate against any school child, and to maintain the public schools . . on a basis of equality . . . without regard to race." Education was a legal matter, he was to remind these boards and officials. But "despite the requirements of the United States Constitution," Georgia had "established and maintained a policy" of denying Negro youth facilities equal to white youth. GT&EA was "determined to work assiduously, and with the use of all techniques, to bring into realization these resolutions."[3]

Mr. Harper pressed the same agenda in his role as president of the Atlanta NAACP branch. Unlike earlier eras, this season of a Supreme Court favored equalizing and integrating schools. This meant that an urban NAACP chapter, such as the one in Atlanta, could speak directly, without having to hide its activities behind citizens committees like the one Mr. Tate had begun in Greensboro. As NAACP branch president, Mr. Harper wrote a letter to officials of the Clayton County schools similar to the ones he had written to other counties under GT&EA auspices. He appealed to the county to "make no racial discrimination providing school facilities for the children." He was quoted in the *Atlanta Daily World* as being "disheartened" to learn that Clayton County had floated school bonds to build two modern high schools for white students at a cost of $440,000 but planned to repair present Negro school buildings and transfer some discarded frame structures from white schools to Negro schools. Such a policy conflicted with "Christian ethics and the laws of the United States," he said.[4]

For Negro education throughout the state, the season represented a glorious era not seen since World War I. Back then, Mr. Hunt could assume the stage at the 1919 NAACP national meeting in Cleveland and speak publicly about the impact of Negro migration on the South. His colleague Lucy Laney, who organized her own school in Augusta and hosted James Weldon Johnson to organize the first NAACP branch in Augusta, could also speak publicly at the national meeting. But those days of public alignment and planning had disappeared in recent decades. Now, though, at the public testimonial dinner given to honor Mr. Harper, the reality and hopes of the current times were evident.

Guests enjoyed the smiling lady ushers in their charming evening gowns, and everyone dined heartily on tossed salad, parsleyed potatoes, broiled chicken, hot biscuits, iced tea, ice cream, and cake. Those speaking before Mr. Harper mentioned the "dense and lethal fog" and depressing gloom of the world wars and the race riots of earlier periods. In his own remarks, Mr. Harper also reminded the audience, which included former students of his, faculty with whom he had worked, GT&EA members, ministers, Robert Carter of the national NAACP, and others, that until recently some Negroes in some counties had attended classes in churches, lodge buildings, and tobacco barns. In one location, Negro children were getting 1 cent of county money while white children received 79 cents.[5]

Mr. Harper certainly appreciated all the remarks and the gifts, including a sterling silver tray to his wife and a $1,000 cashier's check from the Negro-owned Citizens Trust Bank. Yet instead of enjoying these laurels, he emphasized the challenges they still faced. It was true the schools were experiencing a "renaissance, indeed a revolution" in the present era. But Negro teachers, parents, and citizens needed to join him and others to help implement the recent Supreme Court decisions demanding equality in schools. If Negroes could not get "equality all down the line," he solemnly warned, they would begin seeking integration.[6]

And integration is what white southern people feared. When GT&EA appealed directly to state leaders for a legislative program in the 1940s to fully fund public education for both races, white voting Georgians said no.

After he was fired from his school for activities to demand equality, Mr. Harper assumed the role of executive secretary of GT&EA. With Mr. Hunt's death, Mr. Harper became the new leader of educational activity in Georgia. *GT&EA Collection*

Only the increasing array of Supreme Court decisions threatening to chip away at the state's right to maintain segregation reversed their sentiment. Alarmed by the federal climate, some Georgia Assembly members sat around on beds at the Henry Grady Hotel with sandwiches in one hand and glasses of whiskey or cigars in the other, contemplating ways to finance the education bill earlier rejected and, thus, preserve segregation.

Fittingly, they were led by Governor Herman Talmadge, Eugene Talmadge's son. Herman had been hastily elected governor after his father died before assuming office. Eugene had died in late 1946, after being reelected to a fourth term but before being sworn in. In a controversial move, the Assembly had voted to make Herman governor in his father's place, but that decision was ultimately overturned by the state supreme court. Herman, though, was duly elected governor in a special election in 1948 in which "missing" votes cast in alphabetical order by dead people provided the margin to claim victory. And once in office, he alerted white Georgians of the need to implement *Plessy v. Ferguson* to forestall anything worse.[7]

With Governor Talmadge's support of the efforts of the Assembly members, Georgia funded the MFPE with a sales tax increase of 3 percent to begin the task of equalizing schools to preserve segregation. At the same time the legislature sent to Governor Talmadge a bill that would withhold all state financial aid from public schools and units of the university system if any court ordered the admission of Negroes into a white institution. Funds could be withheld from *all* schools if *any* Negro child was admitted.[8]

In a telegram from New York, Walter White of the NAACP taunted Governor Talmadge over the legislation: "You and my native state deserve credit for increasing educational appropriations." Then he crisply noted that the funding increase had come about only because of the court cases. In retort, the governor made no secret of his intent to fund schools as a way of defeating integration. "As long as I am governor," he declared in a return wire to Walter White, there would be no "co-mingling of the races in our schools. Rather than permit this to happen we would return to the system of private schools and subsidize the individuals that go to school."

The governor confirmed this opinion in a response to Mr. Harper and a GT&EA delegation that included Mr. Tate. The governor said he could support equalization, inclusive of salary equalization, but would never support a male Negro principal overseeing a staff that included white female teachers. Such a shift in racial hierarchy would offend southern sensibilities.[9]

Almost overnight, long-standing GT&EA requests for equal educational commitments bore fruit. In addition to money for new buildings, school terms for Negroes lengthened. Textbooks designated specifically for Negro children appeared in local districts—sent by the state—to ensure the new books would not be usurped by white schools. In 123 of the 155 counties where Negroes resided, school boards absorbed Negro transportation at public expense. The pupil-teacher ratio was not yet fully balanced—still one teacher for forty elementary pupils or thirty-five high school pupils—but by the next year the ratio was slated to decrease to one teacher for thirty elementary pupils or twenty-four high school pupils.[10]

The educators knew the MFPE provided tainted money. But much as they'd used the money from the Rosenwald Fund that was designated for industrial schools to create schools that served the community more fully, the educators knew how to circumvent intent. Money for schools was money needed. Even Thurgood Marshall agreed. While the NAACP opposed segregation in any fashion and wanted the "separate but equal" doctrine abolished, Marshall explained that "at the same time, we take the position that in order to assert a right to segregation, there must be complete and absolute equality in the provisions. . . . I see nothing wrong with this position."[11]

That day in April 1951 Mr. Tate left his car in the expansive parking lot and located the gym/auditorium where the GT&EA meetings would be held. With a state membership of seven thousand, the meeting had grown so big that only larger cities such as Macon, Atlanta, Savannah, or Augusta could host the event. As Mr. Tate completed registration, he gathered his souvenir program, put on his badge, and joined colleagues moving toward the auditorium, which could seat two thousand.

For the first time, Mr. Tate entered the annual meeting with the recognition and responsibility of elected leadership. Just eight years in the profession, he was the newly elected director for Region IV. This position paid him no money but made him responsible for overseeing the needs for Negro education for the counties comprised by Region IV. His election as regional director also automatically placed him on the Board of Directors, the GT&EA governing team that met in Atlanta with Mr. Harper and helped to implement the actions of the Representative Assembly.[12]

In his new visible role, Mr. Tate had overseen his first regional meeting a few months back, careful, like other regional directors, to ensure his meeting followed the GT&EA theme and suggested program format. At the Fair Street High School in the cool rolling hills of Gainesville, just an hour north of Atlanta, he had welcomed guests such as the city mayor and city school superintendent, overseen the business and departmental meetings in the day-long event, made sure the logistics worked for the 85-cents-a-plate lunch, and served as a consultant with the Congress of Negro Parents and Teachers. The parents and educators had met in the same place at overlapping times since the old days of Mr. Hunt.

He also welcomed Mr. Harper, who provided the same message at all of the eleven regional meetings across the state. He explained the newly passed MFPE and provided the most up-to-date information on its implementation.[13]

As a new leader in the organization, Mr. Tate strolled into the state meeting, greeting the many people he knew. Mr. Tate always enjoyed seeing Eli Jackson, then the principal of Washington High School. Mr. Jackson had first

With the mentorship of Eli Jackson, a young Mr. Tate was soon elected regional director for Region IV of GT&EA. The position became the first of many elected GT&EA offices he would hold. *GT&EA Collection*

brought him into the profession and introduced him around the state as his "hot shot." Now peers, they had been attending Atlanta University together in the summers as both sought to complete their master's degree. Both would graduate in August, making them eligible for the master's level salary equality that the new state schedule demanded.

Mr. Tate wore his broad smile, paused to listen attentively to some people as they exchanged quiet communications, or reached out a hand to those close and waved to those farther away. He knew these educators; he knew their schools' problems, and they knew his. They saw each other at local, regional, and state meetings, plus principals' conferences and leadership retreats at the new Camp John Hope for Negroes over near Fort Valley. Their paths crossed at the varied athletic and cultural events that linked Negro schools across the state. At the last principals' conference, Mr. Tate had served as one of the group chairmen. He was even beginning to get invitations to deliver commencement addresses at neighboring schools, which provided additional opportunities to connect with his colleagues in their own communities.[14]

He missed seeing some people at this meeting. Dr. Bond had now been away from Georgia for six years as president of Lincoln University in Pennsylvania. The *Herald* saluted him as "Man of the Year" for his contributions to Georgia's education. Mr. Tate also missed seeing his former principal from Elberton, Paul J. Blackwell. Mr. Blackwell had died three years earlier while rushing down the hall to help a teacher with a student, according to his memorial in the *Herald*. Mr. Blackwell was sorely missed at the state meeting, not only by Mr. Tate but by many others. A former regional director and active in many phases of GT&EA advocacy, Mr. Blackwell had used in Elberton the strategies Mr. Tate later learned to deploy in Greensboro. As Mr. Tate came to learn, Mr. Blackwell's veiled work had created the "pretty good school" the young Horace had attended.[15]

The GT&EA 1951 meeting began as the president, Homer Edwards, repeatedly rapped his gavel. Mr. Edwards, who had guided the GT&EA through these years of aggressive and multi-pronged assault on unequal education for Negroes, had already made clear his position on the successes and challenges confronting them in his welcoming address, printed in the bulletin. "As we assemble for our annual meeting," he had written, "we recognize the fact that in the light of recent legislation, we shall soon view the beginning of what we hope shall be an educational renaissance for our state." With the passage and full financing of the new laws, Negro educators could expect expanded educational opportunity for all the children of all the people.

Mr. Edwards had been president during tumultuous times, but he shared the optimism of the state superintendent, who also wrote to the Negro educators about the possibilities ahead. He ended his remarks, "I trust, therefore, that the enthusiasm and inspiration which shall be gathered as we go forth in our deliberations will cause this session to be noted as an epoch-making one in our long and colorful history."[16]

But Mr. Harper, as always, was the person the educators admired. As executive director, he was the educators' spokesman. He personified GT&EA. With pride, he congratulated the educators on their contributions to the teaching profession. They had worked hard in the last decades. In 1936–37, only 10 percent of Negro teachers had certificates based on four years of college work. By 1947–48, 39 percent did, as compared to 52 percent of white teachers.[17]

With the MFPE finally passed, "the Golden Era in Education in Georgia" was on the horizon. It had come after two years of GT&EA encouraging Negro parents in local communities to support the bill and whites reminding their neighbors of the importance of the bill to continue their way of life. With its accompanying Public School Building Authority, the MFPE constituted one of the most advanced steps taken by any state in the Union. If "these laws are administered with justice, as we believe they will be," Mr. Harper continued, the educators would finally gain the cultural atmosphere for educating Negro children that they had not dared dream would be possible in their generation.

"The Spirit of Democracy is insisting upon Equality of Opportunity for all Americans," Mr. Harper expounded to an appreciative audience. Finally, the United States government, through its executive, judicial, and legislative branches, was opening doors "all too long shut" to Negro people. Even Georgians committed to opposing equality could no longer "retard our local and national growth by acts of Prejudice." Justice was finally mounting its throne.

The educators responded with excitement. Mr. Harper explained that with most of the $180 million appropriated by the MFPE appropriated designated for Negro schools, this generation of teachers had the opportunity long prayed for by the educators preceding them. With needed facilities and resources, the educators could better do their jobs well in building strength and character in the youth, directing them into worthy channels, and developing the talents God distributed to people of all economic and racial groups.

"Know the child, his ambitions and aspirations, his fears and frustrations," Mr. Harper explained, "and with this knowledge of him, you will lead him to think, to dare and to do."[18] Mr. Harper spoke of purposeful education. The classroom teachers' job was to overthrow segregation by inspiring students to believe they could participate equally in the American democratic experiment. Mr. Harper's job was to overthrow the structure with activism and litigation.

Now, as regional director and part of the inner circle, Mr. Tate was beginning to learn how advocacy worked. He discovered that in 1950 Mr. Harper and GT&EA member William Boyd had convinced Horace

Ward to be the first Negro applicant to the University of Georgia when the NAACP sought test plaintiffs.[19] Mr. Harper was also behind the highly publicized first desegregation case in Atlanta, *Aaron v. Cook*, that went "radically beyond" the established principle of separate but equal because it asked the federal district court to declare separate schools as unconstitutional and call for their immediate cessation.[20]

As president of the Atlanta NAACP, Mr. Harper was the man objecting to racial segregation. In public, other key people attempted to quell the local indignation and outcry. Speaking at the Hungry Club forum, broadcast on station WERD after the filing, Mr. Harper's colleague Benjamin Mays, the president of Morehouse College, said, "To argue that the suit makes an attack on segregation because the initiators of the suit want Negro children to go to school with white children is to miss the point entirely." He explained that Negroes opposed curtains on dining cars not because they wanted to eat with whites but because curtains were "embarrassing and set them off as inferior." The same was true for schools. The Negro plaintiffs understood that one group of people, whites, made the laws, administered them, held all the public money, and distributed it. They had no history in anyone's memory of dealing fairly with the minority; thus, placing Negro children in their school was one way to ensure equal distribution of funding. Others argued similarly, and Mr. Harper sent out GT&EA newsletters to report to Negro parents and reproduce the comments of white editors supporting equality.[21]

Mr. Tate was beginning to recognize just how stealthy Mr. Harper's efforts were. Mr. Harper engaged Georgia officials in direct appeals consistent with the climate. These leaders liked Mr. Harper, soothed as they were by his gentle persona. But by using other individuals as fronts for legal action, Mr. Harper used the law to force their accommodation.

Mr. Harper would not report to the convened assembly exactly how everything worked behind the scenes, of course. People did still talk, and they sometimes talked to the wrong people. But Mr. Harper knew exactly why Governor Talmadge repeatedly fussed about the national NAACP trying to plunge a dagger into the very heart of southern tradition. He understood the southern climate that led to the five thousand white delegates in attendance at the 1950 Georgia state Democratic convention collectively screaming the rebel yell and unanimously adopting a resolution to fight to the death the Supreme Court's decision in *Sweatt v. Painter* a few months earlier, which held that the separate education offered to the plaintiff did not meet the requirements of the Fourteenth Amendment's equal protection clause. The South's traditions and the educators' agenda, in quiet cooperation with other key organizations, were on a collision course.[22]

Mr. Tate bid goodbye to his colleagues after the two-day convention ended and made his way back along the winding roads to Greensboro. Having listened to the plans of other regional directors across the state and heard Mr. Harper's reports to the board on the cases GT&EA initiated, Mr. Tate left the meeting convinced of the power of the GT&EA to effect changes.

He certainly knew everyone was not happy with the litigation climate. Even some liberal whites were expressing frustration with the lawsuits. The *Atlanta Constitution* reported that the Negro parents behind *Aaron v. Cook* may have "succeeded in alienating the support of a great many who worked continuously through the years for equal school opportunities." Moreover, a year earlier, the GT&EA *Herald* had alerted Negro educators of growing racial tensions everywhere as Negroes made increasing gains in public education. "In many cases, we observe a definite effort on the part of some white citizens to molest members of our group," the writer observed as he suggested they initiate some work in racial understanding. In particular the editor was getting reports that things "looked bad in the rurals" for Negro educators.[23]

As Mr. Tate drove back through the rural countryside toward Greensboro, he did not know one of those discontented whites awaited him.

10

PAYING THE COST

In earlier days when Negroes appeared to know their place in the American social order, the president of the Greene County school board, H.H. Tappan, had been among the whites in the county who supported Negro development and launched an expansive program to support Negro farmers. This program provided the funding for the Negro county agent Mr. Tate had called when he needed to find a phone number for Eli Jackson. In its "Notes from the Field," the local contributor to the *Herald*—probably Mr. Jackson—even commended Mr. Tappan's efforts to help Negroes in Greene County: "Too much cannot be said of the way the leading white people in the county have worked for this program."[1]

Those times of intact Negro and white relationships were changing and, with them, dispositions. Apparently, Mr. Tappan could support the development of Negro farmers in 1939, but his helpfulness appeared to end ten years later when those same farmers—like Mr. Ward—became prosperous and demanded school privileges for their children equal to those provided for white children, and even spoke to him as equals with him during negotiations related to the school bus transportation issue. Their letter to him rejecting the offer of a per diem payment for transportation costs and reiterating their demand for equal transportation options clearly was not acceptable, respectful Greensboro Negro behavior.[2]

As previously noted, the school board and the Negroes eventually settled on an alternative transportation plan that bought the board some time until they could find some other way to deny Negro schools use of the buses. But Mr. Tappan was not pacified. By now he was certain he had identified the leader Greensboro whites had been wondering about for years. Mr. Tate *had* to be behind the audacious requests, sophisticated and direct letters, and the threatened use of legal measures. The confrontation about salary equality had shown Mr. Tate's aggressive manner. And if Mr. Tappan doubted his conclusion, Mr. Tate's more recent reply on the busing matter fueled his certainty.

Mr. Tate had been back in Greensboro only a few weeks before a letter arrived from Superintendent Corry. One week earlier, he and Mr. Corry had had a pleasant, non-confrontational, professional conversation in which the superintendent gave no evidence of displeasure at Mr. Tate's performance and did not critique the Negro principal on any point about his leadership of the school or any other matter.

Unsuspectingly, Mr. Tate slit open the envelope and unfolded the letter inside. He read it slowly, then reread it. Mr. Tate's services would no longer be needed in Greensboro.[3]

"Well, I will be damned." He did not curse often, but this was one of those times. Mr. Tate remembered how the white principal at a neighboring school had been commended for registering voters in the city. Mr. Tate had been behind the registration of 1,300 Negro voters, but was being fired. The invisible leader in voter registration, obtaining the new school, and acquiring transportation had been deemed unfit to run a school.

At least Mr. Tate was alive. Over in Florida, Harry Moore would soon not be. Mr. Moore, too, had been fired for visibly protesting inequality and pushing salary equalization, and he had received threats of violence. On Christmas night in 1951 he spoke with his mother, who was visiting for the holidays, about the threats he had heard, but he dismissed them and told her he hoped to be rehired in a teaching job soon. Then Mr. Moore cut a cake with his wife to celebrate their twenty-fifth wedding anniversary. After the festivities were over, the family said goodnight, and Mr. Moore retired with his wife for the night. Minutes later, a bomb went off under the floor of their bedroom. Their screaming daughter ran from the bedroom next door and alerted the neighbors with whom they had earlier enjoyed Christmas dinner. The neighbors rushed Mr. Moore and his wife to the nearest Negro hospital. He lay with his head cradled in the lap of his mother on the backseat, bleeding, while his wife rode in the front seat. Upon arrival at the hospital, Mr. Moore regurgitated a big spurt of blood onto his mother's lap, and doctors pronounced him dead. His injured wife, who also had been an educator seeking equality and who had been fired from her position in retaliation for her activities, proclaimed she had nothing to live for anymore and died nine days later.[4]

There was also the matter of Lloyd Gaines. Mr. Gaines was the young valedictorian of a Negro high school in 1931 who went on to become president of his senior class at Lincoln University and an honors graduate. His had been the test case the NAACP used to challenge the refusal of the

University of Missouri Law School to admit Mr. Gaines. In 1938, the Supreme Court ruled in Mr. Gaines's favor in *Missouri ex rel. Gaines vs. Canada*, creating an important legal victory that helped the South understand its need to fund Negro schools if it wanted to avoid integration. However, Mr. Gaines lamented the psychological cost to himself, noting that entering the law school was no longer his dream and that he hoped his efforts would pave the way for other Negroes to further their legal education.[5]

Three months after the victory, on a cool evening, Mr. Gaines left his fraternity brother's house in Chicago and never returned. He was twenty-eight years old. Some people who knew him thought he may have escaped to Mexico. Most believed that foul play led to his disappearance.

Mr. Tate was learning the same lesson that people like Mr. Harper and Mr. Gaines already knew: one could not disrupt established segregated patterns in the South and expect a normal life. While Charles Houston emphasized that Walter White should be the "dynamo behind the whole Association" or "the quarterback in charge of the whole show," such statements about maintaining a "hard-hitting" stance could be delivered from the relative safety of New York. Those who operated on the ground in the South understood that the costs to any individual agitator could be great.

Mr. Tate knew that Mr. Harper, whom he admired greatly, had also been fired at one time, and that he had not looked back. So Mr. Tate would not look back now.

Still, when news of his dismissal spread, the parents of his students (no doubt quietly advised by Mr. Harper) wrote a letter of protest to the superintendent. Their May 1951 letter to Superintendent Corry explained that they were patrons of the school system and citizens, and that they protested this action by the school officials. Mr. Tate's eight-year record in the Greene County system—two in Union Point and six in Greensboro—had been exemplary, they argued. There was no criticism of his work, administration, or character, no lack of efficiency or preparation. They were "deeply and favorably impressed" with this school leader.

They emphasized that Mr. Tate was a Christian gentleman and that his conduct in the community had been above reproach. They liked his youth, liked the example he set for their children. He had the "implicit confidence of teachers, greatest respect of his students, the patrons and other citizens."

The parents also argued that Mr. Tate's professional growth was a reason for keeping him as principal. They reminded the superintendent that the four hundred to five hundred teachers in Region IV of the GT&EA had unanimously elected Mr. Tate as their regional director, making him now someone who held an important position in the state teachers association.

"With his outlook on life and his ambition to achieve, he would be able to keep abreast of the times and, if given the facilities, he would give us a school in Greensboro, that would rank among the best in the state," the letter concluded.[6] But the letter did not change the school board's decision.

To replace Mr. Tate, Greensboro hired a man they believed they could trust: Eli Jackson. Some whispered that Mr. Jackson was the half brother of the white superintendent. Even if publicly unacknowledged, familial connections could sometimes generate trust.[7] The result was that Greensboro was willing to maintain a Negro man with a master's degree as principal, but not a man with a master's degree who was also an agitator like Mr. Tate. Little did they know that they had replaced Mr. Tate with a man who had helped train him.

As Mr. Tate came to grips with the reality that Greensboro would no longer be his adopted home, the Tates prepared to head off for summer study—himself to Atlanta so that he could finish his master's degree and his wife, Virginia, to study for the summer at Ohio State. Both Mr. and Mrs. Tate would benefit professionally from a special fund that Georgia, along with other southern states, had set up to pay for Negro teachers to travel to northern or midwestern universities for education not provided by the state—not least because sending them out of state meant that Georgia and the other southern states would not have to integrate their institutions of higher learning. As the elected leader of GT&EA, Mr. Harper had been part of the effort to obtain this money. Over the years, Georgia's appropriation of these funds would increase from $1,044 supporting five students in 1944 to $208,217.90 supporting 1,790 students in 1955.[8] Over the years, both would attend Teachers College and Ms. Tate would complete a master's degree. But the Tates left for their summer study knowing that there would be no jobs awaiting them in Greensboro upon their return.

Getting fired had personal and emotional costs. Mr. Tate had grown considerably in this community of Greensboro. He had moved beyond the young man of Fort Valley interested in the things college boys do, becoming a responsible citizen. He provided leadership to the members of the community who admired and followed his example.

This phase of his life had forced him to reckon with his sense of family, duty, and love as well: he had navigated a first marriage to, and subsequent divorce from, a woman he'd known only briefly in order to ensure their son was not born out of wedlock.

His development into a responsible person and leader had drawn the people of Greensboro to him, and him to them. Leaving Greensboro meant leaving these deep bonds of community respect, caring, and responsibility.

Leaving Greensboro also meant leaving treasured professional relationships. He had enjoyed meeting with a neighboring principal over in Crawfordville, with whom he rode to regional and state principals' meetings. The exchange of ideas about how to forward Negro education had been useful to him.

During these years he had also experienced changes in his family of origin. He had had his first and only "man-to-man" conversation with his father during a return visit to Elberton some years earlier. They had sat up late into the night talking. After they had said goodnight Mr. Tate heard a noise and came running, only to find that his father had suffered a heart attack. He died later that evening. He had never gotten a chance to explain to his son how the key people worked in Elberton, or whether he might have been one of them.

During his years in Greensboro, his mother, who had demanded that he repay her sacrifice for his schooling by helping the children, also died.[9] She had become increasingly ill after the death of her husband and died shortly after her son married Virginia Barnett. But Mr. Tate would treasure for his lifetime her summons to service.

> The new mother, as she looks at the head of the babe in her arms, whispers in her heart: "My child, may you seek the truth. And if anything I teach you be false, may you throw it away from you and go on to a richer truth and a greater knowledge than I have ever known. If you become a man of thought and learning, may you never fail with your right hand to tear down what your left hand has built up through years of thought and study if you see it not to be founded on that which is [true]. In all of your circumstances, my child, may you fling yourself upon the truth and cling to it as a drowning man in a stormy sea

> flings himself upon a little plant and clings to it, knowing that whether he sinks or swims, it is the best that he has. Die poor, unknown, unloved, a failure perhaps. But close your eyes to nothing which seems to them to be the truth."[10]

"Learn this and keep it," she told Horace, as she told all of her children. He did.

Throughout Georgia, it was not unknown for unexplained fires to destroy Negro schools. The *Herald* reported that the shop building of a Negro school had been destroyed in the late 1930s, and the school's depressed principal actively had to work to secure another building. In Atlanta in 1940, the headlines blared, "Cause of Blaze Remains Mystery." The handsome $25,000 ten-room brick building housing the East Point Colored School had been destroyed by a sweeping blaze whose origin remained "shrouded in mystery." By the time firemen arrived, thirty minutes after being called, the entire roof of the structure had caved in and firemen could do little except attempt to save surrounding structures. The principal said the earlier school that had stood on that spot, a twelve-room wooden structure built in 1927, had also burned.[11] Of course, Negro schools were poorly constructed and vulnerable to fire, but Negro children were taught to care for their schools, and many Negroes suspected foul play when a school burned.

And it was not just schools. During the late summer of 1951, while the Tates were still away, they received news that the rented home he and Mrs. Tate shared had burned. Since neither of them had been home, they could not have mistakenly left anything burning. Plus it was summer, so it also could not have been a spark from the heater.

The flames did not appear to be the work of anyone in the Negro community, who knew each other well. Everyone was aware that the home's owner had built the house with the hope that his daughter, employed as a teacher in Savannah, might one day return to live in the house, and in the interim he had rented it to the Tates. The burning of Mr. Tate's home appeared to be foul play. Retaliation had ascended to a new level.

Returning to Greensboro at the end of the summer, Mr. and Mrs. Tate gathered what few items were left. The little furniture they had bought was gone—the living room set, a bedroom set, and a small bed in the other room where Mr. Tate's brother and mother had sometimes stayed. Mrs. Tate had used the smaller room to hang clothes when no one was staying with them, and the line and any clothes left in the house, along with kitchen towels and appliances, all burned. Useless also was the one-eyed jack coal heater that often warmed Mr. Tate when he wearily returned home from those long drives back and forth to Atlanta to get Mr. Harper.

"Don't worry about it," Mr. Tate resolutely told his wife as they loaded their suitcases into the car to begin a new life. They had the clothing they had carried with them for summer study, but little else, as they left Greensboro.

Part II

THE EDUCATION OF NEGRO LEADERS

To loose the bonds of wickedness, to undo the heavy burdens,
to let the oppressed go free.
—Isaiah 58:6

11

JUST TRYING TO BE A MAN

"I am going to run my school!" Mr. Tate said emphatically. He was in Mr. Cousins's office in Atlanta, squaring off with the superintendent of schools for Griffin, Georgia. At issue was whether Mr. Tate would have the autonomy he wanted to run Fairmont High School the way it needed to be run.

Mr. Cousins was the head of the Division of Negro Education. He had often served as mediator between Negro and white educational communities, and he had been helpful to Mr. Tate in the past. He turned, expressionless, to the white superintendent and queried, "Are you willing to let Mr. Tate be principal and run his school?"

The superintendent, Mr. Krudup, weighed his options. Both he and Mr. Cousins knew that even though Mr. Tate had only recently signed an agreement to accept a job in Griffin, he had just been offered another position in a nearby small town, with a higher salary than he would receive in Griffin.

So Mr. Krudup could reject the new principal's demand and lose the chance to build Negro education in his system during an era that called for equality, or he could concede and give the Negro principal the autonomy he was asking for. At heart, Mr. Krudup was a schoolman. He wanted in Griffin the smart principal who had just finished his master's degree, so he conceded: Mr. Tate could run his own school without interference.[1]

Satisfied, Mr. Tate left Mr. Cousins's office.

Several weeks separated the meeting in Mr. Cousins's office and the day Mr. and Mrs. Tate left Greensboro for a new life.

On that day, Mr. Tate nosed the car away from Canaan Street, where their previous home no longer existed, drove past the sparkling new Greensboro school he had written letters all over the country to help build, and turned toward the center of town. Then, instead of heading west to Atlanta, as he had on the many drives to get Mr. Harper, Mr. Tate turned left at the big Coke sign in the center of town and eased onto Route 16. Route 16 was the same highway dotted with the rolling hills and small lakes that he had driven to the GT&EA meeting in Macon only a few months earlier. Today the rural road would deliver him to a new life in Griffin.

Mr. Tate was accustomed to driving and thinking about strategies for equality. Many times he and Mr. Harper had driven past expensive mansions built during slavery, a time when a white man need only be white to obtain free land in Georgia. Now his wife sat in the car beside him, and those strategies for equality had cost him and her dearly.

Southern white people could be strange. Sometimes they actually liked Negroes they knew well. They were neighborly and helpful; sometimes they even let Negroes they liked know when "trouble" was imminent. However, liking an individual Negro did not mean they trusted all Negroes. An individual could be befriended, listened to, or even gifted with a request—so long as the relationship did not disrupt the larger compass of southern relationships. Mr. Tate had noticed this dynamic in his relationship with Greensboro's sheriff.

"I understand you have a voter registration campaign going on," the sheriff had announced to Mr. Tate during an unsolicited visit to the Greensboro school one day. With a gun on his hip and a badge clearly visible, the sheriff was the personification of memories of Mr. Tate's interactions with policemen in Elberton. As he pondered how to respond, Mr. Tate expected trouble.

But to his surprise, the sheriff's conversation was cordial. With Negro voter registration at 1,300 in Greensboro, the sheriff apparently had deemed building a relationship with the Negro school principal advisable. After all, the principal had standing in the Negro community and could influence votes. After their initial conversation, Mr. Tate and the sheriff worked together in friendly yet invisible camaraderie.

As the white constituents in Greensboro expected, the white sheriff regularly arrested Negro people suspected of having broken laws and locked them up in the small brick jail sitting near the center of town. When someone from the Negro community called Mr. Tate to complain that the jailed person had been unjustly accused, Mr. Tate called the sheriff and defended the person. Often after a conversation with Mr. Tate, the sheriff let the accused person go. Negroes gained freedom, and the sheriff gained goodwill from the Negro community without sacrificing his perceived duty to the white community. The system was far from perfect, and didn't align with the NAACP's preference for direct confrontation. But Mr. Tate and many others achieved similar ends by employing this southern relational strategy. With the sheriff, Mr. Tate had experienced a political "friendship" where he was liked and respected as an individual by the sheriff, and their alliance served both constituent groups.[2]

Of course, not all whites formed alliances with Negroes. Instead, some used southern whiteness to assert privilege and, sometimes, abuse the rights of citizens of another hue. Mrs. Tate's father, Mr. Odie Barnett, had been one of the men influenced by the directives of Mr. Hunt and Dr. Du Bois to purchase farms at the turn of the century. Mrs. Tate had confided to her husband that years earlier, sometime after the war had ended, some unidentified whites had stolen her father's cows from their farm in Athens and transported them to the White Pavilion in Atlanta, where they sold them for slaughter. Dismayed at the family loss, Mrs. Tate's brother drove to Atlanta to the slaughterhouse and identified the family cows, Sugar and Bell, amidst the slew of animals. The slaughterhouse owners listened to the story but would not release the animals. Mrs. Tate's brother went back home, picked up his mother, who had worked closely with the cows, and drove back to Atlanta. The mother approached the area where the cows were confined and called out the name of one of the cows. Sugar's head popped up, she made her special noise, and she began to move toward her owner. Thanks to the brother's assertiveness, the family's cows were retrieved. But the brother could not save his father from paying the cost of white retaliation.

About a week later, some young white men broke down the door of the family home late one summer evening, yelling, "Come out!" as they stomped down the dark hall in the center of the house. Mrs. Tate—a teacher at the Greensboro school by this time (though not yet married to Mr. Tate)—was home for the summer and heard the noise from her bedroom upstairs. She climbed through a small door into the attic rafters while her mother stood silently at the top of the stairs with a shotgun. Mr. Barnett aimed another gun from the couple's bedroom on the first floor.

The white invaders and the Negro owners, prepared to protect their property, squared off in the darkness. It seemed as though either Mr. Barnett would be shot defending the prosperity he had amassed as a farmer or he would shoot white boys. Either way, he risked his life. Perhaps the young men sensed their vulnerability in the darkened house, as, after what seemed like a nearly immeasurable time, the white intruders turned and retreated through the door they had broken to enter.[3]

The intruders, presumably angry because the Barnetts had retrieved their cows, disappeared into the night and were never held accountable for stealing or destruction of property. But Mr. Barnett paid a cost. Frightened, he and his wife hastily left their home, family, and church to move to Dayton, Ohio. Mr. Barnett soon planted a garden his northern neighbors admired, but the man who heretofore had never been ill with anything beyond a toothache began to grow feeble. Less than three years later, Mr. Barnett begged to return to Athens for a visit. Shortly thereafter, he died in a Savannah hospital.

Mr. Barnett had joined other Negroes in Georgia who, by 1901, had purchased 66,000 acres of land and added $380,000 to the value of farms. He had been "making a decent living . . . buying land and improving it, building comfortable dwellings, improving the grades of [his] farm animals." Mr. Barnett had been a model of Mr. Hunt's hope that the masses should understand the "absolute necessity for purchasing land" as a way to function independently in America, especially with increasing competition from European immigrants turning southward. Having his own land had not mattered, however. Even if a Negro did everything America and Negro race leaders asked, a Negro man could and often did still pay the price.[4]

As Mr. Tate drove through the rolling countryside, he joined a line of Negroes who had paid the price. Whether one cooperated with the system or tried to challenge the system, being a Negro who wanted to be treated according to America's professed values came at a cost. Every little town he passed on the route reminded him of what America expected of him.

Mr. Tate drove through towns such as Monticello and Jackson. Each one appeared briefly on the rural landscape for less than a mile before the farmland of middle Georgia returned to signal the end of the town. In every one stood a symbol he remembered from his days refusing to get off the sidewalk as he walked to downtown Elberton: a statue of a proud Confederate soldier. The statues varied in height, pose, and materials, but every one of the sculpted soldiers held his gun as though he meant to continue protecting the southern way of life forever.[5]

As he drove to Griffin, Mr. Tate was on a collision course with a deeply treasured heritage among white southerners. At his recent Atlanta University graduation, when he received his master's degree, audience members and graduates sang heartily their refusal to be diminished by southern determination to retain control over Negro citizens. "For still our ancient foe doth seek to work us woe," the Negro voices harmonized. As had been true at Fort Valley, the music fortified the soul of the graduates poised to challenge injustice. "And through this world, with devils filled, should threaten to undo us; we will not fear . . . His rage we can endure, for lo! His doom is sure."[6]

The words of the song spoke of faith and the fight against evil in heavenly places. The choice of the song, like the literature Negroes selected for the curricula of their schools, spoke metaphorically of a fight in earthly spaces. Mr. Tate was no coward. As he entered a new life in an unknown part of the state some hours later, of one thing he was certain: the fight could not end because whites in Greensboro believed they had won the first round.

Mr. and Mrs. Tate entered the quaint mill town of Griffin from the east and drove through the center of town on their way to the Negro community on the other side of the railroad tracks. Down a street on the left was the large, ornate two-story post office. In the town's center was the Confederate monument. Anchoring two corners were two fancy department stores providing fashionable clothing and fabric for women of all hues—so long as they had substantial means. They later learned one store was said to attract women who left their coats open so the lining was visible, in order that others might see the label and admire their purchase.

The Negro community here appeared financially stable. Although in menial positions, Negroes in Griffin boasted jobs in the town's mills. The town even had some Negroes in the professions as well as returning Negro servicemen. With more lucrative income, Negroes in Griffin developed a tight-knit community with several nice homes on an exclusive street near the high school. As Mr. Tate drove to the furnished room he had rented in a private home several miles away as temporary living quarters, he could not help concluding that Negroes here seemed to be more prosperous than those on Canaan Street in Greensboro.

School had not yet begun when the couple arrived, and would not open for another several weeks, but Mr. Tate had moved early to prepare for the first day. Like any good high school principal, Mr. Tate knew he needed to have time to ensure a strong educational program at his school. He needed to survey the school facilities to compare numbers of rooms with numbers of teachers and make room assignments. He needed to plan faculty meetings and guest speakers for assemblies for the year, and prepare a comprehensive calendar for the debating contests, athletic events, Christmas programs, graduation, and other scholastic programs. He needed to walk the campus checking for hazards that could hurt children, prepare schedules for all the students, and plan lunch and transportation procedures. He needed to move into his office, address and initiate correspondence, and coordinate opening activities.[7]

However, unlike the white principals, Mr. Tate also needed to arrive early to get to know the community. He needed to drive slowly through the town to understand its geography and the location of its businesses. He needed to learn those businesses—white and Negro—and make sure business leaders knew him. He needed to find the community leaders, the school leaders, and the student leaders. He needed to visit the churches and talk to ministers and to graduates of the school. Not until he knew the invisible components of community could he determine the level of leadership he would be expected to offer, both inside and outside the school.[8]

Mr. Tate undertook his task with zeal. He was determined to give the people of his new community an honest day's work for a day's pay.

Within weeks of the school's opening, life settled into a normal routine for the new principal. Mr. Tate made his daily trips to the post office to pick up the school's mail. He frequented the drugstore along the row of commercial shops in the town center. He purchased his first new car at the dealership on Route 41 going out toward Atlanta and, as in Greensboro, daily drove the new car to his office after he dropped his wife off at the elementary school where she taught.[9]

He could afford the luxury of a new car. The 1951–52 salary schedule adopted by the State Board of Education in March paid beginning professionals with five years of college training a salary of $2,700. With three years of approved experience, the salary rose to $2,900; with nine years, it maxed out at $3,300. In Griffin, however, Mr. Tate's salary exceeded the state scale. He began at $4,150, then rose to $4,500, and finally got to $4,900 by 1953. Mr. Tate's salary had come a long way in the eight years the GT&EA had been pushing for salary equality. When he first started at Union Point, Mr. Tate had made just over $700 per year. In his last three years at Greensboro, he had made $1,800.[10]

After only a few days Mr. Tate figured out he had accepted a job with a distinct advantage: some school systems provided more resources for Negroes than others in Georgia, and Griffin was one of those systems, thanks to a superintendent who cared something about Negro education. Unlike in Greensboro, where he had had to initiate community support to shore up resources for the Negro school, in Griffin Mr. Tate inherited a community that was already active.

The Griffin community had secured an eight-room Rosenwald frame building with eight teachers and a school term of nine months during the years after World War I when the only way to achieve progress in Negro school buildings was to work with the Rosenwald Foundation. GT&EA had put out the call: "Help us build Rosenwald Schools. Tell your community leaders it is their duty to go before the Board when it meets." This community heeded the call in 1926 and obtained a new school. In the intervening years the community had continued its determination to acquire good schools for Griffin and already had a nice brick school for Negroes by 1951, before the MFPE funds had become available.[11]

The school site included a long, one-story brick building with classrooms on each side. It also had a large two-story gymnasium with an array of windows that connected to the classrooms and a huge trade building looming large behind the classroom building. The physical quality of the new building paralleled the two-story brick school he had attended in Elberton and exceeded the facilities available to most Negroes in the state.

Having a new building provided Mr. Tate a luxury many Negro principals in Georgia did not have. While his counterparts throughout the state focused on how to get the new buildings the MFPE funding was earmarked for, Mr. Tate could focus primarily on actually developing his school's program. He had done so in Greensboro, too, but in Griffin he had more time to devote to making the school work for the community.

Negro schools were as much a part of the strategy to dismantle segregation as was the legal campaign, and foremost on this front was equipping the Negro teacher to inspire Negro children to believe they could one day participate as full American citizens. Someone had to teach the children how to aspire in a society where people and practices daily conveyed negative messages about their place in the American social order. The children at once needed a strong educational foundation and to believe they could achieve outside the school setting.

Negro educators embraced their job with seriousness. Mr. Tate had created teacher study groups back in Greensboro to build the professionalism of Negro teachers and to be sure they knew how to teach and inspire children, and he continued the practice in Griffin. At the regular weekly faculty meetings, many of which lasted for a full two hours, he and the teachers reviewed books on teaching, talked about teaching strategies, or shared new educational ideas learned at professional conferences. They discussed the philosophy of the school and aligned the school's objectives with its philosophy. Professors from Negro colleges visited and talked about educational trends.

The point of the unpaid extra work was the educational excellence of the Negro child. Negro educators called themselves professionals and operated as professionals, committed to getting the work done—the school day for children might end, but that didn't mean the teachers' day ended. Mr. Tate was adamant that no child should graduate from Fairmont High School without knowing the materials he and the faculty had agreed should be learned. He daily walked the halls observing classrooms and quizzing students on curriculum. Sometimes he randomly selected one of his 538 students—all of whom he knew by name—to ask a question on a subject the student should have learned. If the student could not answer, that became a topic for discussion at the faculty meeting. "That child was supposed to know more at three o'clock in the afternoon than he or she did at eight o'clock in the morning," he explained to the teachers at their meetings. "If they don't, the state is wasting money, and we are wasting time."[12]

Since Negro teachers believed white educators operated with greater knowledge and better schools, the principal and teachers at Griffin worked extra hard to be sure their children could compete. "I'm not trying to be a dictator," Mr. Tate said to his staff. "But we are supposed to teach children at this school. Nobody should graduate unless they know certain things."[13]

Mr. Tate acknowledged the disadvantages of being a Negro teacher: low salaries and working hours that extended far beyond the school day. "We must follow the child into his home," he reminded them. "We are expected to be teachers, psychologists, social workers and ministers." Theirs was a professional job akin to a physician's. Negro educators had to be available twenty-four hours a day, seven days a week.

But teaching also had certain advantages, he pointed out, unconsciously echoing lessons taught to him by Mr. Hunt and by Dr. Du Bois at Fort Valley. To Negro teachers had been given the high calling of being leaders in the community, of having high standards. "We must . . . think clearly and we must face the people with the thought that we are willing to help them."

To the teacher was given the job to teach right and wrong. Each student had to be confident that the teachers were giving him the "true facts of life and . . . making him feel that nothing is impossible for him." Teachers needed to understand their influence in the community, be intentional about ways to cooperate with parents, and do anything that would help Negro people in general have a better quality of living. If they loved the children, the children would love them back, he told them. Teachers were to be "deeply concerned" about the children, to consider being entrusted with the children a "great responsibility" they could not afford to dismiss.[14]

At his first GT&EA meeting in 1944, Mr. Tate had heard GT&EA president I.E. Washington proclaim that the professional educator's job was to prepare children "for the world of tomorrow." He had heard these same ideas repeated endlessly at directors' meetings, regional meetings, state meetings, and even at the Griffin-Spaulding Teachers' Association meetings. "So is the teacher, so is the school."

These were the staple beliefs among Negro teachers. Their job was to counter the external negativity of segregation by helping children believe in what they could achieve.[15]

"The power of thought was difficult to estimate," Mr. Tate emphasized, repeating unknowingly Mr. Hunt's objections to "mental puttering." It outweighed inventions both ancient and modern, Mr. Tate explained. He drew on a recent example all remembered, explaining that it was belief that had helped President Franklin D. Roosevelt—who had died not long before in the small town of Warm Springs, not very far away from Griffin—to believe he could be president. President Roosevelt had despaired when he first went to Warm Springs, certain his political aspirations were as withered as his legs. But he had persevered, and years later the world cast its eyes toward Georgia and the Warm Springs Hotel as the late president's body received the solemn salutes of the famous and the unknown on its final trip north.

Negro children also faced handicaps that could leave them without aspirations. Despite the segregation and racism they experienced daily, these children needed to believe in a world they could not yet see in real life, and to help forge that world. To the Negro teacher was entrusted their flexible and impressionable minds. As President Washington had explained at that first meeting, "You will receive no medal; your name will not be emblazoned across the world's great daily papers; your stories of sacrifice and devotion will not be dramatized over the great radio chains." But the world to come would be better because of those educators who had "consecrated life" to help Negro children.[16]

Of course, Negro educators in Griffin could not say outright they were trying to rewrite inclusion into American democracy, just as Dr. Bond could not tell the State Board of Regents he intended to produce graduates at Fort Valley who would challenge inequality in Georgia. Like Dr. Bond, Mr. Tate and Negro educators everywhere had to tread carefully. They had to teach the standard state curriculum and teach it well, for every Negro person understood the need to be twice as good as whites in order to be given half a chance. But the education of Negro children required lessons in democracy so they could see the ways in which America violated its own principles.[17]

Teaching democracy in the Negro school was easy in some ways, since civic education was required in the state curriculum. Negro teachers taught the lessons purposefully, following a script they could not overtly acknowledge but which had been planned in 1919, during the days when the educators and the NAACP operated together openly. Back at the turn of the century, Georgia governor Allen Candler had defended inequality in public schooling by arguing that "God made them negroes and we cannot by education make them white folks."[18] However, educator Lucy Laney, a peer of Mr. Hunt's who helped James Weldon Johnson begin the Augusta, Georgia, NAACP chapter, begged to differ. At the national NAACP meeting in Cleveland in 1919, she spoke directly of a new strategy Georgia educators were adopting to overthrow structures of inequality. "We are going to start anew in a way we know is going to be effective," she said as she acknowledged how the activities of the Negro educators in the post-Reconstruction generation had been shut down by disenfranchisement laws. "We are going to start at the bottom with the children. We'll teach them history, vote, government."[19]

Her strategy defined Negro school curricula across the South. Over in New Orleans, Louisiana, at the Velena C. Jones School, the principal organized the entire school into a democracy in the 1930s, with each room in grades three through seven a state (grades one and two were territories) and officers within each state, including governor, lieutenant governor, treasurer, secretary of state, senators, judges, police officers, and so forth. States had to develop parliamentary procedures, make rules, and pass resolutions for the good of the republic and send these to the senate after being signed by the secretary of state. The teacher was the advisor of the secretary of state, and the principal was the advisor of the senate. Students participated in elaborate election processes, including a primary and final election, and initiated legislation linked directly to the school, such as dividing the school grounds for duty, working with the PTA to fulfill material needs, planning and writing a constitution, and more.

Mr. Harper had taught similarly at Booker T. Washington High School in the decades before he was fired. When the school opened in 1924, Mr. Harper began teaching lessons in political awareness and throughout his tenure involved the entire school and surrounding Negro community in mock elections. One student led the Independent Party and then another the Progressive Party, both running aggressive campaigns. At the end of the elections, the steps and courtyard in front of the school filled with students and community members waving the flags of the winning party, and the school's band provided music as the incoming president was sworn in and gave an inaugural speech to cheers. The annual elections were so inspiring that the *Atlanta Daily World*, a Negro paper, reported in 1932: "If the young of today are trained in the use of the ballot . . . these same young people . . . will not sit passively . . . and let themselves be barred from complete citizenship."[20]

At his school, Mr. Tate followed a plan that had been hatched before he was born. He taught the students they belonged in the American democracy and had a right to participate; he even escorted students to the courthouse to register to vote when they came of age. Mr. Tate's school activities did not make the *Pittsburg Courier* or the local Negro papers, as did the students at Beach High School in Savannah who, in 1951, crafted a project for the students to try to get everyone in the city registered to vote.[21] But the students in Griffin learned as well as those in Savannah and other southern schools the practice of American democracy.

Negro educators also confronted directly the need to teach the children to *believe* they could overcome an America that dishonored blackness. As with civics education and the songs they sang in assemblies, the educators selected European poems that could be easily defended as part of the state curriculum but used them to teach another message to Negro children, one that perhaps had not been intended by the European author. For example, almost everyone in a Negro school across the South learned William Ernest Henley's "Invictus": "Out of the night that covers me, / Black as the Pit from pole to pole, / I thank whatever gods may be / For my unconquerable soul." In their English classes, Griffin's Negro teenagers recited confidently the verse from "Invictus" that spoke of the "bludgeonings of chance"—a poignant reminder of unknown ancestors captured and brought to American shores. They recited the poem's verse about the "menace of the years," which provided an apt summary of the evil of people seeking to preserve segregation in a democratic country. And like many Negro children across the South, they digested the appropriated intent of the poem: "My head is bloody, but unbowed."

"Make sure you listen to the words," one student reported a Negro teacher saying. The message teachers were conveying was that oppressive segregation outside the school walls should not define Negro children. The whites who exulted in their privilege and failed to acknowledge their poor treatment of fellow Americans still did not have the power to diminish Negroes' personhood. With heads lifted, children recited the poem's concluding lines with the conviction Negro educators worked for them to learn: "I am the master of my fate: / I am the captain of my soul."

The students also memorized the lengthy poem "If," by Rudyard Kipling. Across the South, Negro children learned to "keep your head when all around them / Are losing theirs and blaming it on you." Some students also learned Robert Loveman's "April Rain": "It isn't raining rain to me; / It's raining daffodils," thus inculcating the unspoken challenge to refuse to allow life's real circumstances to deprive them of the capacity to be resilient. They learned Edwin Markham's "The Man with the Hoe" and embraced a simple life that reinforced the African belief that they were their brother's keeper. And, even in the middle of the twentieth century, the educators still taught Br'er Rabbit tales, especially the story of the "tar baby," in which a helpless rabbit, seemingly trapped, triumphs over his predator foe.

In Griffin, sometimes the lessons came quietly from the principal in private settings. He once summoned the student he employed to drive his new car back and forth to pick up Mrs. Tate from her school in the afternoons and take her home. "Did you bump into something?" Mr. Tate asked the teenage driver, who cringed, not having seen the dent that had resulted when he tried to show off to friends but wound up driving the principal's new car into a tree.

The principal softly explained to the young man, who was expecting to be relieved of his driving duties, that a man should never ignore a problem. He should go directly to a person to discuss matters.[22] It was a lesson about how to get things done he had learned from Mr. Bond, and it was a way to teach a young Negro man how to behave in life.

Sometimes the lessons came from the principal in the regular and mandatory student assemblies. "He talked about being black all the time," one of the Griffin students recalled. Mr. Tate spoke frankly of the need to love themselves as Negro people, despite the negative images whites portrayed. He told them he liked his tightly curled Negro hair, that he never felt ashamed of it or felt he needed to make himself appear differently to be accepted. He told the students they should think equally well of themselves. He said they were more than the character in the Little Black Sambo books the Rosenwald Fund first put in its Negro libraries, or the *Amos n' Andy* characters that were the only black representation boys and girls in Griffin could listen to on afternoon radio.[23]

Sometimes the lessons about how to achieve in a hostile climate came in gendered assemblies Mr. Tate held, like those Dr. Bond had held at Fort Valley when he talked to young Negro men about dying for a country that mistreated them. While female teachers spoke with the young women, in all-male settings Mr. Tate spoke truths that would help his male students operate in an unwelcoming country. He told young Negro men how to dress and behave as they walked downtown so they would be triumphant in a yet-unrealized country of equality. If they wore their letterman jackets or dressed well, they would be better accepted. One had to know the game. However, the students also needed to be clear that behaviors were just that: behaviors. Wearing the clothes did not make them a better or worse person. In fact, nothing the white South said should ever reduce their personhood.

Sometimes the lessons appeared in the curriculum beyond the state requirement. While GT&EA fought the lack of inclusion of Negro accomplishments in textbooks, Griffin aligned with other Negro educators across the North and South to infuse their classrooms with Negro history and art. Sometimes oratory contests celebrated the poetry of Negro authors and dramatic presentations elevated the music, art, story, verse, and dance of African people and their descendants. Children participated in Negro History Week so the students could learn of the people who preceded them. As Mr. Tate was known to say, the pharaohs of Egypt looked like him, like them.

And the lessons sometimes continued until their final ceremony as high school students. Mr. Tate solicited parents to be certain the Negro students would graduate in formal black caps and gowns, and—as they usually did with Negro principals—the Negro parents cooperated. On the proud last day celebrating their accomplishments, the teachers donned caps and gowns and accompanied the students as they marched into the formal ceremony. One year, Mr. Tate's inspiring speaker, Maynard Jackson—who would later become the first black mayor of Atlanta—awed the soon-to-be graduates as he provided a multitude of examples of how Negro people had participated in every aspect of American life. The final lesson students got from their school was that perhaps Negro people could make a difference in the world. It was the education Mr. Tate knew he had to bequeath to the young people, who had all the questions he'd once had.[24]

Mr. Tate had a secret life, however, while he inspired teachers and students. As a Negro principal, he had to placate his local superintendents at the same time he used the GT&EA to challenge the practices of those very superintendents across the state. Mr. Tate had begun a new life, but his job in Griffin was the same.

12

MOVING ON UP

Why had Mr. Tate sent a requisition for typewriters? The superintendent called to ask Mr. Tate about this request. It seemed odd to him that Mr. Tate would ask for typewriters for the Negro children at the Griffin School. "No one would employ a Negro secretary," he explained to the principal.[1]

The superintendent did not know Negro schools were taking on the arduous work of preparing Negro children to be a part of a world that did not yet exist. Neither did Mr. Tate explain, for there was good reason to keep parts of the curriculum concealed from white eyes. Instead, Mr. Tate challenged the reluctant superintendent based on the South's need to implement the 1896 *Plessy v. Ferguson* ruling. Implementing *Plessy* was the only way the South could avoid implementing *Brown v. Board*, and both Mr. Tate and the superintendent knew it. The white schools had typing classes, Mr. Tate had explained. Why could not the Negro children? The logic convinced the superintendent, and Mr. Tate obtained typewriters for his students.

In another county a principal told the superintendent it would "look bad" for his students to go to a school event at a neighboring county riding in a dilapidated bus. That superintendent had bought a bus for the Negro school.

Mr. Tate next went to work on football games. The white schools had their football games broadcast over the local radio station, WKU. "I want my football games broadcast," Mr. Tate announced to the radio station managers he called, asking why the Negro high school's games were not broadcast.

Yes, the white games were broadcast, the station owners acknowledged. But the white high school had sponsors. Could the Negro principal get sponsors for his school?

"I thought that was your job," Mr. Tate responded. He knew the station obtained the sponsors for the white high school. Nonetheless, Mr. Tate began making the calls to obtain sponsors for the Negro games.

Mr. Tate called a Negro laundry. The owner agreed to be a sponsor. He called a Negro insurance agent for Negro-owned North Carolina Mutual. The agent agreed to sponsor. After a number of phone calls, Mr. Tate mistakenly called a white establishment to obtain sponsorship. He did not realize the owner, who hesitated at his request, was a member of the Griffin Board of Education.

Soon thereafter Mr. Tate received a call from the superintendent. "I understand you are trying to get sponsors to broadcast Fairmont High School football games," the superintendent began.

"Yes sir," Mr. Tate replied.

"Why did you do that?" he queried. "Who gave you permission?"

Mr. Tate bristled.

"Nobody gave me permission," he said in measured tones. "I am principal of this school. You know, you agreed before I took this job. You and I had a conversation. I said I would respect you as superintendent but you would let me run the school." He continued unflinching. "Our people would like to have their football teams broadcast on radio. Parents want it, and I was told the only thing we had to do was get sponsors. So I am trying to get sponsors."

The superintendent capitulated for the second time and, to the delight of the Negro community, the radio station soon began broadcasting Negro games. Attendance grew. Local whites also came to the games at the Negro high school. Although Negro boys were smaller than the white athletes in the town—some said they did not get the same amount to eat as white people did in Griffin—those boys could play, and did so with finesse.

These scrimmages between the principal and segregation's gatekeepers were small victories the community could applaud. Most members of the Negro community knew only that their school leaders went to a lot of meetings. The Negro community could never see the full portrait of struggle for some parts were still carefully concealed from public eyes.[2]

Mr. Tate turned right out of his office, then right out of the school's front door, bidding everyone a pleasant afternoon as he strolled slowly down the cement walkway to his new car. He threw his bag in the car, passed the small, stately brick home he and his wife had built just up the hill from the school, and headed to Atlanta.

Mr. Tate drove the hour north on a route that took him directly through the areas that had provided support for former governor Eugene Talmadge and his son, now the current governor. He passed the old gas station that had belonged to Eugene back during the days when Dr. Bond tricked the governor to keep state money flowing into Fort Valley. The younger Talmadge owned the business now, and he also owned the farmland around it. Negroes whispered that the younger Talmadge had used state money to build the smooth highway on which Mr. Tate drove so that he could more easily get his crops to market.[3]

As Mr. Tate navigated the winding route with its trees and fields on either side of the road, he did not dwell on the shady deals that may have built the rural two-lane highway. Eventually the Senate would reprimand Governor Talmadge for his misconduct. For now, Mr. Tate had other disputes with the governor and other southern political leaders, and those disputes involved the education of Negro children.[4] Mr. Tate was a leader in GT&EA, and leadership meant having the courage to help the organization challenge unfair practices in the state.

Now that Mr. Tate was in Griffin, his school was in Region II on the state map Dr. Bond and Mr. Harper had carefully drawn when they worked together to create a Representative Assembly for GT&EA. But Mr. Tate's term as a director of Region IV had not ended when he was dismissed from Greensboro and had relocated to Griffin. The organization had no history of such a situation and so no policy existed.

GT&EA's regional directors took seriously their unpaid jobs, including sending telegrams to confirm attendance to explain an absence, or reprimanding other directors if they missed consecutive meetings. Board meetings were never simply "yes" conversations. Different directors reported on concerns in their region; they questioned each other politely; they interrupted; they challenged. Sometimes they agreed, and sometimes they agreed to disagree. Regarding Mr. Tate, the other directors had debated how to handle the matter before finally voting to allow the young Mr. Tate to remain as the elected Region IV director.[5]

One of the jobs of a director was to oversee schools in the region, including attending the local GT&EA teacher meetings and reporting back to the directors' meetings the problems occurring within the region. Part of the directors' expectations in allowing Mr. Tate to continue as a director for Region IV was that he would delegate power to oversee the schools in his region when he could not be present, and Mr. Tate had agreed.

An hour and a half after departure from Griffin, Mr. Tate parked his car near the new fourteen-room state headquarters building at 201 Ashby

Street in a prosperous section of Negro Atlanta and confidently ascended the three steps under the white columns framing the door. The new headquarters was originally the property of a Dr. McCoy, but had been bought from his widow at a cost of $25,000 in August 1952. A dedicated building symbolized the growing power of the GT&EA. No longer did the organization share space—first with Savannah State, as in the earlier days, or in Atlanta at the J. L. Holloway and Son Jewelers at 172 Auburn Avenue or the Odd Fellows Building at 250 Auburn Avenue. Now, having increased their membership to eight thousand, the GT&EA had spent $4,414.59 on remodeling, including adding shrubbery and plants lining the walkway outside. The elegant new building provided an inviting place to coordinate the activities of resistance.[6]

Though the youngest of the directors, Mr. Tate approached the meetings with confidence. He settled into a chair around the conference table just under the arc of the curving staircase that led upstairs. Respected colleagues scraped seats across the wooden floor and convened around the table. All believed this body of courageous schemers could navigate the current climate to advocate aggressively for Negro children.[7]

As he had done for more than a decade, Mr. Harper reminded the directors of their responsibilities. In eras when they could speak publicly, the organization did so—as during the days when it united with the NAACP after World War I. But when southern retaliation against advocacy became intense, they continued the work in the tradition of African ancestors, operating behind the scenes, with other people and organizations serving as fronts. Now, at a time when it appeared they had the support of the highest court of the land, the educators could be vocal again. And so they would—through their leader, Mr. Harper.

Negro schools across the state still needed to complete the surveys of facilities so that inequalities could be identified and their districts could apply to erect the classrooms, libraries, lunchrooms, and other essential facilities that were part of the Minimum Foundation Program of Education. The state was rigid about regulations governing space allotments, and the requirements kept changing as the state revised standards. Mr. Harper had sent the specifics of the requirements to all principals in repeated mailings over the year, but regional meetings would host thorough discussions to help communities understand how to go about obtaining state money.[8]

Regional meetings alerted Negro parents to new forms of inequality that southern school districts had ushered into Negro schooling under the guise of promoting equality. Despite the shining promise of MFPE, already Negro parents had "considerable concern" about the places local boards of education purchased to build Negro schools under the plan. It was a "tragedy," according to Mr. Harper. School boards erected new Negro schools worth thousands of dollars on the site of a dump, or adjacent to a guano factory, or at some other undesirable location instead of locations that were sanitary, free from hazards, and convenient to the children. Buses for Negro children remained overcrowded and unsafe, while white students obtained new buses. The point was to make sure Negro children had the same "potentialities as other children—no more, no less."[9] If Georgia wanted to maintain the luxury of separate schools, the time had come for the state to pay for them.[10]

Mr. Tate returned to the important Region IV meeting determined to make sure Negro communities understood that white parents were already pressing the boards of education "for most, if not, all of these additional funds." If Negro parents were not similarly vigilant, the boards would most likely "yield to the pressure of the white groups and our schools will be left without as in the past." The result would be neither "right nor legal." To keep it from happening, Negro parents would need to work together and work with their principals.[11]

If differences existed among members of the Negro community, communities needed to "compose their differences . . . and to work unselfishly and in genuine harmony so that the Negro child may receive from the capital outlay funds all that Justice demand[ed] he should have." They needed to recapture the spirit of years gone by and work together: parents, pulpit, PTA, and citizens committees.[12]

At these regional meetings, directors played critical roles in preparing and organizing Negro communities. They had to remind principals and teachers to bring a group of citizens with them to the meetings. They needed to provide answers for parents to questions about terms such as "15 mill school tax" that would allow them to pursue MFPE in their own communities. Negro parents needed to know the procedures they needed to employ when they approached the local school boards to get the money. And they had to know exactly what the schools needed in order to make their requests count. At regional meetings, parents would learn that citizens' organizations needed to ask for nine-month school terms where they did not have it, for transportation, school desks, running water, indoor toilets where water was available, maps, globes, charts, libraries, cafeterias, science and home economics equipment, and other school facilities of the "same quality and kind provided other children."

"The needs of the Negro school child are the greatest and therefore should be given first consideration," Mr. Harper explained as he attended the different regional meetings across the state, including Mr. Tate's Region IV meeting. The Negro parent had a critical role to play: "The job of the Negro parent is to make his wishes known in courteous but positive tones and he will be heard. The United States Supreme Court hears him and the boards must."[13]

In his years in the profession, Mr. Tate had learned the invisible strategies of GT&EA that connected and coordinated communities and promoted advocacy. However, even as a leader, Mr. Tate did not yet know the world he did not know. When he boldly motioned at a Board of Directors meeting that all of the members of the board set an example of professionalism and integration to teachers and principals by becoming members of both national educational organizations—the black one and the white one—the directors debated the matter.[14]

The National Education Association (NEA) had finally tuned in to a federal climate beginning to investigate inequality for Negroes in the wake of the Second World War and decided to relax its segregation policies and to welcome Negro membership and attendance at national meetings. Negro numbers and dollars were also appealing—they would increase organizational strength. Mr. Tate's suggestion affirmed the importance of GT&EA supporting NEA's steps toward equality.

Two members expressed unreadiness after Mr. Tate's motion was seconded and President Wilkerson called for the vote. One explained that he was already a member of the Principals' Division of NEA. The other expressed concern that the idea would be "dictatorial" to the membership. Their concerns notwithstanding, Mr. Tate's motion passed.[15]

As the Korean War was coming to an end on foreign soil, Mr. Tate stepped into an unknown world of Negro educators fighting their own war at home. He headed to a newly integrated NEA meeting in Miami.

In those days, a trip to Miami for Negroes meant a long ride on a hot interstate in cars with no air-conditioning through south Georgia, into northern Florida, and hundreds of miles down through the Sunshine State. Negroes needed to locate places where they could stop along the way to use the bathroom or eat before finally arriving some twelve driving hours later in the magical city of Miami, with its gleaming lights and brilliant blue-green water. Mr. Tate crowded into a car in Georgia with several other delegates to make the trip.[16]

The 1953 conference was Mr. Tate's first NEA convention and only the second time Miami Beach had hosted an interracial conference of any sort. Ordinarily, Miami was still tightly Jim Crow, but in 1953 Miami had opened to the idea of "taking colored folks' money." The city welcomed the two hundred Negroes attending the NEA meeting into the lounges, swimming pools, fifteen acres of formal gardens, meeting rooms, and elegant dining rooms at Miami's first luxury beachfront hotel, the Roney Plaza Hotel on Collins Avenue between 23rd and 24th Streets. Mr. Tate and the other Negro NEA delegates joined the eight thousand white delegates.[17]

In Georgia, Mr. Tate never fully knew how his white educational colleagues behaved professionally, since he was legally barred from joining the NEA's white affiliate in his state, the Georgia Education Association (GEA). However, in Miami Beach at the ninety-first annual meeting of the NEA, he joined the same white colleagues who did not welcome him in Georgia.

Unlike in Georgia, in Miami the Negro and white delegates picked up registration materials together. Blazoned across the delegates' program were the words "We Pledge Allegiance: To the Welfare of the Nation's Children, to the Ideals of Human Brotherhood, to the Highest Ideals of our Profession."[18] Since they did not operate as brothers in Atlanta, the Miami convention represented a different world.

Over the hot days between June 28 and July 3, Mr. Tate and other delegates attended useful sessions on curriculum and professional development. But more than the curricular talk, the Miami meeting courted Negro delegates with appealing illusions of justice. At NEA, the opening vespers at the Municipal Auditorium on Sunday night elevated the ideals of human brotherhood. Over the next days, delegates and speakers talked openly about how to maintain the public schools in places where segregated schools had become a battleground of "radicalism vs. reaction." NEA even sponsored sessions such as "The New Role of School Boards in Coordinating Support and Defense of Public Schools."[19]

Georgia was one place where public education was in jeopardy, since some whites had determined to abandon the public schools rather than integrate. Prior to the Civil War, Georgia had used public money to fund private schools, and now the state was preparing to do so again, even as white GEA delegates listened to the NEA tout equality.[20] The white GEA colleagues who joined Mr. Tate and other GT&EA delegates in the integrated dining rooms included educational leaders who were gatekeepers for segregation. Among the GEA membership were superintendents who deprived Negro children of their educational rights. GEA also included among its speakers at meetings and in its circle of influence the political leaders who funded the private school plan as a way to forestall integration.

For Negro delegates, as alluring as the sea breezes from the green-tinted Miami waters was the possibility the national NEA might be a way to force the GEA to disrupt segregated southern school customs. White Georgians debated closing public schools and the GEA remained silent on integration. But NEA discussed democracy and considered how public schools might remain open. The National Educational Association's prestige could be used to force the all-white GEA to educate fairly back home in Georgia.

Mr. Tate returned to Georgia with hope that NEA could be a useful accomplice.

The summer of 1953 was a busy one for Mr. Tate, as he was also a delegate to the national meeting for Negro teachers. In 1903 Negro educators had formed the American Teachers Association (ATA, formerly the National Association of Teachers in Colored Schools), and Georgia GT&EA leaders had been among ATA organizers and leaders over the years.

The ATA convention taught Mr. Tate different lessons, especially about the longevity of the educational fight by Negro leaders and the unseen national collaboration that defined the Negro's quest for educational equality. According to Dr. Du Bois and Mr. Hunt—both early members of ATA, with Mr. Hunt among the leaders who rewrote the group's constitution in 1923—the years before the turn of the twentieth century had been ones with better teachers and better possibilities. Negroes had not expected the segregation restrictions and limited education that would come as part of the backlash against Reconstruction. Negroes had been especially distressed to lose the vote.[21] However, when the state Negro educational organizations could make little progress because of hostile climate and loss of political power, these networks joined forces.[22]

The organization founders wanted to seek to solve "co-operatively" the problems arising and to "devise ways and means to solve the problems."[23] In its first ten years, the group had fewer than 250 members across the southern states. Not everyone believed organization could help, and some were overtly distrustful of a plan to fight for better schools and more pay. Some said the group's plans to study and publish the results of inequality in Negro schools, as a way to solve the problems, were too "ambitious."[24]

By its twenty-fifth anniversary in 1928, however, the ATA was five thousand members strong. One member spoke of their collective strength: "Shall we wait for some good angel to bring us longer terms, better salaries, rural consolidation, decent buildings, a willingness to employ better teachers, and other things necessary to real education, while we take not thought for the morrow? Or shall we bring the combined thought of this Association and of all the growing State Associations to bear upon these conditions confidently believing that our combined efforts will be increasingly fruitful of good results?"[25] As far as ATA rhetoric was concerned, separate facilities always led to inequalities. Over the years until Mr. Tate entered his first ATA meeting with Mr. Harper, the goals had remained the same.[26]

The ATA meeting was much smaller than the NEA meeting, and the well-dressed Negro educators attending ATA greeted Mr. Harper and behaved like old friends. Year after year, they convened to share problems occurring across the states and to contemplate solutions. Mr. Tate was a newcomer, but he quickly caught the "irresistible stimulus to good fellowship" that defined ATA meetings.

Old-timers and newcomers slapped one another on the back and grasped hands "in a seemingly vain attempt to express the sheer joy of being reunited after a separation of 12 months." They gathered in groups under trees, in committee rooms, in lobbies, even in bathrooms to share their mutual woes and problems.[27]

Mr. Tate was at Mr. Harper's side for the convening of the fiftieth annual ATA convention, hosted by South Carolina State A&M College in Orangeburg, July 26–28, 1953. Like Georgians before him who had served as presidents or regional representatives, Mr. Harper was well known in ATA circles. Under his tutelage, Mr. Tate walked in the footsteps of President Bond; Dr. Du Bois's friend John Hope, president of Morehouse College; and Mr. Richard Wright, the first organizer of educators in Georgia and one of the organization's first presidents. GT&EA leaders and ATA leaders had overlapped in every generation.

Mr. Tate also engaged in the professional talk of ATA. It differed from that at NEA, where the talk focused on special needs or athletics or juvenile delinquents but did not address directly the special needs of Negro children still victimized by the racial discrimination and legislated inequality. At the ATA meetings, the talk centered on the Negro child. Negro children needed directed play, recess, and medical and dental help. The children needed a good environment and sympathetic teachers who understood children. They needed teaching in Negro history and civics. At ATA meetings, discussions elucidated the ways the Negro child could be developed to become the American citizens NEA only described superficially throughout its 1953 program. Until 1959, NEA would publish not one article supporting integration for Negro children.[28]

Additionally, Mr. Tate soon learned that ATA also had an advocacy agenda for Negro children that NEA lacked. In addition to inspiring professional educators to build better teachers and curriculum that would promote aspirations for Negro children, the ATA embraced the task of making known to the public "the real conditions of salaries, school buildings, heavy enrollment per teacher, poorly supported high schools, inefficient elementary schools, and almost completely starved higher education." How could any lay magazine or organization do the job any better than they themselves could do it?[29]

For years the ATA had worked quietly and cooperatively with the NAACP. Mary White Ovington, the white woman who helped organize the NAACP and named the group's publication, *The Crisis*, had in the 1920s requested that individual NAACP branches provide information on the inequalities in the larger scope of educational problems such as those being challenged in Georgia by Mr. Hunt. She wanted to know about terms, salaries, facilities, and other objective measures of the South's failure to implement *Plessy v. Ferguson*. But the responses she received from the local NAACP branches had been sparse. Branches did not have access to educational information. Educators did, however, and ATA created surveys through its philanthropic friends and quietly funneled information to the national NAACP in 1926. Dr. Du Bois also published detailed information on inequality in Georgia.[30]

By 1953, the thrust of ATA had moved beyond the 1927 expectation of "no difference in standards for white and colored schools" to a full-scale support of the legal campaign of the NAACP. At the convention, delegates reflected on their contributions in the "glorious history of ATA" over the first half of the century, considered the present as "pregnant with opportunities," and looked toward the future. They wanted "equality of educational opportunity for every child," without discrimination based on race, sex, residence, or economic circumstance. They reaffirmed their commitment to "utilize all channels for the implementation of its mission," a commitment that included continuing their annual 10 percent contribution to the Legal Defense and Educational Fund of the NAACP.[31]

Howard University's president, Mordecai Johnson, a longtime member of ATA and advocate for equality in schooling, had hired Charles Houston to direct the law school at Howard in the days when Howard was undergoing a review of its programs and determining whether it would adopt the national standard and move to a full-time law school or continue with its evening school. The university chose to discontinue the evening school, and Attorney Houston had crisply transformed the culture of the law school and produced a cadre of brilliant lawyers before becoming full time at the NAACP.[32]

However, Attorney Houston, a native of Washington who had been schooled at the University of Massachusetts, Amherst, and Harvard Law, was not immediately aware of the long-standing relationship between the educators and the NAACP. In an early trip south to prepare for the education cases, Attorney Houston initially sought logical places for leadership such as churches or clubs, looking at only one school. He mailed letters to fraternities and sororities seeking financial support for the campaign. He did not seek out the state education organization in South Carolina until some unnamed person finally provided him with the knowledge insiders had. Though the relationship was loosely stitched, in part because of Attorney Houston's frustration that educators' meetings were not billed as NAACP meetings, Attorney Houston began communication with the officers of ATA. He had also begun reading President Bond's book on education and attending meetings with the educators.[33]

Houston's student and mentee, Thurgood Marshall, similarly traveled south and eventually learned the nature of intertwined advocacy. For their part, the educators through their education organizations quietly identified plaintiffs and connected them with state and NAACP attorneys. In Charlotte, North Carolina, Attorney Marshall figured out the Negro principal was "very influential" and ready to back a teacher's case. Marshall likewise met with a professor in Winston-Salem who said everything was ready for a case there.[34]

As Attorney Marshall proclaimed after meeting with the presidents of the state teachers' association in North Carolina, the citizens committees they created allowed the teachers to be "completely left out of the pictures and the only members of the committee known to the public are the citizens." The teachers were fully in support of the plan—only their names were kept out of public display—and, as Attorney Marshall added, "the teachers have control over the cases."

Attorney Marshall proclaimed that he was "really surprised" by the spirit of the teachers as he came to understand that the educators functioned as the local, invisible arm of the visible national NAACP agenda. They handled everything from litigation for education to voter registration, and this alliance dominated southern practice despite Attorney Houston's proclamation of the need for local branches to function effectively and take the initiative for coordinating all public-spirited organizations in their communities.[35]

In contrast, when in Virginia seeking plaintiffs for the teacher salary cases, Marshall bemoaned the inactivity of the Virginia state NAACP conference. To revive it, Attorney Marshall suggested the president be instructed to call the meeting at the same time as the state teachers association and arrange for a joint committee to handle salary cases. In this way, the Virginia state NAACP conference could be "built up," Marshall explained to the national office.

Mr. Tate also saw at the ATA meetings that in addition to plaintiffs, the educators provided a steady supply of income for the education fight. By the time Mr. Harper assumed the stage at the 1953 meeting, the ATA was making an annual contribution of $1,600 to the NAACP. The ATA's regular contributions began in 1938–39 after Attorney Marshall wrote a letter to the organization asking for help in arousing teachers' groups and outlining the kind of cooperation the NAACP needed. In response, the ATA pledged its "whole-hearted cooperation" to the NAACP. Through ATA, teachers could contribute to the NAACP without the knowledge of their local superintendents. Over the fifteen-year period since then, the ATA had given a total of $16,690.10 in direct contributions. Now, with the Supreme Court decision in the *Brown v. Board of Education* case looming, other organizations began making hefty contributions as well.[36]

Mr. Tate absorbed these truths as he watched Mr. Harper ascend the stage to make the financial presentation and then stand for a photograph with Attorney Marshall. The two organizations sometimes squabbled over leadership and visibility, but each needed the other.[37] Mr. Tate had first watched Mr. Harper and Mr. Marshall together at the annual GT&EA meeting in 1949, where Mr. Marshall had discussed the Irwin County case, though he had not explained how the relationship between the GT&EA and NAACP worked. Tonight, however, as Mr. Tate watched, Attorney Marshall expressed his "deep thanks" to the invisible collaborators as he received from Mr. Harper the $5,000 additional contribution the ATA was making that year as a result of Mr. Harper's special appeal to the ATA's Board of Trustees. Mr. Marshall confirmed that the contribution was "most heartening" and proclaimed that it "answers the unjust criticisms of our Negro teachers and who are so often the victims of propaganda to the effect that they are only interested in themselves and not in the welfare of their people." He continued, "You and the other officers of the American Teachers Association have set the pace with regular contributions over a long period of years."[38]

Mr. Tate applauded along with all the other educators, both at seeing Mr. Harper in this new role and at the new possibilities for leadership this meeting had revealed. Mr. Tate returned to Griffin in the fall of 1953 with a deeper understanding of GT&EA and its national connections. With its legal relationship with the NAACP and its potential to press NEA, GT&EA just might be able to craft changes in Georgia for the education of Negro children.

13

IN THIS PRESENT CRISIS

Mr. Tate was "Principal of the Year"—as the headline in the February 1954 *Herald* proclaimed. The feature article began with a photograph of a serious-faced Mr. Tate and explained that he had been recognized at the Annual Principals' Meeting of the State of Georgia for his educational training, his useful experience, his achievement, and the progress he had made in the field of education. That year's GT&EA president, R.J. Martin, said he had "watched with great interest the work of Mr. Tate" in the eleven years the young educator had been working in the state.

The article said Mr. Tate had been president of the Greene County Teachers' Association, director of GT&EA's Region IV and chairman of Region IV's Fine Arts Program, and president of District Six of the Georgia Interscholastic Association. He had had an article published from a presentation originally prepared for the Griffin-Spaulding County Principals' Group, "The Effect of Conduct on Grading and Marking," and he held life memberships in the NEA and ATA. In contrast to his brief stint as assistant manager for the Athens District of the Afro Insurance Company, the Griffin principal had become an educational leader, known for his leadership abilities and interest in educators in the state.[1]

Those perhaps wondering how Mr. Tate had fostered "such a live and meaningful program against many handicaps" saw their answer in the *Herald*'s pages. Mr. Tate said he spent "a part of the day in prayer, but the greater portion, in work." He tried to deal with students in ways that made them accept him as a father or brother. As for adults in the community, "I just attempt to do an honest day's work, hoping that by so doing, I will instill some ideals in their children that will live with them daily and even for a lifetime."[2]

The broad announcement of Mr. Tate's selection as principal of the year coincided with an increase in the number of supporters across the state who wanted the young leader to run for vice president of the GT&EA. For those who did not know him, the portrait of Mr. Tate and his activities certainly enhanced his visibility statewide. Or maybe the feature article fueled Mr. Tate's own desire for more leadership responsibilities.

However it came to pass, a run for state leadership soon dominated Mr. Tate's thoughts. Responding to Mr. Tate's letter of April 4, 1954, the director of Region X shared with Mr. Tate the letter he had sent to other districts.

> We are making this last urgent appeal to you and to your delegates to the State Meeting relative to Mr. H.E. Tate, as the State's choice to be elected Vice President of the State Association.... Your influence and support certainly will be appreciated in electing to this high office of our association a gentleman who stands for and has fought for not one or a few but all of the teachers of our state. A gentleman whose record is clean, whose superior knowledge and association with those in position of rank places him far above any other candidate for the office of Vice President at this time.

The writer was confident the recipients of the letter wanted the same kind of sober-minded and intelligent representation as did he and others. Already Mr. Tate appeared to have been endorsed by more than three-fourths of the eleven regions in the state.[3]

Yet not everyone concurred. Some GT&EA members had cautioned an aspiring Mr. Tate in 1952 to wait a few years before seeking elected office. One colleague, who was himself running for vice president, privately asked Mr. Tate not to run against him since he could have a turn to be vice president at a later time.[4]

In 1952 Mr. Tate had not heeded either the advice or the request. Negroes in Georgia were living in a moment of educational opportunity. By spring 1952, the segregationist governor, Herman Talmadge, could report publicly that $135 million had been spent on black and white schools, with the value of buildings and grounds having increased from $99,264 in 1948 to $183,534,980 in 1952. Even before ATA and NEA, Mr. Tate had determined to be a central part of the effort to channel resources into Negro schools. As Mr. Hunt said after World War I, it seemed a "particularly opportune time."[5] And so at the Representative Assembly Mr. Tate had allowed his name to be put into nomination for the post of vice president. Perhaps it was in part due to one of the speeches he had listened to during the annual meeting that year, when Mordecai Johnson, president of Howard University, spoke of the beauty of brown and black people who worked hard but were viewed as animals and relegated to separate spaces. He said brown people did not need to heed white people who said they had to stay in their places. He remembered the pain of mistreatment as a Negro youth, and the quiet anger that bubbled inside. "They [black people] already have their places and all they need is the right to occupy them," Dr. Johnson declared to a spellbound audience.[6] Mr. Tate, who still hated segregation, joined in the applause. As Dr. Johnson said, the time had come to put an end to segregation and slavery. He could join those mourning about continued inequalities at the local level or he could heed the challenge implicit in the haunting spiritual students performed as part of the cultural arts program: "O Mary, Don't You Weep." As the students had compellingly and lyrically recounted, Pharaoh's army had been defeated—drowned in the Red Sea. As far as Mr. Tate was concerned, becoming vice president would be a way to defeat the metaphorical Pharaoh's army of segregation.

He almost won in 1952. Mr. Bacote received 147 votes and Mr. Tate 131 on the first ballot. On the second ballot, Mr. Tate received 180 and Mr. Bacote 200.[7] Mr. Tate had lost the opportunity to become GT&EA's state leader—for the time being. But two years later, the outcome was different.[8]

The GT&EA opened its 1954 annual meeting in the Municipal Auditorium in Savannah on Thursday, April 15, with the convention theme "Expanding Today's Educational Program." Savannah was a beautiful city, with hanging moss and stately old homes. It included the home where General Sherman was quartered when he sent a Christmas present to President Lincoln in the waning days of the Civil War. His headquarters had also been the place where Negro citizens approached him about setting up their own school system for their children. With General Sherman's permission, Negroes in Savannah created a self-sustaining educational system. Although Negro parents subsequently lost control of their enterprise when the American Missionary Association arrived, the Beach School established at that moment in history still stood and was one of the locations for the 1954 GT&EA meeting.[9]

Delegates busied themselves with the usual registration procedures before beginning the first Representative Assembly at noon. They adopted the order of business, the rules of procedures, the minutes of the last meeting, and the report of the Credentials Committee. They listened to the nomination speeches that officially made Mr. Tate a contestant for vice president, then continued with reports from the Auditing Committee, the treasurer, and

Every two years, electing leadership for GT&EA always assumed a prominent role in the meeting. These delegates are participating in the second balloting. *GT&EA Collection*

the Constitution Committee, and finally dealt with new business and announcements. Inside the convention hall, the business was tedious and sessions were long—often too long.[10]

Outside, delegates enjoyed jovial conversations and contests during breaks. The Coca-Cola Company of Atlanta, Georgia, had finally recognized that the dollar coming from Negro hands was cash just like any white dollar. The company had already begun advertising in the *Herald* with large ads of white people enjoying Coke, and in 1954, for the first time, it advertised at the annual GT&EA meeting with a large sign and provided an unlimited supply of Coca-Cola. Its booth offered interesting entertainment, encouraging delegates to stop by. The educators could guess the number of caps to win a "FREE Coca-Cola Cooler!" The strategy worked. Inside, leaders haggled over business. Outside at the booth, the Negro man hired by the company oversaw drawings and Mr. Harper and the retiring

President Wilkerson served as judges while cameras captured pictures of Negro people enjoying Coke.[11]

The year 1954 embodied a new era of possibility and potential new paths to justice, and evidence of that was visible when the delegates returned to business. Although white superintendents or city mayors routinely attended the non-delegate GT&EA meetings and spoke briefly, in 1954 the white president of the NEA, William A. Early, appeared as a major GT&EA speaker. President Early, whose face was plastered across the April *Herald*, assumed the platform at seven-thirty during the open meeting on Friday, April 15, and spoke to the Negro audience. His presence captured the words of inclusion Negro educators wanted to hear. As had been true when Mr. Tate attended the Miami NEA convention the previous summer, Negro educators looked with hope toward the national organization, which purported a desire to include all educators in this new era of anticipated equality.

"Let us say this much to ourselves, not only with our lips but in our hearts. Let us say this: I myself am a part of democracy—I myself must accept responsibilities. Democracy is not merely a privilege to be enjoyed—it is a trust to keep and maintain. I am an American. I intend to remain an American. I will do my best to wipe from my heart hate, rancor, and political prejudice." These words of the prominent author and poet Stephen Vincent Benét were printed on the program of every Negro educator and captured the spirit of the convention. Accompanying them was a challenge by Horace Mann, the man credited with beginning the nation's public school system: "In our country, and in our times, no man is worthy of the honored name of statesman, who does not include the highest practice education of the people in all his plans of administration."[12]

For Mr. Tate, all the possibilities held special implications. At the second vote of the Representative Assembly on Friday afternoon, after the unfinished business, a report from the Election Committee, songs, and reports from the History of Organization Committee and the Resolutions Committee, Mr. Tate assumed the stage with Mr. Early as the newly elected vice president of GT&EA.[13] As the convention concluded, he watched solemnly as the presentation of the gavel from the old vice president to the former vice president and now new president, Mr. Lucius Bacote. By constitutional rules, in two more years Mr. Tate would receive the gavel and become the organization's leader.

During this season of increasing legal victories, when the Korean War was also helping to elevate the idea of democracy in international talk, GT&EA was at its height in public protest. Not since the days of Mr. Hunt and World War I had its link with national actors been so visible. As early as 1949, when Mr. Tate had been driving back and forth to Atlanta to get Mr. Harper, GT&EA talk had started to become more public and uncompromising. The body was committed to the "use of all techniques to bring into fruition these resolutions." In 1952, the Representative Assembly had instructed Mr. Harper that public authorities were to be "reminded again of their obligation and positive duty under the fourteenth amendment of the constitution of the United States and as interpreted by the Supreme Court of the United States not to discriminate against any school child and to maintain the public schools and colleges of the state on a basis of equality of education for all children without regards for race or color." Lest the state's school boards misunderstand their intent, the GT&EA resolved further that these officials should be informed that "any undue temporizing or stalling to avoid implementing these resolutions will leave this body no other alternative than to seek the above objectives by means other than resolutions."[14] In 1953, the delegate body had approved the firm resolutions again.

During the April 1954 meeting, when Mr. Tate was elected, GT&EA voted to petition county boards for a single standard for transportation of children. Through reports to the Board of Directors, the educators knew MFPE was not being applied in all matters related to Negro education, including transportation. GT&EA requested a single standard that included limits on the length of time a child could be on the bus, a maximum load per bus, and quality of equipment. It congratulated the state board on its fairness in the distribution of some state funds, but noted the "disturbing reports" they were receiving about local boards of education approving Negro schools but failing to erect the building, or erecting the building and refusing to add the paint, floor tile, or equipment. Double sessions continued. It also questioned the lack of vocational education for Negro students. White children had vocational education; why not Negroes? The organization wanted the Jeanes teachers who functioned as Negro supervisors for schools to remain. In short, it wanted federal aid to support equality.[15]

One month after the successful GT&EA convention, across the world flashed the news of the Supreme Court ruling in the *Brown v. Board of*

Education decision. By law, America no longer supported the segregation of Negro children. Although the school case in Clarendon County, South Carolina, initiated by a principal there, had been part of the cases comprising the decision instead of the case from Atlanta, black educators in Georgia were no less jubilant about the decision.

In addition to carrying the announcement that H.E. Tate, principal of Fairmont High School in Griffin, had been elected as the new GT&EA vice president, the October *Herald* featured a photograph of a man the educators greatly admired, Thurgood Marshall—and the photo was on the cover, no less. The *Herald*'s biographical sketch celebrated Mr. Marshall and spoke of his education in Baltimore at a segregated school and his various degrees and accomplishments. It did not, however, publicize the money GT&EA had raised to help support the teacher who forfeited his job after the GT&EA had approached him and asked him to become a plaintiff in a lawsuit to challenge salary inequality. It did not name Mr. Harper as an agitator whose job disappeared as a result of his activity, nor did it mention all the other ways the educators funneled money to the NAACP.[16]

The article did, however, celebrate the Supreme Court decision Mr. Marshall had made possible. The new GT&EA president, Mr. Bacote, wasted no time lauding the case in a state where white politicians were stunned by the decision, which they had secretly expected but did not want. President Bacote noted that the world was fast being reduced to a community not more than ten hours' travel distant in the most remote sections, and applauded the general awakening to the "dignity of man" evidenced in the pronouncements of the Supreme Court. Increasingly, citizens would need to be responsible to each other and to the federal government. Moreover, the world would need to be responsible to its citizens, for much work needed to be done to ensure the successful implementation of the decree. As the forces converged to promote the equality expected to follow, GT&EA would continue to build itself into a greater organization—"one so well serving its purpose that at all times there shall not be a question as to the need and purpose of its existence."[17]

The new GT&EA vice president, Mr. Tate, spoke of the decision as well when he addressed students in the closing exercises at his school and others. He reminded audiences that the Supreme Court had "made history" when it pointed out the inconsistency with the nation's foundational principles of democracy if it were to allow segregation to remain. "The tremendous importance of this decision cannot be over-emphasized," he emphasized.

> In view of the fact that you, the Negro boys and girls of Southern schools, represent the largest percentage of the population that will be the beneficiaries of the new endowment, it is reasonable to assume that you are curious to know what the future in public education holds for you. Having been all your lives victims of the fallacy of "separate but equal" school facilities, you are only reacting in a typically human way if you are feeling somewhat bewildered at the prospect of being at long last released from your bonds.

Mr. Tate dismissed conversations they may have heard, discussions on the pros or cons of integration, and stories about the places where it was successfully or unsuccessfully being attempted. "I wish only to remind you that the Supreme Court of the United States has said that they *must* be [integrated], and indications are that they *will* be. In the light of this knowledge, you cannot afford to cling to traditional patterns of thought and behavior. You must be prepared to adjust yourselves to the changed conditions which are sure to come."

Negro students shared the anticipation of their admirable educators. The children knew that, given the opportunity, they could perform as well as whites. The February 1954 edition of the *Herald* congratulated Miss Annette M. Jones, a tenth grader in Macon, for winning the annual Voice of Democracy Speech Contest sponsored by the Junior Chamber of Commerce. The young Negro student's oratory and argument earned first place among all the schools, inclusive of white schools. Negro teachers believed Negro students could compete with, and even outperform, white students when allowed to compete cross-racially.[18]

Now that increasing opportunities loomed, Mr. Tate reminded Fairmont students they were "to make a real contribution to humanity" that would better their fellow man and make the world a better place.[19] He noted the milestone achievements of the past few years, the opportunities created by better school facilities and equipment, and reminded students that he was counting on every one of the graduates to improve society as they improved themselves.[20]

Georgia educators and students were not alone in their hushed expectancy. The national NAACP, jubilant and confident that justice had been served, added a folder on student attitudes in the South to the reports on successful integration it had maintained for decades. Whites afraid to have their names used also indicated they thought white students might respond favorably—even at places like private Emory University. Likewise, the ATA joined in the victory, which saw the success of the agenda they had been pursuing ever since they joined forces across state lines to fight collectively a battle none of them could fight alone. ATA had always been "irrevocably dedicated to the objective of removing race and class barriers from American life," as it would announce at the 1955 annual meeting.

Indeed, while the national NAACP continued the legal campaign, the ATA painted a broad vision for successful integration. The ATA wanted the interest and welfare of the children to receive first consideration as plans were made for public schools to continue as the heart of a democratic way of life. Psychological attitudes and environmental influences could affect the child in the process of total integration, they argued. They wanted classroom climates that supported learning. They urged everywhere a renewed interest in and consideration of the spiritual needs of the child in the new settings.

ATA also wanted educators to take the lead in promoting discussion about integration on local levels. It believed Negro educators should take the initiative in organizing and promoting community discussion groups, based on the principles of fair play and equality, and providing support to governors and other officials who might need advice on creating an integrated, egalitarian society. ATA's unanimous resolutions pointed to the need for school boards to include Negroes, for Negro educators to take the lead in integration by integrating their teacher organizations, and for Negro educators to continue lobbying for other matters such as textbooks that included material on Africa. Most important, it urged "immediate, active compliance" with the decisions of the Supreme Court.[21]

The problem with all of these visionary plans was that southern whites did not see the decision the same way. A year earlier, the *Birmingham News* foreshadowed the response to *Brown v. Board of Education* among some whites in Alabama. If the Supreme Court knocked out segregation, the paper suggested in 1953, "education automatically would become the number one problem—and a terrific headache and pocketbook blow as well."[22]

One problem, an article in *Birmingham News* had said in the late 1940s when the Supreme Court favorably decided earlier cases argued by the NAACP, was that southerners could not get a book published to represent the southern point of view on matters of school integration. The writer said he had been in forty-six states and was pleased by the "amazing number" of people willing to listen to the southern case and who were "sympathetic" to it. However, publishers refused to acknowledge the presence of this widespread sympathy. They deemed the conviction that the two races should be separated in the South to be "too backward for printing."[23] Several years later a Birmingham press decided to step up to represent the southern point of view, and it turned to Herman Talmadge of Georgia to speak forthrightly about the issue. In *You and Segregation,* published by Vulcan Press in 1955, Governor Talmadge used his legal training from the University of Georgia to argue the South's case. "Will you listen, Americans?" he began. "What I have to say is as important to those of you who live in Maine or Michigan or any other state as it is to us in the South." The South had a tradition of segregation, he explained. But more than segregation was at stake: "Make no mistake about it. The issue is your freedom."

Americans lived in an era when a three-way attack was being made on their freedom, especially states' rights. After a detailed historical analysis of the Bill of Rights amendments, the Supreme Court's history, and the intent of the people who populated the Court historically, Governor Talmadge launched into his conviction that the campaign to diminish segregation was nothing more than a "campaign of the federal government to destroy the public school system of the South." The Supreme Court was part of a program to regiment the citizen and his children and to regiment businessmen and their businesses to fix a social pattern. Nowhere under the Constitution was it specified that the federal government have the right to interpret southern schooling patterns, since schools were supported by state and local taxes and were under the exclusive domain of the states.[24]

The governor hated the bloc voting in the South. Bloc voting made it possible in a place like Macon for white newspapers to report the criminal record of Negro candidates, but for those same candidates to receive 80 percent of the Negro votes because of the success of the bloc vote.[25]

The governor did not know that GT&EA maintained meticulous registration records or that principals like Mr. Tate used a variety of citizens clubs to spur registration. Without this knowledge, the governor aimed angry words at the outcome rather than the actors. If the Negro bloc vote continued, he said a Negro might achieve a political coup and win. These were truly "insidious political practices" and it was time for an "aroused White Southern electorate" to halt and defeat these practices.[26]

But most of all, Talmadge was mad at the "communist" NAACP. The NAACP was behind all this bloc voting and the push for integration. The governor explained to his readers that the NAACP national convention had met in Atlanta in 1951, right after the organization filed a suit against the city to end segregation in the public schools. It had been the first NAACP Atlanta meeting since 1920. At the 1920 meeting, white political leaders had invited the organization but then many mysteriously disappeared as the conference began, presumably because of pressure from their white constituents. In 1951 Governor Talmadge was appalled that Atlanta's mayor, William B. Hartsfield, welcomed a group that stated as its objective the plan to wipe out segregation in all facets of southern life. He reminded readers that Mayor Hartsfield had been reelected a few months earlier because he received Negro votes, allowing him to defeat his opponent, who received more white votes.[27]

Governor Talmadge fumed further about the 1951 meeting. He said it had been designed to "throw the fear of the Negro vote into the hearts of Southern politicians" and to "destroy all forms of segregation" in the South. Its "guiding force," Walter White, had said back then—several years before the *Brown* decision was handed down—that it would be "utterly impossible and ridiculous" if the South decided to eliminate public schools as a result of any Supreme Court decision in favor of integration. "Such action will be a calculated and obvious violation of the law and a flaunting of the Supreme Court," as Talmadge recalled White's proclamations.[28]

Now, how could Walter White have known the Supreme Court would decide in their favor? asked Governor Talmadge. Of course, at that time the governor did not know Felix Frankfurter had been a board member of the NAACP prior to his appointment to the Supreme Court or that he and Walter White continued to maintain contact after he was appointed to the Court. However, the governor did know that White's statement had been made years before the Supreme Court decided *Brown,* and he concluded that there had been a conspiracy.

The problem was that the Supreme Court was setting itself up as an "all-powerful legislative body and at the same time as a super-duper national board of education." It had used social science as evidence and usurped the powers of the legislative branches of the federal and state governments to remove school segregation.[29] Clearly, integration in other places had already caused problems. White children abandoned the public schools and attended private schools. Fighting between races occurred; social activities were limited to restrict white and black student interactions. White parents also made demands they deemed in the best interest of their children, demands that white school boards usually heeded.[30]

The governor then delivered the deadliest blow in the shortest chapter. If integration happened in the public schools in the South, the "one group of people who would be hit the hardest would be the Negro school teachers," he proclaimed. There would be no Negro teachers in mixed schools in Georgia, he said. In a private meeting with GT&EA leaders, including Mr. Tate, the governor had once indicated he would support salary equalization but would never support a Negro man being in a position of authority over white teachers. No matter how qualified, a Negro man simply could not be given the supervisory opportunities afforded white men. In the book Talmadge affirmed his statement and threatened retaliation as some unnamed informants helped him figure out the actors behind his state's education problems.

"The NAACP delights in collecting dues and donations from Negro teachers" he announced, "but seems little concerned about their future in the South if its actions in the non-segregated states is any measure." He proclaimed the South wanted to continue to employ the 76,390 Negro teachers in the public school systems. He knew they certainly could not find employment outside the South. But the South had no intention of employing them in integrated schools.

When they lost their jobs, as they surely would as the South imitated what had already been done in California and other places where desegregation occurred, the teachers would have "no one to blame but the NAACP, its leaders and its political friends." Too bad the Negro teachers did not speak out in defense of themselves and their jobs. He concluded they were afraid of the NAACP and its leaders.[31]

The book hit a chord in the white South, especially in Georgia, where the Georgia Education Commission spent $376,000 to promote the "southern point of view."[32] A year later, in 1956, the governor was elected to the U.S. Senate and joined other Georgia congressional delegates working to disrupt the erosion of state rights. Senator Talmadge explained to supporters, writing on U.S. Senate stationery, that his publisher was working with the States' Rights Council of Georgia and was making his book available for free distribution. In fact, the book was so popular the publisher issued a second printing in the same month the first edition was released.[33]

* * *

Mr. Tate had been elected to the GT&EA vice presidency right around the time the state was disintegrating into opposing political positions. As the new vice president, he mulled over the NAACP publications revealing the depth of southern venom. *Dixie Dynamite: The Inside Story of the White Citizens' Councils* chronicled disturbing accounts of southern whites worried about the disintegration of a way of life they cherished. Mr. Tate leafed through the document carefully, musing over the depth of the emotion generated by a case designed to correct inequality. He read of the ways southern anger against federal influence erupted in an explosion of Citizens' Councils and other groups aimed to contest federal imposition on southern norms of race relations.

The anti-integration groups held that candidates for elected office needed to be screened and anyone who favored integration should be denied a spot on the ballot. They would use "economic pressure" and voter registration restrictions to control elections. They would secure information on the activities of the NAACP and "anticipate" any other "concerted action" contrary to their views. After all, the NAACP goal was really only "to open the bedroom doors of our white women to the Negro man." One Citizens' Council organizer eloquently revealed the depth of the sentiment to use politics rather than brawls to address the problem. He rose calmly at the organization of a chapter and responded to a farmer who wanted to "knock [a] nigger in the head with a brick" by saying, "I'll answer you this way. The morning after the White Citizens' Councils organize here, the nigger in Marengo County will be a different nigger. You won't have no trouble then." Eventually the language shifted, with southern whites changing the groups' name from White Citizens' Councils to just Citizens' Councils in an effort to gain respectability.

Mr. Tate was not surprised to read that Georgia had multiple Citizens' Councils. Indeed, Georgia incorporated the Georgia States' Rights Council on December 27, 1954, only a few months after he became GT&EA vice president, and created the white Georgia Citizens' Councils with a "meeting of the high brass" on September 23, 1955. Two hundred of the state's most prominent and influential political and business leaders met and voted to support the movement as "a statewide organization dedicated to the preservation of constitutional government and the maintenance of harmonious race relations." Council members even heralded Georgia's former governor, now a U.S. senator, as "Talmadge, Man of the Hour" and "Talmadge Must Save the South."[34]

Across the state, anguished white response continued. Announcements circulated at an Atlanta auto assembly plant in August 1955 about a revival of the KKK, and the Georgia attorney general, Eugene Cook, published his own booklet comparable to the former governor's: *The Ugly Truth About the NAACP*.[35] But the venom spread far past Georgia.

Mr. Tate read of the new governor of Georgia, Marvin Griffin, debating New York State attorney general Jacob K. Javits at a Harvard Law School forum. Governor Griffin attacked the Supreme Court desegregation decision as a palpable and deliberate usurpation of states' rights. He called the decisions "baseless," claiming that the Supreme Court sought to "transmute socialistic theory into law." He said that it was based on a "ridiculous theory" of Negro children's sense of inferiority in segregated schools and that it "usurped the reserved powers of the states."

Georgia's position on the matter was clear, as articulated by its governor in the Cambridge debate:

> The state of Georgia . . . has reserved to itself the right to operate its public school system by such methods "as in her judgment are conducive both to the welfare of those to be educated and the people of the state generally. . . . Being possessed of this lawful right, she is clothed with power to repel every unlawful interference therewith."

He continued, "No governmental department, no court or other tribunal has the right to dispose of the fundamental liberties of man."[36] Apparently, the right to "dignity of personhood" he proclaimed for himself did not include Mr. Tate, other Negro educators, or any of the children Mr. Tate had been elected to represent.[37]

The battle for educational control in Georgia had begun. While the world toasted a Supreme Court decision intended to free the United States from segregation and repression, Mr. Tate and Negro educators across the South began the hard labor of figuring out how to fight for equality in states determined to resist.

14

SHIFTING SANDS

In Atlanta at his first annual meeting as the elected vice president of the GT&EA, Mr. Tate picked up conference materials and took a moment to peruse the program. On the last page was a large picture of the man Talmadge hated and Negroes admired, with the caption "Walter White: The Story of a Great American." The NAACP leader was recently deceased. Mr. Tate paused appreciatively to read about the life before finding his center-stage seat at the Friday evening session. The Griffin choir would open the evening along with the choir from Mr. Harper's former college, Morris Brown. This was the first session over which Mr. Tate would preside.

A generation was passing. Mr. White's peers had fueled the opening of Pullman and dining cars to Negroes in the South, the end of the white primary, laws to equalize salaries for teachers, an increase in desegregated recreational facilities in many urban centers, and the removal of segregation in many schools, hotels, restaurants, and other public spaces in Washington, DC. Mr. White and Mr. Harper had quietly cooperated in years past after Mr. White left Atlanta to begin the life in New York that pivoted him to the helm of the national NAACP, and they continued their collaborative work until Mr. White's death in 1955. The program in Mr. Tate's hand, probably written by Mr. Harper, who was then a board member of the national NAACP, symbolized collaboration unspoken.[1]

Mr. Tate's first meeting as vice president proceeded routinely. As it had for the past six years, the Representative Assembly passed resolutions on integration at the annual meeting. GT&EA said it believed public education was necessary for a democratic way of life, and any attempt to "supplant public education with private schools constitutes a serious menace to educational progress." GT&EA added to its resolutions an objection to the dismissal of teachers when no charges were proffered, and noted the need for a tenure law.[2] The Negro educators' resolutions directly challenged plans among whites to turn the public school system of Georgia into a private school system if integration occurred. They also directly challenged the threats to fire them in retaliation for their advocacy by demanding the state protect citizens engaged in democratic activities.

Two months after the 1955 state convention, however, state attorney general Eugene Cook retaliated. He demanded the discharge of any public school teacher who contributed to or was affiliated with the NAACP. "I am doing this," Mr. Cook said, "because the NAACP has made a declaration that their entire resources will be used to force mixing of the public schools of Georgia." He knew many Negro teachers were members of the NAACP (and some white teachers also). "They are doing this even to the point of insisting upon imprisonment of responsible Georgia officials who refuse to submit."[3]

The Georgia State Board of Education voted unanimously to revoke "forever" the license of any teacher who "supports, encourages, condones, offers to teach or teaches Negro and white pupils in the same classrooms."[4] It also adopted a resolution against mixed classes upon the motion of its chair, and it did so almost without discussion. Georgia was determined to fight the implementation of *Brown*. While Georgia legislators could not hurt the fancy lawyers in New York who had caused the Supreme Court to discard *Plessy v. Ferguson*, and it could not go after Mr. Harper, who received his salary and directives from GT&EA, it could punish the visible targets—the Negro teachers.

Following the state board's discussion of the resolution to revoke the license of any teacher who retained membership in the NAACP, Georgia sought violators. Politicians demanded bank records from a Negro-owned bank, Citizens Trust Bank, to determine NAACP contributions, still not understanding that the money was channeled through the education organization. They demanded the membership rolls of NAACP chapters so that teachers' names could be identified.[5] Despite the risk, the GT&EA continued its long-standing method of funneling money to the ATA, which then sent it to the NAACP.

Mr. White no longer led the group, but the NAACP moved quickly into overt partnership with the Negro educators and Mr. Harper. Mr. Harper had alerted the National to problems in Georgia immediately after the *Brown* decision. He told the National he needed seventeen hundred copies of the NAACP's statements on the situation of Negro teachers in relation to public school segregation. These copies could be disseminated via the GT&EA network. In response to Mr. Harper's alert, the

NAACP maneuvered to defend its members who were educators, going to court if needed.[6]

In a meeting with the Executive Board of GT&EA in Atlanta in July, which included the new vice president, Mr. Tate, the NAACP conveyed its belief that the proposed regulation targeting Negro teachers was illegal. According to John Davis, a Georgia native, former president of West Virginia State, and director of the newly formed Department of Teacher Information and Security in the NAACP's Legal Defense and Educational Fund, the NAACP stood "ready, willing and able to challenge immediately in the courts these and any other regulations which interfere with the right of Negro teachers to pursue and secure gainful employment in their chosen vocation."[7]

Dr. Davis was well known by the educators and especially Mr. Harper. Dr. Davis was a former president of the ATA, and the program he had espoused in that role had once made Charles Houston fear he would steal the visibility and the thunder of the NAACP in the campaign against educational inequality. By 1954 Dr. Davis had aligned with the legal department of the NAACP. After the NAACP publicly proclaimed its need for "Money *NOW*" and received contributions from a variety of foundations, Dr. Davis's department launched its program to protect Negro teachers from dismissal.[8]

Roy Wilkins, the successor to Mr. White at the head of the national organization, had told Dr. Davis in January 1955 he wanted him to protect the teachers caught in the "backlash of desegregation." Mr. Wilkins explained he would assign field staff to work with him, as they could put into action the "know-how built out of our earlier experiences." Specifically, Dr. Davis would create a liaison with several state associations of Negro teachers and other professional associations, including Negro teachers, and his department would be given legal counsel to draft blueprints for legal action on behalf of teachers.[9]

As Thurgood Marshall had done in collaborations before him, Dr. Davis traveled to the ATA annual meeting in Atlanta in the summer of 1955. A year earlier, at the 1954 ATA meeting, Mr. Harper had provided a special tribute to deceased life members of the association just before the Negro leaders from across the southern states discussed their collective response to integration resistance. Thurgood Marshall was on hand, as usual, to receive the ATA contribution to the NAACP, a check for $1,800. Mr. Harper then presented the ATA Life Membership contribution of $500 to the NAACP Legal Defense and Educational Fund, and Attorney Marshall provided the delegates an "extended analytical and informative presentation" on the present status and the necessary subsequent action incident to the five school cases successfully argued before the Supreme Court.

The collaboration continued. In 1955, Dr. Davis and his colleagues explained the National's plan to respond to threatened Negro teacher displacement. Dr. Davis's colleagues in the national office had already sought information from local NAACP branches on the extent of Negro teacher dismissals in preparation for litigation, unfortunately replaying the same error the NAACP had made in 1923. "We are in need immediately of information concerning dismissals or changes in teaching positions as a result of desegregation of the schools in your area," the NAACP director had written the local branches. The accompanying questionnaire asked about training and experience, whether the teacher read or wrote a foreign language, U.S. military service, and details on desegregation assignments.[10] The response in 1955 mirrored the response in 1923 when Mary White Ovington had sought information from the local branches on the length of term, the salaries, the average daily attendance, the facilities, the number of children in the community, the number of colored and white schools in the community, and whether any schools had double or triple sessions. In 1955, as in 1923, local branches had little access to information on education matters. Educators did, however, and Dr. Davis knew that. So he met with the ATA in 1955 to formulate a plan.[11]

Dr. Davis explained he wanted Negro education organizations in the varied states to press for a teacher law, teacher aid program, and teacher placement bureau. He wanted them to disseminate the plan widely across the South so that Negro state organizations could act collectively in the face of massive southern retaliation against them. While the national NAACP through its Legal Defense and Educational Fund threatened litigation, the Negro education organizations would lobby for tenure.[12]

The National played its role one month later. Roy Wilkins issued the NAACP's public challenge a month after Dr. Davis spoke at the ATA meeting, asserting that teachers could not be fired because of their affiliation with the NAACP. "Aside from the legal aspect of unconstitutionality," Roy Wilkins explained to the South via the press, "this resolution is a reprehensible attempt to terrorize teachers in Georgia."

Mr. Wilkins also made sure that Walter F. George and Richard B. Russell Jr., representing the State of Georgia in the U.S. Senate, understood the need to provide reasoned leadership. On radio journalist Edward P. Morgan's broadcast on August 2, Mr. Wilkins commented, "I realize there are tight emotional problems, bound with the thongs of prejudice and habit, which must be handled on the local level." But he went on to link those local problems to larger issues.

"Yesterday, as you know," he said, "the Board of Education of Georgia, taking its cue from the State Attorney General, ordered all teachers who are members of the NAACP to resign from it by September 15 or have their teaching licenses revoked 'for life.' Let's not dwell, now, on the obvious, even arrogant, threat, which that action poses to the constitutional guarantees of civil rights and civil liberties of Negro schoolteachers in Georgia. Let's explore instead, the threat that action poses . . . at a critical stage in the cold war."[13]

The networks of activists began their work. The national NAACP televised statements about the teacher situation in Georgia and laid a "good foundation" for protests against local Georgia leaders. Meanwhile, Dr. Davis's presence at ATA and with the GT&EA Executive Board, "with his wise and effective suggestions," helped GT&EA leaders chart state strategy.

Of course, the maneuvering also needed the appearance of local NAACP activity. The NAACP still wanted the state branches to be like "interlacing arteries running out from the main office to the most remote part of the organized body." However, local chapters still were not fully operative or organizationally intertwined. Over the decades, visits by New York leaders had spurred big meetings and memberships; the branch paid for the visit, and the branch would collect enough money to be active again. However, even after *Brown* in 1954 and the *Brown II* decision in 1955, ordering that integration be accomplished with "all deliberate speed," many southern branches remained lackluster.[14]

In Georgia, Mr. Harper was the liaison between the educators and local and state NAACP activity, working this time directly with the loose affiliation of local NAACP chapters in the state conference, while the GT&EA officially followed Dr. Davis's suggestions and began to appeal directly to state leaders for tenure laws.

By July 1955, the NAACP Georgia State Conference issued its statement on the matter of threats to Negro educators in direct challenge to Georgia's attorney general, but in perfect alignment with GT&EA beliefs: "We take the position that any American citizen has the civil and constitutional right to join or support any organization whose purposes are legitimate and not contrary to the law of the land." Upon advice of their counsel, "it is our considered opinion that the regulations adopted, as well as the one proposed, cannot be successfully defended whenever and wherever challenged in a court." Echoing the language of Mr. Wilkins, the Georgia state conference stood "today, ready, willing and able to challenge the right of school teachers."

Local NAACP chapters, however, needed information from the National on how to proceed. In private, Mr. Wilkins communicated to W.W. Law of Savannah, the president of the State Council, that he agreed with Mr. Law's suggestion that a conference needed to be held to clarify certain situations that had developed locally. Since local branches did not yet fully connect educational action with the national agenda, local leaders needed a script. "We are thoroughly convinced that many of our branch workers need information and that, in many cases, they must be personally instructed in order to carry out the directive sent out relative to petitions. Oftentimes, local situations have a tendency to confuse them."

Mr. Wilkins said Attorney Marshall would be coming to Macon to meet with branches, even though he had to shift his schedule to do so. Since any moves by the local branches could lead to legal action, the local branches needed the advice of the legal staff, without exception. Mr. Wilkins said Mr. Law would reiterate at the meeting the "intention of the NAACP in Georgia to stand by the teachers of the state who have been threatened by the State Board of Education."[15]

Nothing was said publicly about the health of Georgia's state branches or the quiet relationships with Mr. Harper that, as in previous years, coordinated the national NAACP agenda, the GT&EA advocacy agenda, and the local NAACP branches. In fact, Walter White had solidified the public image of protest in his report at the NAACP annual meeting in 1955, shortly before his death. The "major credit" went to the branches of the NAACP, he said. Although Mr. White knew well the difficulty he had had over the years maintaining branch membership, even resorting to writing threatening or guilt-inducing letters to local branches to compel them to undertake membership campaigns, such matters were not for public discussion. The public script was that NAACP was fighting for the educators whose jobs were under threat. It was in the interest of Georgia educators to let the public believe this untouchable New York target, these "outsiders," were the problem. It freed them up to engage in the professionally accepted behavior of requesting tenure.

Mr. White did mention "many other organizations." But he did not publicly name the educational collaborators. He only paid tribute to the "thousands of unsung heroes and heroines who have done this job."[16] Working quietly together, the decades-old alignments accomplished their goal: Georgia retreated in its plans to penalize any teacher who belonged to the NAACP or advocated racial integration in public schools.[17] But an unforeseen challenge would soon face the coalition when both Mr. White and Mr. Harper died within a span of three months.

Mr. Harper worked until the end. At the March 22, 1955, regular bimonthly meeting of the Atlanta-area Jeanes supervisors at the GT&EA headquarters, they expected to celebrate Mr. Harper's birthday. To their surprise, the Jeanes supervisors arrived to discover that the "unselfish and congenial gentleman" had turned the tables on them, having prepared a dinner in their honor. They discovered the main reception and conference room arrayed with vases of flowers—the fragrance and beauty of which they proclaimed to be suggestive of spring—and appetizing aromas drifting from the kitchen. The group enjoyed a jovial dinner, appreciated the sweet music from a South Fulton High School instructor, and especially appreciated the pianist playing "Let Me Call You Sweetheart" to Mr. and Mrs. Harper. The teachers toasted Mr. Harper in his dapper grayish blue suit, and Mr. Harper toasted them in return before all adjourned to the porch to take pictures at the end of the party.[18]

Perhaps some suspected the aging executive director was growing tired. Mr. Tate had begun soliciting funds for a surprise gift for Mr. Harper shortly after he became vice president in 1954. He reminded educators across the state what Mr. Harper "has done and is doing." He said he hoped the gift from the teachers of the state would show Mr. Harper how much they "wholeheartedly" supported the program he had implemented to help them gain the educational advantages that were rightfully theirs. In October of that year Mr. Tate thanked members for the $2,553.71 in contributions that arrived from across the state.[19]

But as Mr. Harper continued his work in 1955 connecting local and national NAACP branch activity with GT&EA and ATA educational activity, no one was really prepared for his demise. He died in late June 1955, before the summer ATA meeting. The loss was enormous, and all of GT&EA mourned.

The *Herald* saluted the "picturesque character and familiar fighting figure" who had been removed from their ranks. It reprinted an article from the *Atlanta Daily World* about Mr. Harper's death, which said in part:

> Having lived through so many important changing eras and taking his role on the stage of leadership in most of these, he was a veritable reservoir of inexhaustible information and counsel for his generation. Professor Harper's life would read like many a success story of young men coming up from the new-ground farms of backwoods rural Georgia and by sheer push and near genius forged their way to the front to effective and vigorous leaders.

The article reminded readers of Mr. Harper's move from rural Georgia to Atlanta back in the gay 1890s, when Negroes still thought the race would be freed. Mr. Harper had been one of the "moving spirits" responsible for obtaining Booker T. Washington High School, the article said, despite public credit being given to the Atlanta branch of the NAACP. He headed up the GT&EA and led the local Atlanta NAACP. "He was one of the bold spirits that helped to spearhead the drive on segregation which terminated with that famous May 17th Supreme Court Decision—a shot heard around the world."

Morris Brown College president John H. Lewis spoke at Mr. Harper's funeral at Big Bethel—the church in which the sanctuary had been almost destroyed more than three decades earlier when whites discovered it had become the headquarters for the NAACP. "[Mr. Harper] . . . played no small part in that determined onslaught against the walls of segregation, which culminated in the epoch-making Supreme Court Decision on May 17, 1954." The president of Morehouse, Benjamin E. Mays, agreed. Mr. Harper was one of the most self-giving and unselfish men he had known, he proclaimed. "He gave himself wholeheartedly to the cause of human rights" with no thought to "protecting himself when great issues and principles were at stake."[20]

The National NAACP mourned. In a tribute that harked back to 1937, when Walter White had proclaimed himself to be "heartbroken" at the news of Mr. Hunt's death, Attorney Marshall commended Mr. Harper. "Professor C.L. Harper will forever be remembered as a living symbol of devotion to worthwhile causes," Attorney Marshall wrote of the man recently elected to the national NAACP Board of Directors. "There have, of course, been others devoted to causes. However, Professor Harper stood out head and shoulders above many others because of his complete lack of fear of physical or economic repercussions." Mr. Marshall hoped everyone would seek the cause of freedom "at least half as well as Professor Harper did his job."[21]

Mr. Tate also joined the public tributes to the man who was his mentor. He recalled their sitting side by side at the meeting of the state Program Committee in January to plan the upcoming annual conference. It was difficult to believe Mr. Harper's presence at the 1955 state meeting saluting Walter White had been his last.[22]

But Mr. Harper left an imprint, both on the rising new leader and on the direction of the organization. Mr. Harper had once encouraged his students at Booker T. Washington to resist second-class citizenship. Mr. Tate and others determined they would not accept it either. Under Mr. Harper, GT&EA had grown from 2,000 educators to 8,500. The current leadership determined to "carry on in a magnificent manner the work established through heartaches, tireless effort and great sacrifice."[23]

Mr. Harper had said the national NAACP had set a goal of the complete elimination by 1963 of all vestiges of the second-class citizenship from which Negroes still suffered. In his last coordination of agendas, President Harper said in the "Atlanta Declaration" that all branches would be instructed to petition local school boards to abolish segregation without delay. He knew the schools would have administrative problems with implementation of desegregation, but the NAACP was prepared to resist tactics that did not create integration at all levels—including the assignment of teachers.[24]

Meanwhile, he had instructed the GT&EA regional directors in 1954 on how integration needed to be accomplished. They would need to focus on obtaining facilities such as acreage, buildings, and equipment, but they also needed well-qualified teachers. They needed to inspire youth and channel their thinking and activities toward living an efficient and noble life. They needed strong and comprehensive curricula.[25] In other words, successful integration required a holistic approach to ensure that Negro children would acquire the opportunities that previously had been offered only to white children while not losing those elements of the climate of Negro schools that had taught them to aspire. Now that Mr. Harper, the liaison between the instrumental forces of resistance, had died, the GT&EA leadership had work to do.

A stunned GT&EA Executive Board, led by President Bacote and Vice President Tate, began the search for a new executive director. Eventually the board settled on Lucius H. Pitts. Rev. Pitts met most of the criteria they had specified: he was married, he had a master's degree, and although he was a minister, he had some school experience. Board members had questions about his prior work with GT&EA, but the questions were not sufficient to impede his election.[26]

Shortly after becoming executive director, Rev. Pitts met with citizens from Savannah, Columbus, Macon, Coweta County, Albany, Effingham County, and Atlanta and explained in detail the inequities in educational facilities. The group had prolonged discussions and decided that if they could establish their own citizens organization, they could obtain the facts needed to do something about the inequalities and help get that information to the proper people. The group gave itself a name, the Georgia Conference on Educational Opportunity, and decided to draw up a statement to be sent to the Governor's Conference on Education outlining discrepancies and expressing their concern.[27]

Rev. Pitts also continued the GT&EA plan to get information directly to Negro parents. He heeded the Board of Directors when they said they needed citizens meetings at churches to help people learn how to advocate, and he planned for GT&EA to host these local meetings. In four area GT&EA meetings, Negro parents obtained information about the laws governing capital outlay, transportation, and meetings of boards of education and the state board. Rev. Pitts spoke at these meetings and provided information on how to secure needed facilities, supplies, and personnel. He did not have the same community access Mr. Harper had had, but parents were told they could write to him for more information.[28] "Don't go solo or duet. Make it a chorus," the GT&EA literature proclaimed. "Don't trust political chicanery to secure the facilities, equipment and tools for learning. Don't lose your temper—and fuss. Don't give up."

Like Mr. Harper, Rev. Pitts also involved himself with the Atlanta branch of the NAACP. As the branch's education chair, he held meetings at the GT&EA office to review education matters in Atlanta. Eventually he and the committee decided to follow up with the parents in the *Cook* case,

After Mr. Harper's death, Mr. Tate assumed responsibility for creating the mural depicting Mr. Harper and his efforts to achieve quality education. The mural, with its blindfolded Lady Liberty holding the scales of justice, was featured prominently behind the conference table as the Board of Directors met in 1956. *GT&EA Collection*

with whom they had been out of touch since Mr. Harper's death. Rev. Pitts wrote to the parents to extend a dinner invitation so they could all get to know each other.[29]

While Rev. Pitts coordinated community activity and continued to send the educators' monetary contributions to the national NAACP, Mr. Tate's ascension to the presidency began to take shape in late 1955. The soon-to-be outgoing president, Mr. Bacote, commended the directors for "all deliberations with a oneness of purpose." He told them he liked their constructive thinking and action on "the many problems with which they needed to concern themselves." He talked about strategies he employed with the state attorney general to try to engage a meeting that would bring together representative citizens, both Negro and white, to try to solve some of the

The newly elected GT&EA vice president, H.E. Tate, was responsible for planning the annual convention. In 1956, he began responsibilities by convening the State Planning Program Committee for the annual convention. *GT&EA Collection*

problems in the state. Although the attorney general seemed not interested, President Bacote left office with positive affirmations.

"I hope you do not become weary," the outgoing president wrote his colleagues. He confessed he had "come to the point that I recognize that at times I will have to live desperate and with nothing to go upon for encouragement but hope and faith that justice will eventually triumph." But he reminded the Board of Directors that GT&EA would prosper in proportion to the interest they showed as elected advocates for Negro education. "Please keep your regions posted on developments in the organization and let it not lose sight that as never before we need and must have the ardent and unstinted support of every individual."[30]

Meanwhile, Mr. Tate busied himself with his responsibilities as program chair for the 1956 meeting. He worked closely with his committee over a series of conversations between white political leaders and black educators that

In an effort to convince politicians to protect the rights of black children, GT&EA hosted Senator Herman Talmadge at the forty-sixth annual convention. The educators he has suggested firing express little appreciation for his remarks. *GT&EA Collection*

would follow Dr. Bond's model at Fort Valley of trying to gain some accommodations from those leaders by placing them in the position of having to face the constituents to whom they denied equality. As he traveled to the 1956 convention in Augusta, where the gavel of leadership would pass to him, he anticipated the planned greeting from the white Augusta mayor who would welcome the four thousand Negro educators assembled in Lucy Laney High School. He also anticipated the address from Herman Talmadge.

Senator Talmadge had accepted Mr. Tate's invitation. He had once spoken at Mr. Tate's school in Griffin. Mr. Talmadge liked individual Negroes such as Graham Jackson, who had been musical director at Mr. Harper's Booker T. Washington High School and had also played often for President Franklin D. Roosevelt, including at the Little White House in Warm Springs, Georgia. Governor Talmadge had made Mr. Graham the first Negro "official entertainer" for the state. But Governor Talmadge did not want the Negro children he was trying to keep segregated to have democratic opportunities. His visit with the Negro educators at the GT&EA meeting did not change his policies or public discourse.[31]

After the event, Senator Talmadge poses with the GT&EA president and his wife, Mr. and Mrs. Frederick D. Brown. *GT&EA Collection*

Mr. Tate also hoped to force the president of the United States to address the people he refused to fully support. Mr. Tate knew the ATA critiqued President Dwight D. Eisenhower for failing to include *all* citizens and *all* educators—namely, Negroes—in the White House Conference on Education. He had failed to address the continuing inequality in black and white schools in the South, and the NAACP was appalled that he would not specifically address southern states refusing to implement integration.[32] Because of President Eisenhower's unwillingness to contend with Negro educators, Mr. Tate decided to invite him to the GT&EA meeting as well. His letter of invitation was deceptive, as was typically the case when he extended invitations such as these. He said he did not want the president to speak for political reasons, but that he could have a weekend of relaxation from his tension-packed responsibilities. "Augusta will welcome you, Georgia will welcome you, and especially does the GT&EA need you at this time." But Eisenhower did not attend. A heart attack excused him from facing the teachers of the children his White House had ignored.[33]

Undeterred by the lack of senatorial or presidential support, GT&EA maintained its adamant position on integration, and the delegates requested that the organization's leaders communicate their official stance to all relevant authorities. By the meeting's end, there was a new leader who would oversee those communications, a leader determined to fulfill the group's mandates and confident about finishing "the unfinished job which Mr. Harper has handed on to us."[34]

As the new president accepted the gavel during the Friday evening session in the city auditorium in Augusta, he also calmly accepted the daunting challenge of his new role. "Fellow co-workers, as I assume the helm of our state association, I do so with the firm belief that you are my supporters and that you will vigorously provide your aid to all forward looking proposals that will benefit our association." "Tomorrow is here," he reminded them, and with it comes "a demand for action."[35]

15

THE TIES THAT BIND

"Welcome Mr. President," the *Herald* pronounced on behalf of thousands of Negro educators in Georgia, proclaiming its belief that everything pointed to "a highly successful administration of the affairs of the association."[1] The new president still had a school to run back in Griffin as well, but he had been mentored by Mr. Harper and intuitively understood the generational strategies GT&EA applied to address the problems confronting Negro education.

First, Mr. Tate needed to be sure all new directors knew how to run regional meetings. Regional meetings "spurred parents to act for education." He asked a former GT&EA president who had steered the association through difficult years to come to a board meeting and review the methods and techniques of running successful regional meetings. In this new post-*Brown* climate, he also wanted GT&EA's support of integration to be widely known. Following the Representative Assembly's mandate, he had GT&EA staff mail copies of the resolutions passed by the assembly to Georgia's state and local elected authorities. In conjunction with the Board of Directors, he further decided that a political climate prepared to retaliate against teachers exercising their democratic rights also meant GT&EA needed to retain a lawyer for "advice, counsel, and general legal purposes as we move into the days of increased tension."[2]

He had also learned from Mr. Harper the important role of the national education organizations in achieving the fair treatment of Negro children. He had been to meetings, and he understood how litigation worked. He was already mentally preparing for the NEA and ATA meetings he would attend as president. But Mr. Harper had not explained everything.

Only a few months into the job he received a letter inviting him to the National Baptist Hotel in Hot Springs, Arkansas, for a meeting of the National Council of Officers of State Teachers Associations (NCOSTA). He arrived at the venue on September 28, 1956, with Rev. Pitts and joined the group, which was mostly male, at the hotel for Negroes. The attendees representing all the southern states dressed formally, men in suits and ties even in the hot Arkansas September and women similarly smartly attired. The first session began Friday evening at ten o'clock and lasted for over an hour.

In the morning, the representatives reconvened in a loose circle, the blinds in the room all closed—perhaps as a way to keep out the Arkansas heat, or maybe symbolic of the secrecy of their deliberations. Mr. Tate was a newcomer, so all day he merely listened, not uttering a word.[3]

The talk was intriguing. Someone in the meeting reported that the executive secretary of the Virginia Teachers Association, a Dr. Picott, had called to say he had pressing matters at the Virginia legislature and could not be present. Attorney Thurgood Marshall had called to say he was finding it impossible to juggle his schedule to attend the meeting. Apparently this meeting was so serious that any absence had to be explained publicly.

Eventually, a man named Dan Byrd, from Louisiana, spoke on behalf of Dr. John Davis, for whom he worked as an assistant. Mr. Tate knew Dr. Davis. In addition to being the former president at West Virginia State and a champion of inspiring his college students to fight for democracy, Dr. Davis was also a former president of ATA who had used the association to help begin the fight for school equality. Now retired from the college, he led the NAACP Legal Defense and Educational Fund's fight to protect Negro teachers. Mr. Tate had once listened attentively as Dr. Davis spoke to the GT&EA Board of Directors about the National's strategy to have educational organizations seek tenure laws in their respective states.

Mr. Byrd said he wanted this group to develop its full political potential and work to mitigate "some of the evils wrought against teachers." Mr. Byrd reviewed the restrictive legislation passed by states against teachers' connection with the NAACP and argued that united action was necessary. No teacher could stand alone. No Negro state educational association could stand alone, since all were under attack. Backing down or remaining quiet would not be the answer.[4]

Mr. Tate was engaged and invigorated, hearing these people he did not yet know talk about a collective strategy to challenge the troubles Negro educators confronted across the South. Still, he could not exactly fathom the purpose of the meeting he was attending. Neither could Mrs. Sanders, another newcomer. Finally, Mr. Tate attracted the attention of the chair and asked a very basic question: "What *is* NCOSTA?"

The elders patiently explained that NCOSTA "grew out of a need for the state associations during this transition period to pool their resources for cooperative action, to unite efforts in pursuit of common goals, and to compare notes and experiences." Its membership overlapped with ATA's, just as its purpose did. Both were committed to full integration. But this meeting of only the presidents and executive directors of the Negro state teachers associations provided a way to take the pulse of the entire South in one small setting.[5] The executive secretary of the North Carolina teachers' group pointed out that the group was able to invisibly align the agency of individual states and link their collective strength and vision with a national plan.[6] What they did not mention at this point, although Mr. Tate would later learn of it, was why the group had been formed in the first place: since ATA's relationship with the NAACP had become known to political opponents, the educational leaders needed another way, under another name, to coordinate activities between the two groups.

However, Mr. Tate liked the partial answer he was given at this meeting, and quickly accepted the assignment to be part of the Evaluative Committee and assess the extent to which the NCOSTA conference had achieved its goals. He was familiar with this evaluation process; in fact, "evaluation" was the theme of his own Leadership Clinic for GT&EA, scheduled for October 6–7, 1956, at a waterfront camp near Fort Valley with cabins that Mr. Hunt had helped to build.

Since his committee did not report during the NCOSTA session, Mr. Tate decided to submit a few evaluative comments about the meetings to his new colleagues after his return to Atlanta. He thought his points might be useful for future planning. The conference had worked excellently "as a medium of disseminating information regarding problems, operational procedures, how to get it done techniques," he said. He believed actual progress had been made in advertising and teacher placement problems. However, as was often the case in the evaluative critiques of GT&EA, he added that more could have been accomplished if they had adhered more closely to a schedule. Also, the discussion would have proceeded more smoothly if a chairman had been named in advance for the varied discussion groups.[7] Impressed, the officers included Mr. Tate's comments as an appendix to the meeting's minutes.

As noted, the new executive secretary of GT&EA, Rev. Pitts, had accompanied Mr. Tate to the NCOSTA meeting in Arkansas also and participated as a discussant on the panel on teacher placement services.

But, unbeknownst to Mr. Tate, at the meeting the executive secretary had been tasked with exploring how the education associations could still get money to the NAACP. Gladys Noel Bates, an officer of the Mississippi Teachers Association and the secretary-treasurer of NCOSTA, communicated with Rev. Pitts a month after the meeting to explore a mechanism through which NCOSTA could get information to the NAACP Legal Defense and Educational Fund's Department of Teacher Information and Security without public observation. Mrs. Bates said Mr. Byrd had talked with her after the Saturday afternoon session and suggested that the GT&EA contribution be handled by forwarding a check to her for deposit in the NCOSTA treasury. Upon receipt, she said, she would write a check to Allan K. Chalmers, treasurer of the Department of Teacher Information and Security. Mr. Chalmers would deposit the check in his personal account and subsequently issue a check from his account directly to the Department of Teacher Information and Security. The home office would send a receipt to NCOSTA acknowledging remittance after the money had "completed its arduous journey" and finally arrived at its destination.

"It sounds pretty involved to me," Mrs. Bates confided to Rev. Pitts as they considered other invisible ways to channel money to the activities of the Legal Defense and Educational Fund. She wished they had devoted more time in the workshop to working out all the angles or finding or moving the treasury site to a new location. However, she was passing along the information to him, as she had promised Mr. Byrd she would.[8]

Months later, in January 1957, Rev. Pitts and the committee were still struggling to transfer money to the NAACP. Mr. Byrd wrote to Dr. Picott of the Virginia Education Association that he understood his absence from the Arkansas meeting. He certainly had "an overriding obligation" to appear before the Virginia legislative body and give the position of the Negro Teachers Association in Virginia. He needed to do this, even if his presence had no effect on the outcome. But NCOSTA matters still required his attention.

"For reasons known to all of us" the money from the state education organizations needed to get to the NAACP via NCOSTA. Mr. Byrd reminded Dr. Picott the 1956 GT&EA check to NCOSTA for the Department of Teacher Information and Security had never reached the intended recipient. He noted the inhibitory legislation passed by most states already and reported that Georgia's political leaders had gone to the Negro-owned Citizens Trust Bank of Atlanta and demanded the banking records of the Atlanta branch of the NAACP. Because of this kind of hostility, Mr. Byrd believed all banking transactions should be removed from the hostile states.

Mr. Byrd suggested opening an account in Washington, DC, or in New York. He thought a Negro bank in Washington, Industrial Savings, might be an excellent location, since he believed they might be willing to waive the requirement of a signature card in the presence of the bank official. Checks for the Department of Teacher Information and Security could be made out to NCOSTA, which would stamp them for deposit to its account, then issue a check to the NAACP department. He also had other suggestions on the details.[9]

It was crucial for Mr. Byrd to figure out how to get the money to the Department of Teacher Information and Security. As had been true with the teacher salary cases, educators financed the NAACP effort to protect them. Pledges for support for the financing of black teacher security came from across thirteen southern states. In 1957, the support offered by Negro education associations totaled $16,950. The lowest pledge was from Kentucky at $500; Alabama, Texas, North Carolina, and Georgia tied for the highest pledge at $1,800. Louisiana, which pledged only $1,500, had actually paid $1,750 by October 1957.[10]

Of course, as was historically true, some tension existed between the visible educators and the invisible financiers. Dr. Picott, in his role as executive director of the Virginia Teachers Association, had written Thurgood Marshall and Elwood Chisholm of the NAACP Legal Defense and Educational Fund back in June 1956, referencing the suit being planned on behalf of the teachers in South Carolina by the (Negro) Palmetto Education Association. The South Carolina teachers had been told by the South Carolina State Conference of the NAACP that the NAACP would handle the suit if the educators paid all costs associated with the typing and filing of briefs, plus attorney fees and expenses on both the state and national levels.

"We do not object to paying for the services we get," the executive director of South Carolina had said, "but we have given John W. Davis $1,600 of the $17,000 subscribed by state associations." Were the Negro educators not entitled to some services?

Dr. Picott echoed that sentiment in his letter to Attorney Marshall. He was certain Attorney Marshall was familiar with the NAACP's efforts to secure financial support from the Negro educators. Surely he knew the state groups had contributed the amount requested by Dr. Davis and Mr. Byrd at the 1955 meeting of NCOSTA in Nashville and that they planned to do so again in 1956. He reminded Attorney Marshall of Dr. Davis's commitment to protect the Negro teachers in this period of transition from segregated to desegregated schools.

"Permit me to add," Dr. Picott continued, "that those of us who have worked intimately with some of the school cases over the years are keenly aware of the tremendous costs of such litigation. We realize that the few thousand dollars contributed to date to the Legal Defense and Education Fund will not provide too much. Indeed, you will note that the South Carolina group, like most of us, expects to pay." Then he came to the point. "However, the question which has been raised as to the services which will be provided by the Legal Defense and Education Fund is a very real one."

Attorney Marshall responded quickly, replying that Dr. Davis's job and that of his staff would be to get the necessary information when a teacher was denied his or her rights because of race. When a teacher group requested that the NAACP handle the case, the teacher group would "bear the court costs and cost of printing of records and briefs." Attorney Marshall thought it would be helpful if the local group could also take care of hiring a local attorney. However, the Legal Defense and Educational Fund would not charge for its lawyers and, in fact, had never charged for its lawyers—although if the local group could handle transportation, that would be helpful. In other words, the money contributed annually via NCOSTA helped pay for staff support; when a state educational association wanted a case, it would have to pay court-related costs and supply the plaintiffs.[11]

As Rev. Pitts and the executive directors of other states worked out the details of the money transfers and the nature of their relationship with the NAACP attorneys, Mr. Tate was meanwhile attending to the president's functions. In solidarity with the NEA's efforts to assist with the needs of Negro children, GT&EA determined to go to Philadelphia for the NEA's centennial anniversary celebration in 1957. With Mr. Tate's assistance, it chartered a Greyhound bus from Atlanta to Philadelphia.

President Tate and GT&EA delegates boarded the bus in Atlanta on June 23. They rode more than six hours north through South Carolina and stopped overnight in North Carolina at the College Motel near the historically black A & T University. The next morning, they continued for another nine or more hours through rolling countryside as they traversed Virginia, Maryland, and Delaware. Finally they arrived in the City of Brotherly Love. Philadelphia was where the first GT&EA president, Mr. Wright, had begun a successful bank after his departure from Georgia. Mr. Wright was now deceased, but the bank still stood.

For GT&EA, however, the trip was not a time to engage the memories of Mr. Wright. Instead, they joined white NEA delegates in the birthday celebration. NEA had splurged on the event, providing party napkins, a centennial songbook, and other trinkets marking one hundred years of advocacy for education, only a few of which included concerns for Negro children. Still, Philadelphia was an enjoyable city. And for black educators, a new world of opportunity opened.[12]

But more was at stake than NEA's birthday celebration. Georgia's increased NEA membership, inclusive of the membership of newly joining Negro teachers, was now above twenty thousand. Per NEA bylaws, the state was eligible to have two state directors. GT&EA assumed the second director would represent their group. However, in their discussions with their white colleagues in the Georgia Education Association (GEA) in a state-focused meeting during their time in Philadelphia—the two groups had never met in Georgia—GT&EA discovered that the GEA planned to nominate only white men for the second position. Mr. Tate spoke to a group that included the white superintendents creating problems for black education in Georgia to say that the second director should represent GT&EA, and that the GT&EA wished to nominate their president, Mr. Tate. But the mixed-race conversation yielded no mixed-race agreement. In a vote, the numerically superior GEA decided to place only one name on the ballot for the director position, that of a white man.

Undeterred, GT&EA created its own plan to have a voice in the national NEA. In a coordinated campaign, GT&EA members wrote in the name of their choice, President Tate, to hold Georgia's second seat on the NEA Board of Directors. GEA did not discover the strategy until after the vote, whereupon it strenuously objected. The nominee had to be nominated by the *state* to be affirmed in the NEA's Representative Assembly, GEA contended. Furthermore, the white group asserted that "the state's right to a second director" was "permissive and not mandatory." In other words, GEA would rather have no second director than have a Negro second director.

Faced with this conflict, the NEA waffled. Ruth Hamilton of New York spoke for the Bylaws and Rules Committee when she addressed the NEA body. "Some of the Georgia delegates," she asserted—meaning the GT&EA—"did not agree with the majority decision" to name only one director and had written in a name for a second director. However, she reported, the "leaders of the Georgia delegation"—that is, the white GEA—"contend that such write-in votes should not be counted." She reported that the NEA parliamentarian and others had decided that "since the delegates from the state are not even mentioned in this sentence [the Article II, Section I (b) bylaws from which GEA drew its position], it is not the prerogative of the state delegates to determine how many directors that state shall have and that the determination should be made automatically on the basis of the state's NEA membership."

Then she relayed the collective decision of her committee for the NEA to create a plan of action when "reasonable people differ." At this convention, only the ballots for the one director whose position was not in dispute—the white director—would be counted. The other ballots would then be impounded until a final determination could be made by the NEA's Executive Committee as to whether Georgia was electing a second director. If yes, the ballots would be reexamined to determine who had been elected by the write-in votes. Finally, her committee would present to the Representative Assembly a proposed amendment to the bylaws, which would permit directors from each state in the future "to be elected as well as nominated by the delegates from that state."

In other words, Mr. Tate would not be elected for the time being, and perhaps never would; as he mused years later, the "NEA changed [its] rules because of me." The result was that in the future, a state's delegates would vote on its leadership and NEA would accept the result "subject to proper safeguards as to the regularity of their election." As long as the election was fairly executed, NEA would not intervene to see if the election in segregated states with a majority of white delegates denied democratic participation by Negro NEA members.[13] Disappointed, Mr. Tate and his delegation boarded the bus to head home.

Back in Georgia, the GT&EA Board of Directors set to planning how they would influence the NEA to align with black educators. It communicated to Mr. Pitts its desire that he challenge the NEA. As the man elected to represent the interests of Negro education in Georgia, Mr. Pitts agreed.

In short order, he mailed NEA a letter hoping to influence the outcome of its decision making.

The issue, Mr. Pitts wrote to the association's Executive Committee, was whether the constitution and bylaws of NEA "expressly forbid this method" of the write-in vote. Mr. Pitts referred NEA leaders to the pages of the organization's handbook that confirmed Georgia's right to have a second director and affirmed that the laws of Georgia provided that votes for a write-in candidate were valid—possibly a sly allusion to the write-in votes that had been brought into play in the attempt to make Herman Talmadge governor after his father's death a decade earlier. Mr. Pitts quoted multiple NEA documents and Robert's Rules of Order, concluding that "TO DENY GEORGIA A SECOND DIRECTOR IS TO DENY GEORGIA A RIGHT TO WHICH SHE IS ENTITLED"—adding the capitalization and underlining so the NEA president would be clear about his position.[14]

President Lyman V. Ginger responded that the time available for discussion about the second director for Georgia after the annual meeting had been so short that they simply had not been able to address the matter. The NEA Executive Board had discussed the situation at their next meeting and had tasked two attorneys with suggesting an arbitration procedure for Georgia. Their conclusion was that GT&EA should appoint one person to serve as an arbitrator, the GEA should appoint one person, and these two people should appoint a third person. The three arbitrators could then consult and make recommendations to NEA regarding the second director. Of course, President Ginger reminded Mr. Pitts, even having a second director hinged on Georgia maintaining its membership at adequate levels by May 31, 1958, just before that year's convention.[15]

Rev. Pitts and the GT&EA board objected to the NEA position. They believed NEA, not the state organization, already divided by race, should decide. "If the question is left to the state delegates as the occasion may arise there would be varied and sundry opinions which could tend to create disorder and confusion," Rev. Pitts and the board wrote back, and respectfully requested NEA to "so rule and proceed to count the votes for the write-in candidates and declare the Second Director for the State of Georgia."[16]

As president, Mr. Tate participated in all of these state discussions about his non-election as NEA director. As president, he had also participated in the 1957 ATA meeting, held after the NEA meeting, and the affiliated NCOSTA meeting. In the meeting sessions at the James E. Shepard Memorial Library at North Carolina Central in Durham, he began to understand more the history and background of NCOSTA, including its early efforts to get the seventeen southern black state education associations affiliated with NEA in 1952. Attendees also discussed ways NCOSTA could "integrate" the National Association of Secondary School Principals. On financial matters they discussed procedures for sending funds to the Washington bank through the Virginia executive director, Dr. Picott, or the North Carolina executive director, Dr. Greene, via checks labeled "NCOSTA Special Project Fund." Mr. Tate scribbled in his notes his understanding of the problems they confronted: "We are in a terrific fight which involves every Negro teacher in the U.S.—the Negro race and state."[17] But he was not part of the conversations that took place behind the scenes among NCOSTA executive secretaries about a strategic response to the representation problem with NEA that had led to his non-election.

The real issue with NEA was bigger than Mr. Tate, and Mr. Pitts understood that it represented an implicit challenge to all segregated black associations. While Mr. Tate grasped broadly the challenging issues all Negro educators confronted, Rev. Pitts sought help from other NCOSTA executive secretaries on how Georgia should position itself toward the NEA on the matter of Negro representation. He had first looked to his NCOSTA colleagues when he was chosen as executive secretary to "learn how you boys get so much work done."[18] Now, with the NEA matter looming, he had solid relationships with his peers to draw on. Mr. Pitts lost little time consulting them for advice as he prepared to negotiate between his board and the NEA.

Two days after the board meeting, Rev. Pitts drafted his letter to Negro leaders across the South, both NCOSTA and the NAACP, in the well-lit corner office of the executive secretary in the GT&EA office. To all the executive secretaries of NCOSTA, he enclosed the letter from NEA's President Ginger and solicited advice on his response: "Read and let me have your thinking immediately."

Rev. Pitts's own letter pointed out to colleagues the suggestion for arbitration from NEA and noted that Georgia's NEA membership since the debacle the previous year was considerably less, making the second director for 1958 possibly unattainable. Ironically, while GEA's numbers appeared likely to drop, he expected GT&EA's membership to exceed the previous year's. He did not need to comment on the obvious: white membership in GEA had declined. The question was whether the GT&EA should agree to arbitration, as suggested by President Ginger, which would mean engaging with a white organization in a state, Georgia, where there was already a miasma of fear surrounding all matters related to race.

Rev. Pitts believed NCOSTA needed to take a position and express itself as a body "clearly and boldly to NEA policy makers," inclusive of scheduling a conference with the executive director of NEA. "Enough of this crying on the black child in the woods," he ended. "I dry my tears now and await your reaction earnestly and eagerly."[19]

He did not wait long for responses from his NCOSTA colleagues. From North Carolina, an aging W.L. Greene suggested making the NEA president approach the white membership of GEA to obtain answers. From Texas, Vernon McDaniel suggested Rev. Pitts handle the matter without any direct reference to integration publicly, instead centering the conversation on the benefits a second director could provide to the state of Georgia. W.E. Solomon of South Carolina expressed his puzzlement. "Why shouldn't they [NEA] appoint the third person?" he asked about the arbitration. Why would the feuding GT&EA and GEA be expected to agree on a third party? It looked to Mr. Solomon as though NEA was simply stalling for time.

From the NAACP came a response as well. John Davis of the Department of Teacher Information and Security pointed out that NEA appeared to be attempting to place the responsibility for making the decision on the shoulders of someone else. As for the NEA representative who had been suggested as a possible arbitrator, Dr. Davis said that in years of working with him, he had yet to develop the "sufficient confidence" that the NEA spokesperson could mediate on matters of race. Dr. Davis's colleague Dan Byrd put it little less discreetly: "If I did not have respect for your ministry, I could express my first reaction in more expressive language." He believed Ginger's letter a "weak, spineless attempt by the N.E.A. to outmaneuver GTEA" and that the proposal was an insult to his intelligence. "The colossal nerve of them!" The truth was that NEA lacked the guts to rule on the matter. That was the only reason to suggest arbitration. The black Louisiana Education Association, with which Byrd had been affiliated before he accepted the NAACP position, agreed "heartily" with the sentiments Mr. Byrd expressed.[20]

NCOSTA was unified behind Rev. Pitts. So was ATA, its executive director noting it was "anxious to be of service" regarding the second director. In planning for the next NEA meeting, which would be held in Cleveland—and where NCOSTA would also meet, away from the eyes and ears of white NEA delegates—Mr. Solomon, the executive secretary of the Palmetto Education Association in South Carolina, affirmed the need to "follow through on the problems Pitts is having." Even if the Georgia NEA fell short of the membership needed for the second director because of the decline in white membership (a problem Virginia was also having), they needed an "off-the-record meeting to plan joint action and strategy." Mr. Solomon proposed a caucus beginning at 10:00 p.m. in his room at the Statler Hotel during the Cleveland NEA meeting to plan a strategy for their appearance before the NEA Resolutions Committee, the Elections Committee, and any other policy groups whose agenda concerned them. The next night the group would ride the bus about fifteen minutes down 71st Street from the Cleveland Auditorium to a social event and caucus sponsored by the North Carolina delegation at the Chief's Club.[21]

Rev. Pitts's reply to NEA's President Ginger conveyed none of the advice he had received from his NCOSTA colleagues, nor any hint of their suspicions of the NEA and the planning now afoot. He noted only that his board had met and felt the brief they had already submitted to NEA stated their position. Not even Rev. Pitts's Board of Directors knew the details of his collaboration with NCOSTA leaders.[22] Neither did President Tate.

At board meetings, President Tate continued the work that presidents do. He thanked regional directors for their work and parents for the hospitality they displayed when he stayed in their homes while traveling for professional meetings. He crossed the state attending regional meetings and principals' councils. Sometimes he filled the same role that Mr. Harper had, driving out to faraway places after work so that he could discuss with principals the problems in their community that required action. His wife knew he was home when she heard the key turn in the lock.

As the president, he also made appointments to the twenty-five GT&EA committees, responded to personal requests for money from people who needed assistance, nominated teachers for awards, attended committee meetings, and supported college students. In his personal quest to further integration, he sought membership in the World Confederation of Organizations of the Teaching Professions.[23]

In addition to his work as principal at Fairmont High School, Mr. Tate wrote a news bulletin with updates on GT&EA activities for the organization's membership, as his predecessor had done. He submitted an article for publication in a journal for classroom teachers. And following the practice of Mr. Harper and presidents before him, he generated meetings with Georgia's political leaders to press for fair opportunities for all citizens.

He had always paid close attention to the ways southern politicians tried to hamstring Negro education, and so he knew there was a movement afoot to introduce legislation in the Georgia House of Representatives that would block the persistent litigation by Negro groups trying to break down the state's segregation laws. The proposed resolution would set up a six-member legislative committee to investigate school suits filed by Negro parents.[24]

He also paid attention as the state of Georgia readied itself to use state money to pay for private schools for white children if integration occurred. Such a plan was nothing new, as Georgia had used state money to pay for private education before the Civil War.[25]

President Tate especially focused on making sure the Board of Directors stayed abreast of local conditions—not just educational matters, though of course that was their main task, but wider problems of discrimination faced by Negro communities as well. He clipped an account of the criminal assault on a Negro girl, raped in front of her young brother and sister, whose white attacker had been charged only with molesting the girl. He carefully read and filed for later reference the report of a Klan march in Montgomery that boasted a crowd of 1,000 with an estimated 350 robed members of the KKK. One of the speakers had shouted: "The communists would have you believe that the nigger's blackness is only skin deep. . . . All I gotta say to that is they ought to go skin one and find out for themselves."[26] These race problems swirled around the education of Negro boys and girls caught between a *Brown* decision that said they should have equality and a wider society hell-bent on maintaining inequality.

"Please bring to the Board of Directors' meeting any and all outstanding problems of which you have knowledge," he reminded his colleagues as he mailed letters about an upcoming meeting. "These should be problems from your region as well as in your local community."[27] These were the reports he could use to help direct advocacy, both in Georgia and now also through the national networks of which he was a member.

Amid all this activity, he also had to manage the threats back home in Griffin. He was, after all, still a high school principal.

16

PAYING THE COST—AGAIN

"Virginia, I can't stay," a vexed Mr. Tate reported to his wife as the confrontations with the new Griffin superintendent, Mr. C.J. Cheves, escalated. Mr. Krudup, the superintendent he could at least respect as an educational leader even when they disagreed on racial issues, had departed. In his place, the school board had hired Mr. Cheves, a man Mr. Tate did not respect at all.

Mr. Tate increasingly understood the challenges confronting the education of Negro children across the South in places like Griffin. Back in Griffin, though, President Tate was not applauded for his state and national efforts to solve the discriminatory problems confronting Negro children and teachers in the South. In Griffin, he had neither power nor authority outside his school community. And his superintendent did not like him.

Mr. Cheves typified a southern superintendent. While GT&EA directors asked parents and teachers to join the NAACP, some said Mr. Cheves was among the superintendents who in the aftermath of *Brown* asked Negro teachers to sign statements to the effect that they were not members of the NAACP. He certainly called Mr. Tate to his office after the GT&EA meeting at which the attendees passed resolutions supporting integration.

"I didn't know you supported integration," the superintendent announced to Mr. Tate. "What am I supposed to tell the board?"

Mr. Tate replied that the superintendent could tell the board whatever he pleased, and left the room. It was the first of many confrontations with Mr. Cheves.[1]

The two fought over bleachers for the gym in the Negro high school. Mr. Cheves said Mr. Tate could not have money for bleachers for his school. Mr. Tate ordered materials and instructed his shop teacher and students to make the bleachers. The superintendent came to the school and went directly to the shop without alerting the principal of his presence. After confirming that the bleachers were being built, he came to the front office and asked for an explanation. Mr. Tate was furious. "If the barrier had not been there," he told his wife, "I think I would have gone straight to him and hit him."

The two never agreed on anything. As the tumultuous year with the Griffin superintendent approached its end in the spring of 1957, Mr. Tate faced complaints lodged against him and unusual administrative procedures to oust him from his position as principal. Meanwhile, a GT&EA press release spoke of the successful first half of his tenure as president of the now nine-thousand-member organization and spoke with hope about his pending presidential message, to be delivered at the upcoming annual meeting. They believed his message would be "timely, provocative of thought, and above all inspirational." Mr. Tate was weighing his options.[2]

He had retained his job as principal during his first year as president of GT&EA, but he was fully aware he was in a tenuous position. As he delivered the presidential address in Macon on April 12, 1957, to six thousand educators, he spoke with conviction.

> I have a great respect for flowery words, well constructed phrases, and fluent expressions; yet, I have greater admiration for individuals who, in addition to possessing a command of the foregoing, possess to a great degree the spirit of cooperation, the willingness to share, the desire to serve and the courage and creative energy to act. . . . I choose creative energy and planned action from all of us.

He wanted his fellow educators to work at the local level to create opportunities "to give of ourselves for the purposes of aiding the destitute or elevating our society." They were to be mindful of responsibilities and make the upcoming 1957–58 school year a wonderful one for the boys and girls they served.[3]

But in Griffin, the ongoing conflict between himself and the superintendent suggested he would not be able to continue serving black boys and girls as principal.[4]

Mr. Tate contemplated several options, including relocating his family north. Back in August 1955, while the Georgia State Board of Education was first threatening Negro educators affiliated with the NAACP and the national NAACP was compiling information on Negro teachers, he was studying for the summer at Teachers' College at Columbia University.

During that summer, he received a job offer in New York. Mr. Tate had asked Mr. Cousins's advice about relocating, noting that he had already participated in an interview as requested and needed to either accept or reject the position by Wednesday night, August 3. Ultimately, however, the draw to help Negro children in the South was too strong; he turned down the position and cast his lot back with Georgia.[5]

Now, though, as he contemplated how to leave Griffin, Mr. Tate spoke with Mr. Cousins again, emphasizing that if he remained in Georgia he might not have a job long. He sent applications to other schools in Georgia needing a principal. Finally he landed on a viable option. With the Southern Education Foundation granting fellowships to "exceptionally qualified and mature Negro and white students," the time seemed right to pursue a doctorate. Mr. Tate contacted Dr. Bond, recently returned from the Gold Coast, and obtained letters of recommendation, and sent off for transcripts from his earlier educational institutions. He applied to the foundation and became one of twenty students selected.[6]

This time Mr. Tate had to leave alone. As he packed clothing to relocate to Kentucky, he was leaving behind a wife and two young daughters. He knew his mother-in-law would help. She had lived with them since the death of her husband, shortly after the cow thefts. His wife would continue to teach and he would live off a small stipend as he worked toward his doctorate. He would have to travel back and forth between Kentucky and Georgia to continue his job as president of GT&EA, and he would have to miss the precious moments spent when his older daughter accompanied him to the post office to get the mail.

As a graduate student, Mr. Tate also continued his national responsibilities as president of GT&EA. For example, in December 1957, he joined his peers for an NCOSTA meeting in the boardroom of the Virginia Teachers Association Headquarters building at Clay and Fourth Streets in Richmond, Virginia. He listened to information on developments from the legal front: laws attempting to eviscerate the protective features of tenure legislation, laws providing for the closing of public schools in the event of integration, laws making white teachers in private schools eligible to participate in teacher retirement programs so that state money could support private institutions, and laws giving school authorities rights to transfer teachers. Attorney Elwood Chisholm noted the difficulty of obtaining regulations on local educational matters from white state authorities, but emphasized the litigation in place attempting to break down the refusal of authorities to employ

Negro teachers and the "know-how" they were gaining in creating precedents that could be used in non-tenure states. Mr. Tate also presented his Conference Committee report with both Dr. Davis and Mr. Byrd serving on Mr. Tate's committee.[7]

He couldn't call his mother-in-law anymore on special days and ask that his daughter be dressed in her Sunday best so she could ride with him to a town where he was delivering a commencement address for a high school. He would have to assume a traveling lifestyle and separate himself from family as he prepared to fight the fight in new ways.[8] But it was better than being fired again.

Part III

THE EDUCATION OF A PEOPLE

We looked for justice, but there is none. . . . Justice is turned back and righteousness stands afar off. For truth is fallen in the street and equity cannot enter.
—Isaiah 59:11, 14–15

17

WALKING THE ANCIENT PATHS

With Mr. Pitts leaving to assume the presidency of Miles College, the Board of Directors elected Horace E. Tate the new executive secretary of GT&EA. Dr. Tate had traveled back and forth between Kentucky and Georgia for the last several years as he completed the coursework to become the first black doctoral graduate at the University of Kentucky. The board had considered Mr. Tate for the post of executive secretary in the dreary months after Mr. Harper died, but the elders thought him too young and had selected Mr. Pitts. In 1961, when Rev. Pitts announced his departure, GT&EA wanted the continuity of purpose it missed when it had filled the role with someone who had never worked as an educator in the community.

While Mr. Tate finished concentrated dissertation writing at his kitchen table in his home at 2133 North Fourth Street in Griffin during the summer of 1961, the *Herald* lauded the new executive secretary. While Mr. Pitts had done a good job, he was a minister without a history of GT&EA activity and longevity. Mr. Tate would bring the "broad knowledge of association affairs" and an understanding of "procedure gained through working with former leaders of the association over a long span of years."[1]

Indeed, Mr. Tate did. Despite two years studying full-time in Kentucky and a new position as a member of the faculty at Fort Valley, Mr. Tate had never ceased active involvement in the affairs of the organization. With financial aid from the Board of Directors, he completed his term as president, then served as a director at large before the Representative Assembly elected him to the position of treasurer of the association in 1960. His approach toward problems—hammer at them until they were solved—was not disrupted during his years of doctoral study. Once when he was still GT&EA's president, his car had been broken into and clothes stolen on one of the many trips between Atlanta, Kentucky, and Griffin. But Mr. Tate did not worry about it—he still attended the meeting he'd come for.[2]

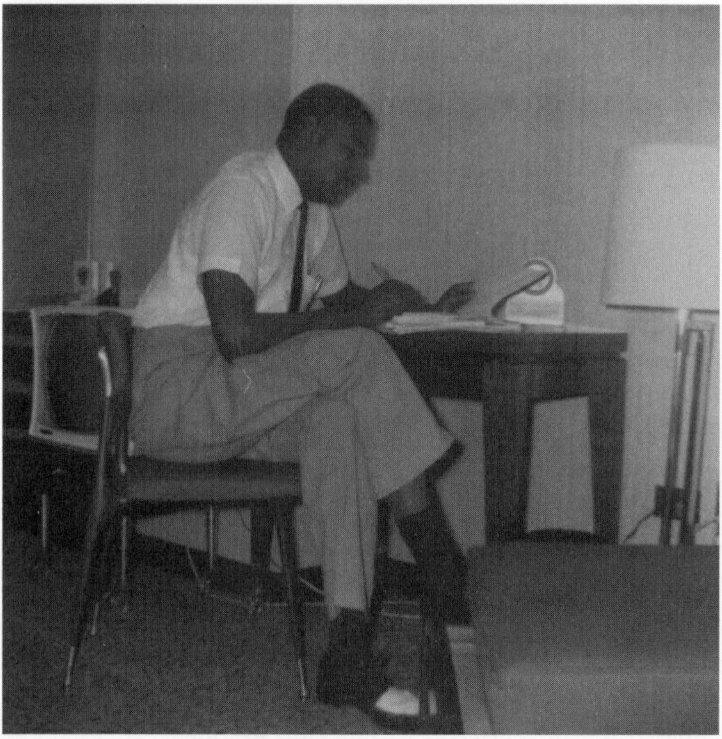

After quitting his job at Fairmont in Griffin, Mr. Tate traveled back and forth between the University of Kentucky and Atlanta to meet his obligations as a doctoral student and as outgoing president of GT&EA. He was appointed to the faculty at Fort Valley after completing his coursework. However, upon appointment to the post of executive secretary of GT&EA, he settled into his family quarters to complete the writing of his dissertation. *GT&EA Collection*

Mr. Tate brought a wide knowledge base about contemporary educational problems to the organization as well. "As all of us so well know," Mr. Tate said in an academic presentation he made as a doctoral student at the University of Kentucky, "the Supreme Court of the United States has ruled that segregation in the public schools of the U.S. based on race alone is unconstitutional and consequently should be eliminated." Drawing data from surveys that addressed school-level concerns, his student group discussed the implementation of integration from the perspective of the teacher, teacher trainer, supervisor, and school principal.[3] His advisor once told him that he had already solved problems the academy was just beginning to address.

In 1961, Dr. Tate became executive director of the GT&EA. *GT&EA Collection*

But neither experience nor academic pedigree could fully prepare the newly minted Ph.D. to walk into the office once occupied by Mr. Harper and Mr. Pitts in the brick headquarters at 201 Ashby Street and assume the duties of executive secretary on July 1, 1961. For the first time, Dr. Tate walked past the open space allotted for Mrs. Reynolds, the office secretary, and assumed the seat of authority in the bright expansive corner office of the executive secretary. Here the heart of the organization pulsated. Flooded by memories, Dr. Tate settled into Mr. Harper's old chair. His was now the job no executive secretary fully discussed with anyone.

Mr. Pitts had fought the good fight, but the quiet battles come with unknown burdens. He had been elected chair of NCOSTA during his tenure as executive secretary of GT&EA, and in 1960 he coordinated a two-day meeting between NCOSTA and the U.S. Justice Department for a briefing on guidelines for implementation of the 1957 civil rights legislation. They would be meeting in the attorney general's suite beginning at 1:00 p.m.

on June 16. "Get your lunch prior to this," Mr. Pitts had reminded delegates. After the briefing with the Justice Department staffers, the NCOSTA members would work long into the night on "material and strategy for NEA and ATA."[4]

While the NCOSTA side of him stayed up late to craft language that might induce NEA members to align with an emerging federal civil rights agenda and support integration during the 1960 meeting in Los Angeles, the Georgia side demanded accountability for his actions at the meeting. In Los Angeles, he had spoken forcefully as part of the heated and lengthy desegregation debate, one unprecedented in time and interest. "We Negroes are not going to live at ease in the South for 50 years. . . . If the N.E.A. doesn't hold the light high on this issue [of integration], then life is going to be difficult for Negroes in Georgia."[5] Rather than taking a stand, however, at the meeting the NEA board had concluded that black and white southern leaders would need to meet to come up with a new statement on integration, one that would be "satisfactory to all."[6] As soon as he returned to Georgia, Mr. Pitts discovered just how difficult this would be. Uncooperative white educational leaders, unhappy with his position, immediately told the white state school superintendent, and Mr. Pitts had to account for his actions.

"There comes a time in life when there is only one choice left," Mr. Pitts said in his lengthy letter to the state school superintendent shortly after his return from the NEA convention. Mr. Pitts expressed gratitude for all the help he received from the state school superintendent and affirmed that it had never been his intention to make it difficult for state leaders to continue their fine work. As the executive secretary of GT&EA, he had never sought to be a "rebel rouser" or "headline seeker." He was writing only to make sure the state school superintendent understood his remarks during the Representative Assembly at the NEA meeting.

Mr. Pitts explained he wanted NEA to take a stronger stand on integration, and that he felt the best way to accomplish this was to change the wording that addressed the importance of integration. Replacing the word "recognizes" with the word "believes" would, in his view, underline the NEA's commitment to the process. In case the state superintendent had heard that he was "pushing for a resolution on integration of NEA affiliates and for integration on the local and state levels"—in effect, a merger of the white GEA with the black GT&EA—he needed the superintendent to know "this is not true."

He confessed he worried that, by speaking, he might "jeopardize the jobs of many Negro teachers in Georgia" and explained he would not continue in his position if it meant the educators would suffer because of his stance. At NEA, he gave the "most impassioned oratory" when he pointed out that the struggle with desegregation "is a struggle with the conscience" of the NEA. "The Negroes only ask that you take a position. Principle must be above personal safety," he urged. And he reiterated his belief that he and the white state leaders could work together through "constant negotiation and creative contact" to "find a reasonable solution" to educate all the children.[7] In more ways than GT&EA leadership knew, Mr. Pitts's unseen work coordinated black educators across states and simultaneously placated and challenged white educators within Georgia.

Unseen by many, Mr. Pitts had also been behind the state's registration of black voters a few years earlier, to help ensure that elected offices—such as that of state school superintendent—were filled with people who would represent the concerns of black communities. "Mr. Pitts has done a wonderful job in handling the committee," the secretary of the Statewide Registration Committee, J. Calhoun, had written in 1957, and noted that two hundred voter registration workers from different parts of the state had attended a meeting a week earlier. To Roy Wilkins, head of the NAACP, Mr. Calhoun reported that the group had county organizers in forty-eight counties and that twenty others had been selected, and that the committee had raised some $2,000 to help get citizens to the polls. They were not operating under the NAACP Georgia State Conference, but the executive committee of the group met weekly.

Of course, Rev. Pitts's role in all this was an enigma to the public. Sometimes stationery listed him as the vice chairman; sometimes his name did not appear at all. "We have not done much with newspaper publicity statewide, for obvious reasons," Mr. Calhoun explained. "The people are so enthusiastic I believe we will get the desired results without publicizing our efforts."[8] In any case, public petitions combined with quiet political relationships and hard data—his files, like Mr. Harper's before him, included exact figures on black and white voter registration as far back as 1950—were part of the executive secretary's multi-pronged efforts to force the South to provide justice for black children. But while Rev. Pitts maintained a conciliatory relationship with the state school superintendent, his role in voter registration, like his role in the larger national fight for integration, could not be disclosed to the superintendent.

Neither could his work with NCOSTA. In December 1960, a few months after he had written his letter to the superintendent, Mr. Pitts had helped plan a meeting of NCOSTA leadership at Howard University as they continued to strategize on ways to petition NEA for more support of integration. They said they needed to meet to "discuss problems peculiar to certain NEA members." In other words, they needed to talk about black people in NEA.

And Rev. Pitts still had to get the money from the educators in Georgia to the NAACP using NCOSTA's elaborate scheme that kept invisible the way black educators continued to support the national office. "Find herein a receipt which you may file at your home or destroy," wrote John Davis to Rev. Pitts as he acknowledged the teachers' financial contribution. Another contribution was referred to similarly, with deliberately vague language: "Find herein two documents which will fit into a file of similar documents in your office." Everything was secret.[9]

Maybe the years of secrecy and fighting had wearied Mr. Pitts. Or perhaps, as he had told the state superintendent in 1960, he did not want to jeopardize the jobs of black teachers in Georgia. As Mr. Tate began to settle into the executive secretary's office for the first time on that July day in 1961, he did not know exactly why Mr. Pitts had chosen to leave that position and accept an offer to be president of a college. He did know, however, that the responsibility of championing black education in Georgia, and beyond, now rested with him.

His eyes surveyed the familiar scene. He knew this office, with the adjoining kitchen where meals were prepared for special GT&EA events. He had seen the big printing press that produced the *Herald*, and he had spent many days at the conference table in the meeting area. He'd even sat on the other side of the desk many times in his position as the organization's president. But being on this side of the desk, looking out through the glass to the parking lot and Ashby Street, was different.

He had a fight in front of him, and he knew it. He needed to fulfill his departing words to the GT&EA assembly when he closed his term as president. Black education remained disarmingly complex, he had said. The times were only recently past when teachers walked five or more miles daily to school to teach in one-room shacks or churches, when children "trudged through mud sleet and rain to get three or four months of learning." However, much had improved as a result of the "founders who loved and labored." Equipment that once had come secondhand from white schools was now sent in new condition directly to black schools. School boards finally assumed responsibility for black teachers' salary and for lunch provision for black students in ways they previously neglected. School facilities that had been "shameful and hideous" had been replaced by modern structures—classrooms were now warmed by efficient heating systems rather than potbellied stoves, which had "circulated the type of heat that allowed pupils literally to burn up in front and freeze behind."

But Mr. Tate knew that the state still had black children "unhoused" or poorly housed. Georgia still tolerated overcrowded classrooms and black children walking too far to school. Moreover, black educators needed to continue to improve instruction and administration so that black children could one day stand "in a new world beside the children of all Nations." Black educators had the dual responsibility of advocating for justice amid persistent inequalities while simultaneously helping eager minds who needed opportunities for expression, originality, and recreation—who needed to aspire to know their individual dignity and human worth.[10]

How would he accomplish the unfulfilled promises of black education in this new position? As the sunlight faded into darkness, Dr. Tate dove into the papers on his desk.

After he had been on the job for two and a half months, Mr. Tate realized that before now he had never fully understood the "responsibilities and demands made upon this office." They were much greater than he had "ever visualized or anticipated." In addition to trying to plan and execute long-term strategies, he had to deal with multiple immediate needs and tasks. He had to contact officials of the State Department of Education in person and by phone to help teachers get properly certified, to aid in getting revoked licenses reinstated, and to help others obtain employment—all matters "of far reaching import to persons involved." He was involved in obtaining aid for displaced persons, beginning teachers, and experienced teachers. He helped sixty-seven teachers obtain employment. He dealt with a stunning number of telephone calls—in just one week, he reported to the Board of Directors, he received and responded to 157 local and 23 long-distance calls, all related to aiding teachers or principals. He dealt with nine insurance agencies, eleven furniture dealers, and janitorial corporations. He assumed the responsibility of editing the *Herald*. He had visited schools in Atlanta, Greensboro, Covington, Madison, Athens, and Watkinsville to talk with unit presidents, principals, and/or teachers and check on local conditions. And he had delivered nine speeches at schools or other educational organizations.[11]

All of this had to be dealt with while he oversaw the GT&EA's move from the 1951 building purchased under Mr. Harper's leadership to the new three-story $270,000 GT&EA headquarters located next to the old building. The new building represented the organization's "expanded educational program." The GT&EA itself occupied a suite on the second floor. Other offices in the building were rented out, including to black State Department consultants who were not located in the downtown quarters with their white counterparts, and the old GT&EA building was

Shortly after Dr. Tate's election as executive director, GT&EA built a new headquarters, which it linked by a back staircase to the original GT&EA building. The old building is in the foreground of this photograph; the new building is attached to the rear. *GT&EA Collection*

leased to the Christian Methodist Episcopal Church; with this rental income Mr. Tate hoped to liquidate debt on the new building quickly, much as Mr. Harper had done with the old building. Mr. Tate involved himself fully in being sure the new building was ready for the conduct of business, including reporting to the Board of Directors on bids for furniture, carpet, landscaping, and telephone service. And he helped collect funding to move the mural of Mr. Harper from the conference room of the old building to a highly visible spot in the two-story foyer of the new building.

He investigated fraud, noting insurance companies who sent materials to black teachers in the early 1950s using the names of GT&EA elected leaders to solicit teacher contributions but who did not have the endorsement of the organization. He involved himself fully in being sure the new building was ready to conduct business. And he sent a letter commending Mr. Pitts for his service to the organization.[12]

That fall Mr. Tate and the GT&EA hosted the annual meeting of NCOSTA. Mr. Tate had been at the previous year's NCOSTA meeting in New Orleans. At that 1960 meeting the group had heard of a distressing situation in Virginia, where sixty-one black teachers had lost their jobs when the Farmville schools closed, and of how the black Virginia Teachers Association had responded; they had also heard of the Louisiana Education Association's legislative and civic efforts in response to laws empowering their governor to close schools to circumvent integration orders. The group had considered the possibility of creating training centers, had discussed the possibility of providing legal advice, and had encouraged teachers to participate in the National Teaching Exam. The meeting had ended with a sober reminder by the Louisiana Educational Association of the importance of continuing to share experiences: "The problem the Louisiana Education Association faces today will come to other minority teacher associations tomorrow."[13]

The preparation for the 1961 meeting followed up on many of these concerns, including the situation in Louisiana. Affiliate members Dan Byrd and John Davis, from the NAACP Legal Defense and Educational Fund, would be joining them to discuss the legal implications of school desegregation.[14]

Dr. Davis, in fact, kicked off the meeting, saluting NCOSTA as "one of the ablest and most important groups of educators in this nation." They were the "grass-roots" educators whose advocacy of total inclusiveness in education was sometimes controversial, he said. They were the new leadership (especially since the voices of state black college presidents were for the most part muffled due to southern states' control of funding for state black colleges). Dr. Davis spoke frankly of his joy at being able "to work with such a galaxy of important men." "You are important," he told them, "because you are close to the people. Your degree of sophistication does not inhibit you—you are yet one of the 'people.'"

In another session Mr. Byrd spoke at a panel on school desegregation. He noted first that the efforts to "cool-down" the promotion of integration were gaining momentum. He referred specifically to his native Louisiana, where new statutes provided for the dismissal of any public employee who advocated integration in elementary or secondary schools. Another panelist, Charles Davis, spoke of the need for teachers to contribute to changing attitudes, values, and ideals. Paul Rilling spoke of the rapid spread of "tokenism" in desegregation in the six years since the Supreme Court decision. "If the courts allow tokenism to continue, we will have a hollow legal victory," Mr. Rilling emphasized. They needed to consider more legal action and mass registration so politicians would know blacks were dissatisfied. They needed community education that would solicit the support of everyone.

Other questions, challenges, and dialogues ensued as the sessions continued through Sunday morning. Across the South, black teachers were still vulnerable to retaliation by dissatisfied state and local leaders. How could their concerns about losing jobs be alleviated? And how should NCOSTA address the situation with the NEA, which even with its waffling stance on integration had provoked political anger—attorney generals in two southern states had announced restriction of NEA membership in retaliation for NEA's tentative support for integration. The officers of NCOSTA viewed such restriction as an "infringement upon personal and professional rights," and they wanted steps taken immediately to secure the rights of the teachers.[15]

Dr. Tate listened intently, welcoming the exchange of ideas. As the Louisiana educators had predicted at the previous year's meeting, the tactic of trying to stymie integration by closing public schools was now spreading to other states. Georgia had already been through a battle over desegregating the University of Georgia. During that struggle Dr. Tate had kept in touch with Donald Hollowell, an attorney who was both litigating the UGA matter and on retainer with GT&EA; in fact, Dr. Tate re-

NCOSTA met regularly during the 1960s. In this photo, NCOSTA members meet with Jim Williams, NEA representative in Atlanta, as tensions mounted between GT&EA and the national organization. Executive directors from across the South convened in the boardroom in the new GT&EA headquarters building. Seated are Ellen C. Watson, South Carolina; Clarence Bozeman, Alabama; Don Mitchell, Washington, D.C.; Elliott B. Palmer, North Carolina; J.K. Haynes, Louisiana; Rosena J. Willis, Virginia; T.E. Patterson, Arkansas; J. Rupert Picott, Virginia; Marion Shannon, Florida; and L.S. Alexander, Mississippi. Standing are Robert Perry, New Orleans; H.E. Tate, Georgia; George W. Brooks, Tennessee; and Dan Byrd, Louisiana. *GT&EA Collection*

called being on a road trip to investigate public school inequality when a bulletin about developments in the UGA case came over his car radio, and he pulled over in some country town to find a roadside phone and call Attorney Hollowell. A plan for desegregating the university had just been achieved, but the problems of primary and secondary school integration still remained, and the state was now threatening to close some of those schools.[16]

In August, just a few weeks before the NCOSTA meeting, newsmen had traveled on air-conditioned buses to observe the peaceful integration of four high schools in Atlanta by nine black students. Unlike neighboring cities, Atlanta showed the world that the progressive city "too busy to hate" would not throw bombs or overtly injure black children. The reports these journalists filed, however, did not address the question of whether the experience of these nine students would be the same as that of the remaining black children in Atlanta, or in the many other cities and towns across Georgia.[17]

Furthermore, there was the matter of the continuing educational inequality in the black schools where most black children still remained. The Minimum Foundation Program of Education, which was supposed to provide "absolute essentials in meeting the needs" of the youth in Georgia, was not adequate, with most systems in the state not yet achieving even those minimum levels of clerical help, instructional supplies, materials, equipment, plant maintenance, or guidance services. Transportation was still a problem as well, with many buses "in a very dilapidated condition" and constantly "dangerously over-crowded." The buses made double runs and covered wide areas, with the result that some children spent three or four hours on a bus each and every day. And there were still localities where black and white teachers received different salaries solely because of race.[18]

When the 1961 NCOSTA meeting ended, Dr. Tate returned to his corner office in the new building with the recently installed green carpet, new blinds, and custom drapes. He pulled his big chair closer to the massive desk. In the sometimes lonely position of GT&EA executive secretary, Dr. Tate had work to do.

18

POLICING THE SOUTH

On November 19, 1963, two years into the job of leading Georgia's black educators, Horace Tate passed through the iron gate at 1600 Pennsylvania Avenue that kept visitors at a distance and entered the Rose Garden, off the West Wing of the world's most famous house. He joined black and white NEA and state education association leaders from across the nation in attendance that day to hear an address by President John F. Kennedy. Here, in a city full of symbols of democracy and freedom, Dr. Tate hoped the administration of the young president would finally promote educational justice for black children.[1]

Dr. Tate greatly admired this president, who gave the appearance to southern blacks of a deep commitment to equality. As the young black children Dr. Tate had taught civil rights had grown to become protesting adults marching in the streets and demanding equality, their actions finally forced the president to speak powerful words from the White House against discrimination. His voice, beamed into living rooms across the nation, helped make southern blacks believe change was possible.

For Dr. Tate, change seemed possible in education also. He joined in the applause greeting the youthful leader who proclaimed that Congress had a "national obligation" to meet the educational needs of its children. The president needed local, state, and national leaders to join him to "get the job done" before Congress recessed the following summer. His goal was to persuade Congress to pass the most substantial acts for education in a century—since the Morrill Acts of 1862 and 1890. The first Morrill Act provided federal land to help states build colleges that focused on "agriculture and the mechanic arts." The second was aimed at the South and required each state to either show that race was not a factor in admission to those land-grant institutions *or* build a separate institution for Negroes.

President Kennedy's public language in 1963 proclaimed the kind of federal support Dr. Du Bois, Mr. Hunt, Mr. Harper, Dr. Bond, the NAACP, and black educators had requested ever since Georgia violated the requirements of the 1890 Morrill Act. At the Atlanta University Conference on Education, Mr. Hunt and Dr. Du Bois coauthored resolutions seeking federal aid to address the continuing inequalities in education. With the NAACP, they had protested legislation in the 1920s and 1930s that would send money into states without "safeguards [that would] prevent unequal and unfair expenditures of funds."[2]

Though the president did not speak directly about the South's continued discrimination against black children, he did address the problems black educators confronted. The need was "very clear," the president said, noting the financial support needed to battle problems in "slum areas, rural areas," including "buildings . . . unsafe, teachers' salaries disproportionately low." The president said he did not know of any problem "more important" and he hoped they could get legislation passed shortly. Too often, in the past, legislation "united enemies instead of friends," he said as the white and black educators in the audience chuckled. The president likely did not know how close that statement came to the truth those educators experienced.[3]

Several months earlier, at the July 1963 NEA convention in Detroit, 10,000 black and white NEA attendees, including 6,800 official delegates, had expressed their views on civil rights in three separate actions. They approved the motions supporting President Kennedy's civil rights program. They proposed a resolution on desegregation that expressed support for the desegregation of the eleven affiliates in southern states where black and white teachers continued to have their own separate organizations. They commended southern affiliates that had removed membership barriers—namely, white associations that had removed clauses in their constitutions that prohibited black teachers from joining. They suggested that the longstanding Joint Committee of the National Education Association and the American Teachers Association meet to discuss the merger of those two groups. On these matters, all agreed.

But differences still divided them in this season of hope for federal support of education. On multiple occasions, white NEA leaders held their own set of private meetings with President Kennedy. They wanted substantial federal support for public education, but they did not see any need for that federal aid to come with restrictions. In contrast, black educators wanted federal aid that would address the inequalities that occurred in local schools. NCOSTA had already critiqued NEA's refusal to stand with black educators in calling for monitoring local conditions. Without local monitoring of the distribution of federal money, the resources allocated would not necessarily help black children. NEA, however, had refused to support a rule for local monitoring that its white southern affiliates rejected.[4]

Now, as the young president concluded his address to the educators in the Rose Garden, he invited the audience to go inside and visit the White House while they were here. It wasn't a "bad education tour," he added jestingly. He also pointed out the trees in the garden planted by Andrew Jackson and John Adams, men who represented the legacy of federal support for education. Shortly thereafter the president thanked his guests and bid them goodbye.

Just three days later, these same educators joined the nation in stunned amazement as newsman Walter Cronkite, wiping a tear, announced to the world that the president—who just two months earlier had told an audience

Just before President Kennedy departed for Texas, Dr. Tate gathered with other educational leaders on the West Lawn of the White House. Dr. Tate is slightly behind the president on the right. *GT&EA Collection*

at the University of North Dakota that "things don't happen, they are made to happen"—was dead. The president had been shot as his motorcade passed the Texas School Book Depository in Dallas.

In Atlanta, an anguished Dr. Tate carefully clipped from *Life* magazine and other publications accounts of President Kennedy's life and death. When the GT&EA Board of Directors assembled, Dr. Tate confessed he was not certain what he could add to the eulogies the president had already been given, but he did want to remind the people assembled in that conference room of the role some unknown educators had played in helping the thirty-fifth president learn respect for human dignity. He emphasized that inspiring others to respect all humans was their challenge as well. "It is up to us," he reminded black teachers across Georgia as they dedicated an issue of the *Herald* to the late president, "to rededicate ourselves to the fulfillment of the goals of education and to the task of assuring all people that the ideals for which John Fitzgerald Kennedy stood, will be fulfilled in this 20th century."[5]

Now, though, a brooding, broad-shouldered southern politician who had had an uneasy relationship with the now deceased president suddenly held the fate of black children in the South in his hands. Writing to NCOSTA members on December 3, Dr. Tate addressed the need for action. Wasn't it time NCOSTA plan to meet with the new president? President Lyndon Baines Johnson had already met with Roy Wilkins of the NAACP and with Whitney Young of the Urban League, and—according to the reports he was getting in Atlanta—he was scheduled to meet with Dr. Martin Luther King Jr. either December 4 or soon thereafter.

"It appears to me," Dr. Tate wrote, "that there are problems facing us in education, which if solved, will aid in eliminating many of the problems which harass society." He knew the executive secretaries of the black teachers associations understood "as much, if not more, about problems facing members of our ethnic groups as other persons in our respective states." And he wondered whether seeking a meeting with the new president might be one way of communicating that understanding to the new president.[6]

Responses to his letter varied. L.S. Alexander, executive secretary in Mississippi, said yes, they should meet, but not too soon. The executive secretary from North Carolina, Charles A. Lyons Jr., apologized on December 19, 1963, for his "late response" but expressed his willingness to go along with the idea if the "other fellows" agreed. Lyons thought Dr. Porter, president of NCOSTA, could make arrangements.[7]

But the new president's policies surprised those who might have made assumptions about how a southerner would handle education now that he was in the White House. While Dr. Tate, fulfilling the mandate given him by the GT&EA board, contacted the governor of Georgia, state officers, and congressional representatives to support the civil rights bill then pending in Congress, the new president met with longtime political acquaintances, called in favors, and got the Civil Rights Bill of 1964 passed.[8] A skillful politician, President Johnson understood America's world leadership status needed the civil rights bill the slain President Kennedy proposed. The new president turned out to be more of an activist liberal in his leadership than Mr. Kennedy perhaps "ever thought of being," reported one politician close to both of them.[9]

President Johnson also successfully navigated the voting rights bill through Congress using every "IOU he had, and it passed," doing so even though he knew "perfectly well we have turned the Southern white over to the Republican party in 20 years' time." He held true to his convictions about education as well, having his first-grade schoolteacher join him as he sat in his old school and signed the Elementary and Secondary Education Act (ESEA) into law in 1965.[10]

The ESEA provided $1 billion in resources for children who had been educationally deprived. In particular, Title I aimed to distribute funds to schools and school districts with high percentages of low-income families. Not only did the legislation fulfill NEA's desire for federal intervention by becoming the government's most comprehensive educational effort, it also fulfilled the desires of black educators for oversight of local implementation. Thanks to the amendments forced into the legislation by black congressman Adam Clayton Powell Jr., federal money would be delivered into the South as long as the South did not discriminate.[11]

When Dr. Tate walked into the White House again in 1964, he came in triumph, joining state school superintendents, state commissioners of education, executive secretaries of white state organizations, and presidents of national PTA organizations. He reported back to the board that President Johnson appealed to all those in attendance to "make every effort to provide equal and quality education for all of the inhabitants of the respective states." When he returned to Georgia, he told the GT&EA Board of

Directors that he believed the new presidential administration was sincere in its efforts to involve all in the problem solving the country needed.[12] Despite the unexpected death of the expected champion for equality, the government of the United States appeared prepared to address southern educational inequalities, even those at the local level.

But local white school boards were unwilling to concede defeat. In Georgia, the small town of Crawfordville symbolized the intensity of local problems that needed to be addressed.

The Crawfordville marches first made the news as another example of civil rights protests. Newly elected Negro Georgia state senator Leroy Johnson headed to Taliaferro County with a delegation of ten other state Negro leaders in early October because of the grave conditions confronting Negroes. He described the situation in the town of Crawfordville "as a potential explosive powder keg caused by determination of Negro citizens there to obtain some degree of first class citizenship and die-hard resistance by whites." As far as Senator Johnson was concerned, "Negroes had a legitimate complaint."

Atlanta newspapers amplified his conclusion. They described angry whites who "roughed up a Negro civil rights worker and a Negro teenager." Three white men reportedly shoved the worker, knocked his glasses off, and snatched his camera. About a half hour later about twenty white men pelted a car with apples, which caused the driver of the car to lose control and smash into a parked car. The white men then "dragged him from the car and pummeled him."[13]

Whites in Crawfordville scuffled with photographers from WSB-TV of Atlanta and the Atlanta bureau of United Press International in an effort to stop them from recording the daily demonstrations rocking the small town. "We don't want you here," someone yelled. "Let's get those cameras!" According to Tom Brokaw of WSB, a small group of white men took the camera of one of the newsmen. The sheriff found a tape of events in the car of a young black youth and then destroyed the tapes. Meanwhile, one of Dr. King's top lieutenants, Hosea Williams, announced plans to mobilize an "all-out movement" that could end in a 120-mile march to Atlanta.[14]

As the weeks passed, the Crawfordville situation worsened. Negroes in the "racial dispute" wanted representation on county and city bodies and nondiscrimination in hiring. Whites claimed to have offered "everything from picking their own policemen to having a voter registration office open five and a half days a week" if that would stop the increasing demonstrations. The white leaders offered to create a biracial committee, get a Negro on the health board, start a food stamps program, and set up an economic opportunity program in the county, as long as a moratorium could be declared on the demonstrations. Led by the SCLC's Mr. Williams, the Negro community rejected the concessions.[15]

Regardless of how it was portrayed in the press, however, the conflict had initially begun when eighty-seven Negro students requested transfer to the all-white Alexander Stephens Institute in the wake of the civil rights bill requiring desegregation. Under the new Civil Rights Act, the school board in the county containing the small town of Crawfordville, Taliaferro County, filed a "freedom of choice" plan approved by the U.S. Education Office that allowed the county to comply with federal guidelines about equality for all children and maintain its federal funding. However, while the school board went through the motions of obtaining federal approval, it simultaneously transferred and bused all two hundred white children in the county to schools in surrounding counties rather than integrate the local white high school, which was named after the former Confederate vice president.[16] Since, as a result of the local school board's actions, no white high school was now available in the county, the school board told black children they would have to continue at their Negro school. In response, about four hundred of the six hundred black students registered at Murden, the black high school, but the other two hundred refused and marched to the courthouse in protest of the inequality.[17]

For days, dozens of black children attempted to board school buses carrying white Taliaferro students to schools in Warren and Greene Counties as state troopers blocked their efforts to integrate the school buses. On day two, a line of twenty troopers armed with pistols and billy clubs turned the children away. White children on the buses cheered when some local white men snatched the camera of a civil rights worker, tossing it to each other as a trooper sought to obtain and return it to its owner. On another day, black children tried to stop the buses by sitting down in the road in front of them as they pulled off. The black children were removed by state troopers.

Undeterred, about ninety black students left the Freedom Schools they had begun attending after being denied equal education within the system, marched to the closed white school, and sat on the lawn singing freedom songs. They said they were preparing to march to Atlanta, where they would present a list of grievances to Governor Carl Sanders. A sour governor announced publicly he would not meet with a "mob representative." Parents needed to make their children go to school, he said. If they couldn't, the state laws could.[18]

But according to Dr. Tate, the story was even more complex, with roots going back to Herman Talmadge's 1951 threat to retaliate for efforts to integrate education. In Crawfordville, the "principal local Negro leader," according to the newspapers, was Calvin Turner, a black teacher in Crawfordville who was one of four whose contracts were not renewed by the Taliaferro County Board of Education. In fact, Mr. Turner was the principal of the black high school, Murden High. And it was purported that the local superintendent had fired him, along with another teacher, Robert Billingsley, because "they were leaders in the local civil rights movement." In a sense Mr. Turner was akin to Dr. Tate, fired in retaliation for having the courage to protest inequality in local conditions.[19]

Whatever the root of the conflict in Crawfordville, the situation had become increasingly volatile. For help, Dr. Tate turned to Martin Luther King Jr. and the Southern Christian Leadership Conference (SCLC).

Dr. King had been one of the children about to enter Booker T. Washington High School when Mr. Harper lost his job because he advocated for salary equality for black teachers. The young Martin lived in the same neighborhood as Mr. Harper and no doubt heard, or heard about, the ringing speech Mr. Harper made at the high school commencement the year before Martin began there. "When others hate, you must respond with love," Mr. Harper explained to black youth in the early 1940s, a time when segregation remained rigid. Moreover, Martin's father had a long-standing relationship with GT&EA as one of the "key people" for the organization, and so the younger man surely had heard his father talk about GT&EA, perhaps around the King family dinner table.[20]

"When the school superintendents did not want to listen to me," Dr. Tate explained of his trips throughout Georgia trying to get local school boards to implement fairly the Civil Rights Act, "I went to see King." No one in a local southern town wanted Dr. King and the SCLC to show up, for the news media would show up as well and broadcast images of the public violation of federal laws.[21]

The *Atlanta Daily World* hinted at the relationship between Rev. King and Dr. Tate when, in an article on a meeting that included SCLC and Dr. Tate, it referred to Dr. Tate as Rev. King's "education advisor." But the paper never discussed the centrality of black educators seeking justice at the local level in Crawfordville.[22] Rather, Dr. King and SCLC were portrayed as the public face of protest.

Rev. King cut short a European trip and publicly announced he was stepping into the "deepening racial crisis at Crawfordville." Plans were made for him to address Negro leaders before speaking at a massive meeting at the Friendship Baptist Church in the small town. The press reported that 120 of Crawfordville's Negroes voted in favor of having the SCLC continue to guide the protests against inequality in their town.

Rev. King and Dr. Tate were quietly working at different ends of a common battle. In a private meeting several weeks into October, Dr. Tate was among the Atlanta leaders meeting with SCLC staff at the SCLC's headquarters at 334 Auburn Avenue. And while Rev. King and Hosea Williams were discussing the situation there in terms of the federal government's failure to carry out court-ordered civil rights legislation, as well as the extended issues of food stamps, evictions, foreclosures, and police brutality, Dr. Tate filed an open letter to the superintendent in his role as executive secretary of GT&EA, chastising the state for the educational crisis.[23] And GT&EA, along with other members of the black community, addressed the problem via litigation.

Unable to come up with a mutually acceptable conclusion that fairly implemented the Civil Rights Act, Negroes in the county filed suit charging "a conspiracy among white officials to violate the 1964 Civil Rights Act." The case was filed by black attorney Howard Moore on behalf of the twenty-nine Negro pupils who found the doors closed when they arrived at the white high school to which they had applied for admission. The suit demanded that Taliaferro "be forced to wipe out all pretense of obeying the 1964 Civil Rights Act and admit Negro pupils freely to its public schools." In retaliation for the black parents' legal action, however, Taliaferro County officials filed a countersuit contending that the civil rights workers were disrupting law and order. Attorney General Arthur K. Bolton asked the three federal judges to restrain the Negroes from continuing the "unlawful boycott of the Murden High School" and from "marching, demonstrating, and singing freedom songs."[24]

The attorney subsequently linked with the Negroes' suit, Attorney Donald Hollowell, was a friend of Dr. Tate's.[25] He was also GT&EA's attorney, having been retained by the organization in 1963. In Crawfordville, Attorney Hollowell worked with Attorney Moore researching the school suit. He was present at the first motion before the U.S. Fifth Circuit Court when Chief Judge Griffin Bell announced that the "rights of Negroes have been evaded and nobody wanted to do anything about it." It was also Attorney Hollowell who filed the amended motion "asking the court to force whites to stop taking Negroes off the school buses going to other counties." Moreover, he and his associate wanted the court to "stop the Taliaferro officials from barring Negros from the gymnasium, science laboratory and workshop at the formerly white school in the county."[26] This litigation effort by GT&EA worked in concert with the efforts by Dr. Davis and the NAACP to protect the teachers through litigation.

According to Dr. Tate's open letter to the state school superintendent, the Taliaferro County School situation "might have been avoided had a statewide teacher tenure law been in existence." Dr. Tate emphasized that GT&EA had for a number of years been attempting to get job protection for teachers.[27]

In May 1963, for instance, Dr. Tate had written to the state superintendent in May 1963, "I am submitting the enclosed Resolutions passed by the Georgia Teachers and Education Association at its 45th Annual Convention in April 1963. As you recall, I made reference to these Resolutions at the last State Board of Education meeting." Dr. Tate said he hoped the state board of education would use its influence to help redress the problems confronting black educators, of which teacher tenure was but one.[28] Before the events erupted in Crawfordville, Dr. Tate had believed the appeals to state officials to implement teacher tenure, and thereby protect black teachers, were making progress.[29] In August 1964, a GT&EA committee met with the Teacher Tenure Study Committee established by the Georgia General Assembly to discuss the teacher tenure bill GT&EA had worked on with Leroy Johnson, the first black elected senator since Reconstruction. Even the GEA had finally linked with GT&EA to support passage of a Georgia state senate bill on teacher tenure under the mutual belief that "educators must have job security."[30] After the bill passed in the 1964 legislative session, GT&EA made public its concern that the bill needed to be implemented "fairly and justly." The state could not allow "devious or discretionary" local administrative policies to influence decisions. The GT&EA expressed concerns as well about a state plan in which the state would pay only a maximum of $5,000 toward each teacher's salary; any amount above that "must come directly from the funds of the local school system." GT&EA had received an "avalanche of telephone calls and letters" from black educators across

Georgia about this concern. If the bill was not fully implemented, "it will not be too much to expect that many small school systems will eliminate many of their teachers thereby using funds that would be paid these teachers to supplement those who are employed. This has happened in the past and will no doubt happen in the future provided the bill is not implemented as written."[31]

Eventually the Crawfordville matter was resolved via federal courts with a victory for the town's black residents. To the dismay of other local school systems across Georgia that wanted federal money but not equality, the courts sided with black educators' concerns about federal oversight. A three-judge federal court in Augusta ordered a "frankly surprised" and reluctant state school superintendent to supervise local educational matters in Crawfordville and to make a decision by October 25 that would achieve equality for black students. Among the choices the court gave the state superintendent were to reopen the all-white Alexander Stephens Institute as an integrated school or provide for Negro children the same free transportation to outside schools that the white children were receiving.[32]

The state school superintendent, who understood the need to be aligned with the U.S. Office of Education's intent for more racial integration, contemplated his options. "We'll be handicapped directing local schools from this office," he protested, "but we'll do our best." Finally he decided to transfer forty-two of the Taliaferro Negro students to previously all-white schools in three neighboring counties that white students from Taliaferro County were already attending. One of those schools was in Union Point, in Greene County—a place prominent in Dr. Tate's memory, as Greene County was the place where he had been fired for promoting equality for Negro children.

Of course, the federal intervention in Crawfordville did not solve all the educational problems. Under GT&EA auspices, Attorneys Hollowell and Moore objected to the state school superintendent's plan, noting that it "brought no relief for some 400 other Negroes who would remain in the all Negro Murden school in Crawfordville." They were overruled, however.

A few weeks after the "quiet" transfers began, Attorney Hollowell again objected when school bus drivers required segregated seating of the black and white children being bused to neighboring counties, charging that it violated Superintendent Purcell's plan, which called for "no discrimination based upon race or color" to be practiced in any school system.

Additional faux concessions were made as the case and Crawfordville slid back into public invisibility. For example, the school board offered the gymnasium at the white school for use by the black students, whose Murden School did not have a gymnasium—"provided it is not now in use [for whites] for any purpose such as storage of furniture."[33] But such concessions did not address local violations of federal matters. While the courts and the president sided with black educators in Crawfordville, the result could not resolve the major differences Dr. Tate had with the white educators he'd mingled with in White House meetings.[34]

19

JUSTICE RESTRUCTURED IN DIXIE

At the spring annual GT&EA conference in 1965, the theme was "Free to Teach." As customary, the convention included a speaker who would address publicly the concerns association members discussed privately. In 1965, a white dean from the University of Florida spoke of the truth that being free to teach meant freedom "from certain conditions and fears." Black educators understood this included freedom from being fired because he or she took a stand for equality.

Sadly, however, the veiled references to the difficulties black educators confronted when they stood for equality were not issues their white colleagues shared, despite one white teacher being fired for reproving students who clapped when President Kennedy was shot.[1] Nationally, NEA aligned its goals with equality. But NEA state affiliates still reflected seething divisions, especially in the South.

The truth was that the white southern educators who were members of NEA were also the local leaders oppressing black education—overtly or by benign neglect. GT&EA had more than twenty years' worth of evidence about Negro teachers who had been dismissed with no official reason. Importantly, teachers most active in their communities appeared to also be the ones whose contracts were not renewed. "In the spring of 1951," Dr. Tate reminisced, drawing on his own experience, "many teachers and administrators who requested more and better materials, equipment and supplies for their schools" were the ones whose contracts were not renewed. In the wake of the mandatory higher salaries called for by the Minimum Foundation Program of Education in 1951–52, Negro teachers who held master's degrees were inexplicably dismissed as four-year college graduates were hired. To protect these black educators from their white GEA colleagues, since 1963 GT&EA had been working on a tenure law, soliciting support from the Department of Education, state senators, and state representatives.

As the Georgia delegation convened for its formal photograph for the NEA meeting in Denver in 1962, they still maintained hope that NEA would help their quest for a fair integration. *GT&EA Collection*

Dr. Tate wanted justice in Baxley, Brunswick, Crawfordville, Dallas, Hogansville, Perry, Roberta, Sandersville, Statesboro, Summerville, Watkinsville, and any of the other places he observed across the state where "white superiority" played a role in teacher dismissals.[2] All the six teachers dismissed in Crawfordville had wanted was a hearing to defend themselves from the charges against them.[3]

Local black and white educators were split over salary equality as well. Despite public perceptions that salaries between black and white teachers had been equalized as a result of the NAACP and black educators' legal campaigns in the 1940s, salary inequality had simply become a local problem. White teachers received salary supplements to maintain higher salaries in some local schools districts; black teachers did not. The GT&EA called attention to these matters at the State Board of Education meeting and Claude Purcell, state school superintendent, had publicly warned superintendents of the need to conform to the criteria outlined by the assistant attorney general. Nonetheless, salary inequality continued.[4]

GT&EA objected and sought the aid of its attorney. "As counsel for the Georgia Teachers and Education Association," Attorney Hollowell wrote to the chairman of the Georgia State Board of Education in October 1965, "it has come to my attention that many county superintendents have failed to complete the execution of Board of Education form A3 (Teachers Salary Payroll Form)," which required superintendents to enumerate teacher salaries. "It appears that there are school systems in this State which have a double standard of payment to Negro and white teachers; that is, that teachers of the same training are not receiving the same pay." Such an action was a breach of regulations and, therefore, illegal.[5]

Dr. Tate had already pressed the matter of local inequality with salaries with the state board for a third time in the spring of 1965, requesting that his white professional colleagues "take immediate steps to eliminate discriminatory practices in the payment of salaries based solely on race" and that other discriminatory practices be eliminated. By December 1965, after GT&EA had made its request seven times, GT&EA leaders declared it appeared increasingly clear to them "that certain local boards of education in this state do not intend to pay Negro teachers the same local salary supplement that they are paying white teachers."[6]

Whether the issue was job security, salary, or the failure to hire black personnel at the State Department or employ them in the Governor's Honors Program in the summer, the dilemma GT&EA confronted repeatedly was the same.[7] Although the state could pass laws that made Georgia appear to be abiding by federal policies, the failure to implement these laws lay at the local level. In local settings, white educators consistently made financial decisions that appealed to their white neighbors.[8]

In matters of justice for black children, GT&EA believed white educators could not always be counted on to support equality. Even when GEA supported tenure in 1964, its reasons reflected national beliefs about teacher security, not GT&EA's concerns about protecting local black teachers caught in the backlash of federal legislation.[9] White educators in GEA were responding to a white community resistant to the racial changes unfolding and the intrusion of federal mandates in local matters.

NEA found itself caught in the middle of the difficulties of its southern white members who did not live in communities that supported the more liberal views held by some of its northern and western members. By 1964, the difficulties with its black and white state organizations were increasingly contentious. At a special one-day meeting called by NEA in 1964, discussion ensued around questions of the effect in a state if NEA came up with a set plan for integration. In particular, NEA was concerned about the effect on its membership if the national body pushed hard on integration. Of course, some attendees at the meeting strongly urged NEA to take a stand for integration "as a principle." NEA needed to set up procedures for desegregation of its associations, provide funds for assisting displaced teachers, and desegregate its own officials and staff. These voices came from places like Washington and Oregon. The South had a different view.

The white Florida educational group reportedly called the idea of consolidation of the white and black educational organizations "utterly impossible." In North Carolina, cautious white leaders advised NEA that any "precipitous action" by NEA could spell defeat of their secret ballot efforts to even remove the restriction clause from their constitutions. Clear to Dan Byrd of the NAACP, who slipped unwelcomed into the NEA one-day meeting, were the tensions between the black and white NEA affiliated groups. The southern white NEA affiliates, he reported to NCOSTA members, "hate any publicity which will show their state association as giving in to any resolution, etc. calling for integration." Indeed, white southern educational associations were following the "Southern Manifesto," rejecting integration "to the letter."

Mr. Byrd, who continued to work in the NAACP to represent the job security interests of southern black educators, observed that "NEA has no intention of desegregating state teacher association[s]." Even worse, he saw the distinct possibility that the NEA national program was "geared to getting as many Negroes in the white association as possible and kill[ing] off the Negro association." To eliminate the Negro association and move Negro members into the white association would be a win/win for NEA, as it would "assure a minimum of membership loss to the NEA," Mr. Byrd hypothesized.[10]

The distinct possibility of extinction of the black educational groups fueled energy in Georgia. GT&EA had never had membership restrictions; only the white organization was in discussion about allowing black members into the local state group. Moreover, according to Superintendent Purcell, Georgia had lost more than two thousand NEA members in 1964–65. Presumably, these lost members were from Georgia's white education association, disgruntled with the policies of the national body. In contrast, from 1961 to 1963, the membership of black teachers through GT&EA increased yearly. Yet GT&EA was being questioned about its affiliate status with NEA. Such matters fueled dissent as GT&EA prepared for the 1965 NEA annual meeting.[11]

At that meeting, NEA assigned days and times for the black and white educators of Georgia to meet in their state delegations. But segregation still ruled in the South, and the black and white educational groups in Georgia were not working well together. "I am sure that you are aware of the fact that Georgia has two state associations affiliated with NEA," Dr. Tate wrote the NEA convention coordinator, noting that only one room was being held for both delegations. "I think I should say in the outset, that the Georgia Teachers and Education Association has no desire to hold a breakfast meeting or luncheon with members of the Georgia Education Association who do not desire such." He wished to be clear that no policy matters should be discussed if *all* members of both associations could not be present.[12]

Dr. Tate's letter captured the mounting tensions between the black and white educational groups. Just before the annual NEA meeting in New York in 1965, an *Atlanta Constitution* article revealed that a group of white Georgia delegates to the NEA was trying to prevent the customary election of a Negro as one of the state's two directors to NEA. GEA remained a much larger group than GT&EA. In June 1965, GEA had 27,000 members compared to 12,000 in GT&EA. At the actual convention, GEA would have nearly 150 white delegates, while GT&EA would have approximately 50. In part, the differences resulted from white educators having smaller classes, thus creating the need for more teachers, and the inclusion of the state's superintendents in GEA membership. The difference in numbers meant that if the group meeting informally decided to elect two white directors, the GT&EA would have little voting leverage.[13]

The efforts in 1965 of white educators in Georgia to preserve segregation and racial superiority in the NEA rankled black educators, who had learned early in their association with NEA to distrust the educators from their own state. While GEA had a history of paternalism toward GT&EA, dating from the days of Mr. Harper and Dr. Bond, it apparently rejected shared power.[14] Dr. Tate, in particular, recalled the 1957 difficulties about a second director, when he had been put up for the post but not seated.[15]

Now that issue was resurfacing as both the black and white delegations prepared for the July 1965 meeting. According to the news accounts, the executive director of the GEA, Frank Hughes, "was one of the leaders in pushing for the election of two white directors" at a convention whose theme was "Education for World Responsibility." Quietly, some blacks said GT&EA was getting too much publicity, exhibiting too much power in Georgia to be left unchecked. They concluded this was the reason the GEA tried to reassert its dominance by insisting on two white directors.[16]

Of course, not all of the GEA members agreed with the president's position. Some whites in GEA believed the "racialized" position the president was taking disrupted the "gentlemen's agreement" that after 1957 had allowed both the black and white educational groups to have a director.[17] But any effort to dismiss black national representation on the NEA board in the wake of the Civil Rights Act raised questions about whether black and white educators in Georgia could lay to rest racial issues.

The accounts in the black newspaper about problems between the black and white educators underscored the unspoken problem surrounding the number of directors: "The controversy, apparently being waged so quietly under the dignity and conservative name of education, is based on the age old attempt of Southern whites to hold on to their traditional strongholds." Consistent with NEA mandates, GEA could remove membership restrictions. However, as the GEA president's failed grasp for power at the 1965 convention revealed, GEA seemed unwilling to change long-standing traditions of racial superiority.[18]

The newest NCOSTA member, Mr. Palmer of North Carolina, challenged the head of NEA before the annual meeting in 1965. He was particularly direct in detailing for him the reports of discrimination since the implementation of Title VI of the Civil Rights Act of 1964, which concerned GT&EA and other southern black educational associations.

"SIR," Mr. E.B. Palmer wrote in a telefax in all capital letters, "WE CALL UPON YOUR OFFICE TO ASSIST US WITH THE PROBLEM OF TEACHER DISMISSALS IN NORTH CAROLINA." In the four subsequent pages, Mr. Palmer described numerous examples of dismissals. One group just received no contracts at all, he explained. "This group reports that, until the assignments could be determined from the 'freedom of choice' reports, no definite assignment of teachers could be determined." In other words, the new Civil Rights Act was being finagled to deny equal protection to black teachers.

Mr. Palmer wanted the executive secretary of NEA to know that the black educational association in North Carolina had already made inquiry with the attorney general of the United States and the attorney general in North Carolina as to whether the practices he was documenting were in violation of the Civil Rights Act. The U.S. attorney general's office had sent an FBI agent to investigate some of the twenty-seven problem areas in the state, inclusive of a small rural area in the Piedmont that housed Caswell County Training School. What, Mr. Palmer wished to know, would be NEA's interpretation of his concerns and how could NEA lend support?[19]

In June 1965, Richard Kennan, the new executive secretary of NEA, scrambled to respond to complaints from its black associations about teacher dismissals. He confirmed to Mr. Palmer that the Civil Rights Act of 1964 must apply to teachers as well as to students. Indeed, NEA's DuShane Defense Fund was already involved in a case supported by the ATA and the black Virginia Teachers Association to prove that the dismissal of the teacher plaintiffs was a clear violation of the Fourteenth Amendment. He answered Mr. Palmer's query about the suitability of retaining white teachers with certificates lower than Class A while firing Negro teachers with Class A by assuring him that the NEA held a well-known position that the best-qualified teachers—without regard to race, color, creed, or national origin—should be employed.

The executive secretary of NEA wavered on some matters, such as whether school consolidation to generate school integration was necessarily implicated in teacher dismissals, but did affirm that the United States Office of Education should be held responsible "for seeing that the various communities are not short-changed educationally by vindictive local school officials acting under the guise of compliance with the U.S. Commissioner's guidelines." Other agencies should be responsible as well, such as the U.S. Civil Rights Commission, state boards of education, local boards of education, and the U.S. Justice Department's Community Relations Service, established as part of Title X of the 1964 Civil Rights Act. But NEA had a role to play also.

"It is the duty of the profession to protect the rights of teachers in the courts or in the spotlight of public conscience," wrote Mr. Kennan. The NEA, as well as the black educational organization in North Carolina, had an "obligation" to be sure teachers were dealt with justly and not dismissed for matters unrelated to teaching capacity. He concluded by suggesting that a "small but articulate committee of executive secretaries, and presidents of the state associations concerned" should come to Washington at the earliest possible moment to confer with officials of the U.S. Department of Health, Education, and Welfare (HEW), the U.S. Office of Education, the Civil Rights Commission, the Attorney General, the Community Relations Service, the Education Committees of the House and the Senate, other key congressional leaders, and, if possible, the vice president. Included in this list was the NEA cabinet.

The president and executive secretaries of organizations affected could "rest assured" the NEA would help protect the teachers in court, he said. NEA had hired Samuel Ethridge, a black man, as assistant secretary for field studies. The organization was protecting black teachers who were fired by other NEA members and "as a last resort" helping relocate displaced teachers.[20]

In terms of language and finances, NEA appeared to be doing its part to protect individual black teachers and to make sure it was planning for the desegregation of its segregated southern affiliates. But black educators interpreted NEA as refusing to take a stand against its white southern members who were creating the problems it said it would fight to solve.

These concerns shrouded the 1965 meeting in New York. As a disgruntled Dr. Tate maneuvered between local and national white educators, his memories of the ways NEA could side with white educators were still fresh. The question was how NEA would translate this language into practice in a southern state when the confrontations between black and white educators played out in tangible disagreements involving schools. He would soon find out.

NEA steered clear of the Crawfordville crisis as schools opened in the fall of 1965. In earlier communications and phone conversations with Dr. Tate, Richard Barnes Kennan, the new executive secretary of NEA, indicated he had someone to coordinate a study of the Crawfordville situation. His commitment came after Dr. Tate got in touch with the NEA office early in the crisis asking for intervention.

To Dr. Tate's consternation, his request for NEA engagement in the Crawfordville crisis inspired some question in the NEA office as to whether his communication was an official request from GT&EA. While acknowledging that individuals might occasionally contact NEA for personal reasons, Dr. Tate noted: "It so happens that the Constitution of our Association specifies that the Executive Secretary when writing a letter of the nature of the one that I wrote must do such in keeping with policies of the Association. Any letter received from the Executive Secretary represents the Association's official position."[21]

Dr. Tate and NEA also had different ideas about how the intervention in Crawfordville should occur. NEA assumed the position that it would investigate without the aid of GT&EA. "Until you telephoned," Dr. Kennan explained, "I had not realized that you wanted this to be a cooperative study with your association." Certainly, though, he was confident that they could work out arrangements for a joint study.[22]

However, no study involving the two organizations was done. In early October, the president of NEA, Richard D. Batchelder of Newton, Massachusetts, visited Crawfordville to "take a first hand look at the situation there as a possible prelude to NEA action."[23] The president toured the racially troubled community where black teachers who sought improved facilities for their students were fired.[24]

From one of the Georgia NEA directors, he could get a hint of what white educators might have been saying about the matter. The state school superintendent, who was in charge of resolving the crisis, had once said publicly that "prolonging segregation might not have been the only reason for the closing of the white school." After all, the school served only fifty-five children in the top four grades, and he knew county officials had been considering closing the white high school anyway because it was so small.[25] In other words, factors other than race could explain the actions of the school officials. GT&EA had a different perspective on events. Fundamentally, from their point of view, the NEA was being asked to examine the outcome of some NEA members firing other NEA members.

After his visit, the president of NEA decided not to intervene. NEA would wait until the court ruled, he concluded. In private correspondence with Dr. Tate, an associate legal counsel for NEA communicated that the NEA Professional Rights and Responsibilities Commission had considered the Crawfordville situation "at length." He said the president had given "a lengthy and thorough presentation of the entire situation" and that, based on the president's assessment and his own recommendation, an investigation would not be productive.[26] One of the "greatest values" of the investigative reports published by the commission in past years was the influence they had on public relations. "When citizens in a community or a state were acquainted with the facts about a situation they have usually taken such actions as were necessary to rectify or remedy the problems." In contrast, Crawfordville had already received so much national attention that "the Commission's reporting function appears to have already been served." The president conveyed the "depth of feeling for all involved in the situation" and reiterated the DuShane Defense Fund's concrete commitment to legal assistance.[27]

Crawfordville had showed GT&EA that NEA would not publicly reprimand the white educators in Georgia who were members of GEA. In the same month when the conflict in Crawfordville was at its height, the national NEA's press release proclaimed that "the National Education Association has offered full backing to the National Congress of Parents and Teachers in its continuing battle with rightist groups." According to the account, Richard D. Batchelder and William G. Carr wrote the president of the PTA: "The nefarious attacks currently being made on the National Congress of Parents and Teachers through propaganda on telephone recordings has shocked the nation. The strategy of your enemies is reminiscent of the smear and the big lie technique used so effectively by Hitler, Stalin, and other notorious enemies of freedom."[28] Apparently, NEA did not feel so passionately about Crawfordville.

Despite questions about NEA's support for local black education, black educators believed they could finally count on the federal government for assistance in securing fair play in local settings. GT&EA appealed to President Johnson to stand firm in demanding accountability for local actions. They wanted the president to present the requirement for desegregation in terms so simple and clear that there would be no question about what needed to be done.[29] The U.S. Department of Education needed to "acquaint all school officials with the fact that integration should not mean 'elimination,' 'tokenism,' nor a one-way stream," GT&EA explained. "The people of America are looking to you, Mr. President, for the administration of justice and the eradication of injustices." GT&EA hoped fervently that the president would not "ease the announced requirement" and thus embolden those who "do not wish, nor intend, to comply." They urged the president to "stand firm" in federal requirements for desegregation.[30]

Because of Johnson's policies, the number of Negro students tripled in one year in the Deep South as a result of the Civil Rights Act, rising to

217,000, or 7.5 percent of the total number of students, up from 2.6 percent in 1964. The federal government appeared to be holding its stand with conviction: Vice President Hubert Humphrey warned that "schools could either comply with desegregation and continue to receive federal funds or fail to comply with the regulations (thus forfeiting the money) and still be forced to desegregate."[31]

Grateful for the federal commitment, GT&EA collected data that could be used to force compliance. Like in Crawfordville, in numerous other local areas compliance was feigned, carefully crafted to make it appear desegregation was in effect when in fact segregation was being carefully observed. It compiled a two-page questionnaire, "Pertinent Information About Georgia Schools," and distributed it through all the regions. The form queried local principals: Did they have a library? A gymnasium? Playground equipment? Did they have janitors, secretaries, and clerical workers? Did they receive local salary supplements? Did they get adequate supplies? Did they have buses—new ones, not secondhand ones?[32]

GT&EA wanted information on whether black and white teachers were meeting together locally, whether black children applying for transfers had been denied, and whether white students were coming to their schools. With only 15.2 percent of Negro pupils enrolled in mixed schools in the fall of 1965, black children and black schools still needed oversight. "Please furnish us the following information," Dr. Tate requested in one of the surveys, because they needed it for the U.S. Department of Health, Education, and Welfare.[33]

GT&EA still believed in September 1965 that if they could demonstrate, with data, that local inequalities still existed, the federal government would address the inequalities. The Georgia State Board of Education had communicated to local superintendents the expectation that they should file desegregation plans in order to receive federal funds. To fail to do so would make the system "liable under the *Brown* case and other decisions of the courts and Title IV of the Civil Rights Act, requiring desegregation of all public school systems."[34] GT&EA planned to use its information to be sure that the plans were not merely filed, as Crawfordville had done, but created with full equality in mind and plans for implementation. "Any local board of education who fails to comply with this simple request," GT&EA announced when the Crawfordville demonstrations were at their height, "will leave us no alternative than to request the Federal

Government to curtail the payment of federal funds to the systems that continue to discriminate."[35]

If the NEA was unwilling to dislodge local discrimination based on race, the federal government would. GT&EA firmly believed the United States was finally willing to make a real commitment to the education of black children.

20

AS FREEDOM TURNS

Harold Howe II, newly appointed by President Johnson in December 1965 as U.S. commissioner of education, believed it was his duty to enforce locally the mandates of the Civil Rights Act. Mr. Howe, jovially called "Doc" even though he never completed a doctorate, was a southerner who was a former superintendent, principal, and teacher. By the time his predecessor, Francis Keppel, introduced him at a news conference as the new commissioner overseeing school desegregation in the South, Mr. Howe had spent several years working in North Carolina to desegregate university faculty. Earlier in December, he had come to Washington to talk with the secretary of health, education, and welfare, John Gardner, and then had been whisked over to the White House to meet with Lyndon Johnson. By the time he left, the president had conferred on this man a position that aligned the new commissioner's office with the hopes of black educators across the South.[1]

With "great pleasure," former commissioner Keppel introduced Mr. Howe to the nation. "Doc," he proclaimed, "it's yours!" With these words, Mr. Keppel ushered himself out of the office after his short stint as assistant secretary of HEW.

Mr. Keppel knew well the challenges in being the commissioner of education. He had served as dean in the Harvard Graduate School of Education since 1948.[2] Surprising many, Mr. Keppel had given up his comfortable job in Cambridge to accept the "scut job with low standing and low reputation" as commissioner of education in 1962, one and a half years into the Kennedy administration. His own wife thought he was crazy since, at best, the Office of Education was viewed as a place to "collect statistics and crank out a few formulas." Mr. Keppel had increased the cachet of the appointment by using his varied philanthropic and political connections to have President Kennedy present when he was sworn into office.

But the public visibility Mr. Keppel sought for the office did not diminish the challenges the office faced. For one thing, Mr. Keppel's staff was dominated by a group of people born within fifty to a hundred miles of the Mason-Dixon line, mostly on the southern side of the line, and they had made their southern position clear to the new commissioner. Civil rights "was absolutely unconnected with education," they let Mr. Keppel know immediately, and he needed to stay out of it. Of course, Mr. Keppel did not share such details publicly as he turned the office over to Mr. Howe, exited the stage, and returned to a quieter life in Cambridge.[3]

The reporters present followed up with a series of questions. "When they interviewed you for the job, what did they tell you they were looking for?" one reporter asked.

"They told me they were looking for me," Doc responded lightly.

What should the public want and expect from the Office of Education? What kind of role would the federal government and this office assume? Who would judge whether a school system was bad?

Doc Howe answered all the questions patiently. His duty was to enforce the provisions that flowed from the Civil Rights Act. He applauded the progress made in the South and believed more progress would occur because of a genuine desire to desegregate, but understood he would probably have to "move in vigorous directions" in working with the compliance provisions. Some of the progress the South would make would flow "from pressures which may have to be created in Washington."

Would the White House back him? Doc Howe hoped so. President Johnson had assured him of his support.[4]

A few months later in Atlanta, in an address before the Georgia Vocational Association, the new commissioner reiterated his hopes that local school systems would comply with the desegregation mandates linked to receiving federal money. If Massachusetts had given birth to free public schools, he said, Georgia had given birth to vocational education. Georgia had taken the lead in passing the Morrill Acts. He did not mention that Georgia also accepted federal money for vocational education while denying equal funding to black students, thus helping to spur the decades of protest during which first Dr. Du Bois and Mr. Hunt and then Dr. Bond and Mr. Harper and a host of others asked the federal government to demand fair accountability within the states. As part of his commendations, Doc Howe commended the state for generating "a national impetus [for vocational education] which has served us well ever since."

His speech appealed to the South's desire to maintain local control even if they needed to adhere to federal guidelines. He wanted southerners to see that state and local agencies could still maintain control, despite federal laws. The new federal laws represented a "partnership in education among the local, State, and Federal governments," he explained. The federal government could provide the leadership and information, but every community would decide how to achieve the national objectives. "Uncle Sam needs you. And he needs you not in Washington, but right here, and right now."[5] The audience applauded his efforts.

They were great words, but not words that would work. In three years, Congress had passed twenty-four education bills. Education had become big business. Across the country, 25,000 public school districts employed 1.7 million teachers to educate 54 million children. Approximately $40 billion annually maintained the education enterprise, one that was bigger than at any point in the previous two centuries in the country. During this period, the Office of Education's budget skyrocketed from $160 million in 1956 to $3 billion in early 1966. Now that the Office of Education had almost twenty times as much money to distribute, southerners wanted their share.[6] So despite their polite applause at the end of Mr. Howe's speech, they adhered to their belief that there should be no federal dictates about how they should expend federal money—especially with regard to race.

Commissioner Howe continued to try to reason with southern leaders. Later in 1966 in Miami Beach at the annual meeting of the Southern Association of Colleges and Secondary Schools, he championed the South's new interest in education. He demonstrated his awareness that, compared to other areas of the country, the South historically had lower teacher salaries, larger classes, per pupil expenditures well below the national average, and colleges with more financial handicaps. He understood the South needed resources for education that were greater than it could "reasonably spare now." He applauded the strength of the South and encouraged it to draw upon every resource it could muster in its new efforts to address education. Then he tried to reason with attendees about federal guidelines.

Among other things, their strength should be applied to "taking a thoughtful, reasoned approach to the issue of school desegregation." He emphasized that 85 percent of Negro children were still attending all-Negro schools with all-Negro teachers in 1966; in some areas, the numbers were closer to 95 percent. School desegregation, he explained, was a matter of law and individual rights but also a way to move beyond the "sense of separateness" in both the North and the South.

Commissioner Howe appealed to the need for federal oversight in an era where growing numbers of private schools were cropping up across the southern landscape. "We do not consider the deferment or withholding of funds a triumph of [the federal government over] the local school system or educational institution," he explained. In fact, he and his office had been "considerably heartened by the amount of progress we have had in avoiding such terminations of Federal aid."

He understood the "difficult social and political environment" in which southern educators worked. "It is indeed a heavy responsibility," he conceded, "but it is also a great opportunity." The dual educational system had "produced a backlog of educational problems for the South." He hoped the Southern Association of Colleges and Secondary Schools would help provide "forthright expression" for southern schools "when individual institutions cannot speak for themselves because of localized pressures."

The Southern Association of Colleges and Secondary Schools had itself desegregated by this time. During the years when they had been excluded as members of the Southern Association, black educators had established their own Association of Colleges and Secondary Schools to help black schools meet the goals of accreditation, but had voluntarily dismantled their parallel organization in 1965 and allowed themselves to be absorbed into the Southern Association. These black colleagues were scattered throughout the audience listening to Doc Howe that day. But numerically, they were powerless to convince their white educational colleagues to heed his appeals that they help the federal government with southern school desegregation. Despite Commissioner Howe's talk, the Southern Association gave no evidence it could be counted on to assuage southern anger against federal restrictions being imposed on southern states receiving federal money.

His efforts at appeasement did not stop the hate letters. He had only been in office a short time before a complaint came from North Carolina saying he was trying to "destroy or hamper the schools . . . on the so-called guidelines set up by your department regarding the racial imbalances in the schools." Howe was from the North. Didn't he realize that after "nearly a hundred years of 'supposing' to be completely mixed, you Yankees are not nearly 'mixed' as you want us to be after such a short time of integrating the schools throughout the nation by the new Negro law?" People in Washington seemed to run absolutely wild, the letter said. Howe needed to remember that more could be accomplished by a little patience than by "listening to such burr heads as Martin Luther King and his kind." It seemed to the average person "that Negroes are doing all the instructing in Washington." They were even "telling the President what to do and he's doing it."[7]

North Carolina was not alone in spewing anger against Commissioner Howe and those attempting to ensure equality in education. From Colorado: Negroes had their civil rights; now they needed to become civilized to "clean their filthy bodies and minds, clean up their own society, improve their character, get rid of their criminals, pimps, whores, dope peddlers and their pack-rat way of life and then and then only will they be welcome by the Caucasian race." From Louisiana: Why was Commissioner Howe "ignoring the constructive criticism and just continuing to PUSH THE STINKING, FILTHY NIGGERS INTO OUR FINE SCHOOLS—regardless of whether they are diseased, mentally incompetent, sex maniacs, or even criminally inclined?" He was an "IDIOTIC DESPOT" who did not even understand education.

The writers of the letters claimed to understand education. Teachers were "avoiding disciplinary action on the sassy, impudent, and insulting nigger pupils" because they were "afraid that the damn federal government will (unjustly) accuse them of 'harassing' the niggers and cause them to lose their jobs." The standards had been lowered in schools. Blacks could not meet the academic requirements "of our white schools." Teachers were "*giving* good grades to the niggers, even though their class-room performance justifies a failing grade," and they were doing this because they were afraid of the federal government accusing them of showing preference to white students. A retired schoolteacher from New York agreed: "Our ghetto schools are not inferior; the pupils are. How can a teacher explain a lesson to students who are disrespectful, arrogant, disinterested in learning?"[8]

The writers personalized the attacks, accusing Commissioner Howe of being in it for "personal gain." They said he was "about the lowest type of humanity imaginable, a renegade white man, a New Englander, a psalm singing hypocrite, treacherous, vindictive, cowardly and degenerate." A St. Louis editorial critiqued Mr. Howe as being "hell-bent" on stirring up a grand mix, as long as his own child—going to a mixed school in Connecticut rather than a school with higher percentages of integration in Washington—did not have to be involved. An Atlanta newspaper headline featured the details of school decisions regarding his son in capital letters:

"EDUCATION CZAR HAROLD HOWE 'BUSES' HIS SON." How dare he deny freedom of choice to other parents who could not afford to pay $2,750 a year but wanted their youngsters to go to public schools "in their own neighborhoods, under local administration?" He should practice what he preached, wrote an angry citizen who sent him a copy of the Atlanta article.[9]

The letters made it clear they did not want "dictation from a nut like [him]." As far as these objectors were concerned, "to hell with the Supreme Court . . . and you." In fact, overt rejection of Commissioner Howe's efforts to oversee the use of federal funds in local schools to create equality generated applause from around the country.[10]

If Commissioner Howe felt the hatred spewing into his Washington office, GT&EA felt it up close, faced with white educators' solidarity in an attempt to preserve white control. Georgia needed the federal funds HEW had said would not be available after June 30, 1965, for systems that had not desegregated, and GT&EA resolved at its annual meeting in April 1965 to call upon the State Board of Education and all local superintendents to file plans for desegregation.[11]

At their annual meeting in April 1966, after Mr. Howe's appointment, GT&EA applauded HEW for issuing guidelines designed to bring about more pupil and faculty desegregation in the 1966–67 school year. At a breakfast meeting the day after the guidelines were issued, Mr. Howe had said "the guidelines meant what they say" and they would be "strictly enforced." As far as GT&EA was concerned, Commissioner Howe's strong words represented the progress they sought. They appreciated HEW's "keen perceptions into the desegregation program" and its "sincerity in structuring guidelines."[12]

GT&EA also continued to alert federal and state leaders to the monetary inequalities in specific locales within Georgia. The money designed to upgrade the educational level of pupils was being "appropriated to and expended by the same group of persons who [had] previously expended and controlled funds and therefore the educational destiny and degradation of minority group pupils." State and local boards of education were using that money to perpetuate the "same practices and patterns that [had] been followed in prior years."[13]

Specifically, it blasted the implementation of Title I of the ESEA, which was to provide funding to local educational agencies to support the education of children from low-income families. GT&EA reported some local

Georgia school systems refusing to take advantage of the grants available under Title I, thus limiting educational opportunities, and other systems taking the grants but having "no real educational purpose in mind." GT&EA resolutions denounced the latter, noting that systems were appointing coordinators for the program "who either don't know what their job is, don't care what it is, or have little interest in it." These appointees spent no time studying the needs of the culturally deprived or conferring with the professionally educated personnel who could help solve the problems. Instead, the money was being expended on portable classrooms, supplies and equipment, or other physical materials.

In one of his regular meetings before the State Board of Education, Dr. Tate represented these concerns to the state school superintendent and requested that the state assume responsibility for making an objective appraisal of the funds received to see if those monies were being used in ways "designed to upgrade the educational level of all culturally deprived pupils." The GT&EA strongly objected to the funds being used for any other purpose. In fact, shouldn't the federal government devise plans to be sure the funds were used properly in local settings?[14]

NCOSTA weighed in on the problem of federal language versus local implementation as well, especially since the problems GT&EA articulated existed in the other southern states as well. After Dr. Tate attended the GT&EA annual conference in April, where the objections to federal policy had been written into resolutions and circulated, he traveled to Louisiana to present a banquet speech for black administrators. He was very "favorably received," according to J.K. Haynes, the executive secretary of the Louisiana Education Association and also president of NCOSTA. But, as Mr. Haynes explained in his next communication, the real issue was to figure out how NCOSTA could quickly meet and discuss the tremendous issues confronting them all. The matters were urgent, the NCOSTA president explained as he sought a site for the meeting.[15] Dr. Tate heeded the call for a meeting, and a press release expressing the collective opinion of black educators across the South followed shortly.

"The executive secretaries of black educators in 11 southern states, representing 75,000 teachers, sent identical telegrams to President Johnson, Secretary John Gardner of HEW and Commissioner Howe to maintain the 1966 guidelines," the NCOSTA press release proclaimed. The executive secretaries pledged full support of school and faculty desegregation, noting that school desegregation could pave the way for community progress if state and local school officials faced up to the existing problems and moved forward rapidly toward full desegregation. But the federal government needed to stand firm. The desegregation of schools for the next twenty-five years would be "dependent upon firm directions and protective guidelines." Drawing on their collective experiences of resistance, the eleven executive secretaries also reiterated to federal officials that local educational officials needed to "accept the federal guidelines" and needed to "cease and desist in tactics of delay, evasion or procrastination in school desegregation."[16]

NCOSTA zeroed in on the guidelines mandating faculty desegregation along with student desegregation. The school environment could not be one-sided in its representation of power. Indeed, faculty desegregation was critical if all students were to be provided the experiences they needed for living in an integrated society. Moreover, *all* teachers' organizations needed to be merged. NCOSTA hoped the upcoming NEA conference in Miami would merge the black ATA with NEA and that the new united group would "plan for and insist upon full desegregation of all teacher units in the United States."[17]

GT&EA and NCOSTA's hopes certainly did not reflect the hopes of white educators in GEA. Caught up in the conflict between a national movement to champion equality for black children, the southern states' needs for federal money for white children, and the objection of many in white communities to racial desegregation, GEA took a contradictory path.[18]

At the GEA's ninety-ninth annual meeting in March 1966 at the Marriott Motor Hotel, the organization voted "overwhelmingly"—according to the newspaper—to remove racial restrictions from membership requirements. The actual vote was 862 to 176, sufficient for the required two-thirds majority needed to pass the removal of the racial restriction clause imposed by NEA but not so much unity as to drown out the faint cries of "No" from some of the 1,038 delegates during the verbal vote. On the surface, the organization appeared aligned with the national tenor in favor of desegregation, supported both by its professional organization, the NEA, and by the federal government. The outgoing president was proud of the move, proclaiming himself to have worked on this goal all year.[19]

But the new GEA president, sworn in the day after the vote was taken, urged the white teachers "to adopt Robert E. Lee as their 'symbol of courage.'" He reminded them that after General Lee lost the battle for his cause, he was still as great a leader to the people of the South as he had been before the war. The new president talked about the need for white educators to roll up their sleeves and create "workable solutions for this day." By this he meant accommodating NEA by removing racial restrictions from GEA membership but also pushing back at a federal government that seemed to want to require quotas that would force their black colleagues not only into their organization but into their schools. The demand for faculty desegregation was based on the "false distinctions we seek to erase," the GEA's resolution on the matter proclaimed. Prejudice could not be "neutralized by the expedient of preferential practices," the group explained as it denounced the "forced integration of faculties in a manner that set established quotas." To accept GT&EA teachers in their schools—it implied without saying so directly—restricted their freedom of choice, violated the democratic process, and arbitrarily aligned federal guidelines about schools with the Democratic Party's platform of 1964. In a veiled threat, the GEA resolutions reminded Georgians seeking public office that the twenty-nine thousand members they represented had "not yet endorsed any candidate for any public office."

And even the dropping of the membership restriction should not create false expectations of a merger of the two teacher groups. GEA leaders explained that dropping the clause did not mean there would be "instant integration." New Negro members might join through local units, they speculated, and maybe a few would come to the one hundredth convention. But a merger of the group with the nine-thousand-member GT&EA group was "unlikely anytime soon."[20]

In its efforts to drop membership restrictions based on race, GEA sought to avoid a furor like that in Mississippi and Louisiana, where state organizations of whites refused to remove clauses barring black members. However, Dr. Tate quickly made public the GEA's lack of full commitment to equality. While the press reported GEA's efforts toward integration, Dr. Tate's press release congratulated the GEA on "doing in 1966 what it should have done in 1867."[21] A few days later, he was more direct. Not only was the action "long overdue," but GEA had removed the restriction "in order to save its image," he chided. "It fact, it seems to be slightly respectable now to have three or four Negroes around as a token show." GT&EA members were not so sure they even wanted to belong to GEA, he said.

In GT&EA meetings Dr. Tate had a lot more to say, and he fully embraced the style and purpose of the executive secretary role he remembered from the days of Mr. Harper. At the GT&EA convention in 1966,

Dr. Tate outlined the ways he had sought to implement the program put in place by the Representative Assembly and the Board of Directors. And he offered his usual unequivocally direct assessment of the local, state, and national scenes as they related to black children and black educators. Drawing on biblical analogies, Dr. Tate said that God had created man last, and He had surely done so with the expectation that man would be able to enjoy all of the creation that had been put in place for him. But man also needed to see the realities in front of him. And Dr. Tate's major concern was that the black educators in his audience that evening needed to see matters confronting them.

Preceding generations of black educators had made possible the current possibilities for desegregation. They were the ones who had had to "hassle and fight" to obtain the benefits for Negro children that local and state boards of education provided white children. "While the boards of education paid the utility bills for those attending schools for whites, the Negro teachers, parents, and pupils were holding fish fries, raffling cakes, and selling soda pops or colored sweetened water in order to pay their utility bills." Negro schools did not have janitors; the children did not have buses or much else needed for education; and Negro teachers did not have a fair salary until GT&EA challenged the inequality in court in 1948 and won. Could the audience *see*?

Gross inequalities remained, and GT&EA was still in the business of investigating those inequalities. Despite the salary case in 1948, and multiple visits to the records division of the State Department of Education by a GT&EA committee beginning in September 1965, and a request from the GT&EA attorney, school superintendents failed to submit the salary requisition forms that would show salary inequality. In fact, in September only one system out of 103 had submitted the forms; in November, when the committee revisited the matter, the forms were still incomplete. In December, while most GT&EA members enjoyed Christmas holidays, the committee spent two days poring over records to prove the suspected violations of state law. The results were clear. In many locales across Georgia, salary discrimination quietly continued. In one setting, the white principal's annual salary was $2,543.16 more than the Negro principal's. Dr. Tate and the committee met with the State Department of Education and HEW to remedy the salary differentials and bring about a solution. Negro teachers, he projected, had lost more than $20 million over a forty-year period because of local southern practices.

But GT&EA had a lot left to do. Referring to a long list, Dr. Tate said they needed to ensure representation on all policymaking bodies, get Negro students into the Governor's Honors Program, get Negroes on the State Board of Regents, secure enforcement of the state sick leave policy, provide housing for retired teachers, and get Negroes employed in the State Department of Education. They needed a real democracy that represented all the races, not just the white race, and they needed a state school superintendent willing to "remedy and correct some of the educational ills of the past, rather than one who will continue to aid those who wish to circumvent policy and law." And that was just part of the problem.

"Approximately two weeks ago, the [GEA] after 99 years, decided to remove from its constitution a racial restriction clause. . . . We had previously told you that this association would remove the racial restriction clause," he explained, "not because they wanted Negroes to join but because they wanted to gain a pseudo-positive image and because it wanted your $10.00." But the GEA did not "see fit to establish plans whereby both associations may come together to form a new one." In fact, "on the same day that the racial restriction clause was dropped, that same association voted overwhelmingly to oppose the new guidelines to desegregate faculties."

The members of the GT&EA needed to see, he said, what the GEA really wanted. "If it wants anything for you at all, [it] is for you to lose the control, direction, and influence which your state organization now has." It did not want integration. GT&EA was already integrated, having never had a restriction clause and always having had some white members. "What you must really see is that there are those who do not want you to have influence, do not want you to speak out, do not want you to lead. If they wanted you to lead, they would be willing to negotiate a plan for merging." Instead, almost every day he heard of how GEA representatives went directly to the presidents of GT&EA's departments and affiliates saying the local units should get together. They wanted the presidents, the counselors, the principals, the classroom teachers, the science and math group, and the Jeanes curriculum directors group absorbed into their departments. But the point was not absorption by GEA, Dr. Tate emphasized; the point was a real merger. He was unconvinced that half a loaf—that is, simply being incorporated into the white group, without having a real say in the organization—was better than no loaf at all.[22]

"I again say to you that what you must finally see is that efforts are being made by persons who are in power and who have always been in power to limit and curtail your influence, direction and control." When talk occurred about coming together or merging, the GEA objected to assurances that Negroes would be represented. To insist on representation would not be democratic, GT&EA was always told. And yet the results in Crawfordville had told the story. "In this system, they presently have no white pupils, nor any white teachers; but the white superintendent and the white board of education continue to hang on" to being the controlling body for Negro education.

"When I look around and see an all-white Board of Education, an all-white Welfare Board and practically all other boards that have all-white members, despite the fact that one-third of our citizens are Negroes, I cannot help but know that it is not full representation and full democracy which those in power want to maintain, but full control." He urged his listeners to look around and see for themselves. Every child deserved the same opportunities and privileges as other children if the American dream was to be accomplished. "God wants you to see," he ended. "Can you see?"[23] He was rewarded with loud applause.

The *Atlanta Daily World*, a black newspaper under managing editor George M. Coleman, also weighed in on the inequalities in school desegregation.[24] While outside observers hailed the great advance of GEA in allowing minority members to join, there was no major rush among black educators to become members. Mr. Coleman quoted Dr. Tate's concern regarding giving up everything the organization had fought for to face an uncertain future. He reported that GT&EA had followed NEA's resolution asking the associations to merge. It had written GEA in 1962 suggesting a joint meeting and repeated its request twice since 1962, but it had never gotten an official response from GEA. As recently as January 1965, GT&EA had requested meetings to set up joint action toward a merger and had suggested topics for discussion, but as of June 1966 no formal reply had been received. Even meetings so that the two organizational leaders could meet each other had come at the request of GT&EA. In 1962 and 1963, the meetings were held, and the groups functioned harmoniously at NEA. But when GT&EA did not ask in 1964, it received no formal invitation from GEA.[25]

The editor agreed with GT&EA that GEA needed to take the first steps in 1966, even though he recognized that it would be hard after ninety-nine years to shift from "wrong to right." He understood GEA had voted to "save face," and it was clear to him from the statements made by both the executive secretary of GT&EA and its president that the organization "was never fooled and would not call upon its members to go flocking to the so-called banner of desegregation." Such was the new state of affairs for the black man. "Once he had to fight for rights . . . Now he has to fight for survival." It was not a pretty picture when framed by "white logic." If no one protested, desegregation would become one where "the Negro will simply switch to a well treated but unimportant group, actually at the mercy of those who wish to revert much more than before." The Negro needed to keep political strength, economic power, and a top post in every organization or nothing would have been accomplished by all the efforts for desegregation. "Such is life in the United States," the editor concluded.[26]

A few weeks later, Mr. Coleman again alerted black Atlanta to the problems with desegregation in education. "Anyone can understand the suspicion of the GTEA officially to allow itself to be merged into the white organization, without guarantees that Negroes will hold high office; that the dark man will not become an unimportant part of the whole machinery, unable to protect himself and his people."[27] But most of America was not listening to a black newspaper or the protestations of a black educational organization.

While the GT&EA and GEA prepared a joint exhibit booth for the NEA meeting in Miami scheduled for June 26 to July 1, 1966, the matters of disagreement about racial equality and local control seethed beneath the surface.[28] And to make matters worse for GT&EA members hoping the federal government would remain an ally, soon the South would make sure Commissioner Howe could no longer have his meddling desegregation hands around their local necks.

21

NOT A TWO-WAY STREET

Back in 1953 Dr. Tate, with hope in his heart, had squeezed in a car with other GT&EA delegates to travel the many long miles from Atlanta to the NEA meeting in Miami. Back then he believed the NEA might provide a mechanism through which justice could be granted to black children in segregated schools in the South. In 1966, Dr. Tate joined other GT&EA delegates and headed to another NEA convention in Miami. This time questions plagued his mind. Although he had encouraged the regional directors at their last meeting to use their influence to send delegates to the meeting, he worried openly about the vexing problems confronting black education. Sometimes the burden seemed too heavy.[1]

Resolution 12 of NEA, a resolution maneuvered and championed by black educators from the South, specified that all affiliated education associations had until July 1, 1966, to comply with removal of restrictions on membership and to present a plan "to effect the complete integration of their associations."[2] As the parent body, NEA had finally determined to take the lead in integration at its 1966 meeting. Having ensured for education the federal money it had long sought, NEA determined to be on the right side of federal regulations.

NEA released press announcements touting its long history in civil rights. It called to the public's attention the fact that after the U.S. Supreme Court struck down segregation, NEA had adopted a policy of meeting only in cities that would accommodate NEA delegates equally, regardless of race. NEA did not mention the nasty fight Mr. Pitts and GT&EA waged regarding an earlier NEA-sponsored meeting where some black delegates boycotted the meeting because of the segregated accommodations NEA accepted.

Instead, NEA described its "fight for civil rights" in the February issue of its *NEA Journal* and reminded readers that blacks had long had the opportunity to speak at its sessions. It noted that Booker T. Washington had been a featured speaker in 1884 and 1904. In fact, in 1857, the same year the Supreme Court had ruled in its *Dred Scott* decision that the Negro was property, the forerunner to NEA, the National Teachers Association, had even allowed Robert Campbell, a Negro, to become a charter member. "Numerous examples," the NEA wrote, indicated the organization's efforts to be a bridge to equality. NEA also employed staff in Washington on a non-discriminatory basis, a step that preceded desegregation in the nation's capital.[3]

Dr. Tate was not so sure about NEA's commitment as he and other GT&EA delegates arrived in the huge Art Deco–style convention center where NEA prepared to stage the triumph of its merger with ATA. Black and white educational leaders shared the stage as the attendees shared a moment of celebration that, at long last, educators at Miami Beach Senior High School, just across the street from the convention center, would no longer be members of separate black and white educational associations. The two national education organizations, separate since their foundation, would merge.[4]

But Dr. Tate and some others frowned as the white leader of the Florida teachers association went to the platform in the expansive ballroom and made the "grandiose" announcement that the black and white professional associations of educators in the state of Florida had also become "one association." Delegates clapped at the announcement, and cameras flashed to record the historic moment.[5] It appeared to be a victory for integration: a southern group of white educators and a southern group of black educators within the same state were professionally united under the NEA umbrella. The Miami convention seemed to bode well for a new era of cooperation and shared educational mission. In fact, during this meeting the NEA amped up its expectations for the merging of other separate black and white state associations in the South.[6]

The largest group at NEA, the Classroom Teachers Association, issued an "ultimatum" during the convention mandating mergers of all NEA affiliates. Black educators from Georgia in the audience heard the decree. White educators from Georgia in the audience heard the decree. The Miami convention unveiled the reality that GEA and GT&EA would have to merge.[7]

Dr. Tate questioned what the mandate would mean in Georgia. As far as Dr. Tate was concerned, the black Florida educational association had been absorbed by the white association. In other words, the white organization would continue with its name and former policies and programs. It appeared to Dr. Tate that the difference was that now it would be bigger and stronger because it admitted black members. The former black association had agreed to be part of the white association but had conceded its former advocacy activities for black education in Florida. It had become part of the white organization with no planning and not a single guarantee for its constituents. Dr. Pitts, the former executive secretary of GT&EA, stated matters more bluntly: "Florida has capitulated." Dr. Tate agreed. "Florida gave up," he said with a shake of his head.[8]

When he returned to Atlanta and was interviewed for local newspaper accounts of the NEA's position on integration, Dr. Tate addressed the issue of the looming merger of GT&EA and GEA. In his estimation, the issue was not GT&EA's unwillingness to merge.[9] "We have been willing to discuss a merger for years," he was quoted as saying. The problem was that GT&EA had "difficulty in getting the white educators to meet with us," he declared. While GEA was making efforts to admit Negro members, he explained, merely admitting blacks as members without guarantees of a voice for GT&EA members would maintain the GEA organization while draining the GT&EA.

It had taken until May 1966 for GEA finally to sit down with GT&EA at the Atlanta Americana Hotel, in a meeting sponsored by NEA, to discuss faculty and school desegregation. Even getting the meeting arranged had been difficult. Dr. Tate had been surprised to hear the executive secretary of GEA announce he had already sent a letter addressed to Dr. Tate noting GEA's willingness to sit down with GT&EA; that letter did not arrive until two weeks after the meeting. And while GEA and GT&EA had indeed sat down together for the purpose of "becoming better acquainted," the sequence of events made black educators suspicious. Dr. Tate worried that the long-overdue meeting had taken place primarily so that GEA could give a good public report to NEA at the Miami meeting, not because of any commitment to the issues of desegregation.[10] Moreover, GEA's intent appeared to be a replay of the Florida model. In other words, GEA removed restriction clauses and admitted black members to meet NEA expectations. It was not interested in the policies, programs, and points of advocacy maintained by GT&EA.

The merger confronting black and white educational associations was tricky, woven as it was into the issue of the importance of an integrated society. The president of Morehouse, Benjamin Mays, captured some of the hushed tensions with which black educational associations needed to contend in his speech to Atlanta's Hungry Club on Auburn Avenue in 1966. In the speech, titled "Desegregate and Integrate: To What End?," Dr. Mays emphatically proclaimed that the goal was not "to be with white Americans." Dr. Mays did not want blacks to believe they had arrived because they could eat in fine restaurants and sleep in swanky hotels or work side by side with whites. If these were the ends, he said they weren't worth the sacrifice. The issue had always been full U.S. citizenship rights. Moreover, Dr. Mays did not want whites to bring with desegregation a false sense of the inferiority of Negroes. "We want to desegregate the South not only to free the Negro's mind, but the mind of the White South as well," he proclaimed.[11]

This fine line of embracing integration while demanding equal partnership was the treacherous one black educators had to walk. GT&EA had always provided a strong professional program for its members, both black and white, centered on supporting black children to aspire to full American citizenship and advocacy for educational discrepancies. "In no case," Dr. Tate had proclaimed emphatically in the *Herald* two years earlier, "can it legitimately be said that the association serving Negroes is inferior to the association serving whites."

As negotiations on a merger began in earnest after the Miami meeting, GT&EA was determined to maintain its power and programs, despite living in a climate where other black organizations were allowing themselves to be discounted and "absorbed" into the extant white structure.[12] Dr. Pitts visited Georgia and told the board of the plight of black educational associations in other southern states that had merged with white educational organizations. For example, Mr. McDaniel in Texas and Mr. Picott in Virginia, both executive directors of the black educators' association in their respective states, long-time members of NCOSTA, and participants in the ATA advocacy efforts that preceded NCOSTA, had lost influence and left their positions when mergers occurred in their states.

GT&EA did not like what it saw among some of its peer associations, and board members came to believe that NEA did not really support genuine integration, either nationally or locally. Dr. Pitts said he believed NEA might "bait the Negroes" by allowing a Negro to become president of the Classroom Teachers Association for one year—a development that had recently occurred. But he did not advise GT&EA to merge "without taking the proper stand as it is done." They should not go with their collective "chin out" but should be standing up like men, standing tall. GT&EA needed to effect a "dignified" merger that could carry them into the future.[13]

Both Dr. Tate and the board were fully in alignment with Dr. Pitts's views. Since the days of Dr. Bond, Dr. Tate had always striven for manhood in a society that denied him equality under the law, and for several years GT&EA had articulated and affirmed its plan to support an equitable merger. They had no objections to a "*real* integration," Dr. Tate declared. It was desirable and the law of the land. But integration should not mean "elimination, extermination, or liquidation of everything controlled by Negroes." GT&EA determined to be deliberate, serious, and thoughtful as it worked out how a merger of black and white associations would occur.[14]

Merger meetings began in earnest on October 4, 1966. Ten members from GT&EA and ten members from GEA comprised the Merger committee. The committee named the two executive secretaries co-secretaries; the two respective organizational presidents were named co-chairmen. At its first meeting, the group decided to record only "definite action"—not discussion—in the minutes. In a foreshadowing of the difficulties the committee would have, even that decision was contentious and would be revisited over the five additional meetings held between October 1966 and April 1967.[15] From their opening conversations, the two organizations clearly had different professional agendas.

GT&EA was adamant that a "merger" meant a new name and creating a new organization that would be "comparable to or better than the program presently offered the members of both associations." It rejected any plan in which one organization would be "expected to come into the other," and it wanted assurances in the new structure of people and programs that merging would really mean integration and not "outergration." To be sure GEA understood, GT&EA created a written copy of the principles it believed should govern the merger discussion and commitments on the night before the first meeting. GT&EA wanted its position clear. The charter of one organization would not be abolished without abolishing the charter of the other: they were creating a *new* organization. They would not tolerate one group soliciting membership from people who were previously members of the other association, and no local mergers should occur until the state merger was completed. The full body of membership needed to approve the merger agreements made by the committee.[16]

GEA was unwilling to address racial inequality directly. While GEA expressed to the public its commitment to salaries, classroom teacher-student ratios, a state-supported kindergarten program, and teacher retirement, it ignored the vexing dilemma of the era: race and desegregation.[17] In fact, GEA did not merely ignore race publicly, but its members overtly operated in local settings based on race. Crawfordville had been a prime example of GEA members and GT&EA members in conflict, and it was not the only problem area.

Dr. Tate regularly reported the problems with these communications to GT&EA's boards. In 1965, for example, Fitzgerald was in an uproar. The city's problems began when Negro teachers and the Negro principal were dismissed and a white principal hired. The Negro teachers were told to resign by 10:00 a.m., but before they could tender their resignations, the newspapers published an article saying that the teachers would be replaced by white teachers. The community revolted. In Waycross, six teachers were not given contracts. Where administrators were being maintained, black men were being ousted in favor of black women. From Region II of GT&EA came reports of the mistreatment of black children sent to a white school for eighth grade. In one region, Commissioner Howe was still holding firm on the refusal to accept visiting part-time teachers as substitutes for integration, but in another region school leaders dodged HEW desegregation guidelines by using only traveling and Spanish teachers to fulfill the requirements for faculty desegregation.

Milledgeville was also a problem. Milledgeville was the forgotten capital of Georgia from the 1800s, shortly after the state's founders claimed they would have no black slaves. But Georgia had turned its back on the policy as surely as local districts shunned federal policy. In the current era, Milledgeville fired black teachers and continued salary inequality. Dr. Tate reported trying to convince the superintendent to reconsider his decision in firing a black teacher and also to pay black teachers the salary supplement they paid white teachers, but his appeals had been to no avail. The only good news Dr. Tate reported to the directors was that most black teachers in the county in which Milledgeville was located had agreed to serve as plaintiffs in a test case against the system.

During this period Dr. Tate traveled across Georgia to investigate conditions in particular localities, generally tipped off by phone calls directed to the GT&EA office from local school districts or problems reported to him by regional directors. He was so busy with investigations he had taken no vacation since he began his duties in July 1961; even after an automobile accident that had resulted in vertebral damage and weeks of extreme pain he had only asked the board's approval for a few days of absence from the office if required by his physician.[18] From his myriad investigations, Dr. Tate reported that twelve local units asked for investigations from the GT&EA office into salary discrimination. There were cases of dismissals, superintendents who refused to submit their reports, Title I violations, problems of black children in schools still all-black, problems of black students in schools previously white. Black teachers complained about having fees for insurance they had not selected automatically deducted from their payroll. In fact, the problems were multiplying so rapidly that some directors said Dr. Tate needed to generate a "manifesto" to alert the country about the violations of federal and state law where desegregation was concerned.[19]

As merger conversations began and local conditions worsened, some GT&EA directors began to question the outcome of integration. They reported the white schools were not as good as they thought they would be. In Region VIII, the middle part of Georgia, which included the majority of counties that had not signed federal guidelines, black children in white schools discovered French was not offered and that the white schools did not even have a band. Both French and band were in the black schools these children had left behind.[20]

With so many local difficulties regarding race, fueled by superintendents who were members of GEA, GT&EA questioned GEA's verbal commitment to a merger and wondered whether the organization could be fully trusted. In November, the president of GEA affirmed to the public that GEA and GT&EA were meeting to lay the "groundwork for future talks which could lead to talks of the two organizations merging." However, a month later it co-sponsored a press conference with the Southern Region of the NEA to announce plans for National Education Week and did not include GT&EA. GEA also announced its equal commitment to both Howard Callaway and Lester Maddox, candidates for the governorship of Georgia. Lester Maddox was a segregation champion akin to former governor Eugene Talmadge.

GT&EA worried that GEA's behavior thus far indicated that it did not intend to deal fairly in merger plans. And as the months passed, more data points confirming its worries appeared. GEA, for example, sought public credit for the teacher tenure bill before the legislature. The tenure proposal reflected the tenor of the times and was important for all teachers, as Dr. Tate and GT&EA committee members had argued in their many presentations before the State Board of Education during the years before GEA supported the bill. But when GT&EA aligned its argument with national rhetoric about tenure, that masked the strategy crafted in the NAACP networks with Dr. Davis and NCOSTA. The plan they'd concocted was to use tenure to provide a legal backstop to prevent local systems from firing black teachers. Now, however, GEA wanted credit for the tenure idea, which whites had decided was important for white teachers as well. Dr. Tate noted in the meetings that the GT&EA directors needed to remind the membership that their organization had originated the early tenure talks.[21]

Equally vexing was that GEA members continued to try to figure out how to accomplish local mergers so they could dilute GT&EA's influence in merger discussions. Over time GT&EA regional directors heard reports about black educators facing pressure from white educators and superintendents to join the organization, essentially circumventing higher-level GT&EA decision makers who would lend valuable insight about the pros and cons of such an action. Region II's director said the local GEA unit in Carrollton had passed a resolution stating that GT&EA members were welcome to membership and that the local superintendent—the one in charge of local black teachers being retained or dismissed—had said that the "Negro and white units should come together." The director saw the gesture as indicating an excellent local relationship, but his peers disagreed. How could a black teacher "tactfully refuse" to join if asked? GT&EA leaders determined that all its leadership needed to be alert "to insidious attempts" to break up their organization. Superintendents, they believed, were out of line. To be sure, they had authority over the school system, but they did not have authority to direct the activities of local associations.[22] All of these matters made GT&EA's elected delegates to the Joint Committee for Merger fume as negotiations for a merger got under way.

A few months into the discussions, the NEA president traveled to Georgia. GT&EA had long believed that NEA needed to set up regulations for mergers and to create national-level directives on integration for its state affiliates. Earlier GT&EA had put forth a resolution requesting NEA action on the matter, and Dr. Tate, instructed by his board, had contacted the

NEA office to ask for additional directions regarding merger efforts. However, the meeting at NEA headquarters that Dr. Tate had attended had not provided sufficient direction for Georgia.[23]

At the December 1966 meeting of the Joint Committee, the NEA president attempted to provide more guidance. President Irvamae Applegate expressed the NEA's goal of establishing one strong statewide association, the structure of which should be "worked out" by the Joint Committee. He wanted no "unilateral planning," and noted the need for monthly committee meetings to work out plans that could be acceptable to both organizations.[24]

The NEA vice president wanted to know if the group had come up with any kind of timeline for merger. The joint answer from GT&EA and GEA was no. The two groups could not even agree on establishing a philosophy for the proposed merged association. As the afternoon shadows lengthened, the leaders finally decided to assign small groups to assemble in workshop sessions at the next meeting to see if a philosophy could be formulated.[25]

GT&EA's frustrations continued to grow over the Christmas holiday. One of the lengthy discussions had been about the guiding principle on which both groups agreed, which was to exchange records. Immediately after the December Joint Committee meeting, Dr. Tate reported to the Board of Directors of GT&EA that the GEA executive secretary had said he was not ready for the exchange of reports, even though he was the individual who had requested them. GT&EA, on the other hand, was ready with its reports.[26] The GT&EA board objected strongly as they convened in the paneled conference room of GT&EA. If GEA wanted records, they should give records first; GT&EA should not "give out information unless [it] received information." Some directors went further—maybe GT&EA needed to let its attorney see any records before they were exchanged. One hoped GT&EA would not unilaterally relinquish the charter the organization had finally received from NEA after Dr. Tate's numerous inquiries; GT&EA should give up its charter only if GEA gave up its charter as well. Dr. Tate tried to assure the board that the GT&EA members of the Joint Committee would not succumb to GEA pressures and were clear that merger would take place only if a satisfactory plan was created and eventually approved by the Representative Assembly of GT&EA.[27]

Through the winter months leading up to the 1967 GT&EA annual convention, the Joint Committee held monthly meetings, which brought some progress. With the help of subcommittee reports, the GT&EA and GEA discussed a shared philosophy, shared objectives, and a transition period. Under NEA pressure, they enumerated the services the new organization would provide. But the negotiations proceeded with continued suspicion, related to both GEA's behavior in the state and NEA's real commitments.

As GT&EA soon discovered, GEA had more access to the NEA than they did. In a letter received by the GEA president on January 30, 1967, President Applegate reminded the Joint Committee that the proposal plan should be submitted no later than May 1, 1967, and that they were targeting a July 1, 1970, merger. But President Applegate had failed to communicate the same information to the president of GT&EA or to Dr. Tate.

The GEA president also provided information at a Joint Committee meeting regarding a conversation with President Applegate in which GT&EA had not been included. NEA's president expressed NEA's desire to see agreement on some basic details of the merger: name, committees needed, assets and liabilities, local associations, representation, officers, and "others." The NEA president wanted to know the dates these items were on the agenda of the Joint Committee meetings in Georgia, the date when agreement was reached, and the proposals for each of the areas. But this desire had been communicated only to GEA. It appeared to GT&EA that NEA was affording GEA special knowledge and privilege.

At the meeting where the GEA president reported on NEA's expectations, GT&EA members challenged the agenda. While the GEA president wanted suggestions in response to President Applegate's proposal, GT&EA expressed its concern that none of NEA's expectations addressed the matters on which they were in contention with GEA.

The NEA letter "could be interpreted to mean that dates for local mergers should be included," one GT&EA member of the Joint Committee pointed out. GT&EA saw local mergers as diluting GT&EA's power to negotiate as a group. However, GT&EA Joint Committee members knew, through Dr. Tate and his inside connections with NCOSTA colleagues, that supporting local mergers was part of NEA's solution to the dilemma of establishing one professional desegregated association in the southern states without offending its southern members. A member of the NEA executive committee had leaked NEA's desire to "bring pressure on county (or local) associations to begin action to comply with Resolution #12," the resolution on desegregation.[28]

GT&EA demanded that its response on the issue of local mergers be written into the minutes despite earlier disputes between black and white committee members about the degree of discussion that could be included in the formal record. The GT&EA members of the Joint Committee emphasized they did *not* want local GEA associations pressuring for mergers. That needed to be stated "again and again," they said. At the very first joint meeting, immediately after introductions, both GT&EA and GEA had agreed there would be no proselytizing. Now GEA, with NEA support, was engaged in proselytizing. For the record, GT&EA said it refused any "merger" talks that really meant "a loss of association members by one of the state associations." GEA members replied that they were telling local members to negotiate a merger "if they want to but we are not proselytizing," and they denied that they were applying pressure for GT&EA members to join "against their will."[29] The discussion was "spirited," especially for blacks and whites around the table unaccustomed to meeting with each other as equals.

Another battle seething beneath the surface remained unspoken: who would lead the new organization? The executive director of GT&EA had a doctoral degree, but the executive secretary of GEA did not.[30] The question of leadership would soon create even more contention.

While GT&EA engaged repeated struggles with GEA, Dr. Tate continued to glean additional context from NCOSTA activities. At the Phoenix meeting in 1966, the executive secretaries of the state organizations updated one another on merger progress across the South, and they contemplated having another late-night meeting at NEA's legislative session in December 1966. In January 1967 they met in Atlanta at the GT&EA headquarters, with each executive secretary bringing a position paper or statement on consolidation or unification with him to share with the other states.[31]

On the night before the serious deliberations with Dr. Davis and Dan Byrd, Dr. Tate arranged for NCOSTA members to meet at Paschal's, the black restaurant known for its fried chicken and from whose corner booth civil rights strategies across the South were mapped. Dr. Davis had said he could not be present with them, but NCOSTA had already pressed Dr. Davis about the help they could expect during these "critical days" of school integration and the management of federal funds in local settings. The

NCOSTA president affirmed that NCOSTA had been "inseparably bound to the Legal Defense and Educational Fund" for nearly a quarter of a century. They had "supported the NAACP in every possible way," GT&EA alone paying $3,000 in 1966, plus the additional $300 special assessment members agreed to tax themselves in order to defend the increasing number of black teachers losing jobs. Like their colleagues a generation earlier, however, NCOSTA leaders wanted the same kind of "clarification and assurance" of a "two-way" accountability from the NAACP that had once been requested of Thurgood Marshall.[32] Dr. Davis had affirmed that ties with the NAACP were "unbreakable," and he had communicated his hope that the seven or eight remaining executive secretaries of black educational associations could continue the work of the larger NCOSTA of earlier years.[33]

Dr. Davis believed intervention was necessary immediately.[34] Fewer than one half of 1 percent of Negro teachers in the South were working in desegregated schools; 83.2 percent of Negro children were still in segregated schools; Negro principals were being "displaced right and left." The National Teaching Exam, originally believed to provide an accurate evaluation of a teacher's performance, was being used unjustly and unfairly to eliminate black teachers or justify lower salaries. NCOSTA *had* to figure out a way to "protect Negro teachers, Negro pupils and the general cause of education in the South and in the Nation."

As much as Dr. Davis and NCOSTA leaders could determine, NEA was not helping matters. At an earlier meeting of the NCOSTA Special Committee, Dr. Davis declared NEA's current leadership "not definitely interested in the Negro teacher." The Negro teacher was controversial for NEA, creating problems with its white southern members.

Black educators needed to be aware of the climate in which they operated. HEW was being challenged by a group of southern politicians calling themselves the Educational Compact of the States, who wanted to do away with the U.S. Office of Education. If the federal government retreated and state organizations of black educators disappeared, what would become of Negro teachers? NEA could not handle all the cases coming in because of legal staff and budget limitations; they were referring cases to the NAACP Legal Defense and Educational Fund. The disturbing result reported by the seven Negro associations left intact was that the interests of the black teacher were "often overlooked."

Dan Byrd, Dr. Davis's associate, was even more direct: "Once a state gets rid of its Negro association, we will find that Negroes have lost both their voice and their jobs. This is the dilemma that we face." Already in Texas, Negro teachers were in "real trouble" because they had abandoned their association. Even if NEA used its funds to defend them, would not superintendents retaliate? And what would the white associations give in return for the merger—some staff positions, some membership on the board of directors? Would a merged association institute a suit on behalf of a black teacher? Who would speak for the needs of Negro educators, and what would happen to black children?

"The Negro teacher must motivate the deprived child because only she knows the situation," he proclaimed. He did not believe that white teachers were psychologically prepared to teach Negro children. They would need to be "trained" to do an effective job. He was tired of the "growing myth of the inferiority of the Negro teacher." NCOSTA members needed to do something—perhaps establish a new organization that would speak for black education.[35]

Dr. Tate had hoped taking his colleagues to the black-owned Paschal's would bring to mind earlier conversations and remind the remaining NCOSTA leadership of the power of black organizations and the ability of blacks to run them. With the exception of Arkansas, all of the other associations for black educators remaining in the South had more members than the entire roster of public school educators in Alaska, Delaware, Hawaii, Idaho, Maine, Montana, Nevada, New Hampshire, North Dakota, Rhode Island, South Dakota, Utah, Vermont, and Wyoming combined. Black organizations brought tailored leadership and programs to their work for black education and needed to be as interwoven into the fabric of professionalism in integrated spaces as other educational groups.[36]

The morning after the Paschal's dinner, the beleaguered NCOSTA executive secretaries debated the unfinished tasks "staring them all in the face." They decided they needed to try to get information from states already having "merged" about the "so-called merger programs" and how they were operating in the states. They needed to think deeply about what "collective voice" would speak for the black teacher and pupil after black and white organizations merged. They also needed to explore whether blacks were leading the education of black children in America, who would support the guidance of black youth, how black youth would be pushed to vote so that education and life could be improved for black people, and how public school integration would support the historical study of Negro life and history in segregated schools.[37] With time, the validity of their concerns would become all too clear.

Some NCOSTA members had previously met with staff from the NAACP Legal Defense and Educational Fund in New York. With Dr. Davis, others had convened at beautiful Hammocks Beach, owned by the black teachers' association in North Carolina. A pristine ocean resort property, Hammocks Beach was an asset of the black teachers already at issue with the white teachers association in North Carolina.

The chairman of NCOSTA expressed the concern dominating all their discussions. Black educational associations had to "face up to the problems of these times," he said as he encouraged them all to figure out how to make integration a two-way street.[38] Old mechanisms of trying to reason with state officials about "past and present racially discriminatory practices"—noting the "unfair and illegal practices" that were still in effect in black education—were not working. Schools still needed basic items, like buses, custodians, and up-to-date equipment. States needed to repudiate the arbitrary scores of the National Teaching Exam as a way to avoid salary supplements for black teachers and stop salary discrimination. GT&EA communicated with the new state superintendent of schools and the governor, and in these communications and in press conferences urged state leaders to address these education matters.[39]

But as had always been true, direct appeal was not enough. Sometimes officials did respond when they were made aware of inequalities, as when Dr. Tate brought pictures to one school board meeting so members could see for themselves the state of black education. In 1966, partly as a result of GT&EA lobbying, all teachers statewide had received a pay raise.[40] Nonetheless, the problems of continuing discrimination were not being adequately addressed by local leaders, states, or the NEA. NCOSTA leaders needed more help to make the public hear the concerns of black educators.

Dr. Tate suggested a mass protest. Black teachers and principals could charter buses to Washington. Then he suggested bringing Rev. Martin Luther King Jr. to black education meetings across the South. Rev. King could make the nation listen.

The idea of a mass protest generated supportive discussion, but concrete plans did not materialize. But Dr. Tate did seek to bring Rev. King to the 1967 GT&EA meeting. "Whenever Dr. Tate wanted Martin, he could get him," one of the GT&EA leaders commented.[41] And get him Dr. Tate did.

22

WE HOLD THESE TRUTHS

The forty-ninth state convention for GT&EA convened in Atlanta as about five thousand teachers, administrators, religious leaders, businesspeople, and others traveled from across Georgia into Atlanta on March 19, 1967. Registration began officially at the Municipal Auditorium from 12:30 p.m. to 5:00 p.m., with GT&EA state office staff carefully overseeing delegate badges to be sure certified delegates from each local unit would have all the materials they needed to make decisions. Unit presidents dined at five o'clock on Wednesday evening at Paschal's. The president of NCOSTA, who was also the executive secretary of the Louisiana Education Association, gave local leaders information they needed from other states. At seven o'clock, the GT&EA session formally opened at the Union Baptist Church, with Dr. Tate delivering his lengthy and precise account of the ways his office had implemented the mandates given by the Representative Assembly during the previous year.[1]

On Thursday morning, GT&EA president James Hawes, principal of Dr. Tate's former high school in Elberton, tapped the gavel to begin the varied sessions that would comprise the three-day conference. On Thursday morning at nine, the Representative Assembly reviewed committee reports and other business matters. At three-thirty that afternoon, Georgia's lieutenant governor greeted the assembly. At eight o'clock that evening, Jack P. Nix, the state school superintendent, delivered remarks about education in Georgia before the delegates disbanded for the evening.

On Friday morning at ten-thirty, Dr. Horace Mann Bond, having relocated back to Georgia and renewed his relationship with GT&EA, introduced Dr. Allison Davis, a black professor of psychology from the University of Chicago. Dr. Bond proclaimed Dr. Davis the "most influential scholar since Dewey." Dr. Davis returned the accolades when he took the microphone, then humorously let the audience stretch before launching into observations about the brilliance of black children.

No matter how black or poor or dirty, Dr. Davis told a room of educators who already agreed with him, the black child had the same brain teachers did and could be taught. Black teachers could and should triumph in teaching the child. They should triumph over meaningless tests imposed on the children and over language barriers separating middle-class and lower-class children. His wisdom echoed other speeches he had given before to black educators as well as words black educators spoke among themselves. Black teachers needed to stop being mad about tests and "be smart." They should "use all the angles." They had to "learn the tricks and work at it" so black children could succeed.

Dr. Davis's address replayed their decades-old pedagogical plan. Black educators taught a state-prescribed curriculum and also sought to discover talent, to direct that talent, and to inspire children beyond the "barrage of obstacles, inconveniences, and disturbances" with the often meager material resources they had. Such talk had permeated black professional meetings after World War I and over the following years was replayed in state meetings of black educators across the South. If a black teacher did not get to know a child, establish a relationship with him, and get "outside his schoolroom and into the community," only a small part of the job had been accomplished. Every child should be able to reach his highest potential. Any child who had learned a language could be taught. Wanting for someone else's child the success a teacher wanted for his own helped determine whether a person was prepared to teach. These ideas defined their vision for educating children treated unfairly by segregated schooling. And, as Dr. Davis had said before, the best way to stimulate desire for success from the pupils was for the pupils to identify with and seek to emulate the teacher.[2]

In addition to their job to inspire children to succeed, Dr. Davis continued, teachers had a difficult pedagogical job. Transferring abstract ideas from their minds to those of the children they taught made the job of the educator more complicated than that of a surgeon who manipulated tangible tissue, he posited. But nobody knew the Negro child better nor knew better how to inspire than they did, he proclaimed. *They* were the savior of black children—little by little, week by week—as they determined to run their classrooms to meet the particular needs of their children.

Through the expansive address, the black educators alternately chuckled or nodded in collective agreement. But attendees also had another speaker on their mind as Dr. Davis concluded. Later that Friday evening, at the eight o'clock session, Rev. Martin Luther King Jr. would speak.[3] Dr. Bond had taught Dr. Tate years ago to go to the top when a matter needed to be addressed. In a few hours, America's top voice for justice would articulate the injustices cleverly cloaked by ostensible efforts at integration.

Some GEA leaders around the state had responded negatively to Rev. King's planned presence at the GT&EA meeting. In one county, the superintendent refused to grant leave for five teachers, all of whom happened to be GT&EA leaders, to attend the meeting. His refusal followed a "growing tendency" to grant spring holidays during the time when white teachers could attend GEA meetings, yet black educators could not be released to attend GT&EA meetings. GT&EA did not want "preferential treatment," Dr. Tate explained in his letter complaining of the practice to the state school superintendent. It did want the same "day off" privileges for its membership that were granted to GEA members.[4]

The county superintendent who was unwilling to let GT&EA leaders attend their professional meetings said teaching in his county was so important he would not excuse them. Dr. Tate objected strongly and publicly that, in addition to the superintendent scheduling the spring break to accommodate the GEA meeting, he was aware of other professional educators (white) in the county who attended other professional meetings during school days. In fact, Dr. Tate said, that superintendent was chairman of the State Board of Education's Standards Committee and that he left school "on many weekdays to carry out his functions."[5]

Dr. Tate's bluntness sometimes offended. In one county a principal discussing with his superintendent a new violation of Title I of the Civil Rights Act reported to the superintendent he would have to call Dr. Tate to get his opinion on the plans being proposed for the local school district. "I don't give a damn about Horace Tate," the irate superintendent responded. "And I don't like Martin Luther King either!"

Apparently neither did many other superintendents. The GT&EA members for whom Dr. Tate had to fight to be present at the Rev. King's event included a president of the State Principals' Group; a vice director for GT&EA's Region VI; a supervisor and chairman of the Spelling Bee Committee, which sent black students to the National Spelling Bee competition in Washington; a principal; an assistant principal; a 1965–66 State Teacher

Dr. and Mrs. King and Dr. and Mrs. Tate applaud the service of GT&EA members during the 1967 convention. *GT&EA Collection*

of the Year; and a president of the State Educational Secretaries Association. Such were the maneuvers necessary to have GT&EA members present for the anticipated "dramatic conclusion" of the 1967 convention—the address by Dr. King.[6]

As the massive crowd of black educators filled seats throughout the Municipal Auditorium, a black high school choir sang eloquently in Latin to open the session. Following warm applause, the president of GT&EA introduced to the audience the speaker who would in turn introduce the keynote speaker for the evening.

"The introduction of the speaker is a big job tonight," President Hawes proclaimed. "So we have selected a big man." With his pronouncement, the organist for the assembly loudly chimed its approval as the man employed by the educators to be their spokesman rose to applause. With his finger on the pulse of educational matters across the state and across the South, this man was something of a black governor in Georgia. His was the task of introducing the world-renowned leader of the civil rights movement.

Dr. Tate responded graciously to the applause greeting him. "That simply means I am supposed to perform those tasks others have forgotten," he mused, refusing to acknowledge the accolades given to him.

Dr. Tate began by recognizing the regional leaders who made the association function through their fearless contributions. Before he concluded, Region IV, the place where Dr. Tate had first been introduced to leadership when he was a young principal in Greensboro, honored him in return. The region presented a monetary gift of $139 "for his own personal use." They spoke their appreciation for his "dynamic leadership" and added prayers that God would protect him as he went around the state trying to defend black children. Surprised, Dr. Tate offered his thanks. He chuckled that it could help with the $265 in expenses he still personally owed a lawyer for a county suit in which he had been named.

He recognized Rev. King's family members on the stage as the audience stood to honor "Daddy" King. It was the name SCLC leaders had given to distinguish the elder Rev. King from his son, Martin Luther King Jr.[7] Beaming proudly on the front row beside Daddy King was his wife, who would eventually be murdered while playing the organ one Sunday morning at the Ebenezer Baptist Church. Seated in the front row with them was Mrs. Coretta Scott King, beautifully attired, and the equally beautifully attired Mrs. Tate.

Dr. Tate recognized his family as well. He thanked his sister Helen, who was in the audience, for having taken care of him as a child and for having sent money to their mother so that his mother could send it to him during his college days when money was tight. He thanked his brother Charlie, who also had given a little money during his college days—"though not as much as his sister." He was not angry at Charlie, though, for Charlie had sold him cheaply the car he'd used to travel back and forth to Atlanta on those lonely nights long ago when Mr. Harper stood in the shoes he now filled.

Finally Dr. Tate turned his attention to the person quietly waiting to approach the microphone. This was the final session of the forty-ninth annual meeting of the GT&EA, and Martin Luther King Jr. was moved to speak to this room of anxious and inspired educators. "This is about all that needs to be said," Dr. Tate began, "for he needs no introduction to any audience in America." He said he would make only a few points before reading and presenting the citation GT&EA had prepared for Rev. King.

Dr. Tate reviewed Rev. King's history of schooling, beginning with Charles Harper's Booker T. Washington High School in Atlanta. The citation spoke of the Rev. King's early "interest and love for the people" and how he had "accepted the challenge to help lowly people" aspire to full citizenship. As a result of his work, "America has not been the same since," for he had made America change.

Dr. Tate recounted the Nobel Peace Prize and the plethora of honorary doctorates awarded him, including one recently conferred by Boston University. He spoke of his books. He elevated Rev. King's philosophy above America's philosophy. America, he said, championed bombing, shooting, and air raids. Rev. King championed nonviolence. "And when the time comes, we are going to put you in office as President of the United States."

The audience applauded wildly. The organ's chimes resounded loudly again, and the audience enthusiastically responded as the famed speaker rose to address black educators in Georgia. In accordance with the NCOSTA strategy, Rev. King had already spoken to teachers in Alabama and Louisiana. The difference was that these Georgia educators were *his* teachers. As he leaned toward the mike to speak, Rev. King knew he was among the people who had helped make him who he was.

"You must be citizens of the world," the principal of Booker T. Washington High School had taught. The teachers at Booker T. Washington had sent a similar message. "You don't have to go be segregated downtown," they told the Negro children. "You can eat at home." Rev. King represented the triumph of the strategy Lucy Laney had spoken of at the 1919 NAACP convention: "We are going to do something in a way that we know will be effective. We are going to teach black children democracy, to vote."

The internationally acclaimed Atlanta resident approached the lectern, which featured shiny silver microphones from several radio stations. He was happy to be here with GT *and* EA, he said. His use of the "and" revealed his relationship to the group. Only longtime members of GT&EA knew to say "GT and EA." The enunciation was a throwback to days forgotten, when Mr. Hunt's new education group and the older education group begun by Mr. Wright had united. That legacy was still honored by pronouncing the acronym for the combined group's name "GT and EA." Outsiders would say simply "GTEA."

After lauding his good friend Dr. Tate, Rev. King too recognized his parents and his wife. He was happy to share a platform with the GT&EA

officers, he said. They represented an organization that had engaged significant work in its forty-nine years of existence, lifting the level of education in the state. He was also grateful for the words Dr. Tate had said about him. He congratulated the audience on its struggle and commended their wisdom in choosing Dr. Tate to lead them. "He is a giant of integrity, of competence and a giant of leadership ability," the familiar voice intoned. Then it was down to business.

The old order of segregation was passing away, he said, but that was bringing with it new challenges. As Dr. Davis had explained the need to teach so black children could pass the test, Rev. King emphasized the need to teach a new generation of American black boys and girls to become part of the brotherhood of an international community. He elevated the interconnections among humanity necessary to make the whole world a neighborhood.

Soon, however, he turned to the education problem America refused to see and to which Dr. Tate hoped his voice could open the eyes of the public. Without question, segregation was evil. But the demise of segregation did not mean accepting integration on just any terms.[8]

Dr. Tate nodded and clapped with the audience. The words expressed exactly GT&EA's concerns. He had received in his office a few months earlier a report of a fifteen-year-old black girl expelled from a white high school after a white boy continually hurled derogatory remarks at her, including calling her "nigger." When the girl tried to protect herself and demanded that he meet her outside to fight, the principal sent her home, while the boy remained in school. Dr. Tate had reported the matter to HEW, but the mistreatment of black children continued around the state.[9]

It seemed the entire system of desegregation in Georgia had been hijacked by those determined to use a new name to maintain old practices of subordination. Dr. Tate daily received reports from black teachers and principals who complained of "well laid schemes" designed "purely for ridding some schools systems, first of Negro leadership (principals) and secondly Negro teachers and other Negro educational personnel." Such reports came from regions across the state. There were tales of Negro students encountering problems in white schools—in one place sixteen of the thirty-eight students attending a white school returned to their black schools, while others simply dropped out, not going to school anywhere. He heard reports of white principals and secretaries sent to Negro schools to "take over." One superintendent who did not want to integrate

In mutual admiration, Drs. King and Tate commend each other's service during the 1967 annual meeting of the GT&EA. *GT&EA Collection*

had told the Negro teachers to expect a "rough, rough time" if they crossed over to the white schools, that the Negro teachers really needed "to leave the problem to us and we'll guide you." Dr. Tate proclaimed the reports to be too frequent to be "accidental or coincidental."[10]

With Rev. King's words to the GT&EA audience projected across the airwaves, Dr. Tate hoped the people listening on local radio would be alerted to the problem. Rev. King insisted on a "genuine, across the board integration." And "integration," he said, should not mean the liquidation of everything begun by Negroes. "We've got to see [it as] genuine integration where there is shared power," Rev. King declared.

Then he turned to the merger problems. The Joint Committee had met in January and February, and while it had missed the March monthly meeting, it was scheduled to meet at the end of this convention. Dr. Tate had reported to the Board of Directors that the Joint Committee still had not formulated any "definite plans" for a merger. He said both the GT&EA

GT&EA reported that Dr. King had "pulled out all of the stops and electrified the convention audience" during his speech at the Old City Auditorium for the GT&EA annual meeting in 1967. *GT&EA Collection*

and the GEA were committed to the merger, and that plans were supposed to be completed and sent to NEA during May—a short two months away. Until then, directors were only to say to local affiliates that all the membership needed to remain intact until the committee accomplished a "real merger."[11]

Rev. King agreed with Dr. Tate and GT&EA that there should be "one organization." But he believed they were on "sound ground" when they said the process should not mean "Negro annihilation."

In classic Rev. King style, he expressed his indignation about integration not being a two-way street. Why should Emory University be preserved while Morehouse or Spelman was discounted? Why should Georgia Tech and Agnes Scott be maintained while Clark and Morris Brown and the International Denomination Seminary were discounted? They did not need to send Negro children to formerly all-white schools while no white children came to Negro schools. "Noooo," he bellowed. "We want it alllllll the way."

That meant a "genuine integration"—one that had black principals at formerly white schools and white principals at formerly black schools. He wanted to stress this because it was "very important": "Integration must lead us to a point where we share in the power that all of our society will produce." As they struggled to end segregation, they also needed to be certain there was a genuine integration with mutual respect.

As he moved toward his conclusion, Rev. King emphasized the ways black children were victims of oppression. The educators facing him needed to put squarely on their shoulders a direct responsibility to help these children make individual and collective contributions to the life of the nation. Especially, educators needed to think about "what the children would inherit" in another generation. For a revolution to be successful, it would need to be brought into the classroom.

"The arc of the moral universe is long, but it bends toward justice," he intoned. Truth might be "crushed to earth," but it would eventually "rise again."

Increasingly unfettered with each statement on educational inequality, Rev. King's voice rose to become the beloved civil rights leader they lauded. "We will hew out of the mountain of despair a stone of hope. With this faith, we will spend up the day when justice will run down like waters and righteousness like a mighty stream." When justice reigned, it would be a great day for America, for the white man, for the black man.[12]

The black men and women in the audience rose to their feet. The organ began a pronounced introduction to "We Shall Overcome," and the black educators joined in the hope that their individual quest for freedom would become an organized public quest for equality in education. President Hawes thanked Rev. King for the "very inspirational message," and the educators also gave Mrs. King another round of applause as the organ chimed.

As announcements reminded them of the plans for the upcoming fiftieth-anniversary celebration, scheduled for April 3–5, 1968, laughter began and friends and colleagues departed for the annual President's Ball. There they would joyfully forget segregation and enjoy themselves until the early morning hours. Privately to Dr. Tate, Rev. King pronounced himself "elated" over devotion being given to the educational interests in the state. All in all, it was a night to remember.[13]

GT&EA began immediately to rouse Georgia's citizens, calling for a conference of GT&EA members from across the state. It was an "important and urgent" meeting and they encouraged attendance. "There is an education crisis in Georgia," the GT&EA publicity announced. The GT&EA board thought the meeting so important for all to attend that they hosted it in the middle of the state, Macon, to balance the driving and encourage everybody who could to come, even if they had to "defray their own expenses."

Black educators and communities were not the only people invited in the initial call. GT&EA also invited the local and state school officers who failed to enforce equality. It invited local and national HEW officials, who were supposed to support federal guidelines for equality. Dr. Tate announced his intention to invite the presidents and executive secretaries of all the national educational groups: NEA, American Association of School Administrators, National School Boards Association, National Department of Elementary School Principals, National Department of Secondary School Principals, National Congress of Colored Parents and Teachers, Georgia Congress of Colored Parents and Teachers, and Georgia School Boards Association. And, of course, Dr. John Davis of the NAACP Legal Defense and Educational Fund would be present.[14] As far as GT&EA was concerned, the violation of integration policies at the local level was serious and needed to be collectively and immediately addressed.

The public call was a strategy reminiscent of Mr. Hunt's in the World War I era and Mr. Harper's after World War II. Then, as now, federal money was available. Then, as now, black children were not getting their fair share. Then, as now, American needed to preserve its image of international leadership by addressing some matters of inequality at home. Black communities in Georgia needed to do what black communities had done throughout the decades: meet and plan. It was "unbelievable" that the elected officials "entrusted with the privilege and responsibility" to provide equal opportunity to all people of the country would "at this time in the history of our country begin laying plans to retard the educational development" of some of the pupils. GT&EA had documentation showing the abuse of federal funds intended for the children but used instead for unauthorized purposes. GT&EA had data on long-serving Negro principals summarily dismissed or demoted to positions of subservience, despite federal guidelines requiring faculty integration. It could document continued salary discrimination. America needed to follow a policy of fairness in integration, and

GT&EA needed people to galvanize around the continuing problems so that inequitable policies could be eradicated.[15]

Dr. Tate made his way to the Macon meeting on May 6, back to Ballard-Hudson Senior High School, which he had first visited as a regional director so many years ago. The state political leaders he had summoned did not join him in Macon. The school superintendents did not show up, having imposed conditions on their attendance. Nor did the other educational stakeholders implicated in perpetuating inequality come to the meeting. But President Hawes greeted the many black educators and parents who did come. Despite having lost 90 percent of his hearing in a fluke accident on his way to the school, President Hawes proclaimed he and others who were part of the planning were "enthused and inspired" by the response of so many in the black community.

Several panelists provided their perspectives on the grave situation confronting black education across the state. Napoleon Williams pointed to the federally funded program Head Start. Ninety percent of the Head Start program consisted of services delivered to black students, he explained. Yet Georgia took the position that Head Start should be in all white schools so that white students could attend and not be discriminated against. White students were not likely to go to Negro schools, officials had explained to Mr. Williams when he challenged them. Now he asked rhetorically, "What does this mean?"

It meant that when the programs were moved to white schools, white directors would be hired, who would—in turn—hire white personnel. And as was the case when black principals were demoted to assistant principalships, the leadership would soon employ more white teachers than Negro teachers in the Head Start programs serving Negro children. As a black educator, he didn't like the unfolding events.

Gwinnett County representatives spoke, reporting a story everybody already knew from countless other places across the state. Superintendents gave white teachers contracts; they did not give black teachers contracts. In one black school, five teachers had been assigned to instruct seven grades, making GT&EA's longtime fight about the student-teacher ratio a problem still not solved. In Gwinnett County, bus drivers could only transport Negro students, and they could only take the students to schools built for whites. Only one of the three Negro teachers in white schools had been assigned as a classroom teacher. Of the many people employed with federal Title I money on the county level, none of them had been Negroes—even though the program was designed to assist Negro children.

Mrs. Gladys Davis Chappel, in her presentation, named discriminatory practices extending beyond hiring and firing. Three times curriculum directors had met in a statewide meeting, she explained, with no Negroes present. When she queried the lack of representation at a professional meeting, she was told the state board and GEA had sponsored the workshops. When she asked if GT&EA could be part of sponsoring the workshops, she received no answer.

A panel of black educators concluded their reports of practices across the state, and President Hawes called on Dr. Tate to provide "first hand information on all of these discriminating practices." During a brief interlude while the Ballard-Hudson chorus sang, Dr. Tate examined his scribbled notes and tried to decide which points to make so that he would not ramble. At last he decided that all of the points were important, and if that meant a lengthy address, so be it.

Black educators, he began, had come to a point where they would "really have to band together or forget it," he said. "To me, it is as simple as that."

Problems that should have been solved had not been solved, he said. Crawfordville was a good example. All Negroes had asked for at first was the opportunity to use the gym in the white school. When the answer was no, that prompted demonstrations, and matters of educational inequality snowballed, eventually leading to publicity on all matters of inequality in the small town. That had been three years ago. Now the Negroes had the gym to themselves because the white school had been given to the Negro children, and no white children attended school in Crawfordville. Integration had never been accomplished.

He and GT&EA leaders had "fussed and fussed and fussed" with the State Board of Education to finally get them to employ some Negroes, or put some Negroes on the Retirement Board. They had put a few, he conceded, but "nothing like the number of Negroes that should have been employed." It seemed to him that "the people in authority are not going to do anything for us unless they are forced to do it."

The black community needed to champion the maintenance of black leadership in schools. Dr. Tate rejected the proposition that changing the administration of schools to let white principals lead was demonstrable progress toward integration, or that it provided a "better quality of education," as the superintendent in Fitzgerald had told him. "All change is not progress," Dr. Tate asserted. To the contrary, to accept these arbitrary dismissals as measures of progress meant that he must also accept the fact that he was inferior.

"We can never accept this," Dr. Tate continued. Black educators were not inferior. They were well qualified and in some states held higher educational degrees than their white counterparts. Moreover, the white educators replacing black educators did not have the same interest in black children black teachers had.

"Let me try to close here by getting back on the point we must know this morning—that we are facing a new kind of slavery." Blacks had experienced "pure slavery," where they were "dominated, controlled," and expected to do what white people told them to do. Segregation had also been used "to make you de-human, make you worse than a dumb animal to keep you subservient." Yet Negroes had refused to be subjugated in either of these oppressive institutions. They had come out with the aspiration to be part of the American dream.

"We want the same aspirations and motivations to continue even in this period that we had within/during the period of segregation," Dr. Tate said. In fact, he believed, the aspirations of black children should be *enhanced* with the increasing opportunities.

But the liberation expected with integration was not happening, either in local school practices or with the GT&EA merger with GEA. GEA was spreading the rumor that GT&EA was trying to curtail a merger. "This is a big lie, one of the biggest lies anybody has every heard." The truth was that GEA wanted black members from GT&EA while dismantling GT&EA's historical advocacy for black education.

"GT&EA members have insisted that if and when we get together, it will be on an equal basis. Nobody will come into this organization on a subservient basis. We've insisted on this." But GEA wanted something different. "They want the president to be white with no guarantee whatsoever that a Negro would ever become president. They want the Executive Secretary to be white with no guarantee that a Negro would ever become [Executive Secretary]." They wanted commissions and committees on paper, with no guarantee that a Negro could ever be a member. With twenty-nine thousand GEA members against thirteen thousand GT&EA members, he believed "majority rule" would defeat black interests from the start.

"Majority rule is fine for the people who are in the majority," Dr. Tate declared. But it did not serve the interests of black people, those in the minority. Black educators in the audience nodded. Many also believed a new educational structure would be another way for white interests to dominate black education.

Dr. Tate ended with a summons to strategies that had worked in black communities in the past. The audience needed to go back into their communities, to reconvene citizens' groups if they were missing. The black community should not be at odds with each other, either in school or out. They needed to "band together," to not let anyone control their thinking. "If he controls your thinking, he, therefore, controls you. He therefore makes you a slave." They should never accept choices from local superintendents that were not real choices. They should demand everything due them in an integrated world.

Finally, Dr. John Davis addressed the audience and echoed Dr. Tate's words. Like everyone else present, he was for integration and merger. In fact, Dr. Davis headed the Herbert Lehman Fund, which helped finance the education of black young people in desegregated colleges and universities, including Emory University in Atlanta. He relied on Dr. Tate and others like him to recommend students to this fund who would integrate white schools.

But Dr. Davis did not want integration to "destroy every vestige of Negro leadership." He did not want black educators in Georgia to turn over their long history of advocacy for black education without negotiating the terms of a new merged association. "Twenty-nine thousand white teachers and thirteen thousand Negro teachers. That's a pretty good size vote that you are going up against. If all of you voted all for one and one for all . . . just remember that there will be twenty-nine thousand votes against you to start with," he reminded the educators. They needed to assert what they wanted *before* any merger happened.

On that Saturday in Macon, black voices aligned with each other and with Rev. King's. With so many continuing problems in black education, Mrs. Marie Dixon proclaimed, they were "fighting bulls—bulls within the pen and bulls out of the pen and every other way, God knows where." But they were going to fight.

Rev. King, the most visible civil rights advocate in the world, shared their stance. The NAACP also aligned with their views. Delivering the education of black children largely into the hands of people who had no historical or present interest in black children was not an option.

23

FIGHTING BACK

The GT&EA leadership referred to the meeting held on May 6, a Saturday, as the "Drive-By Conference," and pronounced this short meeting a success. One weekend later, the principals who constituted the Board of Directors reconvened. They were always meeting these days—hours of drives to Atlanta, innumerable reports to one another of the status of school desegregation in their region, and endless strategy debates on appropriate responses to NEA. Sometimes individual principals called Dr. Tate late in the evening between meetings, and they would talk into the wee hours of the morning. Such were the demands of GT&EA leadership.

On this morning, the principals pulled their cars in the lined spaces in front of the new GT&EA building. In small groups or as individuals, they passed through the glass doors, into the two-story foyer, and up the stairs on the right leading into the GT&EA office suite. Had the situation been less troubling, they might have been descending the stairs in the foyer on the left and going downstairs to the assembly room for curricular meetings or other less urgent discussions. Today, though, each person resolutely turned toward the boardroom. They all passed the larger-than-life mural of Mr. Harper in the historic fight to gain justice for black children.

This generation of leaders had its own fight now. They did not always agree on strategy when they convened in the GT&EA; sometimes they argued into the night. Nonetheless, their common concerns and their courage to be the leaders in their regions bound them together. With the ease of old friends, they pulled the wooden chairs away from the glass-topped table, several making scraping noises on the tile floor. Dr. Tate soon joined them, seating himself at his customary position at the head of the table facing portraits of the previous executive directors. All expected to devote the entire day to discussions of the problems they confronted.

As was the custom, President Hawes opened the meeting with prayer. "Heavenly Father," he intoned respectfully, "we pray that what we do and say today will [be] to Thy name and to the elevation of education in our state." When he finished beseeching God's blessing to guide their discussions, the roll call commenced. "Mrs. Dawson . . . Mr. Martin . . . Mr. Hicks . . . Mr. Ashford . . . Mr. Morgan . . . Mr. Aldridge . . . Mr. White . . ." President Hawes called the names of every one of the nineteen people elected to represent the concerns of the educators in Georgia and waited for an affirmative response before he allowed Mr. Brown to move that the agenda be adopted.

Someone reported having heard that the GEA president and executive secretary already had a copy of the agenda the board had just approved for discussion and, furthermore, that they already knew details of the Drive-By Conference, even though no GEA member had attended. Some unnamed Negro apparently had provided information to the white leadership. Dr. Tate reported it "came back to him" that he had a meeting in Macon "because of an educational crisis and that all the teachers were going down to Macon to discuss the crisis." He was dismayed that, in every crowd, there were some black people who felt it necessary to report to white people what black people knew and everything they were planning.

Not that the board really cared that someone in GEA knew what they were doing. They had invited white people to the public meetings. Unlike the earlier decades of disenfranchisement, this was an era of voting rights, a time when they could participate in American democracy and make their perspectives known publicly. Still, it was disappointing that black people went to report to white people who did not bother to come. They shook their heads and moved on.

In his executive secretary's report, Dr. Tate commended a young student from Region VIII, Miss Glasco, who had won the GT&EA Spelling Bee and was diligently studying with a teacher who was "putting her through the grind" in preparation for the National Spelling Bee in Washington. Despite lack of sponsorship, the student represented GT&EA's first participation in the National Bee. In contrast, the Teachers Agency of Georgia defrayed the expenses of whites attending the National Spelling Bee. In clarification, Dr. Tate explained that the white representatives "have never attended [the bee], but they have taken the trip."

Then the board turned its attention to the upcoming NEA national meeting, which was to be held in Minneapolis. "What has been done about the booth situation?" one board member wanted to know. Were they having a booth with GEA or not? Dr. Tate said he followed the board's instructions and wrote NEA to say GT&EA was planning to have a booth. He had received the reply, and GT&EA was assigned booth 834. The GT&EA booth would be next to the GEA booth, which had already been assigned.

"So they have one already?" President Hawes queried.

Dr. Tate responded affirmatively. "They do this ordinarily," Dr. Tate explained. "They do things without consulting us at all. They aren't going to consult us about anything."

Discussions ensued. Board members believed NEA put the booths next to each other with the hope that the two organizations would agree to merge their exhibits. NEA still was writing to local units saying black and white local units should merge even though black educators had talked with NEA about its need to provide appropriate guidelines on state mergers. The appearance of unity in the booth assignment NEA made ignored the ongoing dissent. It also attempted to minimize its role in encouraging local mergers, which would disrupt the state membership of GT&EA. Basically, someone said, NEA had created a "monster that it doesn't know how to deal with now."

The board discussed the details of the upcoming NEA meeting, such as driving the two and a half days together it would take to get to Minneapolis, but the conversation soon turned to GT&EA's own golden anniversary celebration, coming up on April 3–5, 1968. Undeterred by local superintendents trying again to keep black teachers from attending by raising questions about dates, the board affirmed its desire to use the anniversary to shape GT&EA's image and to maintain morale. Local GT&EA teachers were being besieged about joining GEA and many were being forced to maneuver the directives of their white supervisors to join GEA as they tried to figure out how to keep their jobs. Some situations were so bad that the black educators involved needed counseling. Other black teachers simply avoided saying or doing anything controversial. The board believed the insecurities their members faced could only be addressed by a collective show of strength during the golden anniversary meeting.

They believed the show of organizational strength was important also for negotiations with GEA. Some GT&EA members across the state had already raised questions about the merger conversations. What would happen to the GT&EA assets? What would happen to the GT&EA building? If they merged, how could black people maintain control of the building they

In a mammoth effort to pay off the Ashby Street building and to maintain organizational strength as local officials sought to demand that black educators become members of GEA, small groups met with Dr. Tate in his office to discuss plans for the golden anniversary program. Shown here are Mary Gorden, Charlie Hicks, M.A. Clark, Dr. Tate, and Mr. Hawes. *GT&EA Collection*

had sacrificed to build? Could black teachers continue to own it? Although Dr. Tate and members of the Joint Committee confirmed to the board their intent to preserve GT&EA assets, including Dr. Tate saying he would do anything he could to keep the building in the hands of black people, rumors abounded. The upcoming celebration would be a time to assuage fears and work collectively as the GT&EA officers and board shared openly with the Representative Assembly plans for the merger. In the meantime, the organization would work to pay off the building so that black teachers would fully own it. And, since GEA was continuing its programmatic planning for the next school year with no collaboration across organizations, GT&EA would do the same, especially since GT&EA membership was growing. The board agreed it would begin immediately to affirm the organization's history and contributions to the profession, and would continue until the Friday night of the 1968 convention.[1] Finally, after hours of discussion, the meeting adjourned.

But the group reconvened two weeks later. On May 27, board members from across the eleven regions of the state again drove to the GT&EA building, this time to make a decision on the proposed merger agreement between GEA and GT&EA. Already GEA leadership had allowed some of the information from discussions of the Joint Committee to become public. In contrast, GT&EA representatives on the Joint Committee had followed the confidentiality agreement and remained silent. Today, for the first time, GT&EA members of the Joint Committee on Merger would share the recommendations of the committee.

Board members pored over the materials. Some items appeared perfunctory—details on when both organizations would submit their individual charters back to NEA could be addressed easily. Ways to reconcile the structure of the two organizations and how to include GT&EA services GEA did not provide could all be addressed. But in other areas, board members saw major problems. The fact that GEA had approved the document "word for word" did nothing to encourage them to join in agreement with the document they saw. Neither did they appreciate the news that NEA wanted their approval a few days hence, on June 1.

President Hawes, a GT&EA member of the Joint Committee, agreed to have Dr. Tate, also a member of the Joint Committee, fill in all the gaps as they proceeded through the plan, explaining how each item had been derived. "I want to encourage you to ask questions . . . every question you can ask," President Hawes declared. The board needed no encouragement.

The board expressed its disagreement with GEA's idea of "one man, one vote" since white people would have the majority and would need no protection. Board members wanted guarantees of representation from each organization on committees and in leadership on a rotating basis. The document said they would only have the guarantee for ten years. Ten years was not enough time, they said. NEA seemed to have an "understanding" that first a man and then a woman would be president of the organization. Why could not the new merged organization in Georgia guarantee the same with regard to race? The board wanted a guarantee that blacks would be represented in the merged organization. If they caved on this point, everything GT&EA stood for could be voted down in a decade.[2]

The need to preserve their historic purpose was fresh in the minds of board members after the Drive-By Conference a few weeks earlier. R.J. Martin, a leader in GT&EA for decades, had mentioned at the meeting the reason black educational organizations existed. Black educational organizations were to allow "composite school personnel to come together to look at the problems confronting education . . . and map out programs" to address the problems, he pointed out. If white organizations had expressed any interest in the problems confronting black children or in allowing black members in their white organizations in earlier years, the black organizations would never have had to be created. Black organizations had, of necessity, existed, and they continued to serve as affirmative advocates for black education.

In the current educational climate, he said, from President Lyndon Johnson's office to the Fifth Circuit Court of Appeals and on down, black organizations were getting pressure to yield so that mergers could be accomplished. White people didn't want to yield. "They want you to yield!" Mr. Martin emphasized. He reminded them of the problems he and Dr. Davis and members of NCOSTA already knew of in the so-called mergers that had occurred in other states. Unification might have been accomplished in name, but he could not say the problems had been solved.

In Oklahoma, the black teachers organization went out of business, and immediately Negroes started losing their jobs by the hundreds. "Where was the voice to speak for the Negro teacher? It had gone," he said. "It was buried the moment unification took place." Across the South, he said, all the mergers created was new language for the same old patterns of segregation.[3]

Mr. Martin finally expressed to the board a conviction he had not aired publicly at the Drive-By Conference. "[I have] studied this thing and it's like a nightmare. . . . I don't care how you merge, and I don't care when you merge," but the truth was that "you are going to pay a cost for it."[4]

Mr. Martin was not alone in his worries. Continuing down the list, board members focused on items they believed would hurt black education. They agreed the new organization could not have two executive secretaries, but they did not like the GEA maneuvering to try to get their executive secretary on top.

Dinnertime came and went, and the board members continued to talk to each other. Sometime they talked past each other, or talked over each other. Eventually the group did take a dinner break, and after they reconvened the president asked Dr. Tate to explain again the language of the item pertaining to the executive secretary.

Dr. Tate read from the document: "The executive secretary of the new organization shall be one of the persons now serving as executive secretary of GEA and/or GTEA. Whichever one is not selected shall become associate executive secretary." When he finished reading, Dr. Tate detailed how the respective representatives to the Joint Committee from GEA and GT&EA had attempted to maneuver regarding the statement.

"As you can see, GT&EA voted for this and GEA defeated it. . . . Then GEA came back with the statement: 'The executive secretary of the new organization shall be one of the executive secretaries serving.' The only difference in this statement is that the word 'now' is out." GEA's president had moved to adopt the new language, but GT&EA defeated the motion.

Then Mr. Martin had proposed a new motion: "Any successor to either of the two present executive secretaries before the merger becomes effective shall assume the position of associate executive secretary." GT&EA moved to adopt Mr. Martin's language, but GEA defeated the motion.

Finally, to the vexation of GT&EA members, who did not see why the twenty-member Joint Committee could not resolve the matter, the language about who would serve as executive secretary had been referred to a subcommittee for further review. The executive secretary question had caused so much dissension that, momentarily, the Joint Committee considered missing the NEA deadline and simply not submitting a plan for merger.

"The difference is this," Dr. Tate said. "As of now you have two persons. You have Mr. Hughes and H. E. Tate serving as executive secretaries." In the original language, the organization would have one of these two individuals as the new executive secretary; the other would be the associate. However, Mr. Hughes—who did not hold a terminal degree, as did Dr. Tate—was thinking of retiring soon.

If the two current executive secretaries were evaluated on the basis of experience and education, GEA would be vulnerable in its expectation of continued leadership of the new organization. GEA needed time to hire a leader with Dr. Tate's credentials. Thus the fight over the words "now serving" as candidates for the leadership position.[5]

The board members sitting around the table decoded GEA's quest for leadership of the new organization as another example of replacing black leaders, similar to the replacement of black principals and teachers across the state. They believed the executive secretary with the most experience should lead the new organization.

They also wanted to make sure the white executive director's salary would not exceed Dr. Tate's salary, especially if he was doing less work

As GT&EA and GEA maneuvered to create a merger agreement that would be fair to both groups and to all children, the executive directors of both organizations held a joint press conference. Dr. Tate appears with GEA director Frank Hughes at the GEA headquarters on August 25, 1967. *GT&EA Collection*

because he was not the top pick. Dr. Tate had said publicly in Macon and again today that the salary matters of staff and leadership should "not be about me personally." He reminded the board he had taken a cut in salary to become executive secretary of GT&EA. However, as a negotiation point, salary mattered to the board.[6] Blacks and whites making the same salary for the same job was a matter of long-standing concern.

Then they moved on to other objections. The members appreciated Dr. Tate's leadership but chided him for letting the Joint Committee put in the idea of ten years of rotating positions between black and white. They also raised questions about the future of their assets, especially the GT&EA building. Although GEA had initially expressed no interest in the GT&EA building, the building would soon be fully owned by GT&EA, and GEA was now interested in it as an asset. What would happen to the GT&EA building in the merger?

President Hawes had nudged Dr. Tate under the table during Joint Committee meetings on the matter of the building. To fail to negotiate regarding the GT&EA building was not in the spirit of the "real merger" GT&EA wanted. However, in the present dispute about so many matters representing power and control, the black members of the Joint Committee had decided GT&EA's best interests would be served if GEA did not want the GT&EA building. They had omitted the building as a topic so that GEA's lack of interest would allow blacks to maintain their Ashby Street property.

However, GEA had shifted positions on the building after NEA representatives at the 1967 state convention reportedly provided to GEA the news that made the GT&EA building attractive. NEA representatives heard GT&EA leadership discuss publicly in its 1967 meeting its plans to finish paying for the building during the golden anniversary. A building without a mortgage shifted from a liability to an appealing asset.

Placing their building into the merger negotiations was fair, but board members did not like the idea of GEA controlling the GT&EA building. In other states, such as Virginia and North Carolina, black organizations lost assets in mergers and meeting locations for black educators disappeared.

As the debate continued at the GT&EA meeting, night fell. Finally, one of the regional directors, Mr. John E. Robinson, determined to make his position clear. "I'd like to make a statement, and I'd like to make a motion," he said. "In looking at all the other items that we have acted on here today, giving consideration to some of the guarantees that we want and I would like to say here that unless we are assured of some guarantees in this new association, then I will stand up here until hell freezes over and say we are not going to give anybody our assets." The new merged organization had better ensure "adequate representation." If it did not, it should not get GT&EA assets. And he was ready to make a motion to that effect.

President Hawes sought to remind Mr. Robinson that at least four times during the discussion he had made clear that nothing the board decided on could be made permanent until the Representative Assembly of GT&EA approved it. The merger would have to be acceptable to everybody, the president said.

Mr. Martin agreed that everyone wanted "certain assurances." Perhaps they should hold "in abeyance" the provision about assets and liabilities.

"What is the difference between rejection and abeyance?" an irate board member wanted to know. Either the board was going to agree with the Joint Committee's proposal or it was not.

The clock kept on ticking, and still the cross-talk continued. "There are people in their graves today who were making $57.50 per month but who paid an extra dollar toward the building fund. Those dear old souls would turn over in their graves and say to us, 'Curse it: You gave away what we gave you and what you received in heritage.'"

The president tried to call for a vote on the matter, but more objections were raised. "I don't believe that there is a man here this afternoon who feels that we are so rich that we can just give away something." They needed to "search our hearts and search our minds and come up with some way that we can protect this thing."

At last President Hawes asked for a roll call on Mr. Martin's substitute motion to hold in abeyance the matter of liabilities and assets. "Region I, Yes; Region II, Yes; Region III, No, Region IV, No; Region V, Yes, Region Six, Yes; Region Seven, Yes; Region Eight, Yes; Region Nine, absent; Region Ten, Yes, Region Eleven, No."

Mr. Robinson had been overruled by his colleagues, but he was still angry. "I want the minutes to read that my votes against holding in abeyance was for a strong motion that we should reject [the resolution to put the Ashby Street building into negotiation] altogether." He was sick of "beating around the bush." They had been sitting here all day, and they were all in agreement that they did not like parts of the proposal for merger.

Why didn't they just tell NEA they didn't like particular statements? "We don't want it," he said. "So why keep pussyfooting around?"

And that was the question that had to be finalized before weary regional directors could begin the long drives back home. Dr. Tate had to report to NEA in a few days on their decision regarding the Joint Committee's proposal. What should he say?

The mere question of Dr. Tate's response led to more contention over the items they did not like, especially representation for blacks over the life of the organization, not just for ten years. Ten years was tokenism, some said emphatically; blacks should always be fully involved in the power of the new organization. Moreover, they were tired of people putting one black man on a board and calling it integration.

In fact, NEA was not even well integrated, and GT&EA board members resented that as well. Dr. Tate and two other blacks had been the only blacks present in conversations with GEA and NEA about merger. "And around the table about like this one sat eleven members of the NEA Executive Committee, and around the wall sat about twelve other people, twelve or fourteen staff members from NEA," Dr. Tate recounted, "and even though we were there discussing merger, there was not a single black face on the NEA Executive Committee. Neither did the NEA staff under Dr. Carr [the executive secretary of NEA until 1967] have enough foresight to bring in some NEA staff members who were Negro to sit around the wall."

To Dr. Tate, the NEA model meant that the three black GT&EA members were basically three against thirty-five in the meeting. He felt that NEA appeared to be in alignment with the white GEA. Both appeared comfortable with an integration that involved only a few blacks just so NEA could say it had integrated. "This is what it amounts to," Dr. Tate concluded.[7]

Board members understood there was a battle being quietly waged: words of equality versus justice in practice. They voiced the same objections the NAACP had communicated to Commissioner Howe as it encouraged him not to be swayed by southern outrage against his office demanding equality.[8] But seeing the injustice did not mean they necessarily agreed on a strategy for handling the problem they faced.

"You've got to determine at this point whether you are going to be dictated to by the NEA Executive Committee or whether you are going to exercise in this case sovereignty," Dr. Tate finally noted. NEA had said

GT&EA needed to give its approval to the entire document, and Dr. Tate needed to respond to the NEA. "It is one way or the other," he said.

Mr. Robinson spoke again. "I move that the Executive Secretary send the report as it was acted upon today in our meeting." Someone seconded the motion that NEA be informed about the concerns they raised. Another person raised a question. Then came the vote. The motion carried. Affirming the board's decision, Mr. Robinson said, "I think we ought to not acquiesce. . . . We ought to be forward and stand up and be counted and I think we ought to let NEA and everybody else know that." GT&EA would protect itself without caring whether NEA considered its actions to be obstructionist.

An unnamed colleague echoed him: "This is our organization, not theirs."

As the meeting began to wind down, a few final matters were brought up. One irate board member mentioned he was also tired of HEW sending all these white faces down from Washington telling everybody about how to integrate. "I told [one of them], 'You all ought to practice what you preach.' I said, 'I have never seen a dark face on the group coming down here to discuss programs of education under Title I, in fact, all of the titles under ESEA.'" He told his fellow board members that, to his delight, the federal government under Commissioner Howe had apparently acquiesced to the critique. "Ever since that time," the speaker concluded, "they have brought one or two Negroes with them."

The board also discussed their dissatisfaction with the sums white superintendents withheld from black educators' salaries for insurance products provided by white insurance companies. They decided to endorse an insurance company controlled by blacks. While black educators could in theory choose any insurance they wanted, the board believed they should not feel compelled to go along with the superintendents' decisions.

Finally President Hawes reined in the talk. He extended thanks to the board members for taking time out from their busy schedules to come in and handle the important business of GT&EA, and then he pronounced the meeting adjourned. The weary board members said their good nights, headed back through the heavy wooden door of the GT&EA suite, descended the stairs, and found their cars in the parking lot. On Monday morning, all would be in their respective schools handling school business. They would leave it to Dr. Tate to craft their collective response to NEA.[9]

But tonight they had taken a stand. Whatever the consequences, GT&EA demanded a voice in its own integration. The only problem was that the federal structure needed to support their position on equality in merging were being weakened. Thanks to the southern attacks on him, both on his policies and on him personally, Commissioner Howe, who provided the federal enforcement of student and faculty integration, was on his way out.

It did not matter that black educators in Georgia and across the South supported Commissioner Howe. Some GT&EA board members wrote letters to the president, to HEW secretary John Gardner, and to Commissioner Howe commending them on the federal guidelines and expressing "complete confidence" in Harold Howe and approval "over the manner in which he conducted the affairs of his office." The local black newspaper ran an article with the headline "GTEA Urges Enforcement of School Guidelines."[10]

GT&EA also publicly supported the federal government's actions in the *Herald*. "What manner of man is it," they queried, "and what kind of thinking goes on in the mind of men who receive, for example, $100,000 per year for 50 years for equal distribution between two groups of children and, instead of dividing it, gives $90,000 to one group and $10,000 to the other? What manner of man could steal from, and cheat a group of children out of $2,000,000 over a fifty-year period, then object to attempting to repay it even though the repayment comes from a source not directly his own?"

"Title I funds provide an excellent means for remedying ills that have festered and lingered for years. But evidence shows that there are many who do not want a remedy for certain ills unless, of course, the ills can be treated as they (the unscrupulous) see fit." GT&EA knew local systems needed the money. It also knew the local systems perpetuated inequality and violated federal guidelines. If local systems were left to their own discretion, "the ills confronting black education would not be treated."[11] The federal government needed to remain firm. So said NCOSTA. So said GT&EA.[12]

But the opinion of black educators was becoming less important in a federal climate unwilling to continue to engage black demands for inclusion. Commissioner Howe was imposing federal guidelines for equality in ways that jeopardized federal funding for local school districts, and those districts were not happy.

In Congress, Representative Lucius Rivers of South Carolina expressed particular outrage. Commissioner Howe, or maybe one of his "hirelings," had actually called "down to one of [his] school superintendents" in South Carolina and asked about how they were going to employ faculty. "Mr. Speaker," Mr. Rivers objected, "this man [Mr. Howe] talks like a Communist." The Judiciary Committee could try to review the guidelines requiring desegregation "this idiot has established," Mr. Rivers suggested, but the point was bigger. He needed to be "kicked out," for he was "destroying the schools." In fact, he continued, Mr. Howe had even gone to a black institution and told listening young people that "by exploitation and suffering this Nation was built." Without question, Mr. Rivers concluded, Commissioner Howe was "irresponsible."[13]

The U.S. House of Representatives passed a resolution capturing the response of some U.S. elected officials to Commissioner Howe's insistence that the South to follow federal guidelines: "Resolved that it is the sense of the House of Representatives that the continuation in office of Harold Howe II, Commissioner of Education, Department of Health Education and Welfare, is not in the best interest of public school systems of the United States and that Harold Howe II should be immediately removed from office or be replaced."[14]

Congressmen also turned to President Johnson: "Lyndon, can't you get rid of that son-of-a bitch Howe? He's lousing up the whole country."[15]

President Johnson had been trying to get Commissioner Howe accepted by the South. He had even compelled Commissioner Howe to prepare a letter to GEA congratulating them on their one hundredth anniversary in 1967.[16] But it had no effect on GEA practices or the political avalanche against him led by southern politicians.[17] And those politicians seemed to be reflecting the views of some of their constituents. "Now that you Johnsonian Communists have received another victory over the raped STATES," one irate American citizen wrote, "we have no alternative but to brutally damn the educators for allowing insane Federal officials to curtail STATES' RIGHTS."

Commissioner Howe thought President Johnson tried to "stand up to his old buddies," who wanted to promote state and local governments' ability to self-determine even if the practices created inequality and violated the law. Commissioner Howe even championed the president as the political battle around his own future raged. He admired President Johnson as a southern man who had determined to become president of the whole country rather than simply be a regional politician.

Though one loyal black supporter sent him a Christmas card every year, perhaps as a small thank-you for the president forcing the FBI director to turn his agency's attention away from civil rights activities to the Ku Klux Klan, President Johnson was not the full savior for the black man that his political actions may have suggested.[18] The president could also use racial epithets, including the term "nigra," freely when he talked with southern legislators. Moreover, it was challenging for the president to wage a war for equality when politicians of his own party, including Georgia's Democratic senator Herman Talmadge, described themselves as feeling "sick" when Johnson signed the Civil Rights Act.[19] The Vietnam War was raging, and President Johnson wanted a life beyond Washington. Long before he announced during the State of the Union Address in 1967 that he did not intend to seek office again, he had already shared with close advisors his intention to leave Washington.

Commissioner Howe read accurately the Washington backlash against the federal government championing equality for all citizens. When the president communicated his decision to leave, Commissioner Howe made similar plans. He had been unfortunate enough to believe the South would meet desegregation guidelines in order to get the billions of dollars available. However, the congressional objections combined with the president's departure meant that the federal climate had sufficiently shifted to render him impotent.[20]

Commissioner Howe's predecessor, Francis Keppel, who was now safely back in Cambridge, tried to encourage the beleaguered Mr. Howe. Noting that his morning paper had carried a report of the change in "civil rights matters in HEW," he offered his observation to Commissioner Howe as "an outsider who was once an insider in these matters." Commissioner Howe had "carried the battle to the point where the courts should take over in the (now sharply limited) states that seem determined to resist." Mr. Keppel believed that the "major battle" had been won, and he hoped Mr. Howe would take "personal pride in the whole affair."[21]

Mr. Keppel spoke from the sanctuary of the Harvard Graduate School of Education, an institution that in another year would side with the white South when it aligned with GEA's interests over those of GT&EA. But in Georgia, the federal support needed to stand against inequality had suddenly toppled, and educational opportunities for blacks appeared bleaker.

As Dr. Tate commented to the GT&EA Board of Directors when they met again later in the year to plan the organization's golden anniversary,

"Situations are not getting better for us, they are getting worse." There were not merely perplexing problems of firing and destruction of leadership. There were the age-old problems of salary and buildings and unfairness from every angle. "It is going to take all the ingenuity, motivation, and inspiration that we can muster up to keep ourselves going," he confessed.

They needed to be serious about it, he said. But not too serious. "Otherwise we lose our saneness."[22]

24

A CHARGE TO KEEP I HAVE

The GT&EA golden anniversary commemoration began as a celebration but ended as a protest. Directors across the state had touted the event to the membership and solicited funding to be used to pay off the mortgage on the Ashby Street building, hire additional GT&EA staff, and make Dr. Tate's salary competitive with that of the white executive director of GEA. They were determined to be sure GT&EA could merge with GEA on an equal and competitive basis. In response to the call to strengthen as they celebrated their golden anniversary, approximately five thousand black educators gathered from across the state and registered throughout the afternoon of April 3, 1968.[1]

That evening the GT&EA president tapped the gavel three times to hush the lively talking and laughter that dominated the banquet room of the newly integrated white hotel in which they met, and attendees turned their attention to the head table. With formality, President Hawes declared the first Representative Assembly of the fiftieth annual meeting of GT&EA officially convened.

He explained that some business matters needed to be addressed before guests could enjoy the plates soon to be served by hotel staff. To be served was a leap for black educators, considering that at earlier meetings they filed through the cafeterias of black schools, carefully acknowledging the black women who had prepared the food, and took their own trays out to the student dining room to eat. Tonight, the president reminded them, they simply needed to display their tickets on the table indicating they had paid to attend the banquet or have the money ready to purchase a ticket and hotel staff would serve them. Integration had its benefits.

As the session began, the assembly rose in solemn solidarity for prayer and the presentation of the colors. They listened respectfully to the varied recognitions of the parliamentarian, the state officers, the committee chairs, and the officers of the Department of Classroom Teachers, who

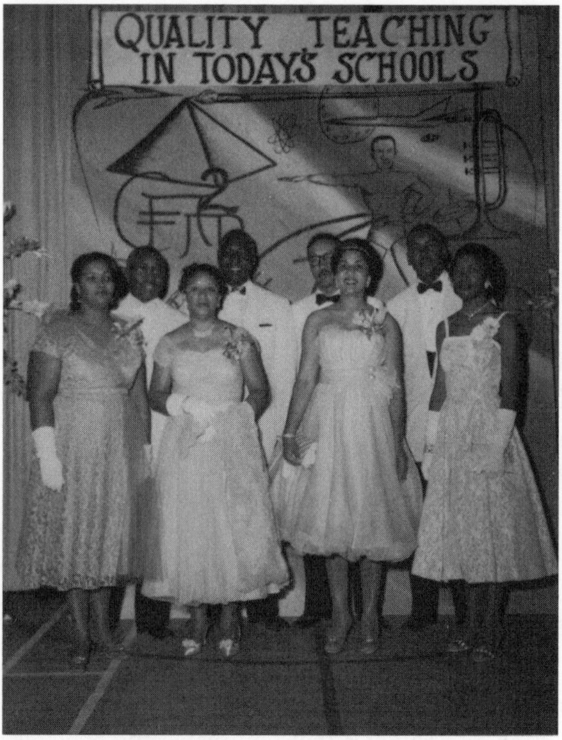

Selecting the annual teacher of the year was a task seriously undertaken by state, regional, and local members of the GT&EA. The regional winners were honored at the state meeting, and the state winner spoke at the annual meeting when a new state winner was named. A recognized educator independent of her husband, Mr. Tate's wife, Mrs. Virginia Tate, was among Georgia teachers honored for her work as a home economist during the years her husband was completing his doctorate at the University of Kentucky. She received a B.S. degree in home economics from West Virginia State College and an M.A. from Columbia University. In this photo, she is shown on the far right. *GT&EA Collection*

were sponsoring the opening meeting for the first time. As the president acknowledged each person or group, the audience dutifully applauded and the piano chimed melodic chords in the background. At the end of the long list, the president encouraged the attendees to applaud all other guests, and the attendees joyfully applauded themselves.

Food aromas drifted into the dining room, but President Hawes insisted that the delegates conduct some business before they ate. Dutifully the delegates approved the rules and adopted the minutes of the meeting. They listened to several committee reports and perfunctorily adopted each.

"Mr. President, I move the adoption of the . . . report."

"Mr. President, I second."

"You have heard the motion. It has been properly seconded. Are you ready for the question? All for the motion, say aye. All opposed?" Only once in the procedural reports did a delegate raise an objection.

"The ayes have it. The motion passes." Then the president moved on to the next item of business. All of the business before they ate related to regional meetings or routine legislation. The president included no committee reports requiring serious debate.

Instead, attendees used the evening to celebrate this golden moment in their history. The president of the Department of Classroom Teachers lauded the GT&EA leadership, past and present. She likened black teachers to English leaders in the 1600s who stood up and did what they believed was right. "We want Dr. Tate and all our leaders to know they are like [those English leaders]. We are proud of them."

When she called for the blessing, the audience laughed, because in the opening prayer, the principal from Madison—a quaint town through which Mr. Tate and Mr. Harper had driven on those long nights going to and from Atlanta—had not just appealed to God to allow them to stand together in this moment of educational crisis but also had already blessed the food to come. "Well, we can't have too many blessings," she quipped. The additional blessing was made, proclaiming thankfulness "for this festive occasion," and at the end the audience laughed again, relieved to finally be able to enjoy their meal to the strains of piano music before the evening's speaker, Ralph McGill, a renowned white columnist for the *Atlanta Journal and Constitution* known for his relatively liberal columns.[2] The gala ended with a tall, tiered fiftieth-birthday cake, candles and all.

The next day, the business of GT&EA proceeded much as it had during the previous fifty years. In sessions that began on Thursday morning at 9:00 and again at 1:00 in the afternoon, delegates patiently listened to committee reports, raised questions about matters of concern, and, with meticulous execution of parliamentary procedure, voted on policies they would support.

Many long-standing educational matters concerning black children and teachers still needed to be confronted at the Representative Assembly in 1968. They wanted the Governor's Honors Program to include more black students and teachers, the state school board to stop excluding Negroes, and the distribution of federal funds monitored at the local level to be sure that superintendents included Negroes among those receiving the benefits of that funding and that they were sensitive to the needs of black children. The black educators pronounced themselves tired of fundraising to pay for items in black schools; they wanted the state to adhere to the mandated student-teacher ratio; they objected to textbooks that did not show Negroes in a positive light and did not appreciate local superintendents who would not let them order alternative books. They wanted the overcrowding of buses and double runs of buses for black children stopped. Consistent with concerns in their national meetings for decades, they believed the testing program for children needed to be aligned with an assessment of physical facilities, curricular offerings, student activities, and financial support.

Throughout the day, the reports and discussions and voting continued. The Committee on Unmet Needs commended the "forward steps" in education resulting from federal money but pointed out the continued needs for school plants, gymnasiums, additional teaching aids, and materials. Citizens needed to be part of regional meetings, and every region needed a public relations committee. Local units, which leadership considered the heart of the organization, needed a legislative committee comprised of people who knew their local representatives serving in the House and Senate and were willing to seek out these people. With the regular updates from Dr. Tate's office describing the ways the welfare of Negro teachers and pupils was jeopardized by local boards of education, local communities should have the information they needed to advocate for themselves.[3]

In some of the areas under discussion, the position of the black educators aligned with the positions of NEA and GEA. Both NEA and GEA were concerned about salary, for example, and black educators who had taught for decades earning less money agreed that increased salary was important. However, unlike GEA and NEA, more of their resolutions related directly to problems uniquely confronting black education. Delegates affirmed their commitment to integration, but also challenged local inequalities. Clearly the desegregation guidelines needed to be "written and implemented in a manner that is just and right to all pupils and educators."[4]

The proposed merger between GT&EA and GEA was not formally debated in this session. The reports from a February meeting in Washington that detailed the experiences of teachers organization in southern

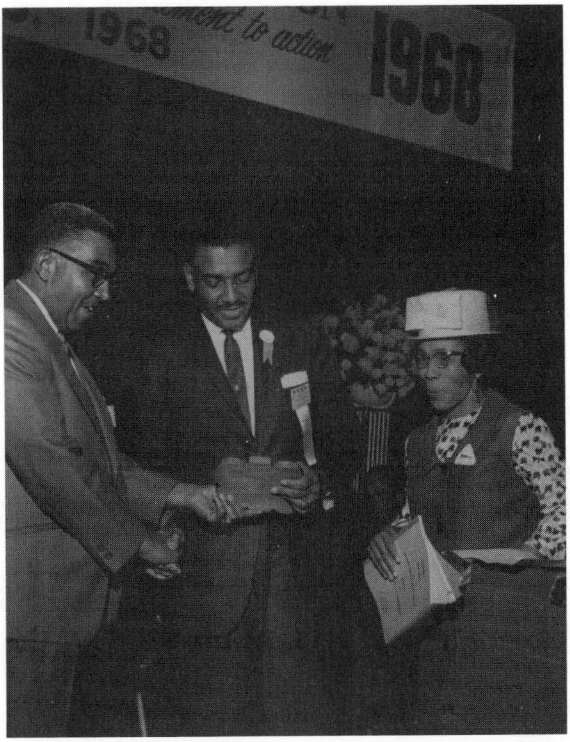

Amid multiple efforts to create a just school integration in Georgia, GT&EA paused in 1968 to salute its executive secretary. Here President Hawes extends congratulations as Dr. Tate receives a plaque from Mary Gorden, curriculum director, Baldwin County Schools. The Citations Committee selected Dr. Tate for the award because of his "generosity to humanity, his service to the profession, and his dedication to the cause of education for all." *GT&EA Collection*

states that had merged confirmed the suspicion of GT&EA leaders that merger simply meant elimination. Most of those reports had been given by white representatives and had been "almost devoid of references about Negroes." However, because no merger proposal by the Joint Committee had been agreed upon by the boards of directors of both GT&EA and GEA, the merger concerns could not be debated on the business floor of the Representative Assembly. Instead, GT&EA disseminated a document in question-and-answer format: "Some Probable Approaches to the Solution of Problems that GT&EA Members Might Face During the 1968–69 School Year." The document provided guidelines on ways to deal with superintendents withholding contracts and with pressure from local GEA

Black educators flood the Municipal Auditorium in Atlanta, Georgia, for the annual convention. *GT&EA Collection*

chapters to join. It also included a statement about GT&EA's commitment to a fair merger.[5]

On Thursday at the Second General Assembly, the educators enjoyed their usual array of informative speakers, including Jack P. Nix, the state superintendent who oversaw Georgia's public schools. They heard reflections on education from the vice mayor of Atlanta, who was also a school superintendent, and from Georgia's lieutenant governor. Special interest groups met. Department and affiliate meetings convened.[6] The final business event of the evening, the Third General Assembly and Cultural Series, was slated to begin at seven forty-five.

After a full professional day, thousands of impeccably dressed teachers and principals pushed through the sets of massive doors and into the lobby of the Municipal Auditorium. Some among them stopped to peruse copies of the glossy history of their organization, *Rising in the Sun*, written by the well-known historian Dr. Horace Mann Bond with a committee of GT&EA leaders. The educators were proud that they had written their own story. Dr. Tate said the books being published by NEA about black educators "did not tell the whole story."[7] A few of those stopping purchased copies of the history, paying the $2.50 to take home a piece of this golden anniversary.

Joviality spread over the auditorium as friends greeted friends from other schools and regions, and voices hummed and echoed across the auditorium. Most of the teachers and principals had traveled to Atlanta from the rural areas of Georgia and the smaller towns and relished spending three days in the lively urban area. After the speeches that evening would come the cultural part of the program, which they all were looking forward to. It would feature musical selections from schools in LaGrange, Rochelle, and Columbus; band selections from Mr. Tate's former school in Griffin, Fairmont; and creative dance and choral performances from Booker T. Washington students. Black teachers leading the groups emphasized artistic precision, and students routinely performed at professional levels.[8] They sang and played gospel and classical, contemporary, and traditional music with equal, nuanced precision under the direction of their demanding teachers.

Finally Rev. James Shropshire led the opening prayer for the evening's program. "We pause to ask for strength in this turbulent world," he began. He sought divine intervention for the agonizing problems they confronted that made it difficult to serve the boys and girls who they hoped would take the reins of citizenship and lead blacks to higher heights. "O God," he pleaded, "if it were not for a God like you, we could not carry on." He hoped they would work to "eventually beat hatred" and "come out victoriously." The organist sounded a soft note as Rev. Shropshire ended and sat down.

Heads lifting, some shifting in their seats, the audience members now focused on the podium as they prepared to listen to the evening's speech recounting the history of the association by Robert L. Cousins, the white man who formerly had been the director of the Division of Negro Education. Tomorrow, they would all watch a dramatic portrayal of the history at the final assembly, but tonight the task of Mr. Cousins, to whom Dr. Tate and others had had to appeal when they needed a white man to mediate between themselves and local superintendents, was to remind the audience of the struggles of previous generations and the progress that had been made.

Mr. Cousins's talk was titled "Recollections of the Highlights During My Association with the Georgia Teachers and Education Association Since 1932." Dr. Tate, the other featured guests seated on the platform, and the audience listened intently. At one time Dr. Tate had trusted Mr. Cousins.

But then Mr. Cousins had asked Dr. Tate and two other GT&EA leaders to an informal meeting to discuss white resistance to integration, and he had asked for a concession from the black educators: that black principals would agree to become principals of elementary schools only, allowing white principals to lead high schools. Mr. Cousins's so-called resolution for the State School Board was his way of addressing the white resistance to integration that led to black principals being fired, yet still continuing to privilege white leadership. Dr. Tate had been unwilling to make that concession, explaining that he could not support any resolution that suggested he was not "educated enough, good enough, [and did not] have enough sense" to lead a high school while a white principal could lead a high school simply because he was white. The proposal never went forward, but a good amount of the earlier respect Dr. Tate had for Mr. Cousins evaporated as a result.[9]

Mr. Cousins spoke thoughtfully about earlier struggles. He referenced names few in the audience knew, including Henry A. Hunt and Charles Harper, well known in previous years but now all but forgotten. He connected the older, struggle-weary Dr. Bond to those now present by recalling Dr. Bond's leading role as editor of their journal, the *Herald*. Of course, Mr. Cousins did not talk about the tricks employed by all these black educators when their direct appeals to southern leaders had not worked. He would not have known.

His recollections moving past the years of world wars, he addressed the years just before the *Brown v. Board of Education* decision and humorously derided the failure of the state education department to provide quality new schools for black children. Built to avoid a mandate to integrate, the new schools that had been constructed had many faults, and black educators had experienced them. To knowing chuckles, Mr. Cousins spoke of the water system that had failed at one of these newly built schools, making it impossible to get a drink or flush a toilet. At another school, the heating system had failed entirely during a meeting of educators, who nevertheless continued on in subfreezing temperatures. In a third location, a failed electrical system caused the chicken for the midday meal to be only half cooked. Some delegates in the audience nodded, remembering the strain of these earlier meetings during the years when the state pretended it was providing equal education for Negroes. Those years had been ones of trial and suffering, Mr. Cousins said, but in his estimation GT&EA had met the challenges with "hard-earned gains."

For Mr. Cousins, 1968 was a moment of triumph as full school integration approached. Only the night before, GT&EA had held its first event in the banquet hall of a white-owned restaurant, the Motor Hotel. It was but one of many signs that the rigid segregated ways were changing in this new progressive day. Mr. Cousins jubilantly applauded the progress and urged the GT&EA to join with the white educators of GEA. Together, the two groups could create a united teaching profession in the state. They would then follow the light of Florida, a state where the two formerly separate racial educational groups had already become one group. Mr. Cousins believed the merger a momentous occasion to be celebrated. From his seat on the stage, Dr. Tate silently questioned whether real progress had been made in Florida—in his opinion, black educators in Florida had simply given up, and he was determined to not allow Georgia to follow the same pattern. But now was not the time to discuss it.[10]

After Mr. Cousins sat down to polite applause, Dr. Tate paid the elder white educator the respect accorded his position and commended Mr. Cousins's role in the history of the education of blacks in Georgia. On another night, he might have interlaced his own story with Mr. Cousins as he reminisced how they'd collaborated to ask for books for his school, or recalled with a smile himself and a white superintendent arguing in Mr. Cousins's office, neutral territory, about a contract. Or he might have hammered on his favorite theme: the contributions of GT&EA to black education in Georgia. He should have been telling them about GT&EA's "amazing and almost miraculous" history: how it had worked to bring about public schools in the state and make certain the schools received the equipment they needed. He loved reminding the young teachers that GT&EA had fought against policies that allowed superintendents to continue to pay white teachers more money, even after salaries between black and white teachers had allegedly been equalized by the state. GT&EA helped parents learn how to advocate effectively to obtain facilities and services for their children. It had fought for buses and books for black children; investigated superintendents who discriminated against black teachers; insisted on black presence in representative bodies; helped fund the educational program of the NAACP; and worked directly with Commissioner Howe and HEW to protect the interests of black teachers, children, and communities.[11]

"No one . . . but GT&EA worked to set in motion [what the children needed] for first class citizenship. No one else has done it for us!" That was the kind of speech those in the audience expected. Such language and reminders would be vintage Dr. Tate in a slot set aside for him to speak, and even sometimes when he was not slated to speak.

But instead of his usual speech, Dr. Tate delivered an announcement no one expected.

Dr. Tate always spoke with confidence. He was a serious man when it came to matters of the organization of black educators, so serious that his elder daughter hardly recognized him at the office as the same attentive father she saw at home.[12] Tonight his voice carried its usual commanding tone as he completed his perfunctory remarks about Mr. Cousins.

But then his voice changed, and he sounded shaken as he called several offices of GT&EA to the platform.

"About twenty minutes ago," he began, "I received the call that Martin Luther King had been shot."

The audience sat in shocked silence.

"We were going to ask Brother Shropshire to utter a prayer that it was not serious and that he would get well," he went on, then paused. He needed composure to deliver the remainder of the news.

"About six minutes ago, I went to the phone and received the news that Rev. Martin Luther King Jr. is dead."

Black educators across the auditorium gasped in a collective cry of pain as the audience erupted in pandemonium. Somewhere someone moaned, "Oh no!" Another called on the Jesus to whom they had just prayed.

Dr. Tate struggled to rein in his own emotions. Had it not been for the conflict with the annual meeting, he and some others would have been present with Dr. King at the Garbage Workers' Strike in Memphis.[13] Haltingly he said that Rev. King had "died for a tremendous cause" but could go no further. The pause lengthened before the esteemed leader of thirteen thousand black educators in Georgia finally said quietly, "Rev. Shropshire, maybe you had better come."

Chimes from the ever-present organ played as Rev. Shropshire returned to the podium to pray. This time, though, his prayer did not celebrate the joviality of friendship. Rather, it expressed collective horror mingled with tears, anguish, and fear. "If a man dies, will he live again?" he began, to quiet sobs from audience members.

In a monotone, Rev. Shropshire asked the Eternal One to give them "the strength to abide by the principle of nonviolence and the strength to be kind." He prayed that all of them be allowed to "catch the spirit of Martin Luther King Jr." and that his death would bring them together.

When the prayer ended, the organist launched a rendition of "Nearer My God to Thee," somberly playing the melody only. It was a far cry from the beautiful spring evening one year ago when Rev. King had spoken majestically and emphatically, affirmed the rightness of their cause, and inspired everyone to believe that black educators could conquer inequality in a climate that spoke of equality but did not practice anything close to it. He had made them believe they would overcome in their demands for full justice because "no lie [could] live forever." For that one moment, they thought they really could transform the nation into a symphony of brotherhood.

Amid the shock and dismay that still pervaded in the auditorium, Dr. Tate called for Ulysses Byas, a leading principal in the state who had resigned in protest rather than accept a meaningless job at the central office while a white principal he helped train became principal of his city's new integrated high school. Mr. Byas headed the Resolutions Committee of GT&EA. From the podium, Dr. Tate assigned him the job of drafting a statement GT&EA could vote on to express its response to Rev. King's death.

President Hawes called an emergency meeting of the officers of the association to determine the direction of the rest of the fiftieth-anniversary celebration, both the remainder of the evening and the next day. Hundreds of black students were present and had prepared to perform in the cultural program. The leaders agreed they must not omit the performances of the four artistic groups that evening, despite the anguish of the moment.

But everyone needed a break. In stunned silence the teachers filed out of the auditorium. No words of any kind could be heard. Only the sound of chairs scraping and feet shuffling sounded for ten minutes or more, until finally, somewhere in the distance, an auditorium door thudded shut.

The teacher who directed one of the student choirs was as dismayed as anyone, but she knew her group must go through a final rehearsal for the evening's performance. Addressing her students without any of her characteristic affirmation and admonishment, she spoke flatly: "Lagrange, take it away."

The students rehearsed their selection. The last song was a haunting melody: "If we don't make it, no one will; if we don't do it, no one will."

As their voices rose to a majestic crescendo with the lighthearted tone that the performance required, despite the pain they felt, the students sang crisply: "If we don't dream it, no one will; if we don't fight it, no one will." Then, in metaphoric imagery, grieving black students sang the chorus: "It is up to us, up to us . . . to build a better world."

In America's memory, it would be up to the black students integrating white schools to build a new world. But in 1968, that time had not yet fully come. GT&EA still existed, and the organization still expected a voice in national and educational matters.

The black educators met in their Fourth General Assembly on Friday morning, April 5, and went through the motions of a meeting. They conducted a planned memorial service to honor deceased educators around the state, a service that now included memories of the slain Rev. Martin Luther King Jr. They listened respectfully to Dr. Deborah Wolfe, of Queens College in New York, as she crisply described the twenty major bills affecting education passed during the 87th, 88th, and 89th Congresses and the major role played by blacks in politics during this period.

When Dr. Wolfe finished speaking, Mr. Byas came forward to read the proposed resolution his committee had drafted:

> Whereas, this country of ours, the United States of America, begs from the Statue of Liberty for the hated, poor, rejected, despised and the down-trodden, and
>
> Whereas, this country of ours, the United States of America, guarantees through our constitution equal rights to all—the color of one's skin and his religious affiliation not withstanding, and
>
> Whereas there are forces operating in this country of ours, the United States of America, who would deny these rights to many of our people, and
>
> Whereas this country of ours, the United States of America, is a major nation dedicated, at least in theory, to basic Christian ethics and morals, and
>
> Whereas, the Moses of our day, Martin Luther King, Jr., a firm believer in all of these high and noble purposes and objectives, and . . .
>
> Whereas, in this convention one year ago, it was evident through our reception and reactions to Martin Luther King's excellent presentation, of our individual and collective commitment to the purposes for which he stood and goals which he sought:

> Therefore be it resolved that this convention eliminate the requirement of formal attire for the 8:00 p.m. session and that the President's Ball be cancelled, and
>
> Be it resolved, that this convention will call for all members present and other interested educators, black and white, to join us tonight at 10:30 p.m. in the city auditorium for the beginning of a silent, peaceful and non-violent march to the state capitol of Georgia for a ceremony, and . . .
>
> Be it further resolved that this convention call upon the President of our United States, the Congress, the Governors and the legislators of the separate states, all public servants and men of goodwill everywhere to re-dedicate themselves, this day, to the total and absolute elimination of prejudice and discrimination everywhere, so that the life given by Martin Luther King, Jr., in this year, 1968, our Golden Anniversary, would not have been in vain.

When Mr. Byas finished reading, he moved to adopt the resolution. Overlapping voices seconded the motion. The resolution, as a statement of the collective views of black educators, carried "without exception."[14]

They still had two hours of meeting before the march would begin, however. The directors reported on the funds raised throughout the eleven regions for GT&EA as part of the golden anniversary: amounts ranged from $2,563.00 in Region IX to $8,928.00 in Region IV. With the $100 contributions of many members to preserve their organization and building, GT&EA had a gross of about $90,000, Dr. Tate announced.

After the installation of the new officers, it was time to recount their own history. The audience stood to sing "America," a song about a land whose good would be crowned with brotherhood, and Mrs. Marie Dixon, a 1956 GT&EA Teacher of the Year, began narrating the well-planned dramatic performance about GT&EA history. Dr. Bond and the History Committee had said in their report that GT&EA needed to consider ways to perpetuate its heritage. Dr. Tate once said if they did not remember their history, in a few decades no one would know black educators had done anything.[15]

The history recounted a story of Negro educators who had been advocating for equality for far longer than the fifty years the GT&EA was celebrated. It named Richard Wright, though it did not fully explain that he had convened representatives from across the state in 1878 to protest the inequality seeping into the distribution of local public school money for

Outgoing officers of the GT&EA did not expect the 1968 meeting would include planning a demonstration in protest of Dr. King's assassination. Shown here are Milton J. White, Region III; W.H. McBride, Region IV; Josie B. Sessoms, Region VIII; J.A. Aldridge, Region II; J.D. Brown, director-at-large; Dane Mack, Region V; Horace Hawes, Region VII; James Hawes, president. Sharing the platform are Martha Wildow and H.E. Tate. Below the stage, members of the student group can be seen in choir robes. *GT&EA Collection*

black children after the federal government turned its back on Reconstruction and allowed southerners to make decisions about local matters. When disenfranchisement disrupted the ability of the organization to advocate directly for equality, Mr. Wright had also sat with Mr. Hunt, Dr. Du Bois, and others at the 1916 Amenia conference at which black leaders had agreed to organize.[16]

When Mrs. Dixon talked of Mr. Wright, she mentioned only that his group had championed professional development. She did not speak of the ways a changing federal climate had shut down the advocacy of Reconstruction-era black educators. She did not know that Mr. Wright, the slave descendant of an African chieftain, had also originated the focus on partnering with black parents by going into communities to tell them about problems, an idea that Mr. Wright had said came to him in a dream when he was discouraged. The current generation of educators thought their focus on school communities came from the white educator John Dewey.[17]

Mrs. Dixon then began the history lesson commonly recounted about forgotten actors as she described Negro citizens incensed and furious in 1917 for not being allowed to participate even on a limited basis in the political affairs of the state. She mentioned Mr. Hunt, who had spent many days of serious thinking about the plight of Negroes in Georgia before he called together a group of leading Georgians to establish a vehicle for attacking the problems. "Something must be done," she quoted him saying. "But what? Someone would have to set into motion a plan to help masses of Negroes, but who?"

Thus began, she said, Mr. Hunt's effort to organize a black organization to speak for education. Their goal had been to get equal salaries for black teachers, better buildings, longer school terms, summer schools, and district agricultural schools. Over the decades, black educators simply wanted for black children the resources and opportunities white educators and communities expected for their children. The audience listened respectfully. Even Dr. Tate did not remember Mr. Hunt, except as the silent grave on the Fort Valley campus.

The presentation lasted two hours as attendees either struggled to absorb names and events or allowed their minds to wander. All of them knew that across America, riots had begun and were worsening as angry blacks violently protested Rev. King's death in multiple cities. Still, the audience applauded politely when the long rendition of their history ended. Then Dr. Tate rose to prepare them for the march.

His words earlier in the day had captured the uncertainty of the moment. "I don't know about people who might join the march," Dr. Tate had said after the assembly passed the resolution. He had been alluding to the potential danger for those who might join him out marching in the streets of Georgia's capital at night. "I decided a long time ago that I am not afraid of dying," he said emphatically. "I don't think anyone is ready to teach unless he is willing to give his life for a worthy cause."[18]

Now the thousands of black educators silently awaited his directions. Dr. Tate reported he had obtained permission from the governor for the march, and that state patrol officers and city policemen had also convened outside the Municipal Auditorium to provide protection. They were to walk in the center of the street as they began the half-mile journey up the hill to the state capitol. He said if they walked outside the Municipal Auditorium and "outsiders intending to loot and destroy property" joined them, they would turn around and come back inside. Their goal was not to give people an opportunity to loot.

As Dr. Tate spoke, the sirens racing by the auditorium in the streets outside punctuated the danger. But the educators listened intently as Dr. Tate concluded, "We're doing what we ought to do . . . to honor Dr. King." And so they all would.

With dress coats and raincoats, heels and suits, hats and scarfs, the black educators linked arms in rows of four or more and marched out the auditorium doors. They descended the marble steps, turned left, and began the slow, silent uphill march to the state capitol. Its golden dome gleamed, even in the evening. Mr. Hunt had helped build the capitol building when he was still a student at Atlanta University. Its grounds now featured statues of people like Eugene Talmadge, a man who shamelessly restricted opportunities for American Negroes.[19]

When everyone had ascended the hill and gathered in the late evening shadows, Dr. Tate extolled the work of Rev. King. Rev. King had stood against all the inequalities and unfairnesses that Georgia and America had sought to keep in place. While America claimed to be defending freedom as it ensnared itself more deeply in the Vietnam War, Dr. King had said to be humble. When America said to kill, Dr. King had said to heal. While America said to bomb, Dr. King had preached nonviolence. He had loved people so well that he could separate the evil in a man from the man himself. Although he had never been president of the United States or mayor of a city, not a councilman or state legislator or U.S. representative, Rev. King was responsible for the signing of many laws that made life better for everyone.[20]

The teachers mourned publicly. Their hearts were burdened and they were "not consoled," even though many across the country joined in their bereavement. They sang the freedom song and reflected on the challenge Rev. King's death left for them. Could they be "so inspired, so rededicated, so motivated, so determined that they could help establish a climate conducive to the atmosphere of brotherhood?"[21]

The educators ended their protest and silently dispersed into the dark night. The golden anniversary was over. Forgotten was the closing prayer offering thanks for the service the organization had rendered for the last fifty years. Black educators had brought black education a long way, one speaker had said earlier before concluding they still had a long way to go. The thousands of black educators in silent lines of protest could not have known that one day they too would be forgotten.

25

JUSTICE BETRAYED

With vigor, GT&EA tried to carry on its defense of black education in the year that followed. Board members believed some political leaders were trying to solve the problems unfolding with desegregation, while others were trying not to solve them. At a Governors' Conference, Dr. Tate reasserted the GT&EA belief that America either believed in justice and would work toward it or it did not. Maintaining segregated schools violated American beliefs. However, the desegregation formula that had been publicly applauded did not fully render justice.[1]

For its part, the GT&EA Board of Directors determined to try to solve problems by demanding justice. As members convened at the conference table in the GT&EA building not long after the march to the state capitol in memory of Rev. King, Dr. Tate provided the executive secretary's report of the matters that had come directly to his office and the ways he had tried to fulfill their mandates since the last meeting. Following his report, each board member adhered to the usual protocol and described educational matters in his or her region. Some said these reports and discussions with their peers were the most meaningful professional engagement opportunity ever provided. Leaders asked questions, argued, and debated as they analyzed and reflected on the status of black education. Dominant in this meeting was the trend of black dismissals and demotions across Georgia and, indeed, across the South.

In the ongoing saga of GEA superintendents supporting GEA's merger ideals, some leaders reported superintendents seeking to disrupt the ability of GT&EA directors to reach the communities they served. The strength of GT&EA had always been in the local educational groups in communities across the 159 counties of Georgia, since the first structural point of complaint for local problems was with the regional director. When superintendents tried to inhibit directors from making the visits across their region that kept them abreast of the region's needs, as one regional director reported was happening, it threatened the network on which the organization relied.

GT&EA had not even merged with GEA, and already the situation in Georgia was starting to look a lot like that in Texas. Since the so-called merger in Texas of the black and white educational organizations, Dr. Davis said, it was difficult for the state's educational leaders to reach the black teachers of Texas. "I hesitated to write to the ones I know personally," his Texas informant explained, "and telephoning has not always proved successful."

In Georgia, the GT&EA board was already having a difficult time reaching black teachers in white schools.[2] Like Texas, where trends showed the non-renewal of contracts of black educators and vacancies filled by white educators, they knew black leadership was being intentionally eliminated in Georgia. Some black principals had been given offices in broom closets or employed to run empty schools while white principals took over black schools. And inevitably with the installation of white principals came the ousting of black teachers, who were accused of poor performance.

The choice the Board of Directors and the members of the GEA and GT&EA Joint Committee had before them was whether to capitulate in the merger discussions and allow GT&EA to follow the model of other white professional groups in the southern states and become "absorbed" into the extant white organization, following its dictates and values, or to fight to preserve its own values and beliefs. Since Florida and Texas, Virginia's black teachers organization had also "given up," and its powerful director, J. Rupert Picott, who had previously led NCOSTA and consulted with President Johnson and HEW on black educational matters, had taken a position with NEA. Mr. Picott had hoped the promise of equality in a merged organization would be fulfilled, and so he had overseen the merger of the black and white educational groups to become the Virginia Educational Association in 1967, but he had been betrayed.[3]

Mr. Picott expressed his disillusionment with the merger in the years after it was accomplished. As he later mused, "absorption" removed a "power base for black teachers" that was not replaced. Teacher transfers and unfair demotion and dismissal continued in Virginia after the merger and "controversial educational issues which involve race" were deemed to be "outside the purview of [the new merged association]." Not only had the history and accomplishments of the hundred-year existence of the Virginia Teachers Association been dismissed by the new white majority, but the merger was never even formally announced, despite a written "understanding" that the union of the two groups would be formally recognized.[4]

Virginia had joined the other merged southern states while its peers, still holding out, evaluated the effect of NEA's requirement that all separate southern black and white organizations become one. Under an NEA executive director in 1968 more open to race matters than his predecessor and with its first black president, Libby Koontz of North Carolina, NEA pressed harder to demand that its local affiliates become one organization. But even with a black president, NEA said little when its white membership and black membership collided over issues of race at the local level.[5]

The times were difficult and "things were changing," Dr. Tate explained to the board members as they discussed Georgia's affairs. He had himself finally directly challenged NEA on its failure to seat him in 1958 as a member of the Board of Directors, now that Libby Koontz was leading NEA and the group's public language reflected equality, and he had won the challenge. In response to the NEA offer to be given his seat for three years with all the "rights and privileges of a Director, except the right to vote," he emphatically declined. One needed the courage to speak and the integrity to not compromise on continued inequality. "If we are afraid," Dr. Tate said to his board, "we may as well leave it all alone."[6]

As 1968 unfolded, GT&EA leaders determined not to be afraid. Many in its membership were "incensed and angry" over the unjust actions of school officials. In LaFayette, Summerville, Canton, Calhoun, Marietta, Douglasville, Decatur, and many other towns, "excellent" school principals were being put under the supervision of white leaders, thereby rendering "the community leaderless."[7] Over the course of the year, the board discussed with Dr. Tate the possibility of a statewide boycott of schools by teachers and students to showcase desegregation problems locally. They issued an "ultimatum" to the state board of education, giving it two weeks to act on GT&EA's complaints.

Dr. Tate continued the hidden networking with SCLC that had begun during the Crawfordville conflict several years earlier. Hosea Williams and two other SCLC leaders demonstrated at the superintendent's desk in Atlanta, even answering his phone. The superintendent called Dr. Tate and asked him to get the people out of his office. Dr. Tate said he would if the superintendent stopped the double sessions some black schools still endured.[8]

But the problems were structural. No widely implemented change occurred. Black educators considered a national protest march to Washington involving black educators from across the South. The latter idea had been proposed by Dr. Tate to NCOSTA. Perhaps Negro educators could convene in Washington and talk with the president, cabinet members, and national legislators. Each state organization could charter a plane or bus and converge for a national meeting. They could also have a hundred teachers from each state meet at the NEA headquarters. By 1968 Dr. Tate was the new vice president of NCOSTA, and now he emphasized to his NCOSTA colleagues some of the points he had already made with the GT&EA board.[9]

"I want to reiterate my belief that many of us are not sensing the seriousness of our plight. Everyone of us can sense that integration of pupils and teachers is not what, in reality, is happening to Negroes in the American society and especially the South. Rather it is *elimination* or as I have further termed it, *outergration* that is taking place. . . . [W]e must either confront the problem with an effort to resolve it or *we can continue to play with the problem*, hoping for the best, while knowing that the worst will result."[10]

The planned national marches and boycotts to bring visibility to the education problem never materialized. But as long as GT&EA existed and local actors could join forces with larger movements, a plan to disrupt the national desegregation script was at least possible. That was what happened in Pike County, Georgia.

In rural Pike County, about an hour south of Atlanta, local protests ignited when a black principal resigned his position and the superintendent replaced the black principal with a white principal at the black elementary school. GT&EA received the usual phone call reporting the problem. Dr. Tate sent Mr. Byas, the displaced principal from Gaines County who was now employed by GT&EA as an associate executive director, to investigate. Under Mr. Byas's leadership, black parents organized the Concerned Parents Group of Pike County. The group said it wanted a black principal at their black school or it wanted a black principal named at the white elementary school.

By registration day for school opening in 1968, the Concerned Parents Group had received no official response. So, like some other black communities in other southern states, they called for a total boycott of the black school. Meanwhile, the president of the parents' group and Mr. Byas met with the superintendent.

"Would you appoint a black principal to an all-white school?" Mr. Byas asked.

"No, definitely not," the superintendent replied.

"Are you afraid the white parents would run you out of town?" Mr. Byas pressed.

"Quite frankly, yes," the superintendent replied.

"Did you and/or the Board give consideration to the feelings, wishes, or desires of black parents in making this appointment of the principal to the East Pike Elementary School?"

The superintendent admitted he had not.

Mr. Byas said that it seemed to him that until the superintendent was ready to employ all people without regard to race, he should continue the policy of employing principals based on the racial composition of the student body.

The conversation escalated as the superintendent said he "had no intention" of making a recommendation to the board to change the principal. Adamant, Mr. Byas rejoined: "I see no reason to continue this dialogue any further." Mr. Byas said he would make his report to the black parents that night. "I want you to know," he said to the superintendent as he departed, "I shall use everything within my power to get our GT&EA Board of Directors to fight this unjust and unequal move and will call upon such other organizations as will lend aid and support in our determined effort."

The organization to which Mr. Byas referred was the SCLC. Even with Rev. King deceased, SCLC had continued its alignment with GT&EA.[11] This time, the critique black educators had sometimes raised in the past about SCLC allowing students to protest during school hours was moot. In Pike County, Dr. Tate led the protests.

The Friday after Labor Day, no more than sixty of the 350–400 students enrolled in the black school reported for class. Meanwhile, 196 people marched two abreast the three-quarters of a mile from the East Pike Elementary School to the courthouse.[12] Marchers prayed and then an SCLC leader, Willie Bolden, delivered a stirring forty-minute talk summing up the "pent-up feelings of repression which many whites of Pike County had forced on the blacks" as the sheriff, his deputies, and five or more units of the state patrol stood silently nearby listening to the "good tongue-lashing."

Three hundred people marched the following day, repeating the rally and the route.

Black teachers across Georgia chartered buses to come to Pike County and its county seat, Zebulon, to march. Dr. Tate's wife, Virginia, rode with Mr. Byas as her husband marched in another problem area. Mr. Byas's little red car had already once been run off the road by local people protesting his interference in local matters. As she and Mr. Byas approached the town the final day of protest, the scene looked harrowing, and she wondered if they would leave alive.[13]

Two public mass marches and demonstrations by black pupils, teachers, and parents and a full week of boycotted classes occurred before the white female principal assigned to the school resigned and "moved into retirement." Inspired by the removal of the principal, the black community group led by Mr. Byas increased its demands. The black community wanted their black secretary back and their aides back. They wanted to be part of the discussions when integration was being "discussed and formulated." They wanted a "voice in formulating the plan."

Since the county was about half black and white, they wanted their principals and teachers retained in desegregation. They wanted overcrowded buses addressed. They wanted unfair maintenance problems addressed. They wanted discriminatory salary practices stopped. "If white folks cannot integrate in a logical manner, we refuse to co-operate with illogical schemes," they said. And they wanted no legal suits brought against them for their actions—either now or in the future.

The local Board of Education was unaccustomed to responding to direct demands from black parents. Dr. Tate drove down to help Mr. Bolden lead a seven-mile march on Tuesday, September 10. Both were scheduled to meet with the Board of Education to negotiate solutions after the march. But when the march went beyond the anticipated ending time of two o'clock, the board "apparently got tired of waiting and disbanded."

Mr. Byas returned early the next morning to represent the demands of the Concerned Parents Group and continue mediation. He was surprised to learn the board had met under cover of darkness the previous night to formulate a response to the parents' written demands. The board did not think it in the "best interests" of education to dictate to a principal whom he should hire. They welcomed citizens coming to their meetings and making petitions but could not guarantee every request would be heeded. They could not guarantee maintaining black teachers and principals, although they would try to comply with federal guidelines. They were working toward the goal of getting modern buildings for everyone. Yes, buses were overcrowded, but none were "dangerously overloaded," and they were working on transportation. They were discussing priority needs for black schools, and salaries came from a formula that included "among other things" duties, number of teachers, job performances, and so forth. And they were not going to sue anyone.

The board's response was not everything the black parents wanted. However, the parents decided it was enough for the moment, especially when a black principal was appointed to the elementary school. The parents also agreed to organize a local SCLC chapter and continue to cooperate with GT&EA until they could get "a complete and total elimination of unfair treatment" of blacks in the county. In the meanwhile, they consented to send the children back to school and to give the board "reasonable time" to work out the rest of the problems. But they said they "would not stop until justice is done." If necessary, they would have a county-wide boycott of all schools.[14]

Reporting at the Region IV meeting in Greensboro with former colleagues and friends, Dr. Tate described Negro teachers and Negro children who had marched seven miles in Pike County. They had succeeded in reversing matters, he believed, because the community stuck together in their demands. In a script as old as Mr. Hunt, he proclaimed that "laymen as well as teachers" needed to "join forces with lawmakers to see that justice prevails in all areas of education."

For a moment in 1968 a ray of hope flickered as a community collectively protested its mistreatment. While some superintendents across the state hated Dr. Tate for these frequent intrusions into local affairs, the GT&EA still wielded the power to organize communities, connect with other advocates, and effect change. As the events in Pike County demonstrated, the collective result could be powerful. As the black high school principal in Pike County, D. F. Glover, pronounced: "Black communities must be well organized so that white people think twice about mistreating a black teacher or student. And if it happens, the black community is going to raise hell."[15]

The black press also applauded GT&EA's public stance for equality as Dr. Tate made the educators' case in multiple public venues.[16] "Because of the known general opposition to desegregation in the white community," the *Atlanta World* wrote, "we assume there will be comparatively few Negroes teaching white children. Therefore, we support the idea that a Negro principal should be in those schools where the majority of the students are of our race. No one is thinking about going back to segregation, but we must have our fair share of principals and teachers in the various public school systems."[17] Like a dying person who rallies a little just before his or her demise, the community activity and public support bolstered increasing hopes about redirecting desegregation.

GT&EA also received another boost in 1968 as its long-standing connections with NAACP lawyers bore fruit. In the years just before the black Virginia teachers association merged with the white Virginia teachers association, a black teacher who was also president of the New Kent County NAACP lent his name to a lawsuit protesting inequitable treatment as New Kent County faced the potential loss of funds under the administration of Commissioner Howe and HEW. The profile of the plaintiff paralleled exactly the activity of Charles Harper in Atlanta and mirrored a GT&EA threatened lawsuit because of the mistreatment of a black teacher. Like Georgia, where Dr. Tate had said publicly that "the association has conferred with its attorneys and top officials of the NAACP's Legal Defense and Education Fund," the black Virginia teachers organization had maintained similar connections with NAACP attorneys.[18]

After the Virginia case's first argument in 1965, the local court accepted the county's "freedom of choice" plan in 1966, and the next year the Fourth Circuit Court of Appeals upheld the lower court's ruling. However, "freedom of choice" plans did not generate equitable integration, so NAACP attorneys appealed the case to the Supreme Court in October 1967. In *Charles C. Green et al. v. County School Board of New Kent County*, NAACP lawyers pointed out the failure in local practices, a failure that had parallels in other reports of local practices available via NCOSTA, GT&EA, and black educational organizations across the South.[19]

When the Supreme Court mandated full integration on May 27, 1968, the victory in the courts that Frank Keppel encouraged Harold Howe to expect materialized. The combining of black and white school bodies needed to address every facet of school operations—facilities, students, faculty, staff, transportation, and extracurricular activities. Full equality should exist across the board, instead of the burden of implementing *Brown v. Board* being unfairly placed on black communities. As Earl Warren, who had been the chief justice when *Brown v. Board of Education* was decided, wrote to the current chief justice, William Brennan, about *Green v. County School Board of New Kent County*, with the new decision it looked like "the traffic light will have changed from Brown to Green."[20]

Of course, no one gave wide publicity to the half million dollars NCOSTA contributed to the Legal Defense and Educational Fund to help litigate this and other cases. Instead, attention turned to continuing to litigate in order to force local units to integrate fairly. NCOSTA referred to the NAACP lawyers as the "best legal organization in the world," and GT&EA determined to have details on local inequalities and dismissals available for Dr. Davis and Attorney Jack Greenberg, the new white head of the NAACP Legal Defense and Educational Fund. In fact, Dr. Tate suspended the usual duties of Mr. Byas and asked him to compile a full research report on problems with faculty integration since 1954 for distribution. Mr. Byas enjoyed the intensive task, even employing a blond female assistant to go to local counties undercover and seek jobs black teachers had been denied.[21]

Mr. Byas's study showed continued dismissals based on race as the district judges placed in charge of implementation placated local concerns despite a federal mandate. The NAACP saluted one Georgia system in 1968 for a desegregation plan that involved all black and white students attending both a formerly black school and a formerly white school. However, massive school integration would not occur for another year. Georgia judges appeared to align with the white North Carolina judge who told a local unit he would give "you boys a year to work things out" rather than forcing upon them an equitable integration in 1968.[22]

GT&EA spoke directly to such matters in its publications. In "Resume on Some Major Issues of Grave Concern to Members of the Georgia Teachers and Education Association," submitted to Georgia school officials on September 15, 1968, GT&EA made its position clear about the need to follow federal mandates in local settings. Aligned with the requirements of the new Supreme Court case, the organization objected to firing black leadership and sought the implementation across Georgia of all the factors identified in *Green*. GT&EA also emphasized the need to involve the black community in the decision making that affected its children as school districts prepared for integration. The publication pointed out that most of the plans for desegregation were being prepared and developed by local boards with no Negro representation even though the plans would affect Negroes as much as they would whites. GT&EA objected to the lack of representation.

"No school superintendent should proceed under the assumption that Negro citizens are pleased and happy to accept a white principal over Negro children, when white parents are not satisfied and happy to have a Negro principal over white children," GT&EA wrote. Instead, Negro citizens needed to play a "vital role" as it formulated school desegregation plans.[23] Surely in 1968, GT&EA thought, black educational needs would be protected. However, as 1969 approached, local matters of inequality continued unabated and even intensified. GT&EA had reason for continued concerns as the federal government, via HEW, diluted the decisions of the federal courts.

Rev. King had once cut short a European trip because of his concern about the crisis in Crawfordville, Georgia. He had said Crawfordville would become "the symbol of token school integration for the nation, just as Selma became the symbol for voting registration difficulties." Rev. King's words represented GT&EA's hope that the educational crisis in black communities could gain public attention and support. But people forgot Rev. King's ninety-minute stay in the racially tense Crawfordville, and the city never came to symbolize educational injustice in the public mind.[24]

For a few months, it appeared to the black community that it had won a voice in school integration in Pike County, especially with Dr. Tate's heated manifesto about the situation. Dr. Tate recorded a forceful critique and set of demands, echoing the dismay of GT&EA and the black parents in Pike County.[25] But the victory soured as the superintendent fired the black high school principal from Pike County, D. F. Glover, apparently in retaliation for his role in the Pike County protest. Dr. Tate returned to the county to protest the firing, paying little attention to the state trooper who came in near the end of the meeting to ask if he was almost finished. Nor did the distracted executive secretary pay much attention to the line of cars parked outside the school board building. As he got in his car, a state trooper pulled out in front of him and another behind him. Dr. Tate did not think much about the police escort until the long line of cars that drove off with him after he left the superintendent's office began to peel off one by one. A little over an hour outside of Atlanta, the thought finally occurred to him: the people in the cars had meant to do him harm. Had it not been for the state patrol escort, the GT&EA executive secretary might not have made it home alive.[26] He dismissed the thought and stayed focused on the struggle. So did the principal the school board refused to rehire.

Jobless, Mr. Glover described in detail in the *Herald* exactly what was happening in local settings where local school boards circumvented a Supreme Court mandate. "The federal government's policing agency, HEW, without Harold Howe or a comparable leader, failed to police the quality of integration," Mr. Glover said. "One time [HEW] was moving in the direction of guaranteeing the elimination of segregation and discrimination based on race." But HEW had "changed direction [after Harold Howe left]" and was now "guaranteeing the elimination of Negro principals, curriculum directors, coaches and others in positions of leadership" as it enforced a new interpretation of the guidelines, which stated that "all *inferior Negro* schools must be eliminated."

Mr. Glover said he knew of no case where a Negro principal, curriculum director, or coach had sufficient qualifications to retain a position of leadership. In some instances, Negro male leadership was being "subjected to insulting treatment" and Negro pupils were being "arbitrarily placed in slow groups" while Negro teachers were assigned to teach, "in some cases, all slow groups." With its new guidelines, HEW was being used to "perpetuate the subjugation of the Negro teachers and pupils" as they approved integration plans submitted by white boards of education.

Mr. Glover reminded black educators of the purpose of the movement to integrate public school facilities: to eliminate discrimination, "to create a favorable atmosphere of respect for the dignity and worth of all races." The heart of *Brown v. Board* was that separate education was "inherently unequal." But "unequal," he said, also included the belief that segregated education was unjust or "unfair."

Mr. Glover believed that in response to *Brown* the South had said, "in so many words to the nation and the world, that we are satisfied with things as they are. We are not going to change. If we are forced to change, the Negro teachers and students will suffer. The Negro students will be relegated to an inferior status because they will not be accepted by the whites. The Negro teachers and principals will lose their jobs."

In 1968, it appeared to Mr. Glover that "these devilish minds and unyielding planners to subjugate Negro teachers and students" had somehow "gotten into the guidelines of the Department of Health, Education, and Welfare. Inadequate and inferior education has become synonymous with Negro education. Inferior and inadequate schools have become synonymous with Negro schools. Inferior and inadequate teachers and principals have become synonymous with Negro teachers. Integration has become synonymous with the movement of Negro teachers and principals from the often time superior Negro school to the white school and the elimination of Negro principals from all schools."

Mr. Glover questioned how HEW could justify its guidelines, especially in the wake of a new Supreme Court case mandating equality. Wasn't it the first duty of "any enforcement agency of the federal government to root out and expose discriminatory practices?" Why had HEW abandoned its earlier position on faculty desegregation? Originally HEW had "inferred that no teacher should lose a job because of desegregation." Those were the days of Harold Howe. "Yet," Mr. Glover continued, "we do not know of a single instance where a system has been denied funds because of unfair practices in faculty dismissal or demotion."

And why did only Negro schools have to be eliminated? "There is some psychology in this," Mr. Glover posited. "If the white child goes to a formerly all-Negro school, which in many cases is superior, it makes him feel that he is no better than the Negro. It also eliminates the myth that all Negro schools are inferior." In contrast, Negro children were being forced into white schools where "all kind of entanglements" awaited them. Without a network of support of black educators, they daily confronted the belief that "white is right."

GT&EA had always been a "combination of a civil rights and a professional organization," Mr. Glover reminded readers. However, as the climate in 1968–69 threatened GT&EA's continued existence, Mr. Glover offered his assessment of the present struggles they confronted. "There is not a single person who has dealt with the southern mind that does not recognize that this devilish mind has discovered a new way to achieve its purposes. The password is HEW."

For clarity, Mr. Glover restated the GT&EA position. GT&EA leaders did not believe in segregation in any form. But to ask the Negro "to sacrifice some of his rights now in order to make a way for the elimination of the dual system, there-by hoping for a better day in the future, is not valid. Tokenism in this country, at the expense of the Negro, is dead," he said. "We refuse to be misled by HEW or any other federal agency."

GT&EA's board and Dr. Tate agreed with Mr. Glover's assessment. GT&EA press releases had protested the U.S. House Appropriations Committee and some congressmen whose goal had been to "restrict, alter, and, therefore, make ineffective the Federal School Guidelines for faculty-pupil desegregation" in the year before the *Green* case. The thirteen thousand members of GT&EA thought it "unbelievable that those elected officials who are entrusted with the privilege and responsibility" to provide equality to all citizens would follow a policy "guaranteeing unequal rights" for some of its citizens. It had wanted the Harold Howe administration of HEW guidelines to continue.[27] However, the climate in the immediate aftermath of the Kent County case revealed that Washington politics had infiltrated HEW practice after Howe's departure and even after the Supreme Court decision.

Dr. Tate mulled the dilemmas confronting them all. He decided to try to extend his scope beyond his influence as executive secretary of GT&EA. As Mr. Wright and Mr. Hunt had believed when they served as delegates to the Republican National Convention in their eras, Dr. Tate hoped black people in political positions could protect black education and other black citizens, especially since white political leaders primarily protected white citizens. He had already run for, and been elected to, the Atlanta school board in 1967 so that he could push the board to seek equality for black children. But because his place on the ballot was challenged on a technicality, he had had to pay attorneys and fight in court to maintain the seat he had been elected to. He had won that fight, and his voice on the school board raised thorny issues the board had to at least listen to, even if it voted differently.[28] He was already familiar with the state capitol, regularly lobbying elected officials to support GT&EA resolutions. Why not blend the larger political, economic, and educational issues in Atlanta and run for a political position that would provide more powerful representation?[29]

With GT&EA support and the "H. E. Tate Campaign Committee," Dr. Tate also put his name in nomination as Atlanta's first black mayoral candidate. Since Negroes had worked hard over the last sixteen years to elect "progressive thinking white mayors," it seemed necessary to form a coalition between whites and Negroes and elect a Negro mayor "to help Atlanta live up to its image." He offered himself as a candidate who could build a coalition between the races through bimonthly meetings of Atlantans across social, racial, and class lines. "We must and we will solve the racial problem," he insisted. He promised to attack inadequate educational programs for all of Atlanta's children by assembling a Mayor's Conference on Education that would create Atlanta schools second to none. He would establish a commission to look at the school integration plans so that

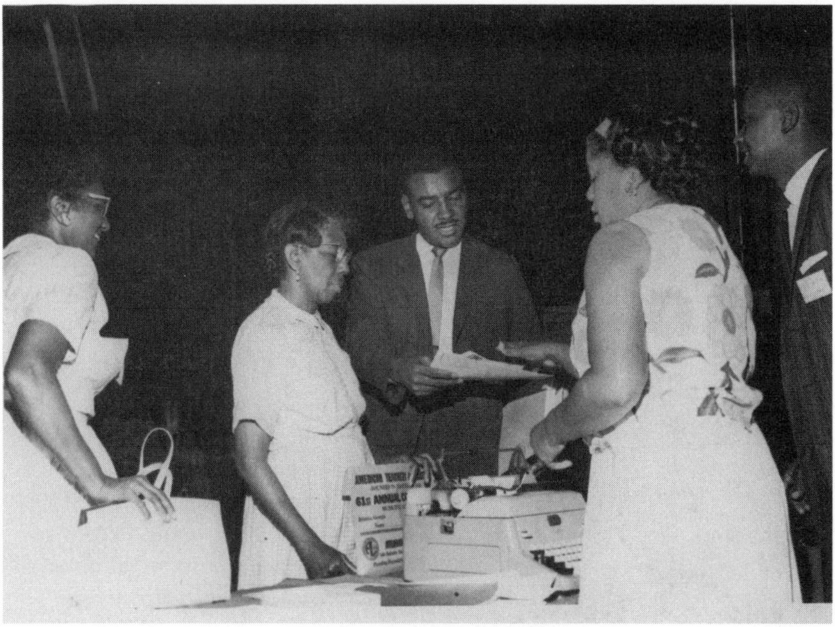

In efforts to gain political power, GT&EA members often quietly organized and supported voter registration campaigns. As the 1960s reduced the need for invisibility, teachers Elmira Black Clayton and Albert F. Vines are shown registering Georgians, including GT&EA's executive secretary, Dr. Tate. *GT&EA Collection*

Atlanta would not become a city of all white people or all black people but one where all people would be proud to live with the opposite race. He talked about using the Justice Department to address wrongful applications of existing laws, and he promised to professionalize the police department so that all would be properly trained in the task they needed to perform. Citing the case of a pregnant woman who had been beaten, kicked, and knocked over by four policemen, he declared that the incident constituted "police brutality" and should not be tolerated. He wanted the Atlanta airport to become an international airport. And he had many other proposals related to housing, business zoning, employment, taxation, and development.[30]

His campaign committee worked hard distributing flyers and announcing his candidacy using a bullhorn mounted to the top of a car and driving through Atlanta's neighborhoods. Survey results showed Dr. Tate with 68 percent of the Negro vote and 16 percent of the white vote. But threats had

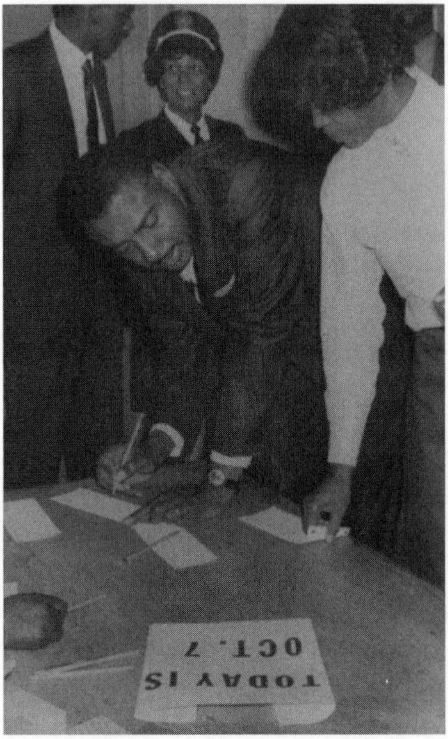

Dr. Tate attempted to gain political power to support black education in Atlanta when he became the first black candidate to run for mayor in the twentieth century. The newspapers reported that Dr. Tate was "favored to be one of the top vote getters and win a spot in a run-off" to be held October 15, 1969. *Associated Press*

been made against him, and people were sufficiently concerned that black men with guns patrolled Dr. Tate's house throughout the night in order to keep the candidate and his family safe.

But on election night, as the votes were counted, it became clear that Dr. Tate was not going to win. His wife called the results "hanky panky." Others contended the votes were manipulated to deny him victory. Ulysses Byas provided a blunt summary: "They stole the race from Horace." In a black precinct where two weeks before the election people remembered him as having been significantly in the lead, Mr. Byas said, on election day they "lost ballots" and Dr. Tate wound up coming in third.[31] In its history Georgia certainly had seen cases of "losing" and "finding" votes before.

Dr. Tate weighed his options. He could contest the results and ask for a recount. However, a recount required money and time.[32] In the end, he decided not to contest the vote, for there were pressing educational matters that commanded his attention.

GT&EA board members continued to report inequalities facing black students. And sometimes people just came to his office to give him a tip about happenings around the state that he could then go and "discover" as problems.[33] In Worth County, a Negro female student in a predominately white school was interrogated by officials from the sheriff's office. The principal said the fifteen-year-old was "unruly, disobedient and discourteous" and that she had used profanity when asked to sit on an assigned seat on the bus. Other students were not assigned seats, but the girl's response landed her in a juvenile home.

In Albany, a black father reported that his fifteen-year-old daughter had left her lunch table for three minutes to telephone her mother. The teacher supervising the lunchroom ordered his daughter's lunch dumped into the garbage pail, even though other students explained she would return momentarily. When the daughter returned, she asked for her 52 cents back or another lunch. Both requests were denied by the principal. Moreover, the principal said the student had been "impudent and insulting," and despite no other offense in school, the girl was suspended. When Dr. Tate investigated, the principal told him she had been suspended for slamming the door when she left his office.[34]

Not only were problems with students multiplying, but Dr. Tate was involved in the problems confronting black educators as well. He entertained phone calls from teachers and principals around the state late into the evening at his home throughout 1968–69. The local pressure to construct an integration that privileged white education continued, and black educators worried as they confided in him the details of the problems in their communities. The stacks of formal complaints continued to mount until they filled file cabinets. What could the umbrella GT&EA organization do to protect its members in a new climate where its local units were compromised and individuals were individually vulnerable if they tried to counter with requests for a fair implementation of the Supreme Court case?

While Dr. Tate listened to the complaints and concerns of educators, he needed to oversee litigation matters as well. He prodded NEA to provide $12,000 from the DuShane Fund to support the GT&EA's case against Mr. Glover's dismissal. Already GT&EA had expended $13,000 of its own funds on the case.[35] There were other cases as well. "Justice Denied in County: GT&EA to Support Appeal," ran a headline in the *GT&EA Reporter*, a new publication of the organization.

Then there were subtle problems with the alliance between GT&EA and the SCLC. Differences of opinion between the educators and the SCLC had sometimes surfaced in the past, but they had not disrupted cooperation. As Dr. Tate had stated publicly, they were all united in their objectives. However, concerns seeped to the surface at one board meeting at which Mr. Bolden of the SCLC explained his intent to go to the corridor of a major interstate and incite school protests. Board members listened to his bold plans with some chuckles, but mostly quietly. It seemed Mr. Bolden imagined himself the leader in the education cases. Dr. Tate finally asked Mr. Bolden if he thought GT&EA was trying to help him or "whether other organizations were helping GT&EA."[36]

To add to the problems, from Valdosta Dr. Tate had received a "very revealing" local report that confirmed his concern that a merger with GEA meant a plan to "take over rather than work together." GT&EA was still working with parent groups to spur equality in local settings and using its Legislative Committee to lobby state politicians for justice. What would happen with these efforts after a merger? Dr. Tate sent a copy of a report by a subcommittee of the Joint Committee of GEA and GT&EA to people like Dr. Benjamin Mays, GT&EA's attorney Donald Hollowell, and Dr. H.V. Richardson, the president emeritus of the Interdenominational Theological Center in the Atlanta University Center.[37] What did they think about the proposed merger? What would happen if these educators disappeared and GEA controlled the destiny of black children?[38]

A year that began with possibilities ended in turmoil. When Mr. Tate led black educators on GT&EA's second three-week European study trip that year (they traveled to England, Holland, Belgium, Luxembourg, Germany, Switzerland, Liechtenstein, Austria, Italy, Monaco, and France), he had still hoped justice would come. After all, he and colleagues Clara Gay and Fred Brown had integrated the State Department of Education cafeteria downtown during a meeting of the Teachers' Retirement Board of Trustees. Despite the governor being alerted before they could even get their food, they did not back down and were the first black people served in the cafeteria.[39]

In Europe, he unknowingly traced materially and metaphorically some of the same paths in those countries walked by Mr. Wright, Dr. Du Bois, and Mr. Hunt during the World War I days when black educators thought they were free. In London, he stood near the Thames River, where Mr. Hunt first described for the Pan African Conference the challenges of education in Georgia. In Paris, he stood beneath the Arc de Triomphe, where Dr. Du Bois and Mr. Hunt had laid a wreath at the Tomb of the Unknown Soldier. In Germany on the Rhine River, he listened with surprise as Germans aboard the boat softly began to sing "We Shall Overcome," perhaps in tribute to their black companions on the same river cruise.[40] Other countries seemed to understand that America's time for justice was now.

But as the GT&EA annual meeting approached in 1969, the words the Germans sang about Rev. King's dream of overcoming became increasingly empty. Dr. Tate urged black educators to attend so that they could discuss the issues facing them, but with so many local, federal, and NEA problems, the dream of black educators for a real integration was fading.[41]

26

A SECOND-CLASS INTEGRATION IT IS

In 1969, the GT&EA delegate body first examined the reports of the Joint Committee on merger as they contemplated whether to give up their organization and merge with the white organization. GEA and GT&EA had reached no consensus by this point, even though NEA's Representative Assembly debated a proposed resolution saying the organization was "deeply concerned over the fact that dual segregated associations still remain affiliated" with NEA. The delegate body said mergers should provide "in writing" all the measures already guaranteed to all citizens under the U.S. Constitution.[1]

GEA and GT&EA could not put the full details of a merger in writing, as not all the disputes had been resolved. GEA said publicly the two organizations should merge, although the group's president acknowledged that communication between the two groups had been difficult and that within his group there was some resistance to the idea that at least every three years the new group must have a black president. But the GEA president emphasized they had gotten some of the protection that they thought they should have—not because "we are white but because we are big."[2] The organization still wanted to avoid race.

GT&EA still believed in merger also, but it continued to hold its longstanding suspicion that white organizations wanted merger but not on equal terms. GT&EA leaders expressed concern that the white race held on to the belief that their philosophy, objectives, programs, and services should be *the* program for everyone. They still worried that an "air" and "tone" of superiority prevailed in the merger discussions, as though "what was good for their association must be the best there is" and that the Negro group should be happy to "accept without question *their* programs, from which [the Negroes had been] for years excluded."[3]

These differences infused the 1969 annual meeting, though they did not disrupt it. All representatives had to do at the meeting on March 17, 1969, was to mark "Against Merger Plan" or "For Merger Plan" on a simple yellow sheet of paper. The delegates did so, and then they continued to act on issues of long-standing concern to the body of Negro teachers.[4]

However, suspicions erupted later in 1969 as the two organizations tried to resolve the question of who would be executive secretary of the merged group. The Joint Committee had agreed that whichever executive secretary was not appointed would become the associate executive secretary of the merged organization. But which leader was best qualified to be executive secretary?

Experience and credentials had created a special problem for GEA since the early years of the merger conversations. Their executive secretary, Frank Hughes, had experience as the leader of their organization but did not have a terminal degree. However, in 1968, Mr. Hughes had resigned and GEA filled his position with Dr. Carl Hodges, who had completed his doctorate from the University of Georgia in 1964. GEA now had a leader with credentials.

Both men had strong school backgrounds. Dr. Hodges had been a superintendent in Fitzgerald until 1963—one of the places GT&EA investigated for discrimination under Dr. Tate's leadership—before receiving his doctorate in 1964. However, Dr. Tate had more professional experience. Dr. Hodges had served only on the Elections Committee of NEA, but Dr. Tate had been elected an NEA director when NEA finally awarded him the seat he had won twelve years earlier.[5] Dr. Tate had research proposals, publications, awards, and recognitions, and he had participated in a series of national educational events. He had given approximately seven hundred speeches, addressing audiences that ranged in size from fifteen to six thousand, in Georgia, California, Michigan, Nebraska, South Carolina, Kentucky, Pennsylvania, and Louisiana. He also had more experience as the director of an education organization. To some, Dr. Tate's comparable degree and broader experiences made him the more viable candidate to lead a merged organization.[6]

GEA accused GT&EA of trying to "blackjack" GEA into accepting Dr. Tate as executive secretary. GEA members had released statements saying Tate wanted "assured channels to the Executive Secretarialship."

GT&EA members countered that they did not want Dr. Tate automatically disqualified from the top leadership position. They said their people were being excluded "solely because of race." GT&EA believed "such exclusion [created] suspicion, resentment, and other detrimental effects which could limit the effectiveness of the [proposed] Georgia

Association of Educators."[7] For his part, Dr. Tate had said he simply wanted "equitable treatment for everybody." He believed positions should be filled based on ability.[8] But race became a deciding factor as black and white educators in Georgia addressed their last hurdle in trying to meet NEA guidelines.

In 1969 NEA stepped in to resolve the conflict between GT&EA and GEA. It appointed a neutral third party to mediate, since GEA and GT&EA's Joint Committee could not resolve the problem of leadership.[9] Thus, Dr. Tate and Dr. Hodges boarded a plane in Atlanta and flew to the Harvard Graduate School of Education so a "special screening committee" could interview both candidates. This committee would determine who would become the executive secretary of the new merged association.[10]

Dr. Tate submitted a bound copy of his resume along with a list containing enumerated statements describing his beliefs about the responsibility of the executive secretary. The document touted his credentials. When he had assumed office in 1961, his staff included only himself and two others, with a new building under construction and over $300,000 of debt to be liquidated. By 1969, the building had been completely amortized; GT&EA had thirteen thousand members; no funds had been borrowed since 1959; and the staff had been increased to thirteen.[11] Dr. Hodges presented no comparable accomplishments to the committee.

After interviews, Theodore Sizer, dean of the College of Education and chair of the evaluation committee, said he believed Dr. Hodges to be the better candidate. Black doctoral students at Harvard whispered the dean had not picked the best candidate. Some believed he thought the time was just not right for a black man to head a merged organization. But none of the backroom talk changed the decision. As the 1970 annual meeting approached, when black educators would vote on the future of their organization, Dr. Tate had been assigned the role of associate executive secretary and Dr. Carl Hodges that of executive secretary. Tate's salary would be 5 percent below that of Dr. Hodges, according to the proposal of Dr. Sizer.[12]

The time had come for the GT&EA delegate body to determine formally whether to accept the proposals of the GEA and GT&EA Joint Committee for a merger or whether to reject them and disaffiliate from NEA. GT&EA members had already joined in a reconvened session of the fifty-first annual meeting to vote on the proposed constitution of the new merged association. GEA met on the same date for a similar purpose. The vote in

GEA had been more than 80 percent in favor of the proposed constitution, specifically 313 for and 73 against.[13] GT&EA had not been so sure, and the questions focused their conversations at their fifty-second annual meeting in 1970.

The convention opened the evening before, with President Charlie Hicks welcoming guests to the Classroom Teachers banquet. The C.L. Harper High School ROTC presented the colors as black educators gathered in the Marriott Motor Hotel in Atlanta. Mr. Hicks was a Fort Valley graduate and a principal of McDougald School in Taylor County. He had been a "rising star" as he moved through the ranks of unit president, regional director, then vice president. President Hawes had passed him the gavel of leadership at the closing ceremonies of the fiftieth-anniversary celebration, which had turned into a silent march protest after the announcement of Dr. King's death. Now finishing his second year as president, Mr. Hicks announced, "The house is now open for business," as the last convention, themed "A Moral and Ethical Integration," began with committee reports.[14]

The Committee on Legislation reported the "unsettled conditions facing Georgia schools" and reaffirmed its intent to foster an additional program to referee controversy in schools and maintain the program of advocacy across a broad spectrum of school needs that had characterized GT&EA since 1917. They had a "heavy responsibility" during this "period of change.

After several other committee reports, the 1970 GT&EA Teacher of the Year came forward to introduce the evening's speaker, Mrs. Ruby Gainer, a member of the board of directors in the merged Florida Education Association. Mrs. Gainer soon turned the topic to merger.[15]

A native of Georgia, Mrs. Gainer spoke of her belief that NEA would come to the aid of any Georgia teacher needing help during the transition, and that it would "expose injustice and seek corrective action" for the educators who fought for change and for people like Martin Luther King Jr. GT&EA members needed to believe men's hearts would change for good in the wake of legislation and court decisions. Black educators could still fight in the merged organization.

"I better not hear tomorrow you decided not to integrate!" she chided those who she worried might "turn their back" on integration.

Dr. Tate spoke after Mrs. Gainer. He commended Mrs. Gainer for her talk: "It was a good one." But he recalled his mother, who had raised fourteen children, and he began by mentioning the poem she had made him and every one of her other children learn: "The new mother, as she looks at the head of the babe in her arms, whispers in her heart, 'My child, may you seek the truth. . . . Close your eyes to nothing which seems to them to be the truth.'"

Then Dr. Tate spoke his truth about what was happening to blacks during this era of public talk about equality. "Mr. President and all of the other persons at the head table and all of you great delegates," Dr. Tate said emphatically, "I want to say to you, this great delegate assembly, to the educators of this state, to the thousands of boys and girls throughout this state and nation and to the millions of people throughout the length and breath of this country and world and to those beings that might be in outer space and to my God Almighty that I, H. E. Tate, presently the executive secretary of the Georgia Teachers and Education Association have not worked and prayed and sacrificed and cried and gone sleepless and almost died for a second class integration—for a second class integration is evil—no matter who thinks otherwise.[16]

"Second class integration . . . is more evil than was segregation," he went on, "because second class integration has a way of striking at the psychic and penetrating the fibers of the brain and depths of the soul to say to a person who has been deprived for over 400 years, 'I will make you think you are equal by passing laws to protect you and your rights, and after I have enacted those laws I will creep in on you. I will creep in on you and make you think you are somebody and make it legal for you to eat at the forbidden lunch counters and then I will creep a little further and take away your jobs so you wouldn't have money in which to buy the food.' . . . Second class integration has a way of saying 'I will creep in on you and surprise you and make you say "Yes sir" and "Yes mam" when you are buying items from my store, but I will creep a little further and charge you 25 cents more than the item is worth. I will let you listen to me tell you that you are equal but I will take away your control; I will take away your power; I will take away your influence; and I will take away your job. But I will tell you that you are equal and integrated.' There can be no first class citizenship with second class integration."

He continued, "Second class integration is evil because it is designed to ease the white man's conscience. It is evil because it is designed to continue the pattern of restraining Negro people . . . It is evil because it is designed to steal from the Negro the black image which has motivated black boys and girls—made them roll up their sleeves and carve out for this nation a new role for democracy. Black boys and girls did this—not white boys and girls. The social pattern, which we have today, was started by black boys and girls taught by black teachers like you, who had the inspiration and aspiration to tell them to push forward, pursue democracy. You can be what anybody else can be. And these [black boys and girls] changed the role of your democracy." Dr. Tate bemoaned black high school principals who gave up their leadership positions and claimed it really was okay with them to become elementary school principals. He questioned the commitment of the people with "legal authority" to protect the interests of either black principals or teachers. And he continued to blast the effects of second-class integration.

"Second class integration is evil because it does not consider the desires, customs and the mores, the traditions and the feelings of black people," he pointed out. White school officials were not concerned about the needs of black children desegregating schools, not even ones five years old. "When they suspend and expel black boys for growing a mustache or wearing their hair natural, or scolding the black girls for the manner of their strutting with the majorette team. Only a second class integration would build in such dehumanizing practice."

His words echoed a discussion at one of the first NAACP conventions, that in Baltimore in 1914. One speaker, Mrs. C.F. Cook, said then that Negro children needed to be guarded, to be fortified in every way possible, if they were to meet a future where inequality was branded early into the consciousness of their little ones and accompanied their growth "day and night, in season and out of season."[17] She had said Negro children were children too and, like all animal life, were sensitive to their surroundings. In fact, children were more sensitive to their surroundings than animals. Negro children needed training in ambition, courage, and love of liberty to offset the humiliations they encountered from childhood when Negro parents had to explain why they could not do the things white people could do. Negro educators, the Negro community understood, needed to take on the added responsibility of fortifying Negro children to be resilient.

Dr. Tate's message affirmed that black educators had taken on these challenges, had risen to them; that GT&EA had protected the interests of black education, and that GT&EA was not second-rate. Harry King, one of the educators protesting in Crawfordville, would still be in Crawfordville rather than at the State Department of Education had it not been for

GT&EA, he said. More than a hundred people served on national committees because of GT&EA. Black teachers had been placed in the Governor's Honors Program and black children allowed to participate. Salaries had been increased. Hundreds of jobs of black teachers had been saved. GT&EA had been part of White House conferences.

"We must make it unequivocally clear that we are not interested in swapping segregation for second class integration," Dr. Tate continued. He referenced a recent testimonial dinner in north Georgia for a black man who had been a principal for fourteen years. Three superintendents, three mayors, and three chairmen on boards of education spoke about the great influence the man had on the school system. Yet, because of integration, they were letting him go. They took half his students and half his teachers, Dr. Tate said, and despite HEW policy to the contrary, they took $3,000 from his salary. Eventually the man was left with only a school building and an office before being transferred to the superintendent's building. There he was placed in an attic room with no windows while the beautiful, just-built school building loomed empty. Humiliated, the black principal turned in his resignation, even as the system announced it had integrated.

"The story is almost always the same," Dr. Tate said, pointing out similar situations in Fitzgerald, Covington, Calhoun, Dalton, West Point—"you name it." In Burke County the school board had already planned to set up a "college prep" school in the all-white high school and a vocational school in the former Negro school because a white mother said she did not want her children "to go to school with the colored." Students would be assigned on the basis of achievement test scores. Negro plaintiffs charged the plan was simply another way to preserve segregation, and the one hundred black teachers of the Burke County Teachers Association adopted a resolution "refusing 'to have any part in the implementation." GT&EA called it "discriminatory, unimaginative and inconsistent with establishment of a unitary school system."[18]

As far as merger of GT&EA with GEA was concerned, he said, the merger committee had worked for three years to structure and approve a plan that guaranteed proper participation by the staff and the members of both associations. Subcommittee meetings had been held and merger committee meetings held throughout 1969, including reports to the Board of Directors, who then gave feedback to the GT&EA members of the Joint Committee. But he confessed, "What is disturbing and confusing to me is a seemingly total disregard for the plan even before the association mergers." He cited numerous violations on matters of personnel and buildings, four of which were reported to him within one hour. Among many matters, the appointed white executive secretary decided to "interview" the black staff, including Dr. Tate, for positions—even though decisions about personnel had already been decided.[19] "This violation of the plan before the merger leads me to only believe one thing. That is, if the plan is violated before a merger—what are we to expect after the merger?"

He was not trying to disrupt the merger, he said. "That's a lie. I want to say here and now I have told nobody in the state of Georgia to vote against the merger plan," despite having been asked numerous times his opinion. Neither he nor GT&EA leaders stood against the merger, and never had. He wasn't against white people. He wasn't against black people. He wasn't against NEA. He had been told some said he was a fool for continuing to seek fair play and justice and equality in the planned desegregation. But if he was a fool, so be it.

"If I am a fool for saying that our association seeks real integration not second class integration, then of course, I am guilty of being a fool." If he was a fool for trying to get equal salary, and keep jobs, and help Negro communities get a fair desegregation plan, then he would just be a fool. It put him in the company of Walter White, who had tried to get discriminatory practices eliminated, and Charles Harper, "who went all over this state trying to end salary discriminatory practices." Since he was doing the same kind of thing, he was willing to be a fool with them too. In fact, Martin Luther King Jr. would have been a fool too, and Dr. Tate was "happy to be in his company."

In his conclusion, Dr. Tate reported that he was no longer as happy about the merger as he had been twelve months or even six months earlier. Then he would have said, "Yes, vote for it," for equality looked possible. But he was not blocking it even now, even though the climate had changed and some black educators wrote him asking about the "many injustices" and questioned the merger.

"I am aware of the fact that the two Georgia educational associations are merging (which is another mistake of us as Blacks)," one GT&EA member had written to him as she protested being dismissed because she was "insubordinate." Another reported dismissal for being insubordinate as well.[20] He listened to the complaints but had not tried to block merger. If he wished, he could have simply encouraged everyone to vote against merger.

He had not. Everyone would have to cast the vote of their own conscience—himself included.

"You are charged," he reminded the listeners. When the Board of Directors was not in session, he was charged as executive secretary to implement the collective will of the black educators. But tonight the Representative Assembly was here, and they would decide on the merger at this meeting.

The next morning, President Hicks recognized all the platform guests to polite applause in the Second General Assembly in Sisters Chapel on the Spelman Campus on April 2, 1970. Atlanta vice mayor Maynard Jackson expressed his confidence in the faith of the judgment of the black educators to make a right decision about merger. Then, controlled, anguished, intense discussions—moderated via Robert's Rules of Order—began as delegates considered whether the proposal was the best merger agreement they could get. Was the document sufficient to ensure black participation, to protect the interests of blacks within the group?

Dr. Threat, recently elected to become the incoming president, said integration was an idea "whose time had come," that they needed to make a "commitment to make democratic promise a reality." They needed to only believe all things were possible. "This is hope we must have," he said as he encouraged the delegates to put their hands to the plow and "don't look back," to "bury the hatchet" and recognize that the likenesses between them and white educators were greater than the differences. The audience applauded as black children sang, "Hello Sunshine."[21]

On the floor of the GT&EA Representative Assembly, Mr. Byas read each item associated with merger, and many delegates voiced their support for the merger. Many believed the merger was necessary, that the beginning was at least "fair." One delegate stated his hope that "black educators can scream and raise enough hell to be heard anywhere" as the body discussed whether black educators would be able to maintain their voice and influence in the new association.

Others were not certain. They needed to take this merger "with a grain of salt," one cautioned. "Who is going to fight for you," queried another, "the NAACP?" Like most of the era unaware of the quiet coalitions, the delegate saw only the visible agency in the state. "GT&EA has been fighting for us," he announced.

The problem, as one delegate said, was the question of whether or not GEA would "fight for the black man." So far as some GT&EA delegates were concerned, fighting was still needed. Earl Warren, the chief justice of the Supreme Court who had supported black education, was gone. The new president, Richard Nixon, failed to support school desegregation. NEA was "not going all the way." HEW was "part of the conspiracy." The "only salvation of the black boys and girls rests in our hands . . . The fight is ours," someone said. "We ought to maintain the only effective weapon we have, and that is GT&EA."

Another person reminded attendees of results in other states. In North Carolina, black educators lost three thousand acres of pristine, sandy oceanfront property that had belonged to their teachers association before it merged with the white state association.[22] Referring to the mergers already accomplished in Florida, Virginia, and Louisiana, he said: "Never go into a hole where all tracks are going and none are coming back." Dr. John Davis of the NAACP's Legal Defense and Educational Fund had once warned of the "struggle" when black educators "went over" into white organizations. "Black teachers have to teach white teachers who don't know anything about how to teach black kids."

Throughout the meeting, individual delegates contemplated the outcome of the secret ballot. Meanwhile, speakers at the convention addressed the ideas the delegates debated. Dr. Jeanne Noble, a black professor involved on myriad national boards, proclaimed she had yet to see or hear all the promises of integration delivered. If they did not "keep some kind of united black power, you will never have the chance to make things happen," she predicted. The price of integration was too high if they lost the muscle they had with GT&EA. She did not mention, nor did Dr. Tate, the waning power of NCOSTA as black executive secretaries of state associations disappeared.

After her, Mr. Leon Edward Panetta, former director of the Office of Civil Rights and special assistant to the secretary for civil rights for HEW, spoke. GT&EA had sent telegrams to the president and education commissioner for help in "securing equal protection for Negro educators and pupils" who were being denied equal protection simply because they were black, but those messages had accomplished nothing.[23] As private schools proliferated across the South, President Nixon made clear he did not support busing to achieve racial balance. In fact, President Nixon had suspended President Johnson's "costly" programs to help poor children and accepted the advice of his special counselor Daniel P. Moynihan, who said the country did "not know how" to achieve equal educational opportunities for minority groups. In response, one black principal said that he *did* know how—and that it was his superintendent who went "from one silly plan to another."[24]

As the current HEW official spoke to the black educators, he acknowledged that district after district was "beginning to back away from their commitment of school desegregation." He said reports from the field indicated that "more and more school officials are waiting it out." But the HEW official blamed the president and the courts. HEW might once have been interested in regulations to protect black teachers and restricting plans calling for the "unfounded closing of black schools," but now the official HEW representative bemoaned the difficulties of overseeing so many school districts in the current era.

To many of the educators voting, it seemed all former alliances supported integration, even a half-cocked version. As individuals, they enjoyed the hotels and transportation options now open to them. They enjoyed attending NEA and desegregated meeting arrangements. With the new resources available in desegregated schools, maybe a trade of organizational power for inclusion was the only viable option.[25] And after all, they could still educate, couldn't they?

At the end of the program talk, President Hicks prepared to announce the results of the voting.

The number of delegates who had voted in favor of the merger was 318; those opposed numbered 101. The belief that integration by any measure was the best path had won. Many knew their votes did not reflect a rejection of all GT&EA had done as a body. They had simply voted the way of hope.

27

NOBODY BUT A FOOL

The last GT&EA state meeting was not finished. In his speech at the closing evening session, President Hicks highlighted the history of the association's opposition to "racial injustices, hate, oppression, segregation, and discrimination in any form." He oversaw the Representative Assembly's approval of a resolution appreciating Dr. Tate's service to the group and resolving to help him in all ways they could as the associate director of GEA.[1] He and Dr. Tate sat together on the stage as an orator from Hunt Senior High School of Fort Valley performed, along with the band from Fairmont High School in Griffin.

When Dr. Tate rose to make his remarks, he spoke directly to the delegates representing the thirteen thousand GT&EA members they served. "GT&EA has, of course, voted to merge with GEA," Dr. Tate said. "I have said to people about four months ago, had it been my organization I would have told you a long time ago what to do. But it wasn't my organization. I felt I would leave this to you as intelligent people. I do believe in the democratic process. You voted to merge and we are going to do the best we can as long as we can."[2]

Then the final GT&EA speaker arose for the last remarks of the day. The Honorable Adam Clayton Powell Jr., slightly inebriated, came to the podium. Former congressman Powell had been one of two black members on the House Education and Labor Committee during the 81st Congress in 1949 when Senate Bill 246, which would have allocated $300 million to public elementary and secondary schools, had failed in that committee because of a deadlock over provisions for aid to parochial schools. He was the congressman who had been punched in the jaw in July 1955 by West Virginia Democrat Cleveland Bailey during an Education and Labor Committee meeting. Among his activities on the committee was the effort to ensure that local oversight was a condition for receiving federal money. At this last annual meeting, he had just won his case before the

Supreme Court, *Powell v. McCormack*, after having been accused of misconduct and unseated by Congress. He was prepared to speak the truth publicly.[3]

Congressman Powell tossed his coat on the seat as a train rumbled in the background and commented that every long freight train had to have a caboose at the end. He was that caboose, he said. More pointedly, he explained, "Someone told me I was coming here tonight to deliver the eulogy." Then he began a rambling but fact-laden and poignant talk.[4]

Congressman Powell mused on the many matters confronting black Americans. He and the audience laughed when he stated the FBI had just proclaimed the Black Panthers the biggest threat to U.S. national security. A few black men exercising the constitutional right to carry guns prompted this much attention? With approximately 232 million black people, the former congressman announced: "You've come a long way, baby!"

Then he spoke pointedly about the education business the body had just transacted. It was no laughing matter, and the congressman made his position clear. The organization had better think this over, he emphasized. Constitutionally, representatives would need to reconvene after the annual meeting to hold a second mandatory vote.

"Nobody but a damned fool walks into an organization where they are immediately outvoted three to one," he proclaimed, dispensing with the language of the cloth. Congressman Powell was also a minister. "Whether it is Harlem or Georgia, I don't join anything where I am outvoted."

In addition to organizational power, the group also had assets. "What is going to happen to your $400,000 in property and money?" he queried forcefully.

Congressman Powell used his speech to reflect on his assessment of how they had come to this point as an organization. "Why don't you try and find out who is the architect of all this?" he asked rhetorically.

"You ought to see their buildings in Washington—steel, stretching into the sky. Not a single high level employee in the NEA is black," he said. "If I am wrong, stand up and tell me." As far as the congressman was concerned, NEA was the architect.[5]

"I was chairman of the education committee," he said. "They [NEA] had to come and kiss my cheek to get certain legislation through. I've been wined and dined by them—had conferences with their high level staff," he said.

"You better think about it, pray about it. . . . All you will get out of this is the right to sit down and have a cup of tea," he said of the *Brown v. Board* decision, which had aimed to help black children but had since been reconstructed to privilege white children.[6]

Congressman Powell said they should not be "fooled by promises." They needed to think about the number of white principals and the few black assistant principals, the already decimated leadership. "It is rough times we are going through. It is not times to be fooled by phrases, promises. Our forefathers went through all of that." As blacks, they would need unity to stand against the discriminations being forced upon them.

The audience concurred with the speech, but the decision had been made. They ignored the ringing words of Congressman Powell and let lie forgotten the words of Horace Mann Bond at one of their conventions just a few years prior.

"The Negro child has been, and is, the victim of a colossal wickedness," Dr. Bond had proclaimed during the 1963 convention, which had carried the theme "Teaching: A Calling to Fulfill." Dr. Bond had quoted the words of Horace Mann, the acclaimed founder of public education in the North, from an 1849 congressional speech to emphasize the point he wished GT&EA to understand: "He who denies to children the acquisition of knowledge," the white Horace Mann had said of white children more than a hundred years earlier, "works devilish miracles."[7]

With the initial vote to close GT&EA, it was unclear what would happen to black children. But the educators could hope equality could still be achieved within the advocacy of a merged group. President Hicks reminded the delegates they would need to reconvene on May 9 in Macon for the mandated final vote. He ended his remarks with the hope they would leave with a "new determination . . . to put shoulder to the wheel and make the new relationship wholesome and productive." And, as they always did, the convention concluded in prayer.

"Eternal God, we come at this hour to thank you for the many hours of devoted service we have been able to render as a group. . . . We ask as when we leave the auditorium that we will be mindful of the fact that all people are children of God—whether yellow, red, black or white, that it is necessary that we attempt to treat all as brothers."[8]

In its last organized effort, GT&EA sent its booklet *A Guide to an Inclusive Integration Plan* to superintendents across the state. GT&EA detailed and expanded the factors that had been outlined in *Green v. County School Board of New Kent County* but which were being ignored, namely the need for system-sponsored sensitivity training for both groups; the need for

Dr. Tate communicated with Presidents Kennedy and Johnson. As school integration as he had envisioned it collapsed, he also met with President Nixon. *GT&EA Collection*

parents of both groups to be involved in integration planning; the importance of a faculty-approved curriculum and textbooks that included multiethnic books; the employment of both black and white bus drivers; the use of all buildings rather than the arbitrary dismissal of the black school building; the need to maintain medals, plaques, trophies, pictures, and certificates from the minority group and not allowing activities such as singing "Dixie" or flying the Confederate flag; the need to create new symbols for all schools; and the need for detailed plans that would ensure representation for students, principals, teachers, department chairmen, counselors, librarians, central office personnel, and lunchroom and maintenance personnel.

The blue GT&EA booklet pointed out that the school systems that had operated schools in a racially discriminatory manner in the past were the ones now working on current plans. "These systems face a tremendous problem because many school officials and boards of education are trying to meet the approval of the law without changing philosophy or practice. . . . [M]ost school officials responsible for integration are reluctant to admit that they have done as little as possible to really develop desegregation or integration plans which are for the best interest of all students, all parents and all school personnel.

"Inasmuch as most boards of education are almost totally white, especially in the South . . . the interest of white students is completely protected. Negro parents, Negro students and Negro professional personnel are made to absorb almost all of the painful burdens of this massive change," it said. "The ultimate test of any school integration plan must be that the opportunities available to all pupils and the active participation of these pupils under proposed integration are greater than those available under segregation."[9]

On May 9, GT&EA delegates reconvened in Macon. Dr. Tate and some others argued that some kind of black organization needed to be preserved, that black children could not go into schools without some form of organized agency because an integrated committee might not well fight the problems of inferior educational opportunities for black children as a black organization would. A former GT&EA president, James Hawes, disagreed. He said the group had been doing things their own way—that is, the black way—for a long time, and "we may as well try it their way," the white way.

Soon Mr. Hawes would lose his job at the Elberton school, where he had been a masterful principal, where he had mentored GT&EA's associate director, Mr. Byas, and where he had courageously led fights for equality on the state and national levels. In the new system he would become a man in charge of buses. Soon Dr. Tate, who knew that Elberton school as his former high school, would also be in the middle of many different battles as the associate director of a merged organization.[10]

But most people cannot read the future well. They make the best decisions they know how to make at the time. And they hope those decisions will be right. After discussion, the delegates quietly voted again.

The final votes were counted and announced. GT&EA members had voted the organization out of existence.[11]

EPILOGUE

THE LAST WORD

"Have you been back to the building?" Dr. Horace Edward Tate repeatedly posed this question to me in the last weeks before he died.

I could not understand why he kept pressing me to return to what he called "the building." He had already shared with me the files Mrs. Tate had attempted to secretly dispose of from their basement—he had triumphantly located them in the trash bin, where they were damp from drizzle, and carefully laid them across the driveway so the sun could dry them before he returned them to the basement.

He had finally shown me the locations of many other materials he had hidden from his wife. Once I had dared tease him about how long it took for him to show me everything. He didn't even smile. He looked at me quizzically and then commanded me to follow him throughout the basement. "I have materials hidden here, and here, and here," he said as he pointed to various ceilings and closets. My own smile faded. That tour was the last time he was well enough to meet with me in his basement.

Then began the repeated question from the confines of his hospital bed in a family bedroom. "Have you been back to the building?" I assured him I would go, but I didn't. I just could not imagine what of use could possibly remain at the old teachers' building.

I did not honor Dr. Tate's command to return to the building until after the icy day in November when Georgia's newly elected governor, senators, and other political and business figures in Atlanta joined elderly black educators to bid farewell to a fallen leader. I had listened earlier in the day as Dr. Tate's death was reported on the Atlanta television stations. I had read the papers announcing his demise as I finalized the remarks for his funeral. One sunny day outside his home, he'd asked me to say a few words at his homegoing. With such a public Atlanta acknowledgment of his death, the acute realization of the status of the elderly, kind gentleman I had come to know was just beginning to take root.

Dr. Tate advocated for Jimmy Carter during the gubernatorial election in Georgia and attended the White House festivities during his inauguration in Washington. The two were lifelong friends, with President Carter calling the Tate home to offer support in the weeks before Dr. Tate's death. *Tate Collection*

When I finally parked again in the driveway of the GT&EA building a month after the funeral and went to the second-floor offices, I told his younger daughter, who worked out of an office next to Dr. Tate's old office, that I did not know why her father had wanted me to return to the building. She was a Georgia state senator occupying the seat her father had left vacant. Distracted, she answered matter-of-factly, "Daddy was talking about the stuff he hid in the attic."

Perhaps I had missed something. I frowned. "The attic?" I finally said. "Where is the attic?"

Even though I remembered Dr. Tate saying he sometimes used an alternative route to escape the press on harried days in the GT&EA office, I never thought to ask him how he had gotten out of his office suite if he did not follow the usual path I knew well by that point. But now his daughter gave me directions. "You know Daddy's office?" she said. I nodded. "Go into the office and look for the door *behind* the door that leads to a hallway. Open that door and make your way down the stairs. It will take you to the old building." After all those visits, I had not known that the old 1951 building was in fact attached directly to the new teachers' building. "The light is out in the stairwell, so be careful," she cautioned me.

In what seemed almost like a dream, I began to follow her directions. I made my way to the end of the hall connecting the old and new GT&EA buildings, avoiding the hole in the floor at the bottom of the stairwell as she had instructed. I turned a corner to the left and stepped gingerly into the empty and dank-smelling room I had seen in pictures. I was standing in the conference room of the 1951 GT&EA headquarters. In a corner across from me, against a sunny windowed wall, was the old printing press for the *Herald*.

Finally, my eyes shifted away from the old press, and I saw the ornate stairway she had told me to use to go to the second floor. I started across the room and began the ascent up the stairs. At the top, I looked carefully and spotted the almost indiscernible attic door.

With more than a little trepidation, I opened it carefully and found a very narrow and very steep staircase. I contemplated not going up, as I was not certain the stairs could hold weight. But I had come this far, so I might as well, as the old folks said, "see what the end was going to be."

I grasped dusty rails and carefully made my way up the squeaky wooden stairs to the attic. When I looked left, I saw what the dying Dr. Tate had sent me to retrieve. Under a broken window were eleven neatly arranged old steel file cabinets. Dr. Tate had removed them from his office and had them brought up here, to a location as far away as possible from prying white eyes. Before me was the full, intact set of GT&EA records. Furthermore, strewn around me across two rooms were boxes and stacks of random books and papers. I spotted multiple, undistributed copies of the GT&EA booklet *Guide to an Inclusive Integration Plan.* I saw trophies ungiven, including one to Ralph McGill, and *Herald*s in stacks. If the file cabinets were neatly placed, the documents looked like the movers had been in a hurry to finish.

After untold minutes I carefully descended the stairs, retraced my route, and emerged back in Dr. Tate's office. A former doctoral student, whom I had asked to wait for me, frowned when she saw me come back through the door. "Are you all right?" she asked after I emerged from the haunts of the old building.

I sank into the closest chair. I was not all right. Once when I had asked Dr. Tate if I could see some of the old minutes to confirm some of the things he was describing, he had simply responded, "Well, I'm sure you're going to find something."

Writing the history of black schools always involved the challenge of finding documentation. People's memories of their own lives were not always infallible, I had learned when I first started writing *Their Highest Potential*, so I sought records. When I first went looking for the school board minutes for Caswell County at the local county office for schools in that area of North Carolina, I was told that the records were missing. But when someone recognized me as the daughter of a former supervisor in the system, the records suddenly "appeared." They had been stored out in an old building, someone said.

Subsequently, I learned that much of black school history was in basements, attics, and back rooms of archives. A North Carolina archivist suddenly "found" principal's reports of the high school about which I was writing after I made friends with him. He said that in the records there were only five left for black high schools, and that they were uncatalogued somewhere in a back hall. I was grateful to have any at all. Mrs. Inez Blackwell, the black parent living closest to the school, had told me that just before integration she had received a call from the school's black secretary instructing her to come over quick because "they are burning everything." Fortunately, Mrs. Blackwell had retrieved some materials I could use. By the time I went looking for the files, all that remained were a few yearbooks.

In the years I spent tromping after Dr. Tate's story, I learned that the problems I'd encountered in North Carolina existed elsewhere. In North Carolina, the last NCOSTA executive secretary, Mr. Palmer, told me he had returned to his office the day after the merger of the North Carolina black teachers organization with the white teachers organization to discover that his files had been summarily removed. When I sent doctoral students on what should have been routine trips to Georgia towns to examine school board records, they returned empty-handed. In Greensboro, Dr. Tate was erased from the record, his successor reported. In Elberton, the black superintendent said he had no idea where the records were.[1]

So as far as I could tell, this intact GT&EA collection that I had just discovered in the attic represented the only untouched, intact set of the records of the activities of black educators' associations.[2]

Dr. Tate had told me before he died that he had purchased the building when the new merged educational association leaders had decided to sell it. He said he paid $100,000 to the black physician who was the original buyer of record. I inferred it was a trick to conceal the real purchaser.

Dr. Tate said he had hoped the black group he tried to put together would want to purchase it collectively, but they were not interested. When they declined, he used his own money to buy the building. He said he always wanted to explain what happened to the building to former GT&EA members, but after the merger the thousands of members were never again together in meetings, so he had no way to explain. During the decades since the dissolution of GT&EA, it had been his personal property.

His wife said he had always hoped that one day black educators would wake up. And when they did, he wanted them to have a place to meet.[3]

AUTHOR'S NOTE

A LOOK IN THE REARVIEW MIRROR

I was a student at the Harvard Graduate School of Education in 1984 when the College Board met with Harold "Doc" Howe to discuss the historic civil rights legislation that had been passed twenty years prior. I was not astute enough to understand either his place in history or my own in that history. I was the black child from a rural school district in North Carolina whom he sought to protect, the one who spent six years in segregated schools. I was also the student integrated into a white school in the second half of my pre-collegiate education, while black educators were "outer-grated." When I began my first foray into writing about segregated schooling shortly after graduation, none of these intersections were apparent to me. Even as I approached this book on segregated schools, my personal lens was immaterial.

I am not sure I could not have seen their carefully concealed story of advocacy had I tried. A former graduate professor, Eleanor Duckworth, spoke thoughtfully as I shared with her the difficulties in mining this story in its early stages. "Sometimes," she said, "historians can help you see things you might not otherwise see, and sometimes historians can keep you from seeing what you otherwise might see."[1]

So it was with me. The experiential history I left uncritiqued blandly accepted the story that most historical accounts wrote and most readers affirmed: that black children had been mistreated until desegregation, when they were rescued from poor black teachers. As Richard Kluger eloquently wrote in one of my favorite books, *Simple Justice*, desegregation laws accomplished justice. Since my own educational opportunities represented the access to new opportunities black parents and lawyers sought, I saw little need to think further about the historical record. Not until I began to spend substantial time in black communities after graduate school asking questions about why they liked their segregated schools (research that resulted in my book *Their Highest Potential*) and spent more years exploring and listening to the accounts of the professional activities of

Dr. Ulysses Byas and reviewing his archival collection (which led to my book *Hello Professor*) did I begin to comprehend the complex story of school climates and professional responsibility embedded in the segregated story I had lived.

I do not criticize history for focusing on only one aspect of the story of segregation and desegregation, or myself for not looking beyond the written word. Historians wrote the story of the public dialogue following the language of the story America postulated. In part, the black educators about whom I write are also implicated in the dominance of the popular story. For most of their years of professional activities, black educators intentionally told the part of the story they wanted the public to know. It was intentional because it allowed them to gain the legal decisions and federal funding desired. The truth is, black educators did such a good job teaching the public the official script that most people never questioned those accounts. Historians cannot fully be blamed for that craftiness. They also cannot be blamed for the widespread destruction of the records of black schools. Without the documents and with little hint of the need to counter a widely accepted story, researchers mostly followed the paths set by their predecessors.

And yet, existing in plain sight if we look carefully, is another story. This account has been written to help us see what we might otherwise have seen had a different lens been applied to history. The account draws upon the tools of historical ethnography to represent the world as experienced by participants. I crafted the term "historical ethnography" when I first sought to tell the stories of black segregated schools in ways that expanded beyond the traditional accounts of inadequacy. My goal was to blend the historian's emphasis on interrogating a historical event in its period with the ethnographic tools of an anthropologist.

The details of this methodology, including the ways in which I account for memories of the participants, interrogate documents, address researcher bias, and draw conclusions, are available in both my previous books on black segregated schools. *Their Highest Potential* provides a general orientation to the methodology and the ways I generalize findings. In *Hello Professor* I elaborate upon and expand the earlier description.

This work held its own particular challenges, and I believe requires another new layer of elaboration on historical ethnography. In particular, because a number of archival records were needed to expand the educators' perspectives, I use this note to provide an abbreviated description of the methodological phases for this work.

In phase one of the project, I functioned in the mode of historical ethnographer. Two years with Dr. Tate provided the initial lens that prompted me to interrogate the historical account differently. I spent approximately three days a week at his home for most of the last year of his life. In the previous year, I had met him on multiple occasions at the building and attended a daylong meeting of former principals he convened there to discuss with me their former activities. The triangulation of his and other oral accounts, along with the documents from GT&EA in his basement, helped me conclude that some black educators played an advocacy role in attempting to obtain just educational opportunities for black children.

I did not, however, understand how the accounts of their activities fit any of the previous accounts I had read. Was the work of the educators complementary with other actors? Supplementary? Competing? And what was the source of the varied ideas they described? These questions led me to phase two of the project. In this phase, I relied on traditional historical methods of archival review to extrapolate the documents related to advocacy from the fifteen GT&EA file cabinets (the eleven from the building and the four others in his basement) and a variety of other documents, which I summarized and placed in chronological order. Once I understood the chronology of events from the GT&EA documents, I began the process of analyzing the activities of other organizations in the same time periods. Specifically, I sought connections between people and events, both locally and nationally. Because I brought an understanding of names and events from the perspective of the teachers' organization, I was able to interrogate documents previously analyzed by historians with a different lens. This lens was particularly useful in the NAACP collection at the Library of Congress, where names like "Mr. Hunt" led me down a different analytical path than that of some of my predecessors who had spent time with the collection.

At the conclusion of the analysis of other archival collections, I aligned the extant archival record with the GT&EA archival record in phase three. This timeline created a discernible record of activism and activities, which I carefully charted. However, the analysis failed to help me understand how local educators worked, especially since the educational actors seemed to say and do different things in different spaces. At this stage of the analysis, the events as solo descriptions made little conceptual sense as a way to understand their activities. To address this difficulty, I developed a "looping methodology" for the third phase of the work.

I understood some of Dr. Tate's motivations from interviews. But his predecessor, Mr. Hunt, I did not understand at all. I particularly could not make sense of Mr. Hunt's relationship with Dr. Du Bois or James Weldon Johnson, especially since Mr. Hunt portrayed himself in other records as aligned with the northern philanthropists' agenda of rectifying the situation of diminished educational opportunities for black children. However, once I could chronicle some similarity of behaviors between Mr. Hunt and Dr. Tate, I began to consider whether the oral motivational report of Dr. Tate might be a lens through which to interrogate the activities of Mr. Hunt.

Mr. Hunt took two years of analysis. In the process, I often wondered why I could not seem to let go of his story. Everywhere he seemed to thread nearly invisibly through multiple documents. However, when I applied Dr. Tate's oral motivational account to Mr. Hunt's activities, the documents congealed and an explanation for Mr. Hunt's advocacy appeared. To my surprise, I discovered the behaviors, values, and curricular emphasis were intergenerational across the leadership of the educational organization, inclusive of Mr. Harper and Mr. Wright. Dr. Tate's descriptive "loop" backward helped locate the details that helped explain Mr. Hunt.

Once I understood Mr. Hunt and the trickster motif, I was able to return to the documents of Dr. Tate and interpret patterns he had never explained. Once I remember Dr. Tate saying as he neared the end of his life, "You will know how to put it together." At the time I did not, and indeed, I frowned at the thought. However, the similarity of generational activity I discovered after I understood Mr. Hunt helped me understand Dr. Tate in ways that extended the descriptions he gave of himself.

The final methodological phase was the crafting of story. The account elevates certain aspects of the story for ease of communication but seeks to rely solely on the triangulated accuracy of the oral accounts and documents to thread the telling. I triangulated Dr. Tate's accounts with each other to check the validity of his memory, his accounts with other oral accounts to triangulate for accuracy, oral accounts with GT&EA accounts for consistency, GT&EA records with other archival records for expansions, and initial themes in varied time periods with extant literature and other researchers to sharpen my critical eye. My goal was to create a story that adhered to historical ethnographical tenants while also expanding the memories of actors beyond their own understanding as I crafted a record of their cumulative work across time.

Is this story generalizable? I am confident the answer is largely yes. The records reveal that black educational associations operated in similar ways in every southern state. The names of these executive directors also appear in the meetings in which GT&EA leaders appeared. While the particulars vary from setting to setting and the actors certainly differ, I think the story of black educational advocacy across states is more similar than different.

My goal in this work has been to provide an overarching landscape of a different story. Importantly, however, the story I tell here leaves many other stories untold. I hope future researchers will grapple with the divergent roads alluded to here and expand the account in the years to come. In particular, I hope the up-close descriptions of southern politicians in federal spaces regarding educational policy, communications between southern white NEA affiliates and the NEA body, and the changing and contradictory role of philanthropists over time will be explored. As well, the documents are so voluminous on meetings, records, arguments, and other events that I hope someone will elevate individual stories of which I have given only an overview and provide them with the nuanced accounting they are due. An understanding of gender is sorely lacking. Women are woefully absent in this accounting.

Historians are reluctant to apply historical ideas to a new generation. I write from the perspective of a historical ethnographer and have fewer reservations. I believe the layering of avenues to seek access over time and the similarity of local and federal response to their petitions deserves grappling with in the current educational moment. As Rev. Warnock, the current pastor of Rev. King's Ebenezer Baptist Church, commented on a Sunday I happened to attend service there, sometimes you have to look in the rearview mirror in order to see a current path better. My hope is that this account assists a new generation to see what it might otherwise have missed.

ACKNOWLEDGMENTS

I once heard the story of an actor whose son was disappointed to learn that a double had been used in some of the scenes he particularly admired in his father's movies. Vexed, the son finally said to his father, "Well, what did *you* do?" The father replied, "I got the credit." So it is with me. Gratitude has many faces. These acknowledgments include only a partial listing of the debt owed to many unseen.

To the Spencer Foundation, which provided an immediate emergency grant during the time of Dr. Tate's illness that allowed me to set up a research site in the basement of his home for the last year of his life, I am grateful. For two to three days a week, I and the first Tate research team—Cheryl Fields-Smith and Mary Elizabeth Kelly—processed files and listened to Dr. Tate's explanation of materials. This year was foundational in helping me to understand Dr. Tate's interpretation of events and to begin the task of outlining a research strategy.

I offer gratitude as well to the Spencer Foundation for the major research grant I later received to support this work. In addition to financial support for research travel, this grant also provided support for the second Tate research team, which met weekly in the basement of my home for several years. I owe a special debt to Michelle Purdy, Tirza White Vincent Willis, Miyoshi Juergeson, Sheryl Croft, and Keisha Greene. These then-doctoral students, now professors, did the hard work of sorting through eleven file cabinets of GT&EA materials to locate documents I needed. They inspired laughter, helped with site visits, offered encouragement, and asked piercing questions that forced me to clarify conclusions. Without their support, I would yet be going through file cabinets.

The final Tate research team of the last two years literally carried me across the finish line. Thank you to Emory University for the research support that allowed Christy Myers to direct the project's completion and to Amber Jones for joining that team. Without Christy, I am not sure anything on these pages would be complete. Discerning and patient, she was an anchor of support.

Although not officially part of any of the Tate research teams, my agent and editor became crucial supporters on whom I also relied. Many thanks to Janell Agyeman of Marie Brown Associates, who invested early and eagerly in helping me think about how to prepare the story for an audience that might reach beyond the academy. Among her goals was to deliver me to an editor who would "get" the work. She did. I can imagine no better editor than Tara Grove at The New Press. Tara is the embodiment of education the way old black educators envisioned it. She has provided humane, enthusiastic, visionary, and tangible support throughout the contract years. I wish for others similar editors. I am also grateful for the diligent and patient support of Sarah Swong, Emily Albarillo, and Susan Warga, all of whom were essential in bringing this manuscript to production.

Many, many others helped also, and I wish to extend my thanks to them as well. I am grateful to colleagues and students in the Division of Educational Studies at Emory University. In this setting, doctoral students, undergraduate students, and faculty learned from and pushed one another to engage in purposeful research. For these dear colleagues and many students over the years, including my most recent wonderful undergraduate students in African American studies, I acknowledge publicly with gratitude your patience and prompting. As we often have said jovially in class and other settings, "He who talks the most learns the most." Thank you for letting me learn better those things I thought I knew.

In ways I did not understand when I first entered the academy, I now realize the central role of scholars around the country in helping launch a research idea. I appreciate many of my colleagues for their suggestions and queries in professional settings over the years, but owe a special thanks to James Anderson for the years of listening to me trying to interpret something that seemed to fit no historical box I understood; Amy Stuart Wells for her gleeful request for annual updates; Jackie Irvine for the continued mentorship and project feedback; Theresa Perry for the multiple ways she demonstrated her belief in the importance of the work; Nathan McCall for his enthusiastic early response and immediate reference to an agent; and Lisa Delpit for providing just the right advice at critical moments.

Many people already knew significant parts of the story I spent years trying to weave into a single narrative. I am grateful to Dr. Tate's colleagues and other people who gave of their time to engage my queries in interviews. I appreciate the many archivists who offered helpful suggestions. I especially thank Ms. Wilmetta Jackson, the archivist at Fort Valley State College. Without the multiple visits and conversations over the years, I would never have had access to the materials that provided a different lens to interrogate Mr. Hunt. And without Mr. Hunt, I could never have unraveled the rest of the story.

On a more personal level, I elevate those family and friends who have surrounded me with their knowledge, support, prayers, and love. Many, many thanks to Marionette Jeffers, Trudy Blackwell, Janice Byrd, Margaret Roane, Marian Elbert, and Mother Tate. These wonderful women read early drafts and gave feedback on an important question: "Does this make any sense?" Thank you also to Polly Nelms, Laverne Byas-Smith, Virginia Burford, Alvin Myers, Sydney Myers, Gloria Henderson, Patricia Pickard, Alice Fink, Priscilla Wilkerson, Rev. McClellon Cox, Rev. Richard Allen Farmer, Claudia Udah, Lora Turner, Veronica Winley, Sandra Baxtor, Alan Mazzaferro, and Paige Stanfield. Every one of you supported me in some stage of this work when I was falling. Thank you to the daughters of Dr. Tate, Ms. Valosia Tate Marsh and Senator Horacena Tate, and a special thanks to many at the congregations of Mount Zion AME and Crossroads Presbyterian.

My family sacrificed and gave the most. Doris "Plum" Wright listened to me most Sunday nights for eighteen years. Her daughter, Brenda, and son-in-law, Shelton, constantly supported me physically and emotionally. My husband, Melford, located on eBay pictures and books I did not know even existed. He encouraged me when I was ready to give up; he put up with some dinner, no dinner, "get your own dinner," "by the way, get me some dinner"—always with humor, patience, and love. He is the half of me who makes me better.

And, especially, I acknowledge with an open heart my daughter, Sarah. This young woman can barely remember life in the Walker home without Dr. Tate or a basement not filled with papers. She gave eighteen years of her mother to this project: waiting patiently as a little girl on the days I was late picking her up from school because I was scurrying from the other side of town, and traveling contentedly with me on varied research trips. I recognize with gratitude her willingness to share her mom with the work. She is the world's most wonderful daughter, but also the graduate student who now says I should announce publicly: "This work is done." I write these last sentences for you, Sarah.

Dr. Tate used to say some things are providential. I have come to believe he was right. I have no real explanation for why he decided to meet with me or to release the documents to my care. I cannot explain the many steps along the way that resulted in new insights or provided direction at critical moments. I am grateful for the providence and grace of God, a Creator who reveals Himself to be one who cares about justice.

Atlanta, Georgia
February 2, 2018

NOTES

Abbreviations

MFPE—Minimum Foundation Program of Education

ATA—American Teachers Association (originally the National Association of Teachers in Colored Schools)

NEA—National Education Association

GT&EA—Georgia Teachers and Education Association

GEA—Georgia Education Association

NCOSTA—National Council of Officers of State Teachers Associations

HEW—Department of Health, Education, and Welfare

Manuscript and Archival Collections

Amherst, MA

Special Collections and University Archives, UMASS Amherst Libraries

Horace Mann Bond Papers, University of Massachusetts, Amherst, MA (HMB)

Atlanta, GA

Auburn Avenue Research Library on African American Culture and History

William B. Matthews Papers (WBM)

Atlanta Public Schools Archives, Atlanta, Georgia (APS)

Atlanta University Center Archival Collection (AUC)

Emory University Stuart A. Rose Manuscripts and Rare Book Library

James Weldon Johnson Papers, Emory University Special Collections (JWJ.E)

Southern Association of Colleges and Universities, Emory University Special Collection (SACU)

Ulysses Byas Papers, Emory University Special Collections (UBP)

Georgia State Archives (GSA)

Education—Negro Education Division—Director's Subject Files, 1928–1996, Georgia Board of Education Files

Robert W. Woodruff Library, Atlanta University Center (RWL)

Horace E. Tate Files, Georgia Teachers and Education Association, Private Collection (HET)

Boston, MA
John F. Kennedy Presidential Library
John F. Kennedy Presidential Papers (JFK)

Cambridge, MA
Gutman Library, Harvard Graduate School of Education
Harold Howe II Papers (HHP)
James Weldon Johnson Collection, Beinecke Archival Library, Yale University

Chapel Hill, NC
Wilson Special Collections Library
The Bulletin: Official organ of the National Association of Teachers in Colored Schools
National Association of Teachers of Colored Schools (NATCS)

Charlotte, NC
Inez Moore Parker Archives and Research Center
James B. Duke Memorial Library (JDML)
Johnson C. Smith Archives (JCSA)

Columbus, GA
Simon Schwob Memorial Library, Columbus State University
Columbus State University Oral History Collection (CSU)

Elberton, GA
Elbert County Historical Society
Elberton Historical Society Collections (EHSC)

Fort Valley, GA
Henry A. Hunt Memorial Library, Fort Valley State University
Fort Valley University Archives (FV)

Greensboro, GA
Greene County Historical Society
Greensboro Historical Society Collections, Greensboro, GA (GHSC)

Morrow, GA
Georgia Department of Archives and History (GDPAH)

Nashville, TN
Special Collections and Archives, Fisk University
Julius Rosenwald Papers (RP)

New Haven, CT
Yale University Library Manuscripts and Archives
James Weldon Johnson Papers, Yale University (JWJ)

Savannah, GA
City of Savannah, Research Library and Municipal Archives
W.W. Law Foundation

Sedalia, NC
Charlotte Hawkins Brown Museum
Charlotte Hawkins Brown State Historic Site

Washington, DC
Records of the National Association of Advancement of Colored People, Manuscript Division, Library of Congress, Washington, DC (NAACP)

Records of the Legal Defense and Education Fund in the Records of the National Association of Advancement of Colored People (LDEF)

Moorland Spingarn Research Center, Howard University (HUA)
American Teachers Association Files (ATA)

National Association of Education Headquarters
National Education Association Archives (NEA)

Interviews by Author

Tate, Horace. Interviews, location, and date separated by;

Dr. Horace Tate Formal Interviews, Atlanta GA, September 1, 2001; October 20, 2001; November 14, 2001; November 20, 2001; December 7, 2001; December 21, 2001; January 9, 2002; February 8, 2002; February 14, 2002; February 21, 2002; March 7, 2002; March 14, 2002; May 9, 2002; May 22, 2002; July 26, 2002; September 20, 2002.

Dr. Horace Tate Review and Document prompted Questions, Atlanta, GA, January 17, 2002; January 24, 2002; April 5, 2002; August 21, 2002; August 24, 2002; September 13, 2002; October 25, 2002; November 14, 2002; November 21, 2002; November 22, 2002.

Tate, Virginia. Interviews. Atlanta, GA, n.d.; June 12, 2002; February 21, 2003; April 10, 2003; August 27, 2009; (phone interview) November 7, 2009; (phone interview) January 1, 2010; (phone interview) October 28, 2010; January 6, 2008; February 21, 2007; March 7, 2008; April 4, 2008; April 28, 2008; May 14, 2011; November 8, 2012; April 23, 2014; February 27, 2015.

Other Interviews:

Beasley, Nancy. Interview, Cartersville, GA, June 23, 2012.

Breeding, William; Henry Brown, Ulysses Byas, Bobby Huff, Horace Tate. Group Interview: Invitational Principals' Retreat, December 1, 2000.

Byas, Ulysses. Interviews, December 1, 2000; (phone interview) March 3, 2008.

Carter, Jimmy. Interview, Atlanta, GA, November 11, 2013.
Davis, Shelton. Interview, Portsmouth, VA, February 21, 2012; February 26, 2012.
Drake, Jennie; Doris Reynolds. Group Interview, Atlanta, GA, February 20, 2003.
Harris, Narvie, Interview, Atlanta, GA, spring 2000.
Hicks, Charlie. Interviews, n.d.
Hill, Oliver. Interviews, Richmond, VA, July 19, 2003; August, 31 2003.
Hollowell, Donald, E. Interview, Atlanta, GA, February 20, 2003.
Hudson, Patricia. Interview, October 18, 2001.
Jackson, Mrs. Phone interview, August 22, 2012.
Vivian, C.T. Interview, June 8, 2015.

Introduction: Finding the Hidden Provocateurs

1. Ulysses Byas is the author of this idea. His work and words are captured in Vanessa Siddle Walker, *Hello Professor: A Black Principal and Professional Leadership in the Segregated South* (Chapel Hill: University of North Carolina Press, 2009).

2. Robert Morton, *What the Negro Thinks* (New York: Doubleday, Doren, 1929), 1–2, 3, 17.

3. Oliver Hill, interview with author, July 19, 2003, August 31, 2003.

4. Donald Hollowell, interview with author, February 20, 2003.

5. Conversations with author, Principals' Conference, GT&EA Building, Atlanta, GA, December 1, 2000.

6. C.T. Vivian, interview with author, June 8, 2015.

1: In the Shadow of His Smile

1. Hazel Poteat, interview with author, May 7, 2013.

2. Horace E. Tate, "The Greensboro Story," unpublished chapter from the unfinished draft of his autobiography, "Just Trying to Be a Man," 20–21, Howard E. Tate papers in possession of the author (henceforth HET).

3. "School Bond Election Held," "Bond Vote Tuesday," "Bond Issue Wins Big Vote," *Herald-Journal*, n.d. but ca. August 1948.

4. Jonathan M. Bryant, *How Curious a Land: Conflict and Change in Greene County, Georgia* (Chapel Hill: University of North Carolina Press, 1996), 184–85; Horace E. Tate, interview with author, n.d.; Virginia Tate, interview with author, n.d.

5. Virginia Tate, interview with author, March 4, 2012; Horace E. Tate, interview with author, n.d.; three author site visits to Greensboro, Georgia. Virginia Tate accompanied the author on one of the visits.

6. Walker, *Hello Professor.*

7. Interview with staff at courthouse during author site visit to Greensboro, Georgia, n.d.; photograph from Library of Congress of original building siding; Greene County Heritage Book Committee, 26, Greensboro Historical Society Collections, Greensboro, GA.

8. Author site travel from Greensboro to Madison, Georgia.

9. Tate, "The Greensboro Story," 7–8; "School Bond Election Held."

10. Tate, "The Greensboro Story," 18.

11. Ibid.

12. Accounts of racial relations in the South are available in numerous books. See, for example, Leon Litwack, *Trouble in Mind: Black Southerners in the Age of Jim Crow* (New York: Vintage Books, 1998); David Carter, *The Music Has Gone Out of the Movement: Civil Rights and the Johnson Administration, 1965–1968* (Chapel Hill: University of North Carolina Press, 2009); Jimmy Carter, *An Hour Before Daylight: Memories of a Rural Boyhood* (New York: Simon & Schuster, 2001); Donald Grant, *The Way It Was in the South: The Black Experience in Georgia*, ed. Jonathan Grant (Athens: University of Georgia Press, 1993).

13. Arthur Raper, *Tenants of the Almighty* (New York: Macmillan, 1943), 348.

14. *Gone with the Wind* at the New Union Theatre, Union Point, *Greensboro Paper*, n.d.; Raper, *Tenants of the Almighty*, 349.

15. Raper, *Tenants of the Almighty*, 338–39. Some scholars limit the agency of black educational leaders, portraying them as self-serving or compromised by finances. See, for example, Kevin Gaines, *Uplifting the Race: Black Leadership, Politics, and Culture in the Twentieth Century* (Chapel Hill: University of North Carolina Press, 1996).

16. Tate, "The Greensboro Story," 19.

17. Author site visit to Greensboro; Noah Bunn, "Day Trip to Madison, GA," *Southern Living* website, https://www.southernliving.com/travel/south-east/madison-georgia; Simon Louvish, *Stan and Ollie: The Roots of Comedy: The Double Life of Laurel and Hardy* (New York: Thomas Dunne Books, 2001), 477.

18. Details of life in Greensboro and Greene County are captured in Greene County Heritage Book Committee, *Greene County County, Georgia Heritage, 1786–2009* (Waynesville, NC: Walsworth, 2009).

19. Report of an oral culture from James Beasley, interview with author, n.d.

20. A detailed story of his interaction with the farmer is provided in Tate, "The Greensboro Story."

21. As examples, see the following items from the NAACP Collection, Library of Congress: W. Pinckney, letter to J.W. Johnson, July 13, 1918 (Part I, B1, G43, F8); W.H. Rowell, letter to W. White, May 22, 1920 (Part I, B1, G43, F1); S.S. Humbert, letter to J.W. Johnson, May 22, 1922 (Part I, B1, G43, F7); Director, letter to J.W. Davis, December 29, 1923 (Part I, B1, G43, F13); S.S. Humbert, letter to R.W. Bagnall, May 22, 1922 (Part I, G43, F7). See also H. Pace, letter to "Dear Friend," July 7, 1917 (Part I, G43, F9); A.D. Williams, letter to M.W. Ovington and J.W. Johnson, January 23, 1924 (Part I, G43, F13); E.F. Frazier, letter to R.W. Bagnall, June 4, 1925 (Part I, G43, F14); R.W. Bagnell, letter to A.T. Walden, September 16, 1929 (Part I, G43, F15); S.S. Humbert, letter to J.W. Johnson, April 27, 1927 (Part I, G43, F7); O.A. Toomer, letter to J.R.

Shillady, August 6, 1918 (Part I, G43, F10); M. Ovington, Memorandum to Conference of Executives, May 1923 (C114, F26).

22. See samples of conflict in NAACP Collection, Part I, B1, C6, F1–3.

23. Atlanta is an example of a city where the NAACP tried to remain active. However, even in Atlanta, difficulties prevailed. See S.S. Humbert, letter to J.W. Johnson, August 10, 1922 (Part I, G43, F7); G.A. Towns, letter to J.W. Johnson, May 18, 1921 (Part I, G43, F11); C.W. Howard, letter to NAACP, November 22, 1922 (Part I, G43, F12); Big Bethel NAACP office photographs, Atlanta (Part I, G44, F11), all NAACP Collection.

24. Georgia Teachers and Education Association, *Rising in the Sun: A History of the Georgia Teachers and Education Association, [1918–1966]: A Half Century of Progress* (Atlanta: Harris Specialty Lithographers, 1966); John Dittmer, *Black Georgia in the Progressive Era 1900–1920* (Urbana: University of Illinois Press, 1980). The history of the "great movement" appears in "Fighting for Better Educational Facilities," *Savannah Tribune*, August 2, 1919, and the reference to churches in that paper on April 30, 1921; the plan for petitioning the state is available in the *Savannah Tribune*, March 2, 1918, and April 24, 1920. See also "Georgia Association for Negro Education," *Savannah Tribune*, May 14, 1921; "Big Educational Meeting Next Month," *Savannah Tribune*, April 19, 1919; "Need Felt for Educational Awakening," *Savannah Tribune*, March 2, 1918. The memorial from Hunt and the educators to the state board is available in State School Board Minutes, Georgia Archives, Morrow, GA, July 2, 1919. For the delegation of black teachers, see "Negro Teachers Claim More Pay: Discrimination Charge by Colored School Teachers in Proposed Schedule for Salary Increases," *Atlanta Constitution*, January 21, 1920. On the letterhead, see H.A. Hunt, letter to J.W. Johnson, May 9, 1921, Part I, G46, F6, NAACP Collection.

25. Tate, "The Greensboro Story," 9, 20.

26. He could have mentioned the brick classrooms white elementary children received from the $75,000 bond issue that built the concrete Negro high school, but he did not. Charles Johnson captures rural life in the South when he includes Greene County, Georgia, among the six communities used to study the rural Negro population in the South. See Charles Johnson, *Growing Up in the Black Belt: Negro Youth in the Rural South* (Washington, DC: American Council on Education, 1941). A full description of Greene County, Georgia, is available in Thaddeus Brockett Rice, *History of Greene County, Georgia, 1786–1886* (Spartanburg, SC: Reprint Company, 1979).

27. Sarah E. Walker, "Pearls of Wisdom: Emily Naomi Williams Beasley," unpublished collection, Atlanta, GA.

28. This report is from a particular regional meeting; however, since the regional meetings always mirrored one another in content, the same details very likely were presented in the other meetings, including the Region IV meeting Tate would have attended. See "Eighth Region G.T.E.A. Meeting," *Herald*, April 1947, 48.

29. Ibid.

30. "Outline of Procedures for Legal Cases," Group II, B110, F3, NAACP Collection.

31. There is no direct evidence on what Mr. Ward grew on his farm; however, the items named are among those described as having been grown in Greshamville. See Greene County Heritage Book Committee, 32, Greensboro Historical Society Collection, Greensboro, GA.

32. Mr. Hunt postulated in 1902 that the Negro occupied a position closer to "farm animal" than farmer during slavery. At slavery's end, blacks embraced education and left farms to acquire education but also began to understand the need of "not only knowing something, but owning something as well," if they were to move beyond the "field hand" stereotype and become farmers. In this context, Mr. Hunt argued they needed to progress from "landless tenant" (which created serfdom worse than slavery) and become "worthy, independent and self-respecting land owners." The farm produced all the necessities of life and allowed independence. Mr. Hunt emphasized "the duty of impressing upon the masses the absolute necessity for purchasing land and the great need, yes, the absolute necessity of doing so *now*." Quoting Dr. W.E.B. Du Bois, he postulated that Negroes in Georgia had purchased 66,000 acres of land and added $380,000 to the value of farmlands. To be an independent farmer was an avenue to independence and manhood in the American landscape. See H.A. Hunt, "Second Paper: The Negro as a Farmer," in *Twentieth Century Negro Literature: Or, a Cyclopedia of Thought on the Vital Topics Relating to the American Negro*, ed. Daniel Wallace Culp (Toronto: J.L. Nichols, 1902), 394. A few years after this speech, Mr. Hunt would move to Georgia and become a leading advocate throughout the state for developing farmers until his death in 1938.

33. Mr. Ward played a role similar to that of Levi Pearson in Clarendon County, South Carolina. An account of school integration in Clarendon County also omits the agency of educators in the school cases, focusing instead on courageous parents and NAACP involvement. Importantly, however, in addition to being a minister, Rev. Delaine was an educator, and Levi Pearson was a prestigious farmer. See Clarendon County Education Association, Retired, *The Growth and Development of Schools for Negroes in Clarendon County from 1670 to 1996*, July 1997. Although important works such as Isabel Wilkerson's *Warmth of Other Suns* (New York: Vintage Books, 2011) have described the reasons blacks migrated north, less attention has been paid to the reasons black farmers remained in the South. Of the decision to remain on the land in the 1920s, one farmer explains he knew little about the North but a lot about the South. "I've always been man enough to take up for my family, and love them, and try to support em, and I just thought definitely I could keep it up. In other words, I was determined to try." This sentiment reflects the support of black parents for black schools widely practiced throughout the South and perhaps explains the sentiment of black farmers who worked with the NAACP to demand equality. For full quote, see Melissa Walker, "Shifting Boundaries: Race Relations in the Rural Jim Crow South," in *African American Life in the Rural South, 1900–1950*, ed. R. Douglas Hurt (Columbia: University of Missouri Press, 2003), 103.

34. Tate, "The Greensboro Story," 32–33.

35. Langston Hughes, *The Best of Simple* (New York: Hill and Wang, 1961), 63.

36. Clifford Kuhn, E. Harlon, and Bernard West, *Living Atlanta: An Oral History of the City, 1914–1948* (Athens: University of Georgia Press, 1990): 95; "A Man with a Vision," *Atlanta Constitution*, October 6, 1985, Atlanta Public Schools Archive, Atlanta, GA (henceforth APS).

37. "Commencement Address" in Booker T. Washington Class of 1931, "Dr. Charles Lincoln Harper, 1877–1955," File—Bio, Harper, Charles Lincoln, APS, 9, 60–61.

38. "A Man with a Vision."

39. Booker T. Washington Class of 1931, "Dr. Charles Lincoln Harper, 1877–1955," 47, 53–54; Lucius Bacote, "Funeral Remarks for Mr. Harper," *Herald*, October 1955, 19, 21 (reprinted from *Atlanta Daily World*, June 24, 1955).

40. Friends say Harper was "always happy when he was about to board a bus or catch a ride" to meet with a small band of Georgians interested in better schools. See "A Man with a Vision." See also Bacote, "Funeral Remarks for Mr. Harper," 21.

41. "A Man with a Vision."

42. Margaret Walker in Booker T. Washington Class of 1931, "Dr. Charles Lincoln Harper, 1877–1955," File—Bio, Harper, Charles Lincoln, APS Files, 56–57.

43. Virginia Tate, interview with author, January 21, 2015. This interview revealed how Dr. Tate filled his time.

44. The driver, Margaret Walker, was tired from a long day when the food menu was unbalanced, the facilities were limited, and only a few people showed up. Margaret Walker, quoted in Booker T. Washington Class of 1931, "Dr. Charles Lincoln Harper, 1877–1955," 2, 56–57.

45. It was not unusual for a couple who were both Negro educators to serve at the same school. Where firsthand reports are available of black men involved in these activities, it seems common that they failed to fully disclose their activities to their wives. In an interview at the "Pursuing the Dreams of *Brown* and the Civil Rights Act" conference at Michigan State Law School on April 10–11, 2014, the wife of Oliver Brown, Leola Brown, spoke about her husband's activities in the case that would help create the *Brown v. Board of Education* decision. To the bewilderment of the moderator, Steven Brown (no relation), who appeared surprised at her admission, the wife acknowledged that she did not know much about the case, as her husband did not discuss it with her. See also Richard Kluger, *Simple Justice: The History of* Brown v. Board of Education *and Black America's Struggle for Equality* (New York: Vintage Books, 2004), 408, for a description of Leola and Oliver Brown. Mr. Harper's demeanor is described in "Tireless Titan" in Booker T. Washington Class of 1931, "Dr. Charles Lincoln Harper, 1877–1955," File—Bio, Harper, Charles Lincoln, APS Files, Atlanta, Georgia.

46. Virginia Tate, interview with author, March 3, 2013.

47. For descriptions of the challenges black educators faced, see John L. Rury and Shirley A. Hill, *The African American Struggle for Secondary Schooling, 1940–1980:*

Closing the Graduation Gap (New York: Teachers College Press, 2015); Henry Allen Bullock, *A History of Negro Education in the South from 1619 to the Present* (Cambridge, MA: Harvard University Press, 1967).

48. To succinctly convey both relationship and purpose, I have blended the title and first sentence of two different communications: Charles Harper, letter to Mr. Marshall, July 24, 1947, and Aaron Brown, E.J. Cranberry, and C.L. Harper, letter to Thurgood Marshall, August 3, 1947, both in Group II, Box 137, NAACP Collection. Some scholars, notably Mark Tushnet and Adam Fairclough, have described some advocacy activities by black teachers. See Adam Fairclough, *Teaching Equality Black Schools in the Age of Jim Crow* (Athens: University of Georgia Press, 2001); Adam Fairclough, *A Class of Their Own: Black Teachers in the Segregated South* (Cambridge, MA: Belknap Press of Harvard University Press, 2007); Mark Tushnet, *The NAACP's Legal Strategy Against Segregated Education 1925–1950* (Chapel Hill: University of North Carolina Press, 1987). However, most scholars omit the role of advocacy in educational organizations. See Katherine Charron, *Freedom's Teacher: The Life of Septima Clark* (Chapel Hill: University of North Carolina Press, 2009); Jack Greenberg, *Crusaders in the Courts: How a Dedicated Band of Lawyers Fought for the Civil Rights Revolution* (New York: Basic Books, 1994); Kluger, *Simple Justice*. Ann Short Chirhart held brief interviews with Horace Tate and captures some of his statements in *Torches of Light: Georgia Teachers and the Coming of the Modern South* (Athens: University of Georgia Press, 2005).

During the year I spent writing this book, I also discussed the advocacy of black educators in peer-reviewed journal articles. See Vanessa Siddle Walker, "Organized Resistance and Black Educators' Quest for School Equality, 1878–1938," *Teachers College Record* 107, no. 3 (2005): 355–88; Vanessa Siddle Walker, "Second-Class Integration: A Historical Perspective for a Contemporary Agenda," *Harvard Educational Review* 79, no. 2 (2009): 269–84; Vanessa Siddle Walker, "School 'Outer-gration' and 'Tokenism': Segregated Black Educators Critique the Promise of Education Reform in the Civil Rights Act of 1964," *Journal of Negro Education* 84, no. 2 (2015): 111–24; Vanessa Siddle Walker, "Tolerated Tokenism, or the Injustice in Justice: Black Teacher Associations and Their Forgotten Struggle for Educational Justice, 1921–1954," *Equity and Excellence in Education* 46, no. 1 (2013): 64–80. I also acknowledge with delight the increasing number of scholarly presentations on black educators and agencies at the American Education Research Association meetings in recent years.

2: Now You See Me, Now You Don't

1. For an example of NAACP matters on GT&EA stationery, see C.L. Harper, letter to Mr. Taylor, March 12, 1947, HET.

2. George Goodwin, "School Suit May Cost 100 Millions," *Atlanta Constitution*, 1949; "Irwin Officers Get Support of Talmadge," undated clipping, no publication listed, HET.

3. John N. Popham, "Negro, White Schools in the South Held $545,000,000 Apart in Value," *New York Times*, January 26, 1949, HET.

4. Walden defended his democratic principles and asserted the governor was attempting to try the case in the court of public opinion. See transcript of Herman Talmadge, "Governor Talmadge's Radio Talk," unknown radio station, October 22, 1949, and transcript of "Atty. Walden's Reply to Gov. Talmadge's Radio Talk of October 22, 1949," both in HET. Walter White also amplifies the governor's belief that the NAACP is behind all the activity in succeeding years as he publicly squabbles with both Eugene and Herman Talmadge during the 1940s and 1950s. For communications between White and Herman Talmadge, see Part II, A 247, F2 and Group II, Box A629, F1, F2, NAACP Collection.

5. For details on James Weldon Johnson, see Clarence Bacote, "James Weldon Johnson and Atlanta University," *Phylon* 32 (Winter 1971): 333–44; Folder, "James Weldon Johnson," Presidential Papers, Robert W. Woodruff Library, Atlanta University Center. Early branch formation in Georgia, including applications for charter and descriptions of initial branch development, are available in Part I, G43–G46, NAACP Collection. For Augusta specifically, see Part I, G45, F10–11, and Johnson, letter to M.W. Ovington, August 20, 1919, Part I, C66, F1, both NAACP Collection. On the increase in NAACP membership between 1917 and 1922, see "Report of the National Secretary," Part I, Box 1, F4; "Press Release," May 18, 1920, Part I, B3, F4, both NAACP Collection.

6. The movement of black citizens north in response to industrial opportunities and the encouragement of black newspapers is chronicled by Adriane Lentz-Smith in *Freedom Struggles: African Americans and World War I* (Cambridge, MA: Harvard University Press, 2009); Patricia Sullivan, *Lift Every Voice: The NAACP and the Making of the Civil Rights Movement* (New York: The New Press, 2009); Isabel Wilkerson, *Warmth of Other Suns: The Epic Story of America's Great Migration* (New York: Vintage Books, 2011). For an example of a principal connected with local branch activity, see James Weldon Johnson, letter to Mary White Ovington, August 20, 1919, Part I, B1, C66, F1, NAACP Collection. See comments about the increase in Georgia lynchings in John Shallady, "Negro Suffrage and the Nation," June 9, 1919, Part I, B1, F11, NAACP Collection. See also "Memo on Georgia," Part I, Box C353, F20, and "Georgia Still Leads," Part I, Box C353, F21, both NAACP Collection. Cameron McWhirter, in *Red Summer: The Summer of 1919 and the Awakening of Black America* (New York: Henry Holt, 2011), has also written in detail about lynching during this period.

The national NAACP repeatedly sought to prompt agency in the South. See Part I, C114, NAACP Collection, for examples of efforts to spur activity. The demise of Georgia branches is evident in Georgia Branch Files, Part I, G43–46, NAACP Collection. See particularly Mrs. Johnson to Mary White Ovington, April 18, 1923, Part I, B1, F11, and M. Ovington, Memorandum to Conference of Executives, May 1923, Part I, C114, F26, both NAACP Collection.

7. NAACP to Storey, June 8, 1920, Part I, C66, F1, NAACP Collection. The presence of a close relationship between educators and the early Georgia branches is evident also in the NAACP national meetings. See Chairman, letter to E.D. Hugg, August 1919; J.W. Johnson, letter to M.W. Ovington, August 20, 1919, Part I, C66, F1, NAACP Collection. For evidence of Henry Hunt and Lucy Laney speaking at the national meeting in Cleveland, see H.A. Hunt, "Rural Conditions of Labor," 1919, Part I, B2, F11, NAACP Collection. Educators were also part of the bid to host the 1920 NAACP conference in Atlanta. See the series of communications in Part I, B2, F4,7, NAACP Collection. Much of the demise of the branches is linked to the political climate in the South, not the lack of southern interest. In another southern state, a local NAACP writes of its inability to use the NAACP name in their work. See Dr. J.W. Paucer to John Bagnall, June 23, 1921, Part I, B4, F7, NAACP Collection. This sentiment captures the experience in Georgia as well.

8. The agendas of the local and national NAACP repeatedly come into conflict. The national NAACP office strongly urged anti-lynching legislation. See, for example, items in Part I, B1, C66, F1–3, NAACP Collection. The National wanted local branches to support this activity by investigating crimes, appealing to legislators regarding lynching, and generally taking the lead in a variety of local matters of discrimination against blacks. More aware of the risk to life and livelihood in the South, the local branches, during their short period of activity, focused more on obtaining membership certificates and conducting drives to have dues to send to the national office. See James Weldon Johnson, letter to branches, March 15, 1021, Part I, C114, F4; Robert Bagnall, letter to Branch, October 11, 1921, Part I, C114, F11; George H. Lawrence, letter to NAACP, September 20, 1919, Part I, C113, F12; R. Bagnell, letter to Executive Committee, February 7, 1921, Part I, C114, F3; R. Bagnall, letter to branches, October 11, 1921, Part I, C114, F11; R. Bagnall, letter to Colored Ministers of America, April 16, 1921, Part I, C114, F5; J.W. Johnson, letter to Branch Secretary, July 25, 1921, Part I, B4, F8; Secretary to Mr. White, September 15, 1922, Part I, G43, F7; letter to S.S. Humbert, September 15, 1922, Part I, G43, F7; see also NAACP, May 22, 1920, Part I, G43, F11, and other communications in Georgia Branch files, Part I, G43–46, all NAACP Collection.

9. Johnson hoped the NAACP could be a clearinghouse for other organizations. James Weldon Jonson to William Pickens, ca. 1927, F14, NAACP Collection. Charles Houston later told Walter White he must be captain and everyone else would have to take orders. White was to be the dynamo, and he needed a "hard hitting well-knit organization" in order to be "the quarter-back in charge of the whole show." In detail, Houston provides the division and subdivisions the NAACP needed, all modeled after the organization of army units. See Charlie [Houston] to White, April 4, 1935, Part I, C64, F18, NAACP Collection. For White's description of his life, see Walter Francis White, *A Man Called White: The Autobiography of Walter White* (Athens: University of Georgia Press, 1948).

10. In earlier years, philanthropists supported the national NAACP. For example, between 1912 and 1916, Julius Rosenwald contributed $1,000 a year. See Part I, C66, F1, NAACP Collection, for communications related to financial support. However, by the 1930s the philanthropic money decreased. See Part I, C230, F6; Part I, C158, F6–7; Part I, C66, F8, F12, all NAACP Collection. Communications suggest their increasing desire to not ruffle southern whites. See George Foster, letter to Walter White, October 9, 1934, Part I, C71, Reel 6. Branches formed in Georgia during the World War I era were not functional, as evident in Part I, G43–46. The national NAACP worked fervently to rebuild its chapters in Georgia in the 1930s. As in the previous era, the national NAACP wanted the local branches to participate in its renewed national focus to stop lynching. See, for example, "Memo," January 7, 1938, Part I, C64, F21. White wanted locals to wire senators regarding lynching. However, after a visit to Atlanta to speak at an effort to coordinate a state meeting, Charles Houston reported that the branches were "at sea" on whether to follow the national program, and he critiqued efforts to build a program using "revival meetings" as the focus. See Charlie [Houston], letter to Walter [White], April 26, 1937, Part I, C64, F21, NAACP Collection.

11. As evident in numerous communications in Group II, C37–41, NAACP Collection, into the 1940s, branches continued to hold membership drives and fund-raising campaigns to send the state money, make requests for their charter and *Crisis,* and send in names of officers, but were inconsistent in membership and showed little activity. However, the local branches lacked ongoing agency related to education. See Group II, C251, F1–5, NAACP Collection. For branches sending money to the National, see Group II, C280, F10, NAACP Collection. In particular, the activity related to Irwin County is instructive. In 1947, when its case originated, Irwin County was asking how to organize, seeking a charter, and complaining about membership overpayment and failure to receive the *Crisis.* No membership was recorded for 1950, and only $31 was sent to the national office in 1951. Of note, Professor Owens ("professor" being the title used for a black principal) is one of the people taking part in communications with the national membership office: Part II, C 39, F31, NAACP Collection.

The lack of activity in the 1940s also describes much branch activity into the 1950s. Particularly in rural areas, Georgia branches had to be reactivated. See Dan Byrd, "Activity Report," Group II, C313, F1; Dan Byrd, "Activity Report," Group II, C313, F4; Dan Byrd, Activity Report," Group II, C313, F5, all NAACP Collection.

Importantly, even when local NAACP branch activity existed, branches focused on broader areas of challenges confronting the black population and less specifically on the details of educational inequality—even in Atlanta, where Mr. Harper led the chapter. For a comprehensive description of NAACP branch activity in Georgia from the formation of the branches into the 1940s and the relationship of this activity to the Georgia educators, see Vanessa Siddle Walker, "Ninth Annual Brown Lecture in Education Research: Black Educators as Educational Advocates in the Decades Before *Brown v. Board of Education,*" *Educational Researcher* 42, no. 4 (2013): 207–22.

In Mr. Harper's own chapter, "education" consisted of giving "moral and financial support to the Citizens Committee of the Urban League in *its* effort to secure equal educational opportunities for Negro Children." "The Atlanta Branch of the National Association for the Advancement of Colored People Observes the Celebration of Emancipation Day," January 1, 1946, Wheat Street Baptist Church, Atlanta, GA, HET.

12. For the formation of the first education protest organization by Atlanta University graduate Richard R. Wright, see R.E. Butchart, *Schooling the Freed People: Teaching, Learning, and the Struggle for Black Freedom, 1861–1876* (Chapel Hill: University of North Carolina Press, 2010). In 1900, black educators were still petitioning the state legislature for equality. See John Dittmer, *Black Georgia in the Progressive Era 1900–1920* (Urbana: University of Illinois Press, 1980).

13. Several scholars capture the plea of northern industrialists to impose industrial education. See Eric Anderson and Alfred A. Moss, *Dangerous Donations: Northern Philanthropy and Southern Black Education, 1902–1930* (Columbia: University of Missouri Press, 1999); James Anderson, *The Education of Blacks in the South 1860–1935* (Chapel Hill: University of North Carolina Press, 1988); James Anderson, "A Long Shadow: The American Pursuit of Political Justice and Educational Equality," *Educational Researcher* 44, no. 6 (2015): 319–35; William Watkins, *The White Architects of Black Education Ideology and Power in America, 1895–1954* (New York: Teachers College Press, 2001). In the context of their work, black educators used philanthropic money to align black communities with agricultural education available for whites under the Morrill Acts and to fulfill their beliefs that land ownership would create economic independence. Mr. Hunt was among the educators who appear to have been a tool of northern philanthropists. However, the portrait of Mr. Hunt is complicated by his focus on both liberal arts *and* industrial education when he worked at Biddle University in Charlotte, North Carolina, and his subsequent inclusion of both foci in his curriculum at Fort Valley. For Mr. Hunt's activities at Biddle, see "Industrial Department," Catalogue of Biddle University, 1892–93, 27, 32, Series 5, Catalogs, Inez Moore Parker Archives and Research Center, James B. Duke Memorial Library, Johnson C. Smith University, Charlotte, NC.

Mr. Hunt's extensive activities building liberal arts curricula to accompany industrial training, as well as his focus on teaching civics education, is available in Unprocessed Henry Hunt Files, including University Catalogs, Henry Hunt Library, Fort Valley, Georgia. An interpretation of black educators within the context of their schools suggests they used the money from northern philanthropists to create equality of industrial opportunity for black students when the Morrill Land Grant Act of 1890 and the Smith-Lever Act of 1914 supporting white students failed to provide the equality espoused in their language.

14. Catalogue of Officers and Students of Atlanta University, File Folder: Henry Alexander Hunt; File Folder: James Weldon Johnson, Robert W. Woodruff Library, Atlanta University Center. For continued relationship, see H.A. Hunt, letter to J.W. Johnson,

October 30, 1916, and H.A. Hunt, letter to J.W. Johnson, October 9, 1931, Folder: H.A. Hunt, James Weldon Johnson Collection, Beinecke Archival Library, Yale University.

15. Program of the Amenia Conference, 1916, Part I, C229, F10, NAACP Collection; "Amenia Conference," in *W.E.B. Du Bois: A Reader*, ed. David Levering Lewis (Markham, ON: Henry Holt, 1995), 380–87, 401–2; David Levering Lewis, *W.E.B. Du Bois: The Fight for Equality and the American Century 1919–1963* (New York: Henry Holt, 2000).

16. Other guests from Georgia included John Hope, the president of Atlanta University; Richard Wright, who created the first educational organization to protest inequality in the distribution of Georgia's resources; and Lucy Laney, a classmate of Richard Wright who founded her own school in Augusta. Program of the Amenia Conference, 1916, Part I, C229, F10, NAACP Collection.

17. Transcribed telephone statement of Jesse O. Thomas, November 17, 1961, HET. James Weldon Johnson uses the same term, "key men," in describing men with whom he spoke at a convention and in the push to have the National "stand strongly behind the locals." See James Weldon Johnson, letter to Mary White Ovington, August 20, 1919, Part I, C66, F1, NAACP Collection.

18. "Fighting for Better Educational Facilities," *Savannah Tribune*, August 2, 1919; "Ga. Educational Society Good Work: Field Secretary's Movements Brings Results," *Savannah Tribune*, August 30, 1919. The strategy also included Mr. Hunt working with Cora Finley, the first principal of the Young Street School in Atlanta, to organize the National Congress of Colored Parents and Teachers Unit in Georgia on May 6, 1921. See Beth Savage, *African American Historic Places* (Washington, DC: Preservation Press, 1984), 186.

19. For Georgia's open climate related to migration, see State Board Minutes, April 10, 1916, April 4, 1917, Georgia Department of Archives and History, Morrow, GA (hereafter GDPAH). See also Donald Grant, *The Way It Was in the South: The Black Experience in Georgia*, ed. Jonathan Grant (Athens: University of Georgia Press, 1993), 292; Dittmer, *Black Georgia in the Progressive Era*, 191; Thomas O'Brien, *The Politics of Race and Schooling: Public Education in Georgia 1900–1961* (Lanham, MD: Lexington Books, 1999), 14.

20. The memorial by Hunt and the educators to the state board is available in State School Board Minutes, July 2, 1919, GDPAH. The Vocational Education Act of 1917 also makes this climate an opportune one to request additional funding for black schools. See *Fort Valley Uplift*, March 1922, H.A. Hunt, Unprocessed Files, Fort Valley State College (henceforth FV). In addition to Mr. Hunt's close relationship with Georgia governor Hugh Dorsey and the support of his institution through the Episcopal Church, Mr. Hunt's school also received support from philanthropist George Foster Peabody. He had little to fear in appearing publicly with this delegation.

21. "Georgia Association for Negro Education Hold Successful Meeting in Atlanta," *Savannah Tribune*, May 14, 1921.

22. Walter White, letter to Roy Nash, February 3, 1917, Part I, B1, F9, NAACP Collection. On James Weldon Johnson's speaking capacity as a college student, see Clarence Bacote, "James Weldon Johnson and Atlanta University," *Phylon* 32, no. 4 (Winter 1971): 338. For detailed description of the relationship between the NAACP and educators, see Walker, "Ninth Annual Brown Lecture in Education Research"; Edgar A. Toppin, "Walter White and the Atlanta NAACP's Fight for Equal Schools, 1916–1917," *History of Education Quarterly* 7, no. 1 (1967): 3–21.

23. Walter White to James W. Johnson, February 22, 1917 (morning); Walter White to James W. Johnson, February 22, 1917 (afternoon), Part I, Box 1, G43, F9, NAACP Collection. The traditional representation of the agency of the NAACP is available in Toppin, "Walter White," and in Jay Driskell Jr., *Schooling Jim Crow: The Fight for Atlanta's Booker T. Washington High School and the Roots of Black Protest Politics* (Charlottesville: University of Virginia Press, 2014), ch. 5.

24. Walter White, letter to Roy Nash, March 19, 1917; Harry Pace, letter to Roy Nash, March 23, 1917; Walter White, letter to Mr. Johnson, March 27, 1917; all NAACP Collection, Part I, G43, F9. The history of this episode attributes agency to the NAACP.

25. Walter White, letter to Mr. Johnson, October 1, 1917, and Acting Secretary, letter to Walter White, December 12, 1917, Part I, Box 1, F9. On branch inactivity between 1917 and 1925, see Walter White, letter to Shillady, July 9, 1918, Part I, F10; Director of Branches, letter to E. Franklin Frazier, January 21, 1925, Part I, G43, F14, all NAACP Collection.

26. "The Atlanta Protest," *Savannah Tribune*, March 10, 1917. Walter White counted the appearance a "protest," where they would "resort to other measures" even if the white people of the town did not think they had "sense enough to use or back-bone enough to try to use" them. In subsequent communications, he refers to "demands" to be made. See Walter White to Mr. Johnson, February 22, 1917, Walter White to Roy Nash, April 12, 1917, all Part I, B1, F9, NAACP Collection.

27. Walter White, letter to Roy Nash, February 3, 1917; Application for Charter of the Atlanta Branch, January 31, 1917; Secretary to Mr. Nash, letter to Mr. White, May 19, 1917; all Part I, B1, F9, NAACP Collection.

28. H.A. Hunt, letter to James Weldon Johnson, May 9, 1921, Part 1, G46, F6, NAACP Collection.

29. On relationships, see H.A. Hunt, letter to William B. Matthews, March 4, 1904, William B. Matthews Papers, Auburn Avenue Library, Atlanta, GA. Confirmation that they were classmates: Myron Adams, *General Catalogue of Atlanta University, 1867–1829* (Atlanta: Atlanta University Press, 1929), 20–26; *Catalogue of Officers and Students of Atlanta University*, 1890, 10, Atlanta University Center (henceforth AUC).

30. H.A. Hunt, letter to John Hope, August 24, 1930; John Hope, letter to H.A. Hunt, September 27, 1930; John Hope, letter to A.T. Walden, September 27, 1930. Presidential Archives, Box 99, F37, AUC.

31. Acting Secretary, letter to Mr. Pace, December 12, 1917; Walter White, letter to Roy Nash, February 3, 1917; both Part I, B1, F9, NAACP Collection.

32. During the period from 1919 to 1924 when multiple bond issues were voted down by Negroes angry because they were not given a fair deal in the proposed tax increases, the Atlanta NAACP was more frequently inactive and, when active, more focused on justice cases and questioning its apportionment with the national organization. The national NAACP press release taking credit, "The NAACP Wins School Bond Issue," was issued on January 11, 1924. The actual Atlanta branch proclaimed itself to be reorganizing on January 18, 1924. Even Walter White expressed his frustration on a visit to speak in Atlanta, noting it was "difficult" for him to turn the attention of the audience to the work of the association. Credit for the 1919 organizing and success of defeat of bond issue is available in T.K. Gibson, Dr. L.C. Crogman, letter to members of the NAACP, February 12, 1919; T.K. Gibson, letter to James Weldon Johnson, March 7, 1919; Atlanta branch, letter to Ministry of Fulton County, February 12, 1919; James Weldon Johnson, letter to Mr. Gibson, March 11, 1919; telegram from John Shillady to R.T.K. Gibson, n.d.; Harry Pace, letter to Mr. Johnson, March 12, 1919; L. Crogman, letter to J.R. Shillady, April 18, 1919; miscellaneous pages of the *Atlanta Independent*; all Part I, B1, F11, NAACP. Credit for the final effort is available in "Negro Vote Against Atlanta Bond Issue: Win 5 New Schools Costing $1,200,000: Atlanta Branch NAACP Heads Fight," press release, January 11, 1924, Part 1, G43, F13, NAACP Collection.

Non-school-related Atlanta branch activity and branch health information is available in Walter White, letter to Rosa Cosby, November 27, 1922; *Atlanta Independent* editorial, May 10, 1919, both in Part I, B1, F12, NAACP Collection. James Weldon Johnson, letter to B.J. Davis, January 18, 1924; B.J. Davis, letter to James Weldon Johnson, January 14, 1924; Walter White, letter to John Hope, January 21, 1924; A.D. Williams, letter to M.W. Ovington, January 23, 1924; A.D. Williams, letter to Robert Bagnall, March 12, 1924; Secretary, letter to Mr. Williams, March 19, 1924; Walter White, letter to A.T. Walden, September 19, 1924; Walter White, letter to A.T. Walden, September 22, 1924; Walter White, letter to George Towns, February 26, 1924; all in Part I, B1, F13, NAACP Collection.

The story of blacks wielding political power and confronting whites is available in "Was Washington First Political Victory," in Booker T. Washington Class of 1931, "Dr. Charles Lincoln Harper, 1877–1955," File—Bio, Harper, Charles Lincoln, APS; Funeral Statement, *Atlanta Daily World*, June 24, 1955, recorded in *Herald*, October 1955, 19. Because the branch records were burned in the fire at Big Bethel, the full details of the "key people" strategy cannot be untangled. However, communications in the materials in Part I, B1, F11, NAACP Collection, include comments noting the difficulty with local branches. In particular, Benjamin Davis, who was part of the 1917 committee to represent the school board, writes that "no local branch is to take charge of the politics of any community." In response, some person at the national office writes on the editorial from the *Atlantic Independent*, ca. 1919, "What is the matter with Ben Davis or the Atlanta Branch?"

33. Dittmer provides important details on black Georgia in the Progressive era, although he does not capture educational trends.

3: My Dear Mr. Marshall

1. Vincent Harris, "Editorial," *Herald*, April 1932, 7.

2. In the 1920s, the GT&EA focused mostly on building Rosenwald Fund schools, and the annual interracial meetings of five hundred or more teachers in the mid-1920s addressed primarily curricular needs. However, as federal money became available again in 1929, the organization reelected Mr. Hunt as president and, immediately after, meetings included details of the federal Smith-Hughes money, plans were developed for creating districts so the teachers would be better organized, and legislative committees appeared. See Georgia Teachers and Education Association Minutes, April 1926–April 1930, HET. On Rosenwald in Georgia, see Jeanne Cyriaque, Keith Herbert, and Steven Moffron, "Rosenwald School in Georgia," National Park Services Form 10-900a, National Register of Historic Places Multiple Property Documentation Form, Georgia Department of National Resources, June 22, 2009, http://www.georgiashpo.org.

3. F.S. Horne and Alva Tabor, letter to Superintendent, July 27, 1935, Unprocessed Files, FV. Mr. Hunt said blacks could not engage in "mental puttering," that members of their generation had to "think straight" to solve problems in the black community. See Henry Hunt, "The Opening Address," *Atlanta University Bulletin*, Series II, no. 61 (November 1925): 7–12, Presidential Files, AU.

4. "Georgia Teachers and Educational Association: A New Deal for the Negro School Child." Both the original typed copy and the trifold copy apparently used for mailing are in Unprocessed Files, FV. Importantly, as earlier educational efforts started to align with state and federal opportunities, this push correlated with increased opportunities in Georgia. See Dorothy Orr, *A History of Education in Georgia* (Chapel Hill: University of North Carolina Press, 1950), 338–39.

5. Mr. Harper maintained files of national NAACP activity, including minutes from Board of Directors meetings. See GTEA Harper files, HET.

6. "Notes on Conference Held December 29, 1942: Representatives of the Georgia Educational Association and of the Georgia Teachers and Education Association," GTEA Papers, FV; "Handbook for Local Units" (revised 1942), Georgia Education Association, GTEA Papers, FV.

7. Factional strife: "The President's Message," *Herald*, February 1942, 3, and "Editors Notes," *Herald*, February 1942, 8. Discussions of district and regions: "What Every Teacher Should Know," *Herald*, October 1941, 9–12. Other state associations: "What Other State Associations Are Doing," *Herald*, October 1941, 12–18; Booker T. Washington Class of 1931, "Dr. Charles Lincoln Harper, 1877–1955," File—Bio, Harper, Charles Lincoln, APS, 52.

8. "Proposed Amendment to the Constitution of the Georgia Teachers and Educational Association. Submitted April 11, 1941 by Horace M. Bond"; Horace Mann Bond to E.J. Cranberry, B.T. Harvey, and C.L. Harper, June 9, 1942; "Fight Looms over Proposed Teacher Reorganization and Amendment: Association Meeting Expected to Develop Spirited Clash Over Bond Amendment"; "Notes on Conference Held December 29, 1942, Representatives of the Georgia Educational Association and of the Georgia Teachers and Educational Association"; all GTEA Papers, FV. Bond is listed as a speaker at the 1941 meeting in "The Recent Meeting Reveals Progress," *Herald*, May 1941, 10.

9. "What President Harper Has Done in a Year," *Herald*, October 1942, 9; Booker T. Washington Class of 1931, "Dr. Charles Lincoln Harper, 1877–1955," File—Bio, Harper, Charles Lincoln, APS, 52.

10. Charles Harper, letter to Mrs. Horace Mann Bond, May 4, 1942, Fort Valley unprocessed GTEA files.

11. In a private telegram, Walter White is emphatic that the responsibility for litigation was the job of the teachers' organization. Telegram from Walter White, July 23, 1940, FV unprocessed GTEA files.

12. See Group II, C37–41, NAACP Collection.

13. Charles Harper, letter to Mr. Marshall, July 24, 1947, Part II, Box 137, NAACP Collection.

14. Franklin H. Williams, letter to Mr. Harper, August 4, 1947; Robert L. Carter, letter to Mr. Aaron Brown, August 5, 1947, Part II, Box 137, NAACP Collection.

15. "Outline of Procedure for Legal Cases: NAACP Branches," September 1943, Group II, B110, F3, NAACP Collection.

16. For the actions described, see the GT&EA original folder "Petitions," HET. Dr. Tate reported having maintained the Greensboro petition. However, this petition has not yet been located in his files.

17. The petition excerpted is from Milledgeville, Georgia, July 1949. However, the GT&EA Harper files include a number of other similar petitions. Dr. Tate repeatedly commented that the court case of Greensboro was among his files. However, although the case is evident in other materials and his petition was no doubt similar to the others, the original document has not yet been located in his files. The original documents are all in HET.

18. H.A. Hunt, letter to James Weldon Johnson, May 9, 1921.

19. On the new headquarters, see Walter White, letter to Rev. A.D. Williams, July 15, 1919. On Mrs. Canady's death, see Drive Director, letter to Rev. Singleton (he calls her "Mrs. Kanady"), May 12, 1921; Rev. Singleton, letter to NAACP, May 4, 1921. On black awareness of white dislike of the NAACP, especially prior to the 1920 convention, see "Annual Report," Rev. Singleton, June 20, 1921. "In Memory of Mrs. Canady" by Rev. Singleton included in Miss Simms, letter to NAACP, June 24, 1921. All in Part I, B1, F11, NAACP Collection. On Rev. Singleton's death, see A.D. Williams, letter to M.W.

Ovington, January 23, 1924; Photograph of Big Bethel fire, n.d.; James Weldon Johnson, letter to Mrs. Singleton, November 26, 1923; James Weldon Johnson, letter to Big Bethel Church, November 28, 1923; James Weldon Johnson, letter to George Towns, November 28, 1923; George Towns, letter to James Weldon Johnson, November 23, 1923, all in Part I, B1, F13, NAACP Collection.

20. James Weldon Johnson, letter to Walter White, September 9, 1921, Part I, C385, F5, NAACP; "A Message from the President of Atlanta University," *Atlanta University Bulletin*, December 1939, 4, Presidential Papers, Atlanta University.

21. "Cause of Blaze Remains Mystery," *Atlanta Daily World*, January 3, 1940; "Unity: Tells Race to Acquire Farm Land," *Atlanta Daily World*, January 2, 1940; H.S. Murphy, "Brass Tacks," *Atlanta Daily World*, January 7, 1940.

22. Frank Horne, "Henry Alexander Hunt, Builder," Biographical File, AUC; "Editorial Comment: Progress in Elimination of Discrimination in White and Negro Teacher Salaries," *Herald*, January 1940, 1.

4: The Balm in Gilead

1. Horace E. Tate speech, Sparta High School graduation n.d., HET.

2. Joyce Davis, *Images of America: Elbert County* (Charleston, SC: Arcadia, 2011), 8, 45; postcard of business center, Elberton, Georgia, ca. 1920s, author collection.

3. Tate, interview by Ann Maurey, March 21, 1995, HET. John Hope Franklin was forcibly removed from a train car when he was six because he accidentally took a seat in the coach designated for whites. James Weldon Johnson was accosted by a conductor wanting to pull him from a first-class train car when he was a teenager. See John Hope Franklin, *Mirror to America: The Autobiography of John Hope Franklin* (New York: Macmillan, 2005), 1:4, 20; James Weldon Johnson, *Along This Way: The Autobiography of James Weldon Johnson* (New York: Viking, 1933), 64–65.

4. Horace E. Tate, interview by author, July 26, 2002.

5. Horace E. Tate, interview by author, May 17, 2001.

6. Horace E. Tate, interview by author, n.d.; Tate, interview by Ann Maurey, March 21, 1995, HET. On his way to Atlanta University, James Weldon Johnson had to switch to speaking Spanish with his friend in order not to be kicked out of the first-class car for which he had paid. He learned that day that any ethnicity was fine, as long as he did not show himself to be a Negro boy.

7. Horace E. Tate, interview by author, July 26, 2002.

8. Horace E. Tate, interview by author, May 17, 2001. Photographs, stories, and descriptions of the history of Elberton are available in Davis, *Elbert County*; Aurolyn Melba Hamm, *Elbert County, Georgia* (Charleston, SC: Arcadia, 2005); *Elberton, Georgia: Points of Interest Pinpoint Tour*, Elberton, GA.

9. Horace E. Tate, interview by author, December 7, 2001.

10. Mr. Hunt worked continually with philanthropists and sometimes sacrificed his salary in his effort to build Fort Valley and keep it in operation. See Hunt Unprocessed

Files, FV, and the series of communications in Box 316, F1, Julius Rosenwald Fund Archives, 1917–1948, Special Collections and Archives, Fisk University, RP.

11. "Advantages," *Fort Valley Message Bulletin*, Summer Session 1929, 3, Unprocessed Hunt Papers, FV.

12. In 1940–41, Tate was a sophomore; 110 of the 324 students were in the sophomore class of the college. Counting the high school enrollment (223), elementary school enrollment (674), and summer quarter enrollment, excluding duplicates (617), Fort Valley total enrollment for 1940–41 was 1,838. *Fort Valley Catalogue*, 1940–41, 54, University Catalogues, FV.

13. "Report of the President," *Fort Valley State College Bulletin* 1, no. 2 (October 1940): 28; "Entrance Requirements," *Fort Valley Message*, 1938–39, 9, FV; Willie Snow Ethridge, "H.A. Hunt Awarded Spingarn Medal," *Baltimore Sun*, July 6, 1930, reprinted in *Bulletin* 11, no. 1 (October 1930), Presidential Archives, Box 99, Folder 6, AUC.

14. In 1942, Bond writes that he "never applied for a job in all my life." H.M. Bond, letter to A.J. Evans, September 9, 1942, Box 10, Series II, Horace Mann Bond Papers, University of Massachusetts, Amherst (henceforth HMB). He also describes an early view of Fort Valley in H.M. Bond, letter to Mr. Doak S. Campbell, November 22, 1937, Series III, Box 72, HMB. His accomplishments are detailed in the student publication, the *Peachite*. See Therman B. O'Daniel, "A Profile of President Bond," *Peachite* 1, no. 1 (June 1943): 3, 7. Faculty support is evident in "Report of the President," *Fort Valley State College Bulletin* 1, no. 2 (October 1940): 28–31, Unprocessed University Files, FV. Wayne Urban has written a biography of Horace Mann Bond. However, it does not delve into his work with students at Fort Valley or GT&EA. See Wayne J. Urban, *Black Scholar: Horace Mann Bond, 1904–1972* (Athens: University of Georgia Press, 1993).

15. J.C. Dixon, letter to Robert Patton, October 9, 1939; H.M. Bond, letter to Edwin Embree, September 26, 1939, Rural School Program, July–December 1939, F4, Julius Rosenwald Fund Archives, Fisk University, Nashville, TN.

16. Among the twelve areas of commendation, Fort Valley rated at the top in faculty organization, teaching load, integration of knowledge in courses, organization and content of curriculum, administrative concern for institution, and adjustment of instructional procedures and curriculum to individual differences. See "Fort Valley Is Rated by Government Survey as Outstanding," *Fort Valley State College Bulletin*, 1942–1943, 12, University Catalogues, FV.

17. H.M. Bond, letter to Embree, August 1, 1945, Box 72, Series III, HMB. Personality traits are in Therman B. O'Daniel, "A Profile of President Bond" and "The Editors Speak: The Fort Valley State College," *Peachite*, n.d., 3, 15, Unprocessed University Files, FV. On Ohio Hall details, see "Plant," Miscellaneous Sheet, 4, Unprocessed Hunt Papers, FV.

18. Horace Tate, interview by author, May 22, 2002.

19. David Levering Lewis documents the life of W.E.B. Du Bois in meticulous detail in *W.E.B. Du Bois: The Fight for Equality and the American Century 1919–1963*. The best portrait of Du Bois's work with education is in Derrick Alridge, *The Educational Thought of W.E.B. Du Bois: An Intellectual History* (New York: Teachers College Press, 2008). For some of his earliest thinking about education, see W.E.B. Du Bois, "Atlanta University," in *From Servitude to Service: Being the Old South Lectures on the History and Work of Southern Institutions for the Education of the Negro* (Boston: American Unitarian Association, 1905), 155–97.

20. Dr. Du Bois had requested that Dr. Bond provide an abstract for the *Encyclopedia of the Negro* and housing for a friend. See Du Bois, letter to Bond, September 10, 1935, Group 411, Series III, Folder 114A, HMB. On Charles Johnson, see John Popham, "Negro, White Schools in the South Held $545,000 Apart in Value," *New York Times*, January 26, 1949, HET.

21. The assessment of Mr. Hunt's activities is in the *Fort Valley Uplift*, March 1922, 50. I have no evidence that Dr. Tate knew of these activities at the time of the speech.

22. The most comprehensive portrait of this era of Mr. Hunt's life is captured in the seminal history by James Anderson, *The Education of Blacks in the South 1860–1935* (Chapel Hill: University of North Carolina Press, 1988), 123–32. Note, however, that his interpretation of the man and the period relies on communications with the philanthropists. Other archival sources were not available. Although Dr. Tate remembered Dr. Du Bois addressing at a later speech his debate with Washington, I have no evidence that Dr. Tate wondered at this particular assembly about the effect of the contradiction in their philosophical views on their friendship. I have inserted the query here purely as a writing tool to alert readers to the contradiction. Likewise, I have no evidence of Dr. Tate's posture during the assembly, although I do have interviews reporting his enjoyment of assembly programs. I learned his facial expressions during the two years I interviewed him and also from more youthful pictures. On John W. Davidson, the real founder of Fort Valley: author interview with Mr. Berry Jordan, August 17, 2010, at Fort Valley.

23. "The Colored Colleges: The Era of Commencements Is at Hand," *Atlanta Constitution*, May 28, 1890.

24. Ethridge, "H.A. Hunt Awarded Spingarn Medal"; "H.A. Hunt Appointed National Farm Administrator," Biographical File, AUC.

25. Adele Logan Alexander, *Ambiguous Lives: Free Women of Color in Rural Georgia, 1789–1879* (Fayetteville: University of Arkansas Press, 1991).

26. White, *A Man Called White*. University of Georgia Press, 1995); Charles Johnson, introduction to *The Autobiography of an Ex-Coloured Man*, Box 1, Folder 6, MSS 797, JWJ.E, Emory University; Alexander, *Ambiguous Lives*.

27. Since Mr. Hunt looked like a typical Georgia white man, Dr. Du Bois explained, he found himself consistently facing situations where he was treated by other whites as

a man and peer only to later face ostracism and insult when they discovered he openly identified himself with the Negro race. The situation was an ongoing challenge to Mr. Hunt—whether to stand on his right to be judged as a man and not tell who he was or to be judged as engaging in "unforgivable deception" if he did not. Yet despite the denigration he received in naming himself, Mr. Hunt refused to be anything other than a Negro man.

28. See Willard Gatewood, *Aristocrats of Color: The Black Elite, 1880–1920* (Fayetteville: University of Arkansas Press, 2000).

29. His brother-in-law was E.A. Johnson, former New York assemblyman. See Frank Horne, "Henry A. Hunt, Sixteenth Spingarn Medalist," Hunt Papers, FV.

30. Observation on Mr. Hunt offered by Dr. E. George Payne, n.d., Biographical File, AUC.

31. John Hope, who resisted Dr. Du Bois's efforts to lure him to New York to live, noting that he could not leave his work in the South, also served on the Spingarn committee, along with Theodore Roosevelt. See Ethridge, "H.A. Hunt Awarded Spingarn Medal"; Official Organ of the National Association for Teachers of Colored Schools in Atlanta University collection.

32. *Annual Catalogue of Biddle University*, 1897–1898, 36, Series 5, Catalogs, Inez Moore Parker Archives and Research Center, James B. Duke Memorial Library, Johnson C. Smith University, Charlotte, NC. The Biddle School climate is available in Inez Moore Parker, *The Biddle-Johnson C. Smith University Story* (Charlotte, NC: Charlotte Publishing, 1975), 8–13.

33. No other information about the job in Africa has been unearthed except the oral report. Ethridge, "H.A. Hunt Awarded Spingarn Medal."

34. Horace Mann Bond, "William Edward Burghardt Du Bois: A Portrait in Race Leadership," Series III, Box 73, HMB.

35. W.E.B. Du Bois, "On the Significance of Henry Hunt," *Fort Valley State College Bulletin* 1, no. 2 (October 1940): 5–16, University Bulletins, FV.

36. Lyrics available at http://www.lutheran-hymnal.com/lyrics/hs889.htm.

37. The significance of spirituals in black culture as a way of creating community is discussed in Lawrence Levine, *Black Culture and Black Consciousness: Afro-American Folk Thought from Slavery to Freedom* (New York: Oxford University Press, 1977), 33, and Donald Matthews, *Honoring the Ancestors: An African Cultural Interpretation of Black Religion and Literature* (New York: Oxford University Press, 1998), 47–78.

38. "Impressions on the Second Pan-African Conference," Part I, C385, F6, NAACP Collection.

39. "H.A. Hunt Appointed National Farm Administrator," Biographical File, AUC. Under Mr. Hunt's tutelage, Negro farmers followed the Danish model he had learned about and formed a cooperative that owned its own reaper and binder. This purchase eschewed traditional reliance on "big farmers"—code for white farmers—and allowed Negro farmers to harvest their own crops. It was also said that no Negro men defaulted

on a federal loan during his tenure, and farm cooperatives developed across the country. See *Fort Valley Message* 11, no. 1, Unprocessed Hunt Papers, FV.

40. Program of the Amenia Conference, 1916, Part I, C229, F10, NAACP Collection; "Amenia Conference," in *W.E.B. Du Bois: A Reader*, 380–87, 401–2.

41. Author site visit, Arc de Triomphe, Paris.

5: A Simple Scheme to Do a "Simple Little"

1. For photograph depicting cafeteria, see *Fort Valley High and Industrial Bulletin* 4, no. 1, unnumbered page; "Celebrating the Journey in Loving Memory of Mrs. Junia J. Fambro, 1894–1999," HET. Ulysses Byas reports Miss Jones, then known under her married name, Mrs. Fambro, recommending him for a job as a principal when he worked for her in the school cafeteria after World War II. See Walker, *Hello Professor*, 67.

2. On the $25 Elberton Alumni Association Scholarship, the money "scraped up" from caddying, and family assistance with tuition costs: Tate, interview by author, December 7, 2001; Tate, interview by Ann Maurey, March 21, 1995, HET.

3. Bond received multiple press releases from the Office of Civilian Defense, Washington, DC, during World War II. The September 11, 1942, release reports the Negro movie house in Vicksburg, Mississippi, leading all Vicksburg theaters for the first two days of a bond drive. Sales totaled $2,175, which was $700 more than any other theater in the city. The same release also shows many Negro homes among the first to receive the V-Home certificate, which indicated all-out participation in the war effort and necessary precautions. See Unprocessed Bond Files, FV.

4. Reminiscent of his own days as a student at Lincoln University, Bond spoke of them as "boys" while well aware that he was training them, as he had been trained, to become real men—not the three-fifths of a man the U.S. Constitution said they were. Tate's description of Bond's meeting with them is from Tate, interview by author, October 20, 2001; see also Charles Harper and Horace Mann Bond, "We Are Americans—At War!!!," *Herald*, December 1941, 3.

5. By 1943, Fort Valley had eighty-nine people—faculty, graduates, and undergraduates—in the armed forces. For descriptions of army life, see *Peachite* 1, no. 1 (June 1943). See also *The Flame* (1945), the first student yearbook, which describes the young men called to the armed forces in 1942 after the Japanese attack on Pearl Harbor on December 7, 1941. Unprocessed Catalogs and Bulletins, FV.

6. The Office of War Information, Office of Price Administration Advance Release, September 27, 1942, noted that merging gasoline and tire rationing programs into a single system would control mileage of the nation's passenger automobiles. See Unprocessed GTEA Files, FV. I am supposing these restrictions, put into place during the time the young Horace Tate was driving Dr. Bond, were the reason he said he was asked to drive faster. The actual meeting Dr. Tate drove Dr. Bond in Nashville to is not confirmed. Dr. Bond was invited to an invitational event at Peabody in February. See "Weekly

Calendar of Events," Fort Valley State College, February 14–20, 1943, Box 327, F1, Julius Rosenwald Fund Archives, Special Collections and Archives, Fisk University, Nashville, TN (hereafter RP). This meeting occurred during the time Tate was a student chauffeur. However, Tate's interviews describe a drive to Nashville at Christmas.

7. For a description of Mr. Hubbard's school and its merger with Fort Valley, see "Then There Was William Merrida Hubard's School, 1900–1938," in Donnie Bellamy, *Light in the Valley: A Pictorial History of Fort Valley State College Since 1895* (Virginia Beach: Donning, 1996), 55–65.

8. For descriptions of Eugene Talmadge and racial politics in Atlanta, see Stephen Tuck, *Beyond Atlanta: The Struggle for Racial Equality in Georgia, 1940–1980* (Athens: University of Georgia Press, 2003); Wayne J. Urban also briefly describes Governor Talmadge's visit to Fort Valley in *Black Scholar: Horace Mann Bond, 1904–1972.* For the complexities confronting African American educators seeking state money during this period, see Joseph Holley, *You Can't Build a Chimney from the Top: The South Through the Life of a Negro Educator* (New York: William Frederick Press, 1948), 112–50.

9. "Gene Talmadge Was a Might Fine Boy—and His Folks Were Might Fine Folks . . . ," *Lavonia Times*, November 29, 1940, GTEA Archives.

10. H.M. Bond, letter to Mr. Wale, May 11, 1941, Box 326, F6, RP; Urban also describes this episode in his *Black Scholar*, 225–31.

11. The transfer of Fort Valley to state control would help ensure the financial support needed for its continued existence. For Mr. Hunt's quiet involvement, see varied communications in Folder 2, Rural School Program—Georgia—Fort Valley Normal and Industrial School, RP. For a report of Fort Valley's reliance on Rosenwald Fund money, see Bellamy, *Light in the Valley*, 67; H.M. Bond, letter to A.J. Evans, September 9, 1942, Box 10, F15, HMB.

12. Dr. Bond reports a Mr. A.J. Evans as the source of his support. When Dr. Bond later refused to work publicly with Dr. Holley to challenge the Board of Regents stance on supporting the three Negro colleges, he also communicated with Mr. Evans about his decision, but that letter is overly self-deprecating in a way that suggests the letter may have been intended as a public face and did not compromise his private alliance with Holley. See H.M. Bond, letter to A.J. Evans, September 17, 1942, Box 10; J.W. Holley, letter to Bond, July 30, 1942, Box 10; J.W. Holley, letter to Bond, September 10, 1942, Box 10, 15C; H.M. Bond, letter to J.W. Holley, September 14, 1942, Box 10, F15C; H.M. Bond, letter to A.J. Evans, September 17, 1942, Folder 10; J.W. Holley, letter to B.T. Harvey, September 27, 1942, Box 10, F15C; all in HMB. Mr. Evans appears to be one of the whites in Fort Valley who quietly provided support for the Negro effort even though he publicly aligned himself with Talmadge. When confronted with matters of retaining his job and keeping money for Fort Valley, Bond turned to Evans. H. Bond, letter to A.M. Evans, September 9, 1942, Box 10, F15, HMB. The *Fort Valley and Industrial Bulletin* 4, no. 1 (n.d.): 9, lists Mr. A.J. Evans as one of Mr. Hunt's references for the work

of the school and notes that he is the president of the Citizens Bank in Fort Valley. In a November 15, 2012, interview with the author, Ms. Wilmetta Jackson, archivist at Fort Valley State College, also commented on Mr. A.J. Evans's involvement with Fort Valley.

13. In looking at writings from Lincoln University more than ten years later, the description of events matches his earlier five-page summary to the Rosenwald Fund, and the picture described was captured in the *Herald*. See H.M. Bond, letter to Clarence Mitchell, October 15, 1952; H.M. Bond, letter to Clarence Mitchell, December 28, 1956, Series III, Box 65, F100, HMB. The two pictures also appear in Bellamy, *Light in the Valley*, 81.

14. Horace Mann Bond, "William Edward Burghardt Du Bois: A Portrait in Race Leadership," Box 173, Series III, HMB; Unnamed Report, 4, Unprocessed Bond Papers, FV.

15. Tate, interview by author, May 22, 2002; H.M. Bond, "What Fort Valley Is Trying to Do in the Field of Rural Education," copy to Edwin Embree, December 7, 1933, Rural School Program, F4, RP.

16. "Founder's and Annual Report Number," *Fort Valley State College Bulletin* 1, no. 2 (October 1940): 27–35, FV.

17. *Fort Valley High and Industrial School Bulletin* 4, no. 1 (n.d.), FV.

18. Horace Mann Bond, "Editorial," *Herald*, December 1941, 10.

19. On Bond's views of his father, see Tate, interview by author, October 20, 2001. Tate does not say what Bond told him about his father. One story recounts the lesson of "Mr. Fee," someone he commends for holding George Washington accountable for his violation of democratic principles by holding slaves. See Robert E. Park, letter to H.M. Bond, January 31, 1929, Box 9; H.M. Bond, letter to Mr. Embree, February 15, 1932, Series III, Box 71, HMB.

20. Tate, interview by author, October 20, 2001; "Founder's and Annual Report Number," *Fort Valley State College Bulletin* 1, no. 2 (October 1940), Unprocessed Catalogs and Bulletins, FV.

21. Bellamy, *Light in the Valley*, 75: "What Fort Valley Is Trying to Do in the Field of Rural Education"; "First Faculty Meeting, 1939–40," Box 326, F4, RP; "The Objectives, Scope and Activities of the FVSC," 8, Unprocessed Catalogs and Bulletins, FV.

22. "Founder's and Annual Report Number," *Fort Valley State College Bulletin* 1, no. 2 (October 1940), FV.

23. Fort Valley High and Industrial School, Leaflet #4, 3, Unprocessed Hunt Papers, FV; "H.A. Hunt Appointed National Farm Administrator," Biographical File, Henry Hunt, AUC.

24. Tate, interview by author, May 22, 2002, and December 7, 2001; Tate, interview by Ann Maurey, March 21, 1995, HET. For additional information on Fort Valley students, see "The Objectives, Scope and Activities of the Fort Valley State College," *Fort Valley State College Bulletin*, 1942–43, 8; "Required Courses in the General College," 13, Unprocessed Catalogs and Bulletins, FV.

25. Horace Bond, letter to Dean W.K. Paine, September 28, 1942, GTEA Folder, FV; "Constitution of GTEA Amendment Procedure Approved," 1942, HET.

26. This is Tate's quote of Dr. Bond's words, not a direct quote from Bond. Tate, interview by author, May 22, 2002.

27. Horace E. Tate, interview by author, n.d., circa December 7, 2001.

28. Memo from Ambrose Caliver and James Atkins to Mr. H.A. Hunt, Dr. Charles H. Thomson, Dean Horace M. Bond (and others), April 23, 1935, Box 8, HMB.

29. J.W. Smith, *Historic Background on the Schools of Atlanta* (Atlanta: n.p., 1927), 17, APS. On Bond at GTEA meeting, see "Weekly Calendar of Events, April 11–18, 1943, Fort Valley," Box 327, Folder 1, Special Collections and Archives, Fisk University, RP.

30. Olive G. Williams, "Whirl in the Social World," *Peachite* 1, no. 1 (June 1943): 31–33; Horace E. Tate, "The College Players Guild," *Peachite* 1, no. 1 (June 1943): 35.

31. Author site visit to President Bond's campus home, August 17, 2010. Photograph of the home as it appeared during the era is available in Bellamy, *Light in the Valley*, 76. For Bond observations about Dr. Du Bois and the Du Bois lectures, see Bond to Embee, May 26, 1943, Rural School Program, F1, RP; "Weekly Calendar of Events March 7–13," Box 327, Special Collections and Archives, Fisk University, RP.

32. For Freshman Week activities, sophomore examinations, and graduation requirements, see *Fort Valley Bulletin*, 1942–43; "The Objectives, Scope and Activities of the Fort Valley State College," *Fort Valley State College Bulletin*, n.d., 11.

33. W.E.B. Du Bois, "Of Mr. Booker T. Washington and Others" (1903) and "Resolutions of the Niagara Movement," in *African-American Social and Political Thought, 1850–1920*, ed. Howard Brotz (New Brunswick, NJ: Transaction, 2006), 516, 538.

6: To Help Our People

1. Jannelle Jones McRee and John McIntosh, "City of Elberton 'Springs' from Humble Beginnings," in *The First 50 Years, 1803–1855: 200th Anniversary Book (1803–2003)* (Elberton, GA: City of Elberton, 2003).

2. The actual house that Horace Tate grew up in was burned down by an unknown person or people. His father rebuilt the house, which was patterned exactly like the original, except the rooms were smaller. Horace Tate, interview by author, May 22, 2002; Virginia Tate, interview by author, September 21, 2017.

3. Horace Tate, interview by author, May 22, 2002; Tate, interview by Ann Maurey, March 21, 1995, HET; "The Objectives, Scope and Activities of the Fort Valley State College," *Fort Valley State College Bulletin*, 1942–43, 8; "Required Courses in the General College," 13, Unprocessed Catalogs and Bulletins, FV.

4. Description of meeting Mr. Jackson and going to Greensboro available in Tate, interviews with author, September 1, 2001, and December 7, 2001. The physical descrip-

tion of Mr. Jackson is from "A Celebration of the Life of Eli J.S. Jackson, Jr.," February 22, 1992, Tate Collection, Atlanta, GA. Possible familial ties are reported in author interview with Virginia Tate, July 22, 2005.

5. Joy Elmer Morgan, "A Tribute to the Teacher," *Herald*, December 1946, 7, Unprocessed GTEA Files, FV; Vanessa Siddle Walker, *Their Highest Potential: An African American School Community in the Segregated South* (Chapel Hill: University of North Carolina Press, 1996).

6. Author site visit to Elberton and to Union Point.

7. Other Union Point teachers were Mrs. Tapley, Mrs. Jackson, Mr. Jackson, and Ms. Susie Davis. Tate, interview by author, September 1, 2001; Greensboro Reunion speech, September 2, 1989, HET; Union Point site visit by author.

8. Tate, interviews by author, October 20, 2001, and December 7, 2001.

9. No minutes are available of the specific meeting Tate attended; however, the agenda was consistent across decades and detailed descriptions of the principals' conference are available in "Annual's Principals' Conference" announcement, November 19–20, 1943, *Herald*, October 1943, 16, and *Herald*, December 1941, 14.

10. Tate, interview with author, October 20, 2001. For ease of flow of the story, I have placed the regional meeting out of sequence. The principals' meeting would actually have preceded the regional meeting, which would not occur until the spring after Mr. Tate had been named principal.

11. Tate, interview by author, September 1, 2001; Horace Tate, address to the University of Georgia, May 25, 1991, HET.

12. Program of Georgia Teachers and Education Association meeting, April 13–14, 1944, HET.

13. I.E. Washington, "Presidential Address," *Herald*, May 1944, 3.

14. Oliver Hill, interview with the author, July 19, 2003.

15. Thurgood Marshall, memo to Budget Committee, December 17, 1940, Group II, B7, F1, NAACP Collection; for additional information on the NAACP description of teachers paying for their cases, see Part II, B2, L1, F13, NAACP Collection. As early as 1913, the NAACP relied on black educators as local agents. See Florida litigation, Group II, Box L38, F6. The teachers raise concerns "that the significance of our efforts have not been publicized as much as the efforts deserve." H.C. Trenholm, letter to Roy Wilkins, April 8, 1953, Part II, A218, F3, NAACP Collection.

16. Questionnaire. Unprocessed GTEA files, Fort Valley.

17. "Executive Committee Meeting," May 13, 1939, HET; Surveys, GTEA Files, FV; Booker T. Washington Class of 1931, "Dr. Charles Lincoln Harper, 1877–1955," File—Bio, Harper, Charles Lincoln, APS.

18. "What Every Teacher Should Know: Personnel Changes in Principalships," *Herald*, October 1942, 17. Citizens Committees were a disguise for advocacy, as the term was less threatening to southern whites. See Mr. Thomas, memo to Mr. Marshall,

December 5, 1942, and Walter White, letter to B.T. Harvey, May 6, 1940, Part II, B177, F3, NAACP Collection.

19. The details of this case are unclear. GTEA is credited with the salary equalization efforts, and this reference appears in its materials. There is no evidence of an appellate ruling.

20. "Negro Teachers Claim More Pay: Discrimination Charged by Colored School Teachers in Proposed Schedule for Salary Increases," *Atlanta Constitution*, January 21, 1920; Program of the Georgia Teachers and Education Association meeting, April 13–14, 1944, Unprocessed GTEA Files–1944, FV; Tate, interview by author, February 21, 2001.

21. Washington, "Presidential Address"; "Georgia Teachers Authorize a Special Fund," *Herald*, May 1944, 5; "The 1944–45 Budget," *Herald*, May 1944, 5.

22. *Atlanta Constitution*, October 2, 1981; Booker T. Washington Class of 1931, "Dr. Charles Lincoln Harper, 1877–1955"; Tate, interview by author, February 21, 2001.

23. Despite being a recognized leader, Mr. Jackson did not typically run the meeting. More often, he would pray or have some other role. See Tate, interview by author, December 7, 2001; Greensboro Reunion speech, September 2, 1989, HET. Tate's recollection of first hearing Harper is described in Tate, interview by author, February 8, 2002.

24. The incident is recounted in detail in "Horace Tate Address to the University of Georgia," May 25, 1991, HET; Tate, interview by author, February 28, 2002. The background on Mr. Corry is available in "Here and There in the Field: As President B.F. Hubert Sees It," *Herald*, December 1938, 21, HET.

25. "H. E. Tate Is Elected Regional Director," undated newspaper clipping, HET.

26. Tate, interviews with author, January 17, 2000, January 24, 2002, and May 17, 2002.

27. Dr. Tate reported the female principal in 1943 saying that white men have opportunities to lead and that it was her belief that black men should also have equal opportunities to lead. He referenced the elevation of black men during this period in an interview with the author on January 24, 2002. Other evidence suggests similar beliefs. For example, in other counties the black patrons said neither they nor the community were "entirely satisfied" with being assigned a female principal because they did not think they got their "money's worth." I have no other data to explain the community's objection. I also do not know whether they were given a male principal in the 1920s.

For parent letters, see Fred Simpson, John Jones, B.F. Lovejoy, and Fisher Lovejoy, letters to Honorable Board of Education, November 8, 1919, author's collection.

28. Tate, interviews by author, January 17, 2000, and May 17, 2002. Accounts of this event differ. His speech to the 1989 class reunion recounts sitting on the porch prior to entering the home; the notes for his book simply describe going into the home. The ten-

sion was resolved in author interview with Tate, January 17, 2000, and the story as told here depicts the resolution: he visited on the porch and was then invited inside.

29. The 1945–46 state salary scale placed a cap on the salary white teachers could receive but still set black salaries at only 75% to 93% of those of the white teachers. "New Salary Schedule," *Herald*, October 1946, 12.

30. W.E.B. Du Bois and Augustus Granville Dill, eds., *The Common School and the Negro American* (1911; reprint, New York: Russell and Russell, 1969).

7: Fighting White Folk

1. Details on inequality between black and white schools are available in Kluger, *Simple Justice*. Hines Lafayette Hill, *Negro Education in Rural Georgia* (MA thesis, Atlanta: Emory University Press, 1939); Archibald W. Anderson, Virgil A. Clift, and Henry Gordon Hullfish, eds., *Negro Education in America: Its Adequacy, Problems, and Needs* (New York: Harper & Brothers, 1962). Georgia's state history of education provides fewer details. Dorothy Orr, *A History of Education in Georgia* (Chapel Hill: University of North Carolina Press, 1950), and Sean Joiner and Gerald Smith, *Augusta, Georgia* (Charleston, SC: Arcadia, 2004).

2. Matthew Bailey, "Rich's Department Store," *New Georgia Encyclopedia*, last updated January 31, 2017, http://www.georgiaencyclopedia.org/articles/business-economy/richs-department-store.

3. Tate, "Just Trying to Be a Man," unfinished autobiography, HET.

4. Tate, interviews by author, December 7, 2001, and July 26, 2002.

5. Tate, interview by author, December 7, 2001; "Greensboro High School Reunion Speech," September 1989, HET. Although both agree on the frame of the story, these two accounts differ slightly on the timing of phone calls and delivery of coal. My summarized account blends the two.

6. Tate, interview by author, December 7, 2001; "Greensboro High School Reunion Speech," September 1989, HET.

7. State School Board Minutes, April 5, 1938, 217, Georgia Archives, Morrow, GA; "An Answer to the Prayers of Teachers," *Herald*, March 1938, 6.

8. Horace E. Tate, interviews by author, September 2, 2001, July 26, 2001, and January 17, 2002. For context on Tate's father and the police, see Dittmer, *Black Georgia in the Progressive Era 1900–1920*. On lineage: E.B. Tate is a celebrated Confederate hero in the town. The lineage is undocumented, though his photograph does show a strong physical resemblance. According to a local Elberton historian, some blacks "could do what they wanted." For a variety of possible reasons, Henry Tate appears to have been one of those blacks, for he never suffered retaliation for his stance.

9. Tate, interview by author, May 17, 2002.

10. All three names are used in speeches and interviews. However, a Bank of Greensboro deposit slip shows the account in the name of the Men's Civic Club; HET.

11. Willie B. Ellis, "History of Ebenezer African Methodist Episcopal Church," in *Histories of Black Churches in Greene County, Georgia* (n.p., n.d.), Greene County Public Library; Willie Patience Brown and Vivian Ellis, "History of Springfield Baptist Church," n.d., Springfield Baptist Church.

12. "Treutlen County," *Herald*, December 1946, 25; "In the Field," *Herald*, October 1946, 14–22.

13. V.H. Harris, "Editorial," *Herald*, April 1932, 8.

14. Untitled index card in "Men's Civic Folder" that appears to be a discussion outline for his presentation, HET.

15. "Standard List of Questions," HET.

16. Tate, interview by author, September 1, 2001; "Greensboro High School Reunion Speech," September 1989; Tate, "Just Trying to Be a Man," HET. As in the coal story recounting, details about the numbers of people at the early meetings vary, but the final number registered does not vary. I have written the account in a way that highlights the activities confirmed in several accounts. "Challenge Negro Registrants Says Talmadge," *Herald-Journal* (Greensboro, GA), June 7, 1946.

17. "Talmadge Address," *Herald-Journal*, June 7, 1946.

18. "Talmadge Speaks Today," *Herald-Journal*, May 31, 1946; "Challenge Negro Registrants Says Talmadge"; "Talmadge Address."

19. "Talmadge Wins in State: Gene Makes Great Race in Greene Against Block 850 Colored Votes," *Herald-Journal*, July 26, 1946.

20. Ibid.

21. "Outline of Procedures for Legal Cases," Group II, B110, F3, NAACP Collection.

22. Untitled sheet with meeting notes in "Men's Civic Club" Folder, HET; "Greensboro High School Reunion Speech," September 1989.

23. Tate note outline for Men's Civic Club Meeting: "Men to go get building." Note on "Get your vision," see "Civic Club" Folder, HET.

24. Tate, "Just Trying to Be a Man."

25. Postcard of Greensboro courthouse in 1940s, author collection.

26. "Colored Schools (1947)," in Thaddeus Brockett Rice and Carolyn White Williams, *History of Greene County Georgia* (Washington, GA: Wilkes, 1973), 221.

27. See the series of letters directed to Mr. Tate in Greensboro File, October 16, 1947, HET.

28. John N. Popham, "Negro, White Schools in the South Held $545,000,000 Apart in Value," *New York Times*, January 26, 1949, HET.

29. Ibid.

30. "Talmadge Memorial Fund," *Herald-Journal*, January 23, 1948; Tate, "Just Trying to Be a Man."

31. Du Bois and Dill, *The Common School and the Negro American*.

32. Tate, "Just Trying to Be a Man."

33. "Bond Issue Wins Big Vote," *Herald-Journal*, August 20, 1948.

34. Horace E. Tate, letter to Mr. Harper, January 13, 1949; Men's Civic Club, letter to Mayor and Council, January 13, 1949; Charles L. Harper, letter to Mr. Tate, January 25, 1949; Horace E. Tate to Mr. Harper, February 4, 1949, all HET.

8: Out of the Public Eye

1. Georgia Teachers and Educational Association, "Highlights of the Annual G.T.E.A. Meeting," *Herald*, October 1949, 15–17.

2. Ibid.

3. Tate, "Just Trying to Be a Man."

4. Georgia Teachers and Educational Association, "Highlights of the Annual G.T.E.A. Meeting."

5. H.E. Tate, letter to H.A. Henderson, September 20, 1949, HET.

6. The number of people registered is from Tate, interview with author, September 1, 2001, and is confirmed in Tate, interview with Ann Maurey, March 21, 1995, HET. See also Thomas O'Brien, *The Politics of Race and Schooling: Public Education in Georgia 1900–1961* (Lanham, MD: Lexington Books, 1999).

7. Tate, interview with unnamed author, March 21, 1995, HET.

8. "Editorial," *Ocilla Star*, n.d.; "Distortion of Facts Won't Solve This Problem," *Atlanta Journal*, October 26, 1949; George Goodwin, "Negro Law Suit No State Case—Cook," *Atlanta Journal*, August 19, 1949, all HET.

9. The clippings for the Irwin County case include: George Goodwin, "School Suit May Cost 100 Millions: Valdosta Litigation Asks Equalization for Negroes," *Atlanta Journal*, 1949; Ralph McGill, "Chapter Two on Segregation," *Atlanta Constitution*, November 14, 1949; Ralph McGill, "The Chickens Are Coming Home to Roost," *Atlanta Constitution*, November 13, 1949; "Georgia Seeks Dismissal of Irwin County Suit," *Atlanta Constitution*, October 2, 1949; "Press Viewpoint on School Suit," *Oscilla Star*, n.d.; George Goodwin, "Negro Teacher Suit No State Case—Cook," *Atlanta Journal*, August 19, 1949; "Irwin Officers Get Support of Talmadge," n.d.; "The School Suit in Irwin," *Atlanta Constitution*, October 24, 1949, all HET.

10. McGill, "The Chickens Are Coming Home to Roost"; McGill, "Chapter Two on Segregation."

11. J.C. Jackson, letter to Mr. Harper, October 5, 1949; no name (Citizens Committee), letter to Mr. H.H. Tappan, October 12, 1949.

12. No name (Citizens Committee), letter to Mr. H.H. Tappan, October 12, 1949.

13. Georgia Teachers and Education Association, "Treutlen County," *Herald*, December 1946, 25.

14. Georgia Teachers and Education Association, "State Aid to Transportation," *Herald*, November 1947, 13, FV.

15. Canceled checks and reports are in HET. The summary was calculated by a member of my research team, October 4, 2002, HET.

16. Robert L. Cousins, letter to Horace E. Tate, July 6, 1949, HET.

17. Tate, "Just Trying to Be a Man."

18. H.E. Tate, letter to H.A. Henderson, September 20, 1949, HET.

19. On the football field use, see "Greensboro High School Reunion Speech," September 2, 1989, HET.

20. The particulars of Tate's retort differ. One report has him saying "as long as he lives." The other says "over his dead body." See Tate, interview with unnamed author, March 21, 1995, HET.

9: Seasons of Opportunity

1. Horace Tate, "The Negro Comes Back," circa 1950s, HET. Two versions of this talk exist, one in notes prepared for a community that focuses on registration, economic needs, elevating one another as blacks, and getting education and religion; the second is a typed text apparently delivered at church. Although titled the same, the substance varies. This reference is to the typed version.

2. "New Bibb County Negro High School," *Herald*, April 1949, 20–21.

3. "Report of the Resolutions Committee," GTEA, April 13–15, 1950, HET.

4. "Harper Calls on School Heads to Equalize Facilities," *Atlanta Daily World*, June 13, 1950, HET. For additional details on Harper's activities first as vice president and then as president of the Atlanta branch and of recognitions he received in the national office, see Part II, C37, F1, F6; Part II, A547, F8; Part II, A130, F13, NAACP Collection.

5. "Testimonial Dinner Honoring Professor Charles Lincoln Harper," June 13, 1950; "Georgians Join Atlantans in Tribute to Mr. Harper," *Atlanta Daily World*, June 14, 1950; "Harper's Tribute Set at Y Tonight," *Atlanta Daily World*, June 13, 1950; B.V. Hodges, "Prof. Harper to Be Honored for Long Service," *Atlanta Daily World*, April 30, 1950, all HET.

6. Although Mr. Harper supported integration of public high schools, his reference is to integration in higher education in this speech.

7. "Educational Achievement in Georgia Shows Vast Gains During Past Five Years," *Albany Herald*, December 28, 1952, reprinted in *Herald*, February 1953, 6. Thomas O'Brien provides detailed insight on the politics of the passage of the MFPE and the finances accruing to Georgia schools as a result in *The Politics of Race and Schooling: Public Education in Georgia 1900–1961*.

8. Clarence Mitchell, letter to Walter White, January 19, 1951; "Georgia Acts to Bar Funds in Bias Battle," *Atlanta Constitution*, February 16, 1951; all in Part II, A247, F4, NAACP Collection.

9. Herman Talmadge, telegram to Walter White, February 26, 1951; Walter White, telegram to Herman Talmadge, February 26, 1951; "White Attacks, Talmadge Defends

Georgia Jim Crow Education Bill," press release, March 1, 1951, all in Part II, A247, F4, NAACP.

10. "Some Facts About Negro Education in Georgia During 1950–51 and the Prospects for 1951–52," HET.

11. Thurgood Marshall, letter to Dan Byrd, December 6, 1946, Group II, B7, F2, NAACP Collection.

12. Size of meeting: "1951 G.T.E.A. Convention," *Herald*, April 1951, 4; Horace E. Tate, letter to Roline Boss, February 1, 1950, HET.

13. "Program for Region IV," February 9, 1951, HET; "New Bibb County Negro High School," *Herald*, April 1949, 20–21, HET.

14. On the principals' conference: Robert Cousins, letter to Mr. Horace Tate, November 14, 1949, HET.

15. "Dr. Horace Mann Bond: Man of the Year," *Herald*, November 1945, cover; "Elbert County Highlights," *Herald*, October 1944, 21; "Paul J. Blackwell," *Herald*, October 1948, 5.

16. Homer Edwards, "To the Teachers of Georgia," GTEA Souvenir Program, April 12–13, 1951, HET; "Harper Greeting to Teachers," GTEA Souvenir Program, April 12–13, 1951, HET.

17. "Negro Education in Georgia (Excerpts from 76 and 77th Annual Reports of the State Department of Education)," *Herald*, February 1949, 17–18.

18. I have attributed Harper's remarks during the session to the written remarks he made prior to the meeting. See "Harper Greetings to Our Teachers," GTEA Souvenir Program, April 12–13, 1951, HET.

19. Mr. Ward would suddenly be called into service in the armed forces before the case could be litigated. Six years later, the University of Georgia leaders would say it was too late for him to be admitted as a student since he was already matriculated at another university. When he became an attorney, Mr. Ward would sit at the table with the first black students who were admitted to the University of Georgia. Horace Tate, speech to the University of Georgia, HET.

20. Mr. Harper informed the National in 1949—writing on GT&EA stationery—that the local branch needed to do something about education: that everything should not always rest in the hands of "fly-by-night citizens councils." Mr. Harper might have been referencing citizens committees in general, but more likely he was referring to the Citizens Committee established in Atlanta one year before: the Atlanta branch had formed the committee to work on education issues, instead of doing so using the NAACP name. The case did not originate at that time. In 1950, when the *Aaron v. Cook* suit was filed, it was said to have been filed by the "Education Committee" in cooperation with the Atlanta Urban League. By 1950, the branch had money and had arranged with the national NAACP to keep its money instead of sending it all in as assessments, and had retained Mr. Walden and NAACP lawyers. Mr. Walden was not happy with the other younger NAACP lawyers coming in trying to disrupt his long-standing

advocacy, but the case was labeled a "most outstanding event." See "Atlanta Branch NAACP Annual Report of the President," December 13, 1949, Group II, Box C37; Charles Harper, letter to Glouster Current, February 22, 1949, Group II, C 37, F8; Annual Report of the Executive Secretary, Atlanta Branch, 1950, Group II, Box 38, F1; Lucille Black, letter to Charles Harper, January 10, 1949, Group II, C37, F9; memo from Robert Carter to Walter White, Thurgood Marshall, and Gloster Current, September 21, 1950, Group II, Box C38, F1, all NAACP Collection.

A similar anti-segregation lawsuit was filed in Clarendon County, South Carolina. However, the Atlanta case was expected to be heard earlier than the Clarendon County case and become the test on racial segregation in the public schools to head to the U.S. Supreme Court. See "The Deep South: Suit to End Racial Segregation in the Schools Draws Fire," *New York Times*, September 24, 1950, HET.

21. Dr. Benjamin Mays, "Oct. 4, 1950 Hungry Club Broadcast," WERD, HET.

22. "South in Turmoil over Sweatt Rule," *Austin American*, June 6, 1950, www.houseofrussell.com/legalhistory/sweatt/as/as060650a.html; "The Deep South: Suit to End Racial Segregation in the Schools Draws Fire," *New York Times*, September 24, 1950. The report of the Democratic convention is in Walter White, memo to Thurgood Marshall, September 8, 1950, Part II, A246, F7, NAACP Collection.

23. "Racial Tensions," *Herald*, February 1949, 6.

10: Paying the Cost

1. "Greene County Launches Big Program Among Negro Farmers," *Herald*, February 1939, 15.

2. Unsigned (carbon copy) letter to Mr. H.H. Tappan, with copies to Mr. Corry and Mr. Cousins, October 12, 1949, HET.

3. Tate, interview with author, December 7, 2001.

4. James C. Clark, "Civil Rights Leader Harry T. Moore and the Ku Klux Klan in Florida," *Florida Historical Quarterly* 73, no. 2 (October 1994): 166–83; Leedell Neyland and Gilbert Porter, *History of the Florida State Teachers Association* (Washington, DC: National Education Association, 1977), 100–101; Florida Office of the Attorney General, "Preliminary Statement," http://myfloridalegal.com/moore.nsf/WF/JFAO-6SQHVY/$file/MooreReport.pdf.

5. On Lloyd Gaines, see David Stout, "A Supreme Triumph, Then into the Shadows," *New York Times*, July 11, 2009; Chad Garrison, "The Mystery of Lloyd Gaines," *Riverfront Times*, April 4, 2007.

6. Unsigned (carbon copy) letter to Mr. F.T. Corry, May 1951, HET.

7. Mr. Tate was also once saved from harm in a racial dispute when a store owner identified him as a descendant of one of Elberton's leading white figures. Virginia Tate, interview with author, September 22, 2017.

8. William Pirkle, "A Study of the State Scholarship Aid Program for Negroes in Georgia, 1944–1955," Ph.D. diss., Alabama Polytechnic Institute, 1956, 140–41.

9. Report of Resolutions Committee, 1952, HET.

10. Horace Tate, interview with unknown author, n.d., HET.

11. "Here and There in Georgia as President B.F. Hubert Sees It," *Herald*, March 1939, 13; "Cause of Blaze Remains Mystery," *Atlanta Daily World*, January 3, 1940.

11: Just Trying to Be a Man

1. The new position would have increased his salary by $2,500. Although he never provided a rationale other than the desire to control his school, Mr. Tate could also have been explicit about his demands in the hopes that the superintendent would not agree and cancel the Griffin contract, allowing him to take the new job. No data exist to explain the superintendent's acquiesce. I have triangulated the climate of the era and the repeated report about his commitment to education to represent his reasons. Author interview with Dr. Tate, May 18, 2000; Atlanta University diploma, August 9, 1951, HET.

2. Horace E. Tate, interview by author, September 1, 2001.

3. Mrs. Tate, interviews by author, January 13, 2015, and March 11, 2016.

4. Mr. Hunt created the first Negro farmers conference in North Carolina. Henry A. Hunt, "Second Paper: "The Negro Farmer," in *Twentieth Century Negro Literature*, ed. Daniel Wallace Culp (Atlanta: J.L. Nichols, 1902), 394–98.

5. Author site drive from Greensboro to Griffin on Route 16.

6. Summer Convocation Program, Atlanta University, August 9, 1951, HET.

7. Dr. Horace E. Tate, interview by author, May 23, 2002.

8. "Political Actors," Tate's handwritten notes in spiral notebook, circa 1991, HET.

9. Griffin State site visit with Mrs. Tate on February 27, 2015.

10. State Salary Schedule for 1951–52; Professional Development Record reviewed on April 9, 2002, HET.

11. Dr. Tate, interview by author, February 28, 2002; "The Negro Common School, Georgia," *The Crisis*, September 1926, 60, Part I, C288, NAACP Collection.

12. Dr. Tate, interview by author, February 28, 2002; notebook list of faculty meetings in Griffin, 1956, HET. Mr. Tate's school is not unusual. The professionalism of black educators is documented. Walker, *Hello Professor*.

13. Dr. Tate, interview by author, April 9, 2002.

14. Back in Greene County, without him, the teacher study groups reported that to be effective, a "good teacher" needed a sympathetic mind, a genuine interest in children, an insight into the development of a child's mind and its ability to grow to its fullest capacity, an intrinsic liking for children, a fine sense of humor, an emotionally mature nature, and a willingness to stay "intellectually alert." Articles in the *Herald* pointed out that, as professionals, teachers adjusted their working hours to meet their responsibilities, did not transfer responsibility to others for failure, and continuously sought

additional professional knowledge and skills. See "Notes from the Field: Greene County," *Herald*, December 1952, 37–38; "From the Editor's Desk: What Makes a Professional Worker?," *Herald*, February 1953, 3–4, reprinted from *Alberta Teachers Association Magazine*, December 1951, 23.

15. The care ethic in black schools is repeatedly documented in case studies. See Lazarus Bates, Preston Royster, and W.C. Edwards, *The Education of Black Citizens in Halifax County: 1866–1969* (Springfield, VA: Banister Press, 1979); Titus Brown, *Faithful, Firm and True: African-American Educational in the South* (Macon, GA: Mercer University Press, 2002); Curtis Morris and Vivian Morris, *Creating Caring and Nurturing Educational Environments for African American Children* (Westport, CT: Bergin and Garvey, 2000); Curtis Morris and Vivian Morris, *The Price They Paid: Desegregation in an African American Community* (New York: Teachers College Press, 2002).

16. Griffin-Spaulding Teachers Association: Evaluative Summary of Group Meetings, May 12, 1955, HET; Dr. Tate, interview by author, April 9, 2002; author site visit to Warm Springs, Georgia.

17. I.E. Washington, "Presidential Address at the 1944 GTEA Convention," *Herald*, May 1944, 3.

18. Ulysses Byas, interviews by author, December 1, 2000, and March 3, 2008; Lucy Laney, "The Negro and the Vote," Part I, B2, F11, NAACP Collection.

19. Mrs. Tate, interview by author, April 6, 2014.

20. For evidence of black educators at the NAACP conventions, see Chairman, letter to E.D. Hugg, August 1919; J.W. Johnson, letter to M.W. Ovington, August 20, 1919. For evidence of Henry Hunt and Lucy Laney speaking at the national meeting in Cleveland, see Hunt, "Rural Conditions of Labor," 1919, Part I, 2, F9, NAACP; Lucy Laney, "The Negro and the Vote," 1919, Part I, B2, F11, all NAACP Collection.

21. Velma Horne, "Registering Voters 18 Years Old and Over—A Project," *Herald*, April 1951, 16.

22. Dr. Philip Hood, interview with author, April 13, 2015.

23. Horace Bond advocated the need for textbooks with a "systematic treatment of Negro educational problems." He believed it would have a good market. Horace Bond, letter to Mr. Trenholm, June 4, 1932, Folder 2A, HMB.

24. Dr. Tate, interview by author, May 23, 2002.

12: Moving on Up

1. Mrs. Tate, interview with author, September 24, 2006.

2. Horace Tate, interviews by author, July 26, 2002, December 7, 2001, and December 21, 2001.

3. Virginia Tate, interview by author, February 27, 2015.

4. Author site visit to Griffin, Georgia.

5. Minutes of the August 26, 1951, Board of Directors meeting. On explaining an absence, see E.J. Cranberry, letter to Mr. Harper, July 17, 1952, HET.

6. "GTEA Purchases a Home," *Herald*, October 1952, 20–21. On the joint office with the NAACP, see Mr. Harper, letter to Madison Jones, October 27, 1945; Charles Harper, letter to Miss Baker, September 26, 1944, Part II, A547, F8, NAACP Collection, and author site visit; Harper letter draft, August 18, 1952; Harper, letter to E.J. Cranberry, September 10, 1952; GT&EA news release, no. 1, HET. Original portrait of headquarters as it looked in the 1950s: back of GT&EA Program, April 15–16, 1954, HET.

7. Photographs of directors' meetings in headquarters, HET.

8. For introduction of segregation law, see Clarence Mitchell, letter to Walter White, January 19, 1951, Part II A 247, F4, NAACP Collection; Mr. Harper, letter to "Our Supervisors, Principals and Unite Presidents," September 19, 1951; Mr. Harper, letter to teachers, May 8, 1952 in "Holidays, July/August," GTEA Publication, GTEA news release, no. 1, HET.

9. Mr. Harper, memo to superintendents and boards of education, June 23, 1953, HET

10. J.S. Wilkerson, "President's Message," *Herald*, April 1952, 9; J.S. Wilkerson, "President's Message," *Herald*, October 1952, 6; radio broadcast by Dr. W.N. Boyd, WERD, Atlanta, September 22, 1950, HET

11. M.D. Collins, letter to superintendent, February 28, 1952; Mr. Harper, letter to teachers, May 8, 1952, in "Holidays, July/August," GTEA publication; GTEA news release, no. 1, all HET.

12. Mr. Harper, letter to teachers, May 8, 1952, in "Holidays, July/August," GTEA Publication, HET; Mrs. J.S. Morgan, address over WERD radio station, September 7, 1952, included in Mrs. J.S. Morgan, letter to Mr. Harper, September 9, 1952, HET.

13. H.T. Edwards and Mr. Harper to teachers, January 4, 1952, GTEA news release, no. 1, HET; "From the Editor's Desk: Laymen Interest," *Herald*, October 1951, 4.

14. "American Teachers Association (Formerly the National Association of Teachers in Colored Schools)," *Herald*, March 1945, 11–12; "NEA Platform to Strengthen Schools," *Herald*, December 1948, 12–13, HET.

15. Mr. Tate made another motion that the annual overnight clinic, a retreat for GTEA leaders, be held at Camp John Hope in the fall, a facility close to Fort Valley and named in honor of the former GT&EA member and Morehouse president. Mr. Harper would create the program, and include in it the topics suggested by the board, including the MFPE and concerns about salary and supplements. The motion passed.

16. I have no evidence that these delegates actually used the Green Book, a guide for Negro motorists. For information on the Green Book, including an image of the 1954 edition, see *The Green Book Chronicles: A Documentary About the First Black Travel Guide*, http://www.shoppe.black.us.

17. For a full report of Dr. Tate's first NEA meeting, see NEA, *Addresses and Proceedings*, vol. 91, 1953. Dr. Tate's materials from the ATA Convention, including his letter to attend, are available in the "ATA 1953" folder, HET.

18. See Nathan Daniel Beau Connolly, "By Eminent Domain: Race and Capital in the Building of an American South Florida," Ph.D. dissertation, University of Michigan, 2008. On the Roney Plaza in 1953, see "Roney Plaza Hotel—Miami Beach's First Oceanside Grand," http://janesbits.blogspot.com; Delegates' Manual and Program: National Education Association of the United States, June 28–July 3, 1953, Miami Beach, Florida, HET.

19. Delegates' Manual and Program: National Education Association of the United States, June 28–July 3, 1953.

20. A comprehensive description of Georgia's efforts to dismantle its public schools is in Jeff Roche, *Restructured Resistance: The Sibley Commission and the Politics of Desegregation in Georgia* (Athens: University of Georgia Press, 1998). See also Thomas V. O'Brien, "Georgia's Response to 'Brown v. Board of Education': The Rise and Fall of Massive Resistance, 1949–1961," April 1993, ERIC ED360454.

21. W.E.B. Du Bois, *The Negro Common School* (Atlanta: University Press, 1901).

22. Vanessa Siddle Walker, "Organized Resistance and Black Educators' Quest for School Equality, 1878–1938," *Teachers College Record* 107, no. 3 (2005): 355–88. For the official history of ATA, see T. Perry, "History of . . . Constitution and By-Laws of the National Association of Teachers in Colored Schools," *Bulletin* 10, no. 2 (January 1930): 5–6, National Association of Teachers in Colored Schools (henceforth NATCS).

23. "Purpose and Program of the National Association of Teachers in Colored Schools," *Bulletin* 10, no. 1 (November 1928): 6.

24. Ibid., 5–6.

25. W.A. Robinson, "Taking Thought for Tomorrow," *Bulletin* 8, no. 1 (n.d.): 4, NATCS.

26. T. Perry, "History of . . . Constitution and By-Laws of the National Association of Teachers in Colored Schools," *Bulletin* 10, no. 2 (January 1930): 5–6, NATCS.

27. "The Editor's Page," *Bulletin* 10, no. 1 (December 1929): 11, NATCS.

28. Al-Tony Gilmore, *All the People: NEA's Legacy of Inclusion and Its Minority Presidents* (Washington, DC: National Education Association, 2008). NEA's history is also in Wayne Urban, *Gender, Race, and the National Education Association Professionalism and Its Limitations* (New York: Routledge Falmer, 2000).

29. "Purpose and Program of the National Association of Teachers in Colored Schools," 7; Robinson, "Taking Thought for Tomorrow"; "Resolutions for the National Association of Teachers in Colored Schools," *Bulletin* 8, no. 1 (October 1927): 8, NATCS; "Civic Education," *Bulletin* 8, no. 2 (November 1927): 18, 20, NATCS. The reference to "civic education" here addresses the need for the child to properly respect law, order, and authority. Respect saved individual lives. This focus appears not to diminish the commitment to teaching children about democracy. See "Introduction to Civic Project: Valena C. Jones School," *Bulletin* 10, no. 7 (June–July 1930): 5–6. Black educational organizations across the South mirrored one an-

other in their efforts to address inequality in southern schools. See John Potts, *A History of the Palmetto Education Association* (Washington, DC: National Education Association, 1978); Thomas Patterson, *History of the Arkansas State Teachers Association* (Washington, DC: National Education Association, 1981); Ernest Middleton, *History of the Louisiana State Teachers Association* (Washington, DC: National Education Association, 1984); Leedell Neyland and Gilbert Porter, *History of the Florida State Teachers Association* (Washington, DC: National Education Association, 1977); Ancella Bickley, *History of the West Virginia State Teachers Association* (Washington, DC: National Education Association, 1979); J. Rupert Picott, *History of the Virginia Teachers Association* (Washington, DC: National Education Association, 1975).

30. The Mary White Ovington requests are available in Part I, Box 288, F2, NAACP Collection. W.E.B. Du Bois's detailed data on the schools in Georgia appear in James Weldon Johnson, letter to Dorothy Guinn, February 28, 1927, Part I, Box 288, F12, and "The Negro Common School," Part I, Box 288, F11, NAACP Collection.

31. The American Teachers Association, Office of the Executive Secretary, July 30, 1953, Secretarial Memorandum #11, HET.

32. Rayford Logan, ed., *Howard University: The First Hundred Years 1867–1967* (New York: New York University Press, 1969).

33. During the post–World War I era, when black educators and the NAACP began coordinating activity, Charles Houston was still a law student and offering his services for free. See Charles Houston, letter to James Weldon Johnson, Part I, C113, F20, NAACP Collection. His later initial efforts to locate support for the NAACP's legal campaign to defeat school desegregation are evident in Houston, letter to White, November 2, 1939, and Itinerary of Charles Houston and Edward P., 1934, B64, F12, NAACP Collection. His work with the National Black Education Association begins in 1935, when he provides the Legislative Committee with a report of legal pleas. Mutually, they agree to launch a legal case challenging teachers' salaries. See "Report of the Committee on Legislation," *Bulletin* 14, no. 1 (November 1935): 49, NATCS. His understanding that connections with educators needed to remain confidential is evident in his communications to Oklahoma teachers; see Part I, C290, F8, NAACP Collection.

34. Memorandum to Office from Thurgood Marshall, October 17, 1937, NAACP Admin Files, Box 179, Folder 6, NAACP Collection.

35. Marshall, letter to Leflores, September 15, 1937; Marshall, letter to Shores, May 11, 1938; Houston to NAACP Branches, January 17, 1936; Thurgood Marshall, letter to Louis Berry, June 15, 198, Group II, B7, F2; Thurgood Marshall, memo to Budget Committee, December 17, 1940, Group II, B7, F1, all NAACP Collection.

36. "Teachers Association Gives $5,000 to Education Cases," August 6, 1953, Part II, A218, NAACP Collection.

37. The collaboration between the NAACP and the ATA was not always smooth. In North Carolina, some educators supported the NAACP and Attorney Marshall and others supported the long-standing advocacy measures of direct appeal to elected politicians utilized by their state educational association since Reconstruction. The NAACP engaged in direct appeal also, but it did so on the federal level with congressional leaders and the president. It was not pleased when members of the North Carolina Teachers Association continued these procedures on the state level and did not welcome their help, even with litigation—instead billing them as "outsiders." The NAACP and ATA also fought over the regional school plan the southern states proposed as a way to get around the admission of Negroes into graduate schools in southern states. The NAACP sharply denounced the plan, arguing that the fact that Georgia legislators supported it was a case in point as to why the governors should not be believed in their public proclamations that they were not trying to circumvent the *Gaines* decision. The ATA likewise publicly proclaimed its disagreement with the plan as a way to circumvent integration. However, the NAACP regularly questioned the loyalty of some educators and their motives, suggesting they were more concerned about building their own institutions than advocating the NAACP desegregation agenda, and some educators angrily questioned the goals of the NAACP, reminding national leaders they *were* the NAACP and did not want political fights that jeopardized students' abilities to be educated in the schools. See, for example, Part II, A247, F1- F3, NAACP Collection. Private squabbles also erupted over the NAACP's concern about who would receive national credit. John Davis was president of the ATA during the same time Attorney Houston utilized NAACP money to film inequalities in South Carolina. Attorney Houston acknowledged to his fan and colleague Walter White that Davis—who traveled with him to South Carolina to film injustices—had a "swell" conference in 1935 and that the NAACP needed to put on one that was a "bigger and better show." He emphasized to White the need for the NAACP to receive the credit for the films. See communications in Part I, C64, F17, NAACP Collection. Public credit was reasonable for the larger the organization. After all, it represented a large number of people and was the voice of the Negro in appealing to presidents and congressional leaders. For educators, credit was not a major concern. In this period, they did not want their role widely publicized in the South. If the NAACP wanted credit, the collaboration worked for educators, who did not want local credit. For Harper and his close association with the National NAACP, see Part II, A130, F13; Part II, A547, F8, NAACP Collection.

38. "Highlights of the Annual GTEA Meeting," *Herald*, October 1949, 15.

13: In This Present Crisis

1. "Principal of the Year," *Herald*, February 1954, 18; H.E. Tate, "The Effect of Conduct on Grading and Marking," speech to the Griffin-Spaulding County Principals Group, n.d., ca. 1953.

2. "Principal of the Year."

3. Leonard N. Rodgers, letter to Mr. Tate, ca. early April 1954, HET.

4. A fellow principal supporting Mr. Tate announced his willingness to use every "ounce of [his] influence" to get Tate elected. H.E. Tate, letter to John Clark, March 16, 1952; J.E. Clark, letter to Mr. Tate, April 2, 1952, Folder Miscellaneous C, HET; Tate, interview by author, n.d.

5. "Educational Achievement in Georgia Shows Vast Gains During Past Five Years," *Albany Herald*, December 28, 1952 reprinted in *Herald*, February 1953, 6. O'Brien in *The Politics of Race and Schooling*, 53–65, provides detailed insight on the politics of the passage of the MFPE and the finances accruing to some Georgia schools as a result.

6. *Herald*, October 1952, 17, HET.

7. Untitled report, 1952, Delegate Assembly National Meeting, HET; Tate, interview by author, September 20, 2002.

8. Bruce I. Blackstone, "Before You Accept the Nomination," reprinted in *Herald*, December 1954, 11, HET.

9. Du Bois, *The Negro Common School* (reprinted by Arno Press and *New York Times*, 1969).

10. "1954 GTEA in Annual Session at Savannah," *Herald*, April 1954, 20–21, HET.

11. "Coca-Cola Display at Convention," *Herald*, April 1954, 31–32, HET.

12. "1954 GTEA in Annual Session at Savannah," 21.

13. Ibid.; "GTEA Vice President," *Herald*, October 1954, 9, HET. During the convention one candidate for the same position circulated the truth that Mr. Tate had a son prior to his marriage to Mrs. Virginia Tate. Reportedly, the candidate thought this statement might help his own campaign. However, Mr. Tate had married the mother of his son prior to his birth so that the child might have his name, with the understanding that the couple would soon divorce. He never lived with his first wife, and the circulating report of a son from a prior marriage was one the people "did not pay any attention to" as they decided on leadership. Author interview with Mrs. Tate, August 27, 2009.

14. Report of Resolutions Committee, April 10–11, 1952, HET.

15. Report of Resolutions Committee, April 21–22, 1954, HET.

16. "Biographical Sketch of Thurgood Marshall," *Herald*, October 1954, 7. While the teachers' organizations supplied the money for any educator willing to litigate, the national NAACP also recognized the individual sacrifices involved. "All the weight of the NAACP should be thrown around those who were sacrificed in the wage equalization fight and a special note will [*sic*] be added on their behalf," wrote an NAACP staffer. The letter spoke of the resumes the NAACP had of other educators who lost jobs, including J. Rupert Picott of Virginia. See Leon Scott, letter to Norma Jensen, August 21, 1945, Part II, A24, F2, NAACP Collection. Mr. Harper was this early agitator in Georgia and, like others, he sacrificed his job. See Booker T. Washington

Class of 1931, "Dr. Charles Lincoln Harper, 1877–1955," File—Bio, Harper, Charles Lincoln, APS Files.

17. "Letter from Lucius T. Bacote, President, to Fellow Teachers," *Herald*, October 1954, 5, HET.

18. Cover of *Herald*, February 1954; "From the Editor's Desk," *Herald*, February 1954, 8, HET.

19. Author interview with Dr. Tate on segregation, May 18, 2000; George Coleman in Booker T. Washington Class of 1931, "Dr. Charles Lincoln Harper, 1877–1955," File—Bio, Harper, Charles Lincoln, APS Files.

20. H.E. Tate, Principal's Message (1953, 1954); Message to the 1953 Graduating Class, HET. The *Herald* editor also reflected on his amazement at the number of new facilities across the state ("From the Editor's Desk," *Herald*, April 1953, 8, HET). Consistently, students were cautioned not to abuse them. The pride they took in having the facilities others "prayed, worked, bled, and died for" likely helps explain the repeated emphasis on respect for school property and school personnel that is commonly remembered by blacks throughout the South. Patricia Pickard, interview by author, September 29, 2017.

21. These resolutions also speak to teacher security, a topic addressed later in the text. See "Resolutions Adopted Unanimously by the American Teachers Association in Annual Convention, Houston, Texas," July 26, 1955, Part II, A247, F6, NAACP Collection. At the 1954 meeting, delegates to ATA began their Monday morning session with a report on the status of education as reported by the joint committee with their expected colleagues, NEA. On Tuesday morning, fourteen departments staged concurrent discussion sessions on the sub-theme "How Teachers Can Help Our Children in the Transition Crisis." See ATA Secretary Memo #17, July 31, 1954, HET.

22. Hugh W. Sparrow, "Alabama Politics—Education Seems Destined to Become the Major Problem for the 1953 Legislature," *Birmingham News*, January 4, 1953.

23. "This Afternoon," *Birmingham Post*, May 22, 1947, Part II, A 247, F4, NAACP Collection. In subsequent years publishers would print accounts of the South's interpretation of *Brown*. For perspectives on southern values, see William Douglas Workman, *The Case for the South* (New York: Devin-Adair, 1960). Other contemporary accounts are available in *With All Deliberate Speed: Segregation-Desegregation in Southern schools*, ed. Don Shoemaker (New York: Harper, 1957); Virgil T. Blossom, *It Has Happened Here* (New York: Harper, 1959); Thomas Buford Maston, *Segregation and Desegregation: A Christian Approach* (New York: Macmillan, 1959); Melvin Marvin Tumin, *Desegregation: Resistance and Readiness* (Princeton, NJ: Princeton University Press, 2015).

24. Herman Talmadge, *You and Segregation* (Birmingham, AL: Vulcan Press, 1955), 1–13.

25. Ibid., 23.

26. Ibid., 24–25.

27. Ibid., 30–31.

28. Ibid., 32.

29. Ibid., 57.

30. Ibid., 60.

31. Ibid., 64–65.

32. Reed Sarratt, *The Ordeal of Desegregation: The First Decade* (New York: Harper & Row, 1966).

33. Herman Talmadge, letter to "My dear Friend," n.d., author's personal collection.

34. NAACP, *Dixie Dynamite: The Inside Story of the White Citizens Councils* (New York: NAACP, 1957).

35. "A Special Report from the Southern Regional Council: Pro-Segregation Groups in the South," November 19, 1956, (mis)filed in Tate Folder: The Self Philosophy Class, HET.

36. "Griffin Raps Court Edict as 'Usurpation of Rights,'" *Augusta Chronicle*, April 14, 1956, HET.

37. Ibid.; "Mayor Today Will Greet 4,000 Negro Educators," *Augusta Chronicle*, April 12, 1956, HET.

14: Shifting Sands

1. Program, GTEA Annual Convention, April 20–24, 1955, HET.

2. Report of Resolutions Committee, April 21–22, 1955, Tate P Folder, HET. At Teachers College, Mr. Tate had written a class paper about the implications of southern integration for program planning. See 1955 Curriculum Class Paper, Graduate Training Folder, HET. At GTEA, the matter was not academic but practical. He said he knew discussions in his graduate class here and other places were not right, but that he had to complete the classwork. Horace Tate, interview by author, January 24, 2002.

3. Telephone call from Ted Poston to NAACP, July 12, 1955, Part II, C427, F7, NAACP Collection.

4. Ibid.

5. Ibid. Ultimately, the state attorney general's office would back down on its 1955 efforts to retaliate. See "NAACP Hails Action Rescinding Teacher Purge," press release, August 8, 1955, Part II, C427, F7, NAACP Collection.

6. Roy Wilkins, letter to GTEA, June 1, 1954, Part II C427, F6, NAACP Collection.

7. "Statement by Dr. Davis at Atlanta Meeting on July 16, 1955, with the Executive Committee of the Georgia Teachers Association," Part II, C427, F7, NAACP Collection.

8. Gloster B. Current to NAACP Officer, May 18, 1955, Part II, A247, F6; Dr. John Davis as Head of Department of Teacher Information and Security, see Byrd, letter to Dr. Hatch, January 15, 1955, Part I:8, F4 (LDEF); "NAACP Legal Defense Fund Needs Money Now, 1953," March, press release, Part II, A247, F9; Roy Wilkins, letter to

Robert Klein, December 12, 1954, Part II, A247, F9; Robert Klein, letter to Roy Wilkins, December 3, 1954, Part II, A247, F9, all NAACP Collection.

9. Mr. Wilkins, memo to Dr. Davis, October 17, 1955, Part II, A247, F6; T.R. Speigner, letter to John Davis, April 5, 1955, Part I:8, F4 (LDEF), NAACP Collection.

10. Gloster Current, letter to NAACP Officer, May 18, 1955; Questionnaire on Dismissed Teachers, Part II, C427, F6, NAACP Collection.

11. Mary W. Ovington, letter to Executive Committee, February 26, 1923, B1, C288, F1, NAACP Collection. Branches' responses to the question about dismissal varied widely and did little to provide comprehensive data. See communications in Part II, C427, F6, NAACP Collection.

12. "Proposed Statement of John W. Davis to ATA, Houston, Texas, July 25, 1955," Part II A247, F6, NAACP Collection.

13. "From Edward P. Morgan's Broadcast—August 2, 1955," Part II, C427, F7, NAACP.

14. A.P. Marshall of Missouri complained to Gloster Current, director of branches, that being devoted to the NAACP cause was costing him dearly that year. He had advice on how to create programs that would increase membership because they were active and interesting, but he wasn't sure he could continue the work. He had not even received expenses. Gloster Current, letter to A.P. Marshall, May 31, 1955; A.P. Marshall, letter to Gloster Current, May 29, 1955, Part II, C427, F6, NAACP Collection.

15. Roy Wilkins, letter to W.W. Law, August 3, 1955, Part II C427, F7, NAACP Collection.

16. Remarks by Walter White, Executive Secretary, NAACP Annual Meeting, January 3, 1955, Group II, Box A59, F1, NAACP Collection.

17. Memo to Mrs. Marion Bluitt from the NAACP Legal Defense and Educational Fund, n.d. (response to Memo to Dr. Davis from Mr. Wilkins, October 17, 1955), Part II A247, F6, NAACP Collection.

18. "Jeanes Teachers of Atlanta Region Enjoy Party," *Herald*, October 1954, 25. For a description of Georgia, see Rebecca Davis, Maenelle Dempsey, Ethel Knight, Madie Kincy, Susie Wheeler, Josie Sessoms, and Ella Tackwood, *Jeanes Supervision in Georgia Schools: A Guiding Light in Education: A History of the Program 1908–1975* (Athens: Georgia Association of Jeanes Curriculum Directors and the Southern Education Foundation, 1975).

19. H.E. Tate, "Report of the Harper Fund Solicitation Committee," *Herald*, October 1954, 19–20.

20. John H. Lewis, "Statement at Professor Harper's Funeral," *Herald*, October 1955, 18, 40; Benjamin Mays, "They Knew Charles Harper," *Herald*, October 1955, 40.

21. Thurgood Marshall, "They Knew Charles L. Harper," *Herald*, October 1955, 19. On the Hunt connection, see Thurgood Marshall, letter to Dr. Henry Hunt, August 23,

1934; H.A. Hunt, letter to Walter White, June 18, 1937; Thurgood Marshall, letter to Forrester Washington, July 26, 1937; H.A. Hunt, letter to Thurgood Marshall, August 27, 1937, Part I, G44, F37, all NAACP Collection; reprint from *Atlanta Daily World*, June 24, 1955, in *Herald*, October 1955, 19, HET.

22. "Professors and Projects on the Georgia Educational Front," *Herald*, October 1955, 22–23.

23. L.T. Bacote, "Reflections," *Herald*, October 1955, 21.

24. "The Ninety-First Anniversary of the Emancipation Proclamation Celebration, 1955," HET.

25. C.L. Harper, memo to Regional Directors, December 23, 1954, Director of Negro Education Subject Files, Group 12, Series 71, Unit 3, Location 439-04, Georgia State Archives, Morrow, Georgia (GSA).

26. Rev. Pitts had some prior association with GT&EA since he appeared at the April 23, 1955, board meeting, when Mr. Harper was still alive. His presence is unexplained. See Board of Director Minutes, April 23, 1955, and October 15, 1955. See also "Memo to Board of Directors from Committee on Criteria for Selection of an Executive Secretary," August 22, 1955, and "Agenda for GTEA Board Meeting," August 27–28, 1955, Item 7, Tate Folder: GTEA Board of Directors, HET.

27. This Georgia Conference on Educational Opportunity differed from the State Conference of the NAACP, which focused itself with plaintiffs and litigation for equality. "Notes," received in the office November 19, 1956, Tate files, loose, HET.

28. "Meeting of the Board of Directors Agenda, August," March 10, 1956, Tate Folder S; "Area Citizens Meetings, 1957, of the GTEA," Tate Folder: Black Teacher Salary, 1957, HET.

29. See "NAACP Correspondence NAACP" Folder, GTEA Collection, HET.

30. Lucius T. Bacote, letter to Directors, September 15, 1955, Tate Folder: Directory—Regions 1–4, HET.

31. State Program Planning Committee Minutes, November 5, 1965, Tate Folder: 1956 Miscellaneous Materials; "Planning Committee Meeting at GTEA Office," February 18, 1956, Tate Folder: GTEA Minutes; "Georgia's Official Negro Musician," n.d., Tate Folder G, all HET. Talmadge visit was discussed in Mrs. Tate's interview with author on January 16, 2008. Talmadge once told Tate that he would never support a white lady working for a black man; Horace Tate, interview by author, November 14, 2002.

32. ATA Flyer, February 2, 1955, and ATA Flyer, February 12, 1955, Tate Folder: American Teachers Association, HET. The NAACP objected to the conference in a series of communications, noting the failure to include sufficient blacks in the discussions and the failure to address directly school integration. See Part II, A247, F7, NAACP Collection.

33. H.E. Tate, letter to President Eisenhower, September 16, 1955; Walter George, letter to Vice President Tate, September 30, 1955, Tate Folder, HET.

34. R.L. Cousins, "They Knew Charles L. Harper," *Herald*, October 1955, 20.

35. "President's Message," *Herald*, Fall 1956, HET.

15: The Ties That Bind

1. Edward J. Odom Jr., "Welcome, Mr. President, Editorial," *Herald*, Fall 1956, 6, Tate loose files, HET.

2. BY ORDER OF THE PRESIDENT, Dear Sir, n.d., Tate Folder S; L.H. Pitts, memo to Members of the Board of Directors, September 20, 1956, Tate folder: GTEA Board of Directors, 1956; L.H. Pitts, Progress Report and Recommendations to the Board of Directors, Tate Folder: GTEA Board of Directors, 1956, all HET.

3. G.L. Porter, letter to Mr. Tate, September 13, 1956, Tate Folder: Miscellaneous F, HET; NCOSTA Minutes, Fall Workshop, September 28–29, 1956, GTEA Folder: NCOSTA, HET; "NCOSTA Holds Two-Day Workshop at Hot Springs," *Mississippi Educational Journal*, November 1956, 33.

4. NCOSTA Minutes, Fall Workshop, September 28–29, 1956, GTEA Folder: NCOSTA, HET. See Potts, *A History of the Palmetto Education Association;* Patterson, *History of the Arkansas State Teachers Association;* Middleton, *History of the Louisiana State Teachers Association;* Neyland and Porter, *History of the Florida State Teachers Association;* Bickley, *History of the West Virginia State Teachers Association;* Percy Murray, *History of the North Carolina State Teachers Association* (Washington, DC: National Education Association, 1984).

5. NCOSTA Minutes, Fall Workshop, September 28–29, 1956, GTEA Folder: NCOSTA, HET.

6. Dr. E.B. Palmer, interview by author, June 22, 2002.

7. Ninth Annual G.T.E.A. Clinic, October 6 & 7, 1956, Tate Folder: GTEA General, HET; Appendix II, NCOSTA Minutes, Fall Workshop, September 28–29, 1956, GTEA Folder: NCOSTA, HET.

8. Gladys Bates, letter to Mr. Pitts, October 2, 1956, GTEA: NCOSTA Folder, HET.

9. Dan Byrd, letter to J. Rupert Picott, January 9, 1957, GTEA Organized Folder: NCOSTA, HET.

10. The national NAACP was relieved when a plea was formulated. "Glad you will *soon report through NCOSTA*," John Davis writes to Mr. Pitts, October 1, 1957, Part I:9, F1 (LDEF), NAACP Collection; NCOSTA Minutes, December 7–8, 1957, GTEA Organized Folder: NCOSTA, HET.

11. Virginia Teachers Association, letter to Thurgood Marshall and Elwood Chisholm, June 8, 1956; Thurgood Marshall, letter to Rupert Picott, June 11, 1956, GTEA Organized Folder: NCOSTA, HET.

12. Trip Itinerary of Henderson Travel Services; Memo from Paul Street to Professional Leaders, February 15, 1957, Folder: National Education Association, HET.

13. For description of events, see "Addresses and Proceedings of the Ninety-Fifth Annual Meeting Held at Philadelphia, Pennsylvania, June 30–July 5, 1957," National Education Association Proceedings, 1957, volume 95, 140, 141, 180, 181, 448, 449, HET; Tate, interview by author, December 7, 2001.

14. Brief submitted to the Executive Committee of NEA by GTEA, Folder: 1958/NEA/GTEA/NCOSTA, HET.

15. Lyman V. Ginger, letter to Mr. Pitts, March 17, 1958, Research Summary Folder: NEA/GTEA/NCOSTA, 1958, HET.

16. Brief submitted to the Executive Committee of NEA by GTEA, Folder: 1958/NEA/GTEA/NCOSTA, HET.

17. Minutes of the NCOSTA Meeting, July 29, 1957, Folder: NCOSTA, HET.

18. Mr. Pitts, letter to Robert C. Hatch, March 12, 1956; Mr. Pitts, letter to G.W. Brooks, March 12, 1956; Mr. Pitts, letter to Walker E. Solomon, March 12, 1956; Mr. Pitts, letter to Mr. W.L. Greene, March 12, 1956, Folder: NCOSTA, HET.

19. Pitts, letter to Executive Secretaries of NCOSTA, March 19, 1958, Folder: 1958/NEA/GTEA/NCOSTA, HET.

20. W.L. Greene, letter to Mr. Pitts, March 21, 1958; Vernon McDaniel, memo to Mr. Pitts, April 15, 1958; W.E. Solomon, letter to Mr. Pitts, March 24, 1958; John Davis, letter to Mr. Pitts, March 26, 1958; Dan Byrd, letter to Mr. Pitts, March 22, 1958; J.K. Haynes, letter to Mr. Pitts, March 28, 1958, Folder: 1958/NEA/GTEA/NCOSTA, HET.

21. W.L. Green, letter to Executive Secretaries of State Teachers Associations Affiliated with NCOSTA, June 3, 1958; Trenholm, letter to Rev. Pitts, March 31, 1958, Folder: 1958/NEA/GTEA/NCOSTA, HET.

22. L.H. Pitts, letter to Dr. Ginger, June 10, 1958. No evidence exists of discussions with his board or his conversations with NCOSTA executive secretaries. According to Dr. Palmer, the last executive secretary in North Carolina, executive secretaries utilized the information they received from colleagues in their states but did not usually name the source. Dr. Palmer, interview with author, June 22, 2002.

23. I provide here a sample of his activities. For regional classroom teachers' conference, meeting of the trustees and committees, PTA office space, communication with the governor, see Tate Folder: G, HET. See also H.E. Tate, letter to Mrs. Ethel W. Knight, January 23, 1957, Tate Folder: Region II GTEA, HET. For examples of thank-you letters, see H.E. Tate, letter to C.A. DeVillars, April 23, 1957, Tate Folder: Miscellaneous D, HET; H.E. Tate, letter to R.J. Martin, April 24, 1957, Tate Folder: GTEA Minutes, HET. For committees, see "Committees," Tate Folder: GTEA Minutes, Tate Folder: Committees GTEA; Tate Folder: Miscellaneous, HET; H.E. Tate, letter to Mrs. Ruth Pickens, March 13, 1956, Tate Folder: P; Tate and Pitts, letter to Members of the Board of Directors, February 15, 1957, Tate Folder: GTEA Board of Directors, HET; Nomination of teacher—Tate, letter to Mr. Peterson, June 8, 1957, Tate Folder:

Communications, HET. For commencements, see Tate Folder: Commencement Programs, HET. For integration of associations, see: Carl Megal, letter to Mr. Tate, January 2, 1957, Tate Folder: ATA, HET; H.E. Tate, letter to Mr. B. Lawler, April 17, 1957, Tate Folder: Communications, HET; Vanett Lawler, letter to Mr. Tate, April 30, 1957, Tate Folder M, HET.

24. N.C. Chriss, United Press Staff Correspondent in Atlanta, "Bill Would Put Teeth into Georgia Law Against Stirring Up Law Suits," n.d., ca. 1957.

25. Edward J. Odom Jr., "Welcome, Mr. President, Editorial," *Herald*, Fall 1956, 6, Tate loose files, HET; "Burden Left to Communities," *Atlanta Journal-Constitution*, February 27, 1956, Tate Folder: Newspaper Clippings, 1955–56, HET.

26. Samuel L. Adams, "Girl Charges Criminal Assault but Man Only Held for Molesting," *Atlanta Daily World*, February 27, 1956; Bob Ingram, "Klan Stages Ritual Here," November 25, 1956, Tate Folder: M, HET.

27. H.E. Tate, letter to Mr. DeVillars, March 1, 1957, Tate Folder Miscellaneous D, HET.

16: Paying the Cost—Again

1. Horace Tate, interview by author, February 21, 2002.

2. News release, April 9, 1957, and other communications in Tate Folder: H.E. Tate, HET.

3. "Message to the Georgia Teachers and Education Association," n.d., HET. This message is with Tate's 1957 materials and, though typed, has his signature. Because only one presidential speech would be given a year, I am assuming this speech can be matched with the date provided in the text. I also rearranged portions of the text for ease of telling the story.

4. "School Board Re-elects Principals," *Griffin Daily News*, February 12, 1957, HET.

5. Horace E. Tate, letter to R.L. Cousins, July 31, 1955, Tate Folder: Correspondence, HET; Mary Sullivan, letter to Walter White, June 7, 1955, Part II: A 247, F6, NAACP.

6. News Release, April 9, 1957, Tate Folder: H.E. Tate, HET; Ibid.

7. NCOSTA Minutes, December 7–8, 1957, GTEA Organized Folder, HET.

8. See communication exchanges in Tate Folder: Southern Education Foundation, HET; Tate, interview by author, April 5, 2002.

17: Walking the Ancient Paths

1. "H.E. Tate Elected to Executive Secretary of GTEA," *Herald*, Spring 1961, 8, HET.

2. Mrs. Tate, interview with the author, October 7, 2017.

3. Horace E. Tate, "Opening Statement: What Are the Implications of Desegregation for Program Planning?," Folder: University of Kentucky, 1958–59, HET.

4. L.H. Pitts, letter to NCOSTA Executive Secretaries, June 3, 1960, Folder: NCOSTA, HET.

5. L.H. Pitts, letter to Claude Purcell, July 29, 1960, Folder: Peters, James F., HET; NEA 1960 Convention from "Washington, December 16 Meeting: NEA and School Desegregation," GTEA Files; "N.E.A. Convention," *The Nation's Schools* 66, no. 2 (August 1960), HET.

6. For Pitts nationally, see "Washington, December 16 Meeting: NEA and School Desegregation," GTEA Files; "G.T.E.A. Leaders Attend A.T.A. at Daytona," Folder: ATA Convention 1958; Pitts, letter to NCOSTA Executive Secretaries, June 3, 1960, Folder: NCOSTA, all HET. On Pitts in Georgia, see Henry A. Stewart, letter to Dr. Pitts, Sept. 14, 1960, Folder: Correspondence; "Statement to Georgia State Board of Education," by L.H. Pitts, June 14, 1961, Folder: L.H. Pitts; L.H. Pitts, letter to Dr. Claude Purcell, May 20, 1960, Claude Purcell, letter to Mr. L.H. Pitts, May 24, 1960, Mr. Pitts, letter to Mr. Purcell, June 3, 1960, James S. Peters, letter to Dr. L.H. Pitts, May 14, 1960, James S. Peters, letter to Mr. Pitts, April 6, 1959, and George P. Whitman Jr., letter to GTEA, March 15, 1957, all in Folder: Peters, James S., HET. Letter to superintendent and superintendent response: Mr. Pitts to Mr. Purcell, July 19, 1960, Claude Purcell to Mr. Pitts, July 29, 1960, HET.

7. L.H. Pitts, letter to Claude Purcell, July 29, 1960, Folder: Peters, James F., HET.

8. J. Calhoun, letter to Mr. John Wesley Dobbs, March 20, 1957; J. Calhoun, letter to Mr. Roy Wilkins, March 20, 1957, Statewide Registration Committee of Georgia: Summary of Changes in Number of Registered Voters in Counties Organized, Folder: Peters, James S., HET.

9. John Davis, letter to Rev. Pitts, April 25, 1960; John Davis, letter to Mr. R. Picott, December 7, 1959. Part I: 9, F7 (LDEF), NAACP Collection.

10. H.E. Tate, "Lest We Forget: President's Message," *Herald* XXIV, no. 3 (Winter 1958): 2.

11. "Executive Secretary's Report, Board of Directors Meeting, September 15, 1961," *Herald* XXVII, no. 1 (Fall 1961): 3, names H.E. Tate as the journal's editor.

12. Ibid.; "Executive Secretary's Report, Board of Directors Meeting, December 16, 1961."

13. National Council of Officers of State Teachers Associations, Proceedings of the Annual Meeting, September 23–25, 1960, New Orleans, Louisiana, HET.

14. Memo from W.E. Solomon to NCOSTA members, September 20, 1961; T.W. Coggs, letter to Mr. H.E. Tate, September 20, 1961; Robert H. Hatch, letter to Dr. Tate, September 18, 1961; Daniel E. Byrd, letter to Dr. H.E. Tate, September 16, 1961; H.E. Tate, letter to NCOSTA Members, September 18, 1961; Telegram from NCTA to H.E. Tate, September 20, 1961; Telegram from Vernon McDaniel to H.E. Tate, September 22, 1961; C.J. Barber, letter to Dr. H.E. Tate, September 22, 1961; Telegram from

W.R. Collins to H.E Tate, September 21, 1961; NCOSTA Roster of Arrivals; Messages from Dr. Gilbert L. Porter and T.V. Glover, n.d., all HET.

15. NCOSTA Minutes, September 22–24, 1961, Atlanta, Georgia, GTEA Files, HET.

16. For a full discussion, see O'Brien, *The Politics of Race and Schooling*, 135–93.

17. Ibid., 189–91.

18. Report of the Resolutions Committee to the Representative Assembly, April 8, 1960, HET. Some of these items are crossed out, perhaps because the assembly did not adopt the language. However, they provide an accurate report of educational conditions for black children at the beginning of the 1960s.

18: Policing the South

1. Author site visit, April 2016. For a record of President Kennedy's remarks to the Georgia educators, see John F. Kennedy, "Remarks to Officers of State Educational Associations and the National Education Association 19, Nov. 1963," November 19, 1963, JFF WHA-240-007, JFK.

2. See "Discrimination in Expenditure of Public School Funds," February 22, 1929, March 11, 1929, June 10, 1929, and September 9, 1929, Minutes of the Meetings of Boards of Directors, 1909–1959, Reel 1, NAACP Collection. See also Houston, letter to Spingarn, March 5, 1937, Part I, C64, F20, and a variety of other communications in the Board of Directors Files, Part I, A1–17, NAACP Collection. Importantly, southern states routinely sent money into local counties where the money was diverted to support white schools. According to Fred McCuistion, Negroes were cheated out of $600,000 a year in public money. See Frank Horne, "Paper on Present Day Education of Negro," 1936 Howard University yearbook, Unprocessed Files of Henry Hunt, Fort Valley.

3. "The White House Message on Education," White House press release, January 29, 1963; "Remarks to Officers of State Education Associations," November 19, 1963, JFF WHA-240-007, JFK.

4. "National Education Association 101st Annual Meeting, June 30–July 5, 1963," press release, GTEA Files, HET.

5. *Herald*, Winter 1963, 2.

6. H.E. Tate, letter to Mr. L.S. Alexander, December 3, 1963, HET.

7. Charles A. Lyons Jr., letter to H.E. Tate, December 19, 1963, HET.

8. GTEA Resolutions, April 3–5, 1963, HET.

9. Jim Killacky and Mary Catherine Conroy, "ESEA Twenty Years Later: A Talk with Francis C. Keppel and Harold Howe II," *College Board Review* 138 (Winter 1985–86): 7, Box 1, F2, Harold Howe Papers, Harvard Graduate School of Education, Cambridge, MA (henceforth HHP).

10. Ibid.

11. "Federal Aid to Education," *Herald*, February 1950, 5.

12. Dr. Tate reports the meeting in Executive Secretary's Report, September 18, 1964, HET.

13. Harmon G. Perry, "Taliaferro County's Racial Condition Is Grave Says Johnson," *Atlanta Daily World*, October 5, 1965; "2 Negroes Roughed-Up Wed. by Angry Whites in Crawfordville," *Atlanta Journal*, October 5, 1965, HET.

14. Richard B. Leggitt, "Negroes, Newsmen Attacked by Mob in Crawfordville," *Atlanta Daily World*, September 29, 1965; "Police Bar Bus to Taliaferro Negroes," *Atlanta Constitution*, September 29, 1965; Mike Barron, "King Aid Vows Wide Boycott," *Atlanta Constitution*, September 30, 1965.

15. Joe Brown, "Taliaferro Faces New Issues," *Atlanta Constitution*, October 19, 1965; Reg Murphy, "Negroes Reject All Concessions," *Atlanta Constitution*, October 11, 1965, HET.

16. Ed Rogers, "Taliaferro Closes Its Only White School as All Students Transfer Out of County," *Atlanta Constitution*, September 2, 1965.

17. Joe Brown, "Taliaferro Crisis May Go to Board," *Atlanta Constitution*, October 16, 1965. For discussion of African American children's participation in school protests, see Rebecca De Schweinitz, *If We Could Change the World: Young People and America's Long Struggle for Racial Equality* (Minneapolis: University of Minnesota Press, 2009). See also Vincent DeWayne Willis, "Rhetoric, Realism, and Response: *Brown*, White Opposition, and Black Youth Activism, 1954–1972," PhD diss., Emory University, 2013.

18. "Rev. King Planning Visit to Taliaferro Next Week," *Atlanta Constitution*, October 6, 1965; "2 Negroes Roughed-Up Wed. by Angry Whites in Crawfordville"; "Taliaferro Negroes Say No to Sanders," *Atlanta Journal*, October 7, 1965; Richard B. Legitt, "Dr. King Says He Is Stepping into Crawfordville's Crisis," *Atlanta Daily World*, October 7, 1965, HET.

19. Reg Murphy, "Governor Seeking Taliaferro Truce," *Atlanta Journal*, October 8, 1965; Walker Lundy, "Taliaferro Protest Aimed at Georgia's 'Token' Integration, Says Williams," *Atlanta Constitution*, October 10, 1965; Brown, "Taliaferro Faces New Issues," HET.

20. Author site visit, Martin Luther King Jr. childhood home.

21. Dr. Byas also described this relationship. Ulysses Byas, interview by author, November 15, 2001.

22. "Crawfordville Suit Before U.S. Panel," *Atlanta Journal*, October 12, 1965; Brown, "Taliaferro Faces New Issues"; Brown, "Taliaferro Crisis May Go to Board."

23. Reg Murphy, "Negroes Say Ruling Can't Calm Taliaferro," *Atlanta Constitution*, October 8, 1965, HET; "SCLC President Discusses Fate of Taliaferro," HET.

24. "Crawfordville Suit Before U.S. Panel"; Brown, "Taliaferro Faces New Issues"; Brown, "Taliaferro Crisis May Go to Board."

25. Reg Murphy, "Suit by Taliaferro Charges Rights Plot," *Atlanta Constitution*, October 8, 1965; Murphy, "Negros Say Ruling Can't Calm Taliaferro," HET.

26. "'Rights of Negroes Have Been Evaded' Says Circuit Judge," *Atlanta Daily World*, October 14, 1965; GTEA Resolutions, April 3–5, 1963, HET.

27. "Dr. Tate Blames Non-Tenure for Crawfordville," *Atlanta Daily World*, October 15, 1965, HET.

28. H.E. Tate, letter to D. Claude Purcell, May 16, 1963, HET. Among other requests, they wanted the salary equality that had never been resolved, even when the state established a statewide salary scale. Local boards had simply begun to offer supplements to white educators. They wanted to cease having to devote classroom time to fundraising to supply the needs in black schools; the state should have provided the buildings and resources the children needed. Dr. Tate went about the task with zeal. The state board appeared not to want his presence at their meetings. "I am writing to express my opinion concerning an incident of the May 21 meeting of the Board," Dr. Tate wrote to the State Board of Education office in June 1964. The meeting had been scheduled for 10:00 a.m. "At approximately five minutes before 9, I received a telephone call informing me that the time had been changed from 10 o'clock to 9 o'clock." It was "virtually impossible" for him to be on time. It was "embarrassing to be tardy at a meeting for which I had long planned to attend, especially since my tardiness was by no fault of my own." He hoped such a situation would not recur. H.E. Tate, letter to State Board of Education, June 1, 1964.

29. Dr. Tate reported to his NCOSTA colleagues that the state petitions—in a climate of open advocacy—were having some effect. The state school superintendent and the state board chair published their own pamphlet in September 1963, "Time for a New Break-Through in Education in Georgia," HET, which suggested some constitutional changes for Georgia—though none that directly railed against inequality.

30. Executive Secretary's report, September 18, 1964, HET.

31. Among the other GT&EA requests: "That no allocation of auxiliary personnel be left to local administrative discretionary influence, but that an objective formula for allocating certificated personnel be utilized, that this formula be the same as that specified in Senate Bill 180"—one auxiliary person for every two hundred pupils—and "that the present salary schedule already approved by the State Department of Education and the State board of Education be adhered to and implemented." See "GTEA Appeals to Governor for Educational influence," GTEA news release, January 13, 1965, HET.

32. Al Kuetner, "U.S. Court Halts Busing Crawfordville Pupils: Crawfordville School System Called Bankrupt," *Atlanta Daily World*, October 15, 1965; Joe Brown, "Federal Court Orders Purcell to Take Over Schools in Taliaferro," *Atlanta Constitution*, October 15, 1965; Walker Lundy, "Purcell Gets 3 Alternatives," *Atlanta Journal*, October 15, 1965; "Purcell to File School Plan," *Atlanta Constitution*, October 22, 1965; "Purcell Proposes Transfer of 88," *Atlanta Constitution*, October 26, 1965.

33. "Overrules Negro Attorneys: Federal Court Accepts Plan for Taliaferro School Desegregation," *Atlanta Daily World*, October 29, 1965; "Attys. Hollowell, Moore Object to Purcell's Plan," *Atlanta Daily World*, October 28, 1965; Achsah Posey, "Taliaferro Bus Segregation Charged," *Atlanta Constitution*, December 1, 1965. On his reasons, Purcell responded that interviews with parents of the eighty-eight original children indicated that forty-seven no longer wished transfers. Only seventeen students asked to integrate; the others chose Negro schools. "U.S. Judges Okay Taliaferro Plan," *Atlanta Journal*, October 28, 1965. A second report of the gym episode makes no reference to the restrictions; see Joe Brown, "Purcell's Bus Plan for Negro Pupils in Taliaferro Wins U.S. Court Okay," *Atlanta Constitution*, October 29, 1965.

34. The GT&EA document does not expressly point to the educator as white. However, in public statements supporting tenure, Dr. Tate characteristically applied the broader national reasons in explaining why tenure should be granted *all* teachers. This broad process helped him achieve the support of the white association for the bill. Since blacks uniformly supported President Kennedy and his policies, it is a stretch to imagine a classroom setting where black children would have applauded his death, thus leading me to characterize the incident as involving a white educator. For reference, see "Statement Given to Instruction Committee of the State Board of Education by a GTEA Tenure Committee," December 14, 1965, HET.

19: Justice Restructured in Dixie

1. Harmon G. Perry, "'Teachers Must Scale Hurdles' Says Educator," *Atlanta Daily World*, October 14, 1965.

2. "GTEA Asks State Education Officials to Enact Job Protection Law for Teachers," inclusive of H.E. Tate, letter to Claude Purcell, October 12, 1965. In his GT&EA report of actions to obtain tenure, Dr. Tate acknowledged that firing employees without formal charges might be acceptable in business but should not be utilized for employees whose salaries initiate from tax sources; the report also provides detailed descriptions of events occurring in each of the counties named. See "Report of Selected Cases Involving Subjective Personnel Practices Utilized in Dismissing Educators," n.d., HET.

3. "An Incomplete Account of the Dismissal of———" by———, various dates, HET. The names have been withheld to preserve anonymity.

4. Claude Purcell, letter to Superintendent, April 23, 1965; "Racial Discrimination in Payment of Local Salary Supplement Abhorred," press release, December 22, 1965, HET.

5. Donald L. Hollowell, letter to James S. Peters, Chairman, State Board of Education, October 28, 1965, HET.

6. "Statement to the State Board of Education, Meeting in Session April 21, 1965, by the Georgia Teachers and Education Association," HET.

7. GT&EA complaints about these and other matters are evident in a variety of documents. See, for example, "Statement to the State Board of Education, Meeting in Session April 21, 1965, by the Georgia Teachers and Education Association"; "Resolutions Passed by the Representative Assembly of the Georgia Teachers and Education Association at its 47th Annual Convention, April 7–9, 1965, Pertaining to Teacher Tenure and Retirement"; Memo from GTEA to Members of the State Board of Education, July 22, 1964 (which also reminds the board of its history of other objections to practices related to school buses, janitors and janitorial supplies, teaching supplies and equipment, textbooks, library books, and school facilities); H.E. Tate, letter to Dr. Purcell and each of the members of the State Board of Education, April 16, 1964; H.E. Tate, letter to State Association Executive Secretaries, May 26, 1965 (wants them also to push for more blacks in State Department); "GTEA Appeals to Governor for Educational Influence," GTEA news release, January 13, 1965, ALL HET.

8. For example, Senate Bill 180, designed to create tenure, suffered from amendments proposed that would make local systems have to finance salaries above $5,000. The amendment touched off a firestorm of letters and calls in the GT&EA office since smaller school systems would not be a position to defray the costs, thereby creating a loophole that would create a state tenure law but allow inequality to continue locally. See H.E. Tate, letter to Governor Sanders, January 13, 1965, HET.

9. Executive Secretary's Report Submitted to the Board of Directors at the September 18, 1964 Meeting, HET.

10. Robert H. Wyatt, letter to Mr. Haynes, May 6, 1964; Dan Byrd, "Special Report: Integration of Teacher Associations, May 28, 1964," HET.

11. Claude Purcell, letter to H.E. Tate (with "Have You Joined the NEA" attached), October 6, 1965; Executive Secretary's Report Submitted to the Board of Directors at the December 21, 1963 Meeting, 17, HET.

12. H.E. Tate, letter to Lois V. Rogers, February 21, 1964, HET.

13. Sam Hopkins, "Teachers Act to Bar a Negro," *Atlanta Constitution*, June 24, 1965, HET.

14. "The Relationship of the Georgia Education Association to Negro Education," *Herald*, February 1946, 7, HET.

15. The account of the second director is available in NEA, "Addresses and Proceedings of the Ninety-Fifth Annual Meeting Held at Philadelphia, Pennsylvania, June 30–July 5, 1957," Washington: NEA; Tate, interview by author (notes written on the address), ca. October 2002.

16. Mrs. Tate, interview by author, September 25, 2015; Hopkins, "Teachers Act to Bar a Negro."

17. Hopkins, "Teachers Act to Bar a Negro"; Memo from H.E. Tate to GTEA Members Attending the NEA Meeting, June 15, 1965, HET.

18. George M. Coleman, "GTEA Has a Problem in the Current Face of 'Change,'" *Atlanta World,* April 11, 1965.

19. Telefax of telegram from E.B. Palmer to Dr. Richard B. Kennan, May 26, 1965, HET. For the story of Caswell County, see Walker, *Their Highest Potential.*

20. Richard Barnes Kennan, letter to Mr. E.B. Palmer, June 3, 1965; HET. Samuel Ethridge would also work closely with the black educational associations and use his position to try to spur NEA to support black educators. Clarence A. Laws, Regional Director of the NAACP, letter to Mr. Samuel Ethridge, June 2, 1965, HET. For description of the inclusion of free legal funding in the NEA resolution, see author interviews with Dr. Ulysses Byas, December 1, 2000; (phone interview) March 3, 2008.

21. Dr. Tate, letter to Dr. Kennan, October 19, 1965, HET.

22. Dr. Kennan, letter to Dr. Tate, September 30, 1965, HET.

23. Reg Murphy, "Governor Seeking Taliaferro Truce," *Atlanta Journal*, October 8, 1965.

24. "NEA Holds Off Till Court Rules in Taliaferro," *Atlanta Constitution*, October 8, 1965.

25. Walker Lundy, "Purcell Gets 3 Alternatives," *Atlanta Journal*, October 15, 1964.

26. "NEA Holds Off Till Court Rules in Taliaferro"; Richard L. Morgan, letter to Dr. Tate, October 28, 1965, HET.

27. Richard L. Morgan, letter to Dr. Tate, October 28, 1965, HET.

28. "NEA Backs PTA in Fight of Rightist Groups," *Atlanta Daily World*, October 7, 1965, HET.

29. "Almost 217,000 Negro Students in Dixie's Desegregated Schools," *Atlanta Daily World*, October 7, 1965, HET.

30. "GTEA Asks Johnson to Stand Firm on Education Position," *Atlanta Daily World*, May 19, 1965, HET.

31. "Mass Integration Is On at Schools," *Atlanta Constitution*, August 30, 1965, HET.

32. "Pertinent Information About Georgia Schools," questionnaire, GTEA, completed form received September 28, 1965, HET.

33. Horace Tate, letter to "Dear Principal," September 10, 1965, HET.

34. Claude Purcell, letter to "Dear Superintendent," April 28, 1965 (with "Resolution" appended), HET.

35. GT&EA Press Release: "Racial Discrimination in Payment of Local Salary Supplement Abhorred," December 22, 1965, HET.

20: As Freedom Turns

1. Killacky and Conroy, "ESEA Twenty Years Later: A Talk with Francis C. Keppel and Harold Howe II," 4–7, 27–29.

2. Ibid., 4; "Mr. Howe Meets the Press," December 22, 1965, Box 1, Folder 2, HHP. Keppel's perspective on education is available in his *The Necessary Revolution in American Education* (New York: Harper & Row, 1966).

3. Killacky and Conroy, "ESEA Twenty Years Later: A Talk with Francis C. Keppel and Harold Howe II," 4–5.

4. "Mr. Howe Meets the Press."

5. "Recruiting for the New Partnership," Address Delivered at the Annual Breakfast Meeting of the Georgia Vocational Association at the Marriott Motor Hotel, Atlanta, GA, March 18, 1966, Box 1, Folder 13, HHP.

6. "Integration and Academic Quality," Address by Harold Howe II for the United Negro College Fund Symposium, Washington, DC, March 28, 1966; Harold Howe, "Tolstoy and Teachers," *NEA Journal* 55, no. 5 (May 1966), Box 1, Folder 25, HHP.

7. Alvin Tucker, letter to Harold Howe, April 9, 1966, Unnumbered Box: Anti-Howe Letters, 1966–68, HHP.

8. I categorize these letters by location to show the array of non-southern protest. Colorado: letter to Harold Howe, October 12, 1966; Louisiana: letter to Harold Howe, December 1, 1966; New York: letter to Harold Howe, February 8, 1967, Subseries B, Unnumbered Box: Anti-Howe Letters, 1966–68, HHP.

9. Philadelphia: letter to Harold Howe, April 3, 1967; Ohio: letter to Harold Howe, February 11, 1967; Hot Springs: letter to Harold Howe, February 1, 1967; St. Louis: letter to Harold Howe, February 8, 1967, Subseries B, Unnumbered Box: Anti-Howe Letters, 1966–68, HHP.

10. Hot Springs: letter to Harold Howe, February 1, 1967, Subseries B, Unnumbered Box: Anti-Howe Letters, 1966–68, HHP. Importantly, some of the letters supportive of Howe are also in this correspondence.

11. GTEA Resolutions, April 21, 1965, HET.

12. GTEA Resolution XXXII: Guidelines, April 21, 1965, HET.

13. One solution GT&EA sought was to have grants delivered directly into its account so that representatives of the minority group might administer the funds in the way that best would help solve the problems of the Negro children, most of whom were still segregated. Resolution XXX: Federal Grants to Education Associations, April 21, 1965, HET.

14. GTEA Resolution XXXIII: Abuse of Federal Grants; Presentation to the State Board of Education by the GTEA, April 20, 1966, HET.

15. J.K. Haynes, letter to Dr. Tate, March 4, 1966; J.K. Haynes, letter to Dr. Tate, May 2, 1966, HET.

16. NCOSTA Press Release, Atlanta, Georgia, ca. May 1966, HET. See Walker, *Hello Professor*, for a description of the network that allowed black educators to be aware of activities across the South.

17. NCOSTA Press Release, Atlanta, Georgia, ca. May 1966, HET.

18. *Herald*, convention issue 1966, front page; "GEA Head Seeks Ease on Guidelines," *Atlanta Journal and Constitution*, March 24, 1966, HET.

19. "GEA Head Seeks Ease on Guidelines"; Joe Brown, "GEA Admits Negroes by 4–1 Vote, Denounces New U.S. Guidelines: Says Integration Rules Curb Freedom of Choice," *Atlanta Constitution*, March 19, 1966, HET.

20. "GEA Head Seeks Ease on Guidelines" and "GEA Admits Negroes by 4–1 Vote, Denounces New U.S. Guidelines: Says Integration Rules Curb Freedom of Choice."

21. Ibid.

22. The full text of the speech is H.E. Tate, "Let Us See," Executive Secretary's Address to the Forty-Eighth Annual Convention of the Georgia Teachers and Education Association, Atlanta, GA, March 30, 1966. The reference to the GEA denial is available in Minutes of the Joint Committee-GTEA-GEA, June 15, 1966, in *Minutes: Joint Committee, Georgia Education Association, Georgia Teachers and Education Association* (bound volume), HET. GEA would deny it was trying to proselytize members a few months later—claiming it was simply removing racial restriction clauses in the local units.

23. H.E. Tate, "Let Us See." Tate did not mention in his groups of people who comprised the GTEA his recent formation of an "Educational Secretaries" group in Region XI. This group proposed to create study groups to learn federal guidelines, to meet regularly, and to stress the secretary's image relative to administrators, pupils, parents, lay persons in the community, and others. See Constance S. Pullen, "Educational Secretaries of Region Eleven," *Herald*, convention issue 1966, 27, HET.

24. Program of the Annual Convention, *Herald*, convention issue 1966, 26; "GEA Head Seeks Ease on Guidelines."

25. Georgia Teachers and Education Association, "Presentation of Pertinent Practices Relating to Resolution 12," June 20, 1966, HET.

26. George M. Coleman, "Dr. Brown, Dr. Tate Never Felt the GEA Would Act Fair," *Atlanta Daily World*, March 29, 1966, HET.

27. Coleman, "GTEA Has a Problem in the Current Face of 'Change.'" In the same editorial, this author also races the questions that permeated public understanding—that the Negro educator could also be inferior and unable to measure up to white standards when desegregation became an actual fact.

28. "GEA-GTEA Joint Exhibit Booth," 1966 NEA Convention: Expenses, HET.

21: Not a Two-Way Street

1. Board of Directors Minutes, May 21, 1966, HET.

2. "1964 NEA Resolution No. 12: Desegregation in the Public Schools," HET.

3. "NEA Has Long History in Civil Rights Move," *Atlanta Daily World*, February 16, 1967, HET. The release is from the NEA headquarters, Washington, DC.

4. *Honoring Our Legacy of Inclusion: The NEA-ATA Merger*, DVD, National Education Association, 2006; author site visit to Miami Convention Center in spring 2011.

5. For a visual of the history of ATA, see *Respect-Equality-Hope . . . The Journey of a People*, VHS, American Teachers Association, Washington, DC.

6. For a description of the influence of black education associations on NEA, see Carol F. Karpinski, *"A Visible Company of Professionals": African Americans and the National Education Association During the Civil Rights Movement* (New York: Peter Lang, 2008).

7. "NEA Issues Ultimatum on White-Negro Merger," *Atlanta Constitution*, June 29, 1966; "NEA Warns Teacher Units Must Merge," *Macon Telegraph*, June 29, 1966.

8. Horace Tate, interview by author, February 14, 2002; Board of Directors Minutes, April 2, 1966, HET.

9. "NEA Issues Ultimatum on White-Negro Merger"; "NEA Warns Teacher Units Must Merge"; "Presentation of Pertinent Practices Relating to Resolution 12 by the Georgia Teachers and Education Association," June 20, 1966, HET.

10. Minutes of the Board of Directors, March 6, 1965; "Presentation of Pertinent Practices Relating to Resolution 12 by the Georgia Teachers and Education Association," June 20, 1966.

11. Benjamin E. Mays, "Desegregate and Integrate TO WHAT END?," *Herald*, convention issue 1966, 13–15.

12. Horace Tate, "Will There Be a Merger? Decide for Yourselves," *Herald*, Winter 1964, 27.

13. Minutes of the Board of Directors, April 2, 1966, HET.

14. Minutes of the Board of Directors, March 6, 1965; 1966 Annual Meeting Report, HET.

15. "Summary of Actions of the Merger Committee," n.d. (ca. spring 1968), HET.

16. "Presentation of Pertinent Practices Relating to Resolution 12 by the Georgia Teachers and Education Association," June 20, 1966; "Suggested Principles That Should Be Considered in Negotiating Merger Agreements," October 3, 1966, HET.

17. Harmon G. Perry, "GEA and GTEA Laying Ground for Talks Concerning Merger," *Atlanta Daily World*, November 4, 1966, HET.

18. Minutes of the Board of Directors, March 6, 1965, HET.

19. Minutes of the Board of Directors, March 18, 1967, HET. GT&EA was filing suit also in Fitzgerald. See Minutes of the Board of Directors, December 10–11, 1965 [incorrectly dated 1966]; Minutes of the Board of Directors, May 21, 1966, HET.

20. Minutes of the Board of Directors, September 16, 1966, HET.

21. Minutes of the Board of Directors, April 2, 1966; March 18, 1967, HET.

22. Minutes of the Board of Directors, May 21, 1966; December 10–11, 1965 [incorrectly dated 1966], HET.

23. Minutes of the Board of Directors, March 6, 1965, HET.

24. Minutes of the Joint Committee of the GEA and GTEA, December 20, 1966, HET.

25. Ibid.

26. Minutes of the Board of Directors, December 16, 1966, HET.

27. Ibid.

28. W.E. Solomon to NCOSTA Presidents and Executive Secretaries, August 31, 1966, HET.

29. Minutes of the Joint Committee, February 17, 1967, HET.

30. Services included teacher welfare, legislative program, professional services, working conditions, recruitment and placement services, public relations, development of educational policy, and organizational services. See "Report of Sub-Committee on Services That Should be Rendered by the New Organization," appended to the Minutes of the Joint Committee of the GEA and GTEA, January 12, 1967, HET.

31. Joe L. Reed, letter to J.K. Haynes, December 6, 1966, HET.

32. J.K. Haynes, letter to Dr. Davis, March 7, 1966, HET.

33. Joe L. Reed, letter to J.K. Haynes, December 6, 1966; C.T. Vivian, interview by author, June 8, 2015.

34. Vernon McDaniel, letter to NCOSTA Members, June 10, 1966; Financial Statement from NCOSTA Projects to GTEA, June 10, 1966; Vernon McDaniel, letter to Dr. Tate, June 17, 1966; J.K. Haynes, letter to Dr. Davis, March 7, 1966, HET.

35. Minutes of NCOSTA's Special Committee, August 26–27, 1966, HET.

36. J.K. Haynes, letter to NCOSTA Member, January 18, 1967; NCOSTA Meeting Agenda, January 21, 1967; Memo from John Davis to J.K. Haynes and NCOSTA Members, January 19, 1967. Samuel Ethridge of NEA was also in contact with John Davis and attempted to gain advantages for Negro teachers when he could. See John W. Davis, letter to Samuel B. Ethridge, January 17, 1967. Author interview with Horace Tate on February 14, 2002, during the NCOSTA board meeting tape review. On teacher associations: "Welcome GTEA Members," *Atlanta Voice*, April 2, 1967, HET.

37. John W. Davis, letter to J.K. Haynes, March 9, 1966, HET.

38. J.K. Haynes, letter to Dr. Tate, August 18, 1966; John W. Davis, letter to Mr. Haynes, August 15, 1966; Meeting of NCOSTA's Special Committee, August 26–27, 1966, HET.

39. For the ongoing nature, see Executive Secretary's Report submitted to the Board of Directors, May 16, 1964. GT&EA members wanted split summer sessions for black children abolished; they wanted blacks employed in strategic positions in the State Department; they wanted "unfair administrators" to deal "fairly and justly" with black teachers and principals and, if they could not, to have those administrators removed. Direct appeal continued into 1967 with the same items addressed. See Press Release (inclusive of letter to Mr. Jack P. Nix), January 6, 1966; "GTEA Executive Urges Governor, Lawmaker to Up Teachers' Pay," *Atlanta World*, February 17, 1967; Augustus

Hill, letter to Dr. Tate, July 19, 1966; H.E. Tate, letter to Mr. Eberhardt, June 17, 1966; H.E. Tate, letter to Dr. Aderhold, June 17, 1966; H.E. Tate, letter to Dr. Simpson, June 17, 1966; Press Release: Statement by the Georgia Teachers and Education Association—Presented at a News Conference, January 7, 1966, HET.

40. GTEA News Release: "The Governor Has Just Given a $500 Raise to all Teachers," July 28, 1966, HET. Mrs. Tate, interview by author, October 7, 2017.

41. Ulysses Byas, interview by author, March 3, 2008.

22: We Hold These Truths

1. "Welcome GTEA Members," *Atlanta Voice*, April 2, 1967; Executive Secretary's Report, March 18, 1967.

2. 49th Convention, March 31, 1967, GTEA Audio File, HET. For examples of the beliefs of black educators and their statements in public settings, see Leland Stanford Cozart, *A History of the Association of College and Secondary Schools, 1934–1965* (Charlotte, NC: Heritage Printers, 1967), 92–153.

3. Minutes of the Board of Directors, March 18, 1967; "Welcome GTEA Members"; 49th Convention, March 31, 1967, GTEA Audio File, HET. I have no evidence that they nodded. However, a black cultural tradition is to nod in affirmation, and the audio file depicts verbal assent.

4. H.E. Tate, letter to Mr. Nix, March 28, 1968, HET.

5. H.E. Tate, letter to Dr. Shaw, February 16, 1967; Statement by Dr. H.E. Tate for Immediate Release, February 17, 1967, HET.

6. GTEA Press Release, February 17, 1967; "GTEA President Hawes Says Organization Has Long Journey," *Atlanta World*, April 1, 1967, HET.

7. C.T. Vivian, interview by author, June 8, 2015.

8. 49th Convention, March 31, 1967, GTEA Audio File, HET.

9. H.E. Tate, letter to U.S. Department of Health, Education, and Welfare, January 12, 1967, HET.

10. GTEA News Release, May 24, 1968; "Questionnaire" [stack of filled-out forms with reports from across the regions, most dated May 6, 1967], HET.

11. Minutes of the Board of Directors, March 18, 1967, HET.

12. Dr. King's address was broadcast by all the major radio stations. A summary of the speech is also provided in "GTEA President Hawes Says Organization Has Long Journey," *Atlanta World*, April 1, 1967, HET.

13. Schedule for meeting: Executive Secretary's Report, May 13, 1967; 49th Convention, March 31, 1967, GTEA Audio File, HET.

14. James Hawes, memo to Principals, Curriculum Directors, Unit Presidents, Teachers and Other Educators Affiliated with the Georgia Teachers and Education Association, April 21, 1967; GTEA News Release, May 24, 1968, HET.

15. Released by the Board of Directors, GTEA, May 13, 1967; GTEA News Release, May 24, 1968; GTEA News Release, May 28, 1967, HET.

23: Fighting Back

1. Minutes of the GTEA Board of Directors, May 13, 1967, HET. The chronology of this chapter follows loosely the order of the meeting. To avoid redundancy, I linked some conversations that occurred in different locations in the original minutes. I have also imported minutes of other meetings as necessary for elaboration of ideas. Whenever this is done in the subsequent discussion, an additional endnote is added.

2. Minutes of the Special Meeting, Board of Directors, May 27, 1967.

3. Minutes of the Special Meeting–Members of the Georgia Teachers and Education Association, Macon, Georgia, May 6, 1967.

4. Minutes of the Special Meeting, Board of Directors, May 27, 1967.

5. Ibid.

6. Minutes of the Special Meeting–Members of the Georgia Teachers and Education Association, Macon, Georgia, May 6, 1967.

7. Special Meeting of the Board of Directors, May 27, 1967.

8. "NAACP Endorses Decentralized School System," *Atlanta Daily World*, December 23, 1967; Jean Fairfax, letter to Mr. Howe, September 26, 1966.

9. H.E. Tate, letter to Dr. Applegate, May 28, 1967.

10. "GTEA Urges Enforcement of School Guidelines," *Atlanta World*, May 16, 1967.

11. "General Aid a Subterfuge to Eliminating Aid to Title I," *Herald*, Winter 1967, HET.

12. NCOSTA members held meetings with Commissioner Howe, directed a White House conference, and appeared before the Senate Judiciary Committee. The organization asserted strongly that the federal government could not abdicate the need to provide leadership in the integration process. See J.K. Haynes, letter to "Dear Co-Worker," July 7, 1966; D. Steven Mitchell, letter to J.K. Haynes, July 1, 1966; Statement of J.K. Haynes, President of the National Council of State Teachers Associations, before the Constitutional Rights Subcommittee of the Senate Judiciary Committee in support of the Civil Rights Act of 1964 (S. 3296), July 19, 1966. For Picott, executive director of the Virginia black teachers association, directing a conference upon the invitation of President Johnson and Commissioner Howe, see J.K. Haynes, letter to Dr. Tate, August 4, 1966, HET.

13. Congressional Record—House, September 30, 1966, Subseries B: Unnumbered Box, Congressional Record Clippings, HHP.

14. Killacky and Conroy, "ESEA Twenty Years Later: A Talk with Francis C. Keppel and Harold Howe II," 4.

15. Ibid., 28.

16. Minutes of the Board of Directors, May 21, 1965, HET. For Howe overtures to GEA, see "Statement for the Georgia Education Journal (No. 1), 1967 January," Series I, Box 2, F30, HHP.

17. Carter, *The Music Has Gone Out of the Movement.*

18. 50th Convention, GTEA Audio File, HET.

19. Adam Serwer, "Lyndon Johnson Was a Civil Rights Hero. But Also a Racist," MSNBC, April 12, 2014.

20. Killacky and Conroy, "ESEA Twenty Years Later: A Talk with Francis C. Keppel and Harold Howe II," 28; Wolfgang Saxon, "Harold Howe, 84, Fighter Against Segregated Schools," *New York Times*, December 3, 2002.

21. Francis Keppel, letter to Harold Howe, May 11, 1967, Subseries B: Unnumbered Box, Correspondence, HHP.

22. Minutes of the Board of Directors, September 15, 1967, HET.

24: A Charge to Keep I Have

1. "Report of the Credentials Committee," Reports of Committees and Commissions of the 50th Annual Meeting, April 3–5, 1968, HET.

2. 50th Convention, GTEA Audio File, HET.

3. Ibid.; "Integration Used as a Guise to Oust Negro Principals," GTEA Press Release, March 28, 1968, HET.

4. Report of the Committees and Commissions of the 50th Annual Meeting, April 3–5, 1968, HET.

5. Ibid.; Executive Secretary's Report Submitted to the Board of Directors, March 2, 1968, HET.

6. Executive Secretary's Report Submitted to the board of Directors, March 2, 1968, HET.

7. H.E. Tate, interview by author, November 10, 2000.

8. Minutes of the 50th Annual Convention, April 3–5, 1968, in 51st Annual Meeting of the Georgia Teachers and Education Association: Reports of Committees and Commissions, March 26–28, 1969, HET. The precision of black choral groups' performances is evident on the audio files of varied GTEA meetings.

9. When Dr. Tate was vice president, Mr. Cousins had asked to speak with him, Mr. Homer Edwards, and Mr. Wilkinson at an unusual meeting location, the Butler Street YMCA, on a Sunday afternoon. Upon arrival, Mr. Cousins said, "Gentlemen, I have something to put before you. But I have to have your permission . . . I have been thinking of ways we can save the black principal." Then he told them his plan. "I have come up with a resolution that I have written that I am going to take to the State Board, if you agree with it." The resolution was a statement saying that, when integration came about, high schools would be headed by white principals and elementary schools could be headed by black principals. Both Mr. Wilkerson and Mr. Edwards agreed with Mr. Cousins as a preemptive way to save black leadership. "When he got to me, I said, 'Mr. Cousins, read the resolution again please.'" He read it, and Vice President Tate responded: "While I don't think I know more than anyone in here—I may know the

least—and while I may not have the experience these other principals have, and while I may sometimes be called radical, I think you are really asking me, Mr. Cousins, to say to people everywhere that I don't think I'm educated enough, good enough, have enough sense to be a principal of a high school but I do have enough to be principal of an elementary school. . . . I appreciate what you are doing to try to save black principals. But I can't agree. I can't say, because someone is white, they can be principal of a high school and I will be principal of an elementary school." In response to the Tate statement, Mr. Cousins said he wanted unanimous consent before taking the idea to the State Board. Without it, he withdrew his planned resolution. Horace Tate, interview by author, February 14, 2002.

10. Horace Tate, interview by author, May 22, 2002.

11. At the opening session the night before when Dr. Tate recounted some of these ideas, he also talked about GTEA's influence on higher education. Remembering, though not naming, Mr. Hunt's feverish backroom efforts at Fort Valley in the week before his death to ensure the institution's continuation by having the state assume financial responsibility, Dr. Tate spoke of the struggles in the school that gave him a start. "It was up to us to work out agreements for private two-year colleges that were constructed and equipped by the perseverance, blood, sweat, and tears of our great grandparents, to be completely deeded to the state of Georgia debt free so we could attend a four-year college at state expense." 50th Convention, GTEA Audio File, HET.

12. Valocia Tate Marsh, interview by author, October 6, 2017.

13. Ulysses Byas reports GTEA having some unnamed role in the garbage workers' strike and contends that GTEA would have had a presence in Memphis if it were not for the annual meeting. Ulysses Byas, interview by author, March 3, 2008.

14. 50th Annual Convention Program; Minutes of the 50th Annual Convention, April 3–5, 1968, in 51st Annual Meeting of the Georgia Teachers and Education Association: Reports of Committees and Commissions, March 26–28, 1969, HET.

15. The History Committee Report, Report of the Committees and Commissions of the 50th Annual Meeting, April 3–5, 1968: 15, HET. The events in North Carolina are an author memory of the events at her own school.

16. Mr. Wright also was a delegate to the Republican National Convention, the highest black officer during World War I, an acquaintance of U.S. presidents, and a scholar who traveled to Europe to document black soldiers in the world war. He read French and German nightly from a Bible he kept beside his bed, and he retired from education to move to Philadelphia. There he attended the University of Pennsylvania business school and eventually became a very successful banker, finally putting into practice the economic lessons he said he had tried to teach his students. For details on the life of Richard Wright, see Presidential Papers, File Folder: Richard Wright, AUC. See also Elizabeth Haynes, *Unsung Heroes: The Black Boy of Atlanta:*

Negroes in Domestic Service in the United States (New York: G.K. Hall, 1997), 281–535.

17. "Growing and Glowing in the Sun," A Narrative Presentation of the Historical Accounting of the Georgia Teachers and Education Association at the Closing Session of the Golden Anniversary Year Program, April 5, 1968, HET.

18. 50th Convention, GTEA Audio File, HET.

19. Ibid.; "March to Georgia State Capital in Tribute to Dr. Martin Luther King, Jr.," *Herald*, Spring 1968, 36, HET.

20. Horace Tate, "Honoring Martin Luther King, Jr.," Camilla, Georgia, Citizens Group, April 4, 1969. The march to the capital was reported in the journal of another black education organization but no text remains. I have used other memories to reveal his orientation toward Dr. King and suggest the type of remarks possible. Virginia Tate, interviews by author, September 18, 2012, and October 6, 2017.

21. No audio record exists of the event at the capitol. The sentiment attributed to teachers is from Helen Johnson, "The King Is Dead! Long Live the King!," *Herald*, Spring 1968, 26, HET.

25: Justice Betrayed

1. Governor's Conference, GTEA Audio File, HET.

2. Vivian R. Bowser, letter to John Davis, May 21, 1968 [copied to Dr. Tate—information from Dr. Davis, May 31, 1968], HET; Board of Directors Meeting, May 4, 1968, GTEA Audio File, May 4, 1968.

3. Additional details may be found in Dwana Waugh, "'The Issue Is the Control of Public Schools': The Politics of Desegregation in Prince Edward County, Virginia," *Southern Cultures* 18, no. 3 (Fall 2012): 76–94.

4. Picott, *History of the Virginia Teachers Association*, 222–27.

5. The William Carr papers of the NEA demonstrate repeatedly his unwillingness to champion race. Although he was very concerned about international affairs and about getting federal money for public education, as late as 1960 he applauded school board members who suffered from "public denunciation, often cruel and vindictive." William Carr, *Collecting My Thoughts* (Phi Delta Kappa Educational Foundation, 1980); Executive Office, William G. Carr Papers, Folder 1060, NEA.

6. Board of Directors Meeting, May 4, 1968, GTEA Audio File, HET. Dr. Tate repeated on several occasions the story of NEA's denial of his seat. Tate, interviews by author May 22, 2002, and December 7, 2001. He also told it to Elaine Bolton in a class paper for Dr. Wayne Urban. The copy of the paper in his files reflects his detailed correction of people and events.

7. "Integration Used as Guise to Oust Negro Principals," GTEA Press Release, March 28, 1968.

8. Virginia Tate, interview by author, February 8, 2015. Ulysses Byas names Bolden, King, and Williams as GTEA contacts.

9. Minutes of the Board of Directors Meeting, May 10, 1969; "Ultimatum Is Issued by Negro Teachers: State Board Given 2 Weeks to Act on Group's Complaints," *Atlanta Constitution*, June 20, 1968, HET.

10. Memo from E.B. Palmer to NCOSTA, April 26, 1968; Memo from H.E. Tate to Past and Present Executive Officers of NCOSTA, April 29, 1968, HET.

11. Ulysses Byas, interview by author, March 3, 2008.

12. Detailed description of community protest in North Carolina is available in David S. Cecelski, *Along Freedom Road: Hyde County, North Carolina and the Fate of Black Schools in the South* (Chapel Hill: University of North Carolina Press, 1994).

13. Virginia Tate notes, October 21, 2013; Ulysses Byas, interview by author, March 3, 2008.

14. "GT&EA Helps Pike County Parents Win Their Point," *GT&EA Reporter* 1, no. 1 (December 1968); GT&EA Report: The Pike County Case, August 21–September 11, 1968, HET; Ulysess Byas, interview by author, March 3, 2008. Zebulon was located in Pike County in middle-west Georgia, a rural community of family farms and two or three industries. Of the 159 counties in Georgia, Pike was 132nd in population with roughly 55 percent of the population white and the other 45 percent black. For earlier history on the role of black newspapers, see William G. Jordan, *Black Newspapers and America's War for Democracy, 1914–1920* (Chapel Hill: University of North Carolina Press, 2001).

15. "Dr. Tate Asks Layman's Help," *Atlanta Journal*, October 10, 1968; Region IV Meeting, October 10, 1968, GTEA Audio File, HET.

16. Memo from C.K.H. to Jack Greenberg, June 3, 1968; John W. Davis, letter to H.E. Tate, June 24, 1968. For examples of Virginia desegregation, see Matthew D. Lassiter, *The Moderates' Dilemma: Massive Resistance to School Desegregation in Virginia* (Charlottesville: University of Virginia Press, 1998). See also Waugh, "'The Issue Is the Control of Public Schools': The Politics of Desegregation in Prince Edward County, Virginia," 76–94.

17. See, for example, "Dr. Tate Speaks Again on Displacement of Teachers," *Atlanta World*, June 25, 1968; "Newly Elected Superintendents Hear Dr. Horace E. Tate," *Atlanta Voice*, December 22, 1968, HET.

18. "GTEA Probes Negro Teacher Transfer, Threatens Lawsuit," *Athens Banner-Herald*, December 3, 1967, HET.

19. Encyclopedia Virginia (www.encyclopediavirginia.org/Green_Charles_C_et_al_v_County_School_Board_of_New_Kent_County_Virginia) provides the detail that the plaintiff was a teacher.

20. Oliver Hill, interview by author, July 19, 2003; J.K. Haynes, letter to Dr. Davis, July 29, 1969, HET.

21. E.B. Palmer, memo to NCOSTA, April 26, 1968; Ulysses Byas, letter to J.K. Haynes, August 6, 1968; H.E. Tate, memo to Past and Present Executive Officers of NCOSTA, April 29, 1968, HET.

22. "NAACP Accepts Plan on Schools in Walton," *Atlanta World*, August 2, 1968, HET.

23. In a study done only three years earlier, GT&EA found evidence that many systems were still paying Negro employees less than white employees. GT&EA had confronted the State Board of Education with these findings and been told by the state attorney that such inequalities were illegal "even by Georgia law." GT&EA said it wanted local boards to stop discriminatory salary practices based on race. They also objected to systems closing to favor GEA meetings but not closing for GT&EA meetings, especially since, in the past, school systems had closed for both meetings. "Resume on Some Major Issues of Grave Concern to Members of the Georgia Teachers and Education Association," September 15, 1968, HET. The North Carolina example is from Oakwood Elementary School in Caswell County and reflects my remembered experiences as a student. I was also the child who naively asked the principal to support the one hundredth anniversary at my church and was reprimanded by my mother, a black teacher at the school.

24. Al Kuttner, "Dr. Martin L. King Cuts Short European Trip; Racial Crisis," *Atlanta Daily World*, October 26, 1965; Walker Lundy, "Negroes Hold Short Sing-In," *Atlanta Journal*, October 12, 1965. Sara Parsons briefly describes the Atlanta school board while she and Dr. Tate served. See Sara Parsons, *From Southern Wrongs to Civil Rights: The Memoir of a White Civil Rights Activist* (Tuscaloosa: University of Alabama Press, 2000), 127. Although litigation awarded Dr. Tate his seat, his selection to the Board of Education was contested. See "Tate Seat Upheld by High Court," *Atlanta Constitution*, January 6, 1967; Horace Tate, interview by author, February 14, 2002. For mayoral campaign speech, see "Atlanta Mayoral Campaign Speech," HET. For mayoral campaign literature, see pamphlet "For Mayor: I Am H.E. Tate," October 7, 1969, HET.

25. Virginia Tate written notes, July 22, 2005.

26. Virginia Tate, interview by author, February 21, 2007.

27. GTEA: For Immediate Release, May 13, 1967, HET.

28. Robert S. Morley sought to remove Tate from the school board by arguing that he had qualified as a candidate without paying an entrance fee. The Supreme Court of Georgia ruled that the entrance fee was not necessary. "In a unanimous decision the tribunal said Tate was elected by a majority vote in a general election and it is firmly established in the law that attacks on irregularities must be made before the election." "Tate Seat Upheld by High Court." For contentions on the School Board, see Tate files of School Board meetings.

29. Executive secretary reports and minutes throughout this period indicate the interest of the GT&EA board in a variety of issues facing blacks in Georgia. They discuss issues related to economics and retirement, including seeking money to help support affordable housing. Horacena Tate, interview with author, March 6, 2008.

30. Atlanta Mayoral Campaign Speech; "For Mayor: I Am H.E. Tate," campaign brochure; H.E. Tate to "Citizens Interested in Good Government," September 25, 1969; "Will Atlantans Elect Black Mayor in 1969?" *Atlanta Journal and Constitution*, April 23, 1969, HET.

31. Minutes of the Board of Directors, May 10, 1969, HET. On the contest for Tate's vacated school board seat, see "Dr. B.E. Mays Seeks a Seat on School Board," *Atlanta Daily World*, August 15, 1969; "Dr. Middleton Runs for Seat on Board," *Atlanta Daily World*, August 21, 1969; "Rev. C.W. Jackson Announces for Dr. Tate's Board Seat," *Atlanta Inquirer*, June 26, 1969; "School Seat Sought by Zion Pastor," *Atlanta Journal*, June 28, 1969; "3 Enter Race for School Post," *Atlanta Constitution*, July 15, 1969. For information on Tate mayoral race, see "Sen. Johnson Urges Negro Vote to Select a Candidate for Mayor," *Atlanta Journal and Constitution*, April 22, 1969, HET. On "hanky panky": Virginia Tate, interview by author, April 4, 2010. Dr. Tate had become increasingly active in urging black educators to vote for candidates who would serve their interests and provide car pools for others, if necessary. His comments extended to presidential campaigns and gubernatorial campaigns, particularly Jimmy Carter. See Press Release from H.E. Tate, November 1, 1968, HET.

32. On Tate response to election, Virginia Tate, interview by author, May 6, 2017; Ulysses Byas, interview with author, n.d.

33. Ulysses Byas, interview by author, June 3, 2003.

34. Executive Secretary's Report, submitted to the Board of Directors at the March 8, 1969, Meeting; Horace Tate, "Roadblocks to Equal and Adequate Educational Opportunities: A Panel Presentation Made to the NEA Summit Conference on Education, January 24–27, 1969." For Dr. Tate's version of differences between educators and the SCLC, see "Dr. Tate's Speech #126a and #126b," Audio Files, HET.

35. "Justice Denied in County: GT&EA to Support Appeal," *GT&EA Reporter* 2, no. 1 (September 1969): 1; H.E. Tate, letter to Mrs. Scott, November 6, 1969; Active Black Citizens of Haralson County, "An Informational Mass Meeting," May 21, 1969.

36. H.E. Tate, GTEA Speech, circa 1969; Minutes of the Board of Directors, May 10, 1969.

37. Executive Secretary's Report submitted to the Board of Directors at the May 9–10, 1969 Meeting; H.E. Tate, letter to Mrs. Myles, May 7, 1969; H.E. Tate, letter to Dr. Richardson, March 11, 1969; H.E. Tate, letter to Attorney Hollowell, March 11, 1969; H.E. Tate, letter to Dr. Benjamin Mays, March 11, 1969, HET.

38. Board Meeting Minutes, March 2, 1968; "Resume on Some Major Issues of Grave Concern to Members of the Georgia Teachers and Education Association," September 15, 1968. Dr. Tate explicitly establishes the connection between black leadership and black pupils in the audio files. See, for example, W. Mitchell, CME Church, 1970, GTEA Audio Files. It is not explicit in the document for superintendents.

39. Dr. Tate recalled that about ten to twelve whites and three blacks were part of a meeting at the State Department. A member of the group, Jim Williams, suggested they pause to get lunch and return at one-thirty. This time period was not sufficient for the black committee members to go all the way to the black-owned Paschal's and return. Dr. Tate noted others going upstairs and said, "Let's go eat there." At the door, a man standing there said they needed a pass to come in; Dr. Tate said he did not hear him ask other people for a pass. The man said "they knew somebody," and Dr. Tate responded: "Well I don't know anybody, but we plan to eat." When the man asked him to step aside so he could call the manager, Dr. Tate announced he was not going to step aside. People behind the three went downstairs and came up on the other side. Some stayed behind. Word went to the governor that they were standing there, and finally they were told they could enter as members of the Teachers' Retirement Board of Trustees. Although Dr. Tate recognized others' claims to having integrated the cafeteria downtown, he says this event preceded many others. Horace Tate interview by author, n.d.

40. U.S. Passport, Mrs. Virginia Tate; "Come with Me: GT&EA Golden Anniversary European Study Tour," *Herald* XXXIV, no. 3 (Spring 1968), 28.

41. "GT&EA Golden Anniversary European Study Tour"; U.S. Passport, Mrs. Virginia Tate; Mrs. Virginia Tate, interview with author, October 2, 2017.

26: A Second-Class Integration It Is

1. NCEHR—Proposed Desegregation Resolution, July 1, 1969. Dr. Tate's handwritten notes are on the back of this resolution, which suggests it may have been part of the historic maneuvering of black delegates from across the southern states to gain from NEA the equality of protection they desired.

2. "GEA Leaders Urge Approval of Merger," *Atlanta Journal-Constitution*, April 24, 1969, HET.

3. "Suggestive Topics for Discussion Relative to Merging of State Education Associations in Georgia," GTEA publication, circa 1969, HET.

4. Harmon Perry, "New GTEA Chief Tackles Big Spot: Quality Education, Teacher Welfare Still Group's Goal, Hicks Vows," *Atlanta Journal*, April 10, 1968.

5. "Injustice of 12 Yrs. Corrected: Dr. Horace Tate Seated on NEA Board of Directors," *GT&EA Reporter* 2, no. 1 (September 1969): 1; "GEA Leaders Urge Approval of Merger."

6. No comparable materials are available for Dr. Hodges. Biographical Data, Executive Secretary of Georgia Association of Educators, 1970; Biographical Sketch of Dr. Horace Edward Tate prepared for Dr. Zack Henderson, Dr. R.J. Martin, Dr. Theodore Sizer, December 12, 1969, HET.

7. Report of the Sub-committee, Joint Committee on Merger, March 5, 1969, Appendix I, Joint Salary Committee Meeting and Joint Board Meeting, February 21, 1970.

8. "Not Pushing Tate, GTEA Leaders Say," *Atlanta Constitution*, June 16, 1967.

9. Executive Secretary's Report Submitted to Board of Directors at the September 15, 1967 Meeting; "Criteria for Evaluating Merger Plans and Compliance with Resolution 12," in Executive Secretary's Report submitted to the Board of Directors at the December 14, 1968 meeting. After complying with the demands of black educators to have a "protective responsibility as well as a supporting responsibility" in affiliate mergers in 1967, NEA had provided "Criteria for Evaluating Merger Plans and Compliance with Resolution 12" in 1968 in order to assist its affiliates in forming "fair and workable organizations for the achievement of a strong united teaching profession." After meeting at the Air Host Inn in Atlanta with non-merged southern affiliates, NEA agreed that the spirit of Resolution 12 required the termination of both previous organizations; procedures for resolving disputes; maintenance of rights for the minority group to hold office and participate in all activities; plans for merger that eliminated the "proselyting of members of each association," especially at the local level, until mergers were accomplished; maintaining black and white personnel in the new organization; and creating an objective procedure for selecting the executive secretary.

10. For NEA perspective on Georgia merger events, see Allan M. West, *The National Education Association: The Power Base for Education* (New York: Free Press, 1980), 138–41.

11. Biographical Sketch of Dr. Horace Edward Tate prepared for Dr. Zack Henderson, Dr. R.J. Martin, Dr. Theodore Sizer, December 12, 1969, HET.

12. Press Release from GEA and GT&EA, December 13, 1969; Theodore R. Sizer, letter to Board of Directors, GTEA, December 12, 1969; Horace and Virginia Tate, interview by author, n.d. In conversation with the author (New York, n.d.), Dr. Sizer confirmed that he believed Hodges to be the better candidate in 1969.

13. "Georgia Teachers and Education Association Proposed Merger Plan," Ballot; H.E. Tate, letter to Delegates, December 3, 1969, HET.

14. Harmon Perry, "New GTEA Chief Tackles Big Spot: Quality Education, Teacher Welfare Still Group's Goal, Hicks Vows," *Atlanta Journal,* April 10, 1968; H.E. Tate, letter to GT&EA Principals, January 15, 1970, HET.

15. Minutes of the 52nd Annual Convention; "Teacher of the Year Banquet" Program, March 6, 1970, HET.

16. In the minutes, he says "very, very evil." This apparently revised text contains the record of the convention, including his speech. See "Georgia Teachers and Education Association 52nd Annual Convention," Folder of Dr. H.E. Tate, HET. General scholars have captured the multiplying of difficulties confronting black schools in communities during desegregation. See, for example, Robert Crain, *The Politics of School Desegregation* (New York: Anchor Books, 1969); Anna Victoria Wilson and William E. Segall, *Oh, Do I Remember!: Experiences of Teachers During the Desegregation of Austin's Schools, 1964–1971* (Albany: SUNY Press, 2001); Orlando Patterson, *The Ordeal of Integration Progress and Resentment in America's "Racial" Crisis* (Washington, DC:

Civitas/Counterpoint, 1997); Curtis Morris and Vivian Morris, *The Price They Paid: Desegregation in an African American Community* (New York: Teachers College Press, 2002); Nancy St. John, *School Desegregation Outcomes for Children* (New York: Wiley, 1975); Peter Irons, *Jim Crow's Children: The Broken Promise of the* Brown *Decision* (New York: Penguin, 2002). For a theoretical interpretation of the implementation of the *Brown* decision, see Derrick Bell, *Silent Covenants:* Brown v. Board of Education *and the Unfulfilled Hopes for Racial Reform* (New York: Oxford University Press, 2004).

17. C. F. Cook, "The Problem of the Colored Child," May 4, 1914, and G.R. Walker, "The Color Problems of Baltimore," 1914, Part I, B1, F4, NAACP Collection.

18. "Confusion and Anxiety Mount in Delay of Burke Integration," *Atlanta Constitution*, February 3, 1970.

19. Minutes of the 52nd Annual Convention. For details on merger disputes and GEA pushback, see Carl V. Hodges, letter to Members of the GEA Governing Board, April 7, 1970; Carl V. Hodges, letter to Dr. Tate, January 5, 1970; H.E. Tate, letter to Dr. Hodges, January 14, 1970.

20. ———to Dr. Tate, May 7, 1970; H.E. Tate to———, May 11, 1970;———to Dr. Tate, April 13, 1970, HET. The names have been withheld to preserve anonymity.

21. 52nd Annual Convention, GTEA Audio File, HET.

22. E.B. Palmer, letter to Executive Secretary of NCOSTA, April 1, 1970.

23. Bob Hart, "6 Governors Discuss Busing," *Atlanta Constitution,* February 25, 1970; Fred Heller, "Panel Okays Bill on Busing: Maddox Plan Would Outlaw Transfer for Race Balance," *Atlanta Constitution*, February 18, 1970; "Nixon Supports Same Integration for All, No Busing: He'd Treat North and South Alike," n.p., n.d. (ca. spring 1970); GTEA for Immediate Release, February 19, 1970; Boyd Bosma, letter to Horace Tate, March 10, 1970.

24. ———to Mr. Tate, February 19, 1970. Dr. Tate also maintained a file cabinet of complaints, the details of which cases are not discussed to preserve confidentiality. "Pres. Proposes New Agency to Probe Schools Failures," *Atlanta World*, March 5, 1970; "Dixie Wins Battles on Busing, Guidelines," *Atlanta Constitution*, February 20, 1970, HET.

25. Virginia Tate, interview by author, February 15, 2017.

27: Nobody but a Fool

1. Minutes of the 52nd Annual Convention; Charlie Hicks, "President's Address," April 1–3, 1970, HET.

2. Minutes of the 52nd Annual Convention; 52nd Annual Convention, GTEA Audio File, HET; Horace Tate, interview by author, November 10, 2000.

3. Rachel L. Swarns, Darcy Eveleigh, and Damien Cave, "Unpublished Black History," www.nytimes.com/interactive/projects/cp/national/unpublished-black-history/dr-martin-luther-king-jr-portrait-1963; "Powell, Adam Clayton, Jr.," United States

House of Representatives History, Art & Archives, http://history.house.gov/People/Detail/19872.

4. "Federal Aid to Education," *Herald*, February 1950: 5; Minutes of the 52nd Annual Convention; 52nd Annual Convention, GTEA Audio File, HET. Another perspective on GEA and GT&EA merger is available in West, *The National Education Association*, 139–40.

5. Libby Koontz was the first black NEA president. However, she was not an employee. See Urban, *Gender, Race, and the National Education Association*, 226; Gilmore, *All The People*, 87.

6. The interspersed statements, referred to as the "Desegregation Compromise" and the reinvention of the *Brown* decision, are not part of Powell's address. This language represents conclusions imposed by the author.

7. Horace Mann Bond, "Teaching: A Calling to Fulfill," *Herald*, Convention Issue, 1963, 5.

8. 52nd Annual Convention, GTEA Audio File, HET.

9. GTEA, "Guide to Developing an Inclusive Integration Plan," 1970, HET; Responses from Bessie McCloud, letter to "Dear Sir," March 6, 1970; M. Hayes Mizell, letter to Dr. Tate, February 20, 1970, HET.

10. Virginia Tate, interview by author, February 15, 2017; Horace Tate, interview by author, February 14, 2002.

11. Another perspective on GEA and GT&EA merger is available in West, *The National Education Association*, 139–40.

Epilogue: The Last Word

1. Author and Tate research team site visits to local school districts; Mr. Palmer, interview by author, June 22, 2002; Mr. Breeding, interview by author, December, 1, 2000.

2. I later learned the Virginia Teachers Association (VTA) collection is housed at Virginia State. However, the VTA merged prior to GT&EA, making its records not as extensive as the GT&EA files.

3. Mrs. Tate, interview by author, October 7, 2017.

Author's Note

1. Eleanor Duckworth, personal communication with author, June 2, 2008.

INDEX

Italic page numbers indicate photographs.

ABOUT THE AUTHOR

Vanessa Siddle Walker, a professor at Emory University, has studied the segregated schooling of African American children for more than twenty years. She has won the prestigious Grawemeyer Award in education, is a member of the National Academy of Education, and is the 104th president of the American Educational Research Association. She lives near Atlanta.

PUBLISHING IN THE PUBLIC INTEREST